WILKIE COLLINS IN CONTEXT

This collection of essays by international scholars celebrates the 200th anniversary of Wilkie Collins's birth by exploring his unconventional life alongside his works, critical responses to his writings and their afterlife, and the literary and cultural contexts which shaped his fiction. Topics discussed include gender, science and medicine, music, law, race and empire, media adaptations, neo-Victorianism, disability and ethics. Along with an analysis of his novels, the essays included also recognise the importance of his short stories, journalism and contributions to Victorian theatre, most notably illuminating the strong connections between sensation fiction and melodrama, as well as exploring his influence on film and television. Engaging with yet also delving far beyond the famous novels, this volume promotes awareness of Collins's remarkable and diverse writerly achievements and paints a vivid portrait of an author whose fluctuating reputation among contemporary critics stands in stark contrast to his immense and still-enduring popularity.

WILLIAM BAKER is Distinguished Chair Qiantang River Professor, Hangzhou Normal University China, and Distinguished Professor Emeritus at Northern Illinois University. A scholar of British literature, he is the author and editor of numerous articles and books, including *Wilkie Collins's Library: A Reconstruction* (2002), *A Wilkie Collins Chronology* (2007), *The Letters of Wilkie Collins* (with William M. Clarke, 1999), *The Public Face of Wilkie Collins: The Collected Letters* (with Andrew Gasson, Graham Law and Paul Lewis, 2005) and *The Collected Letters of Wilkie Collins* (with Paul Lewis, Andrew Gasson and Graham Law, 2019).

RICHARD NEMESVARI is Professor of English and former Dean of Arts at Wilfrid Laurier University, Canada. He has published widely on Victorian fiction, including the works of Thomas Hardy, Wilkie Collins, Mary Elizabeth Braddon and the Brontës. He is General Editor of the Cambridge Edition of the Novels and Stories of Thomas Hardy.

WILKIE COLLINS IN CONTEXT

EDITED BY

WILLIAM BAKER
Hangzhou Normal University and Northern Illinois University

RICHARD NEMESVARI
Wilfrid Laurier University, Canada

Shaftesbury Road, Cambridge CB2 8EA, United Kingdom

One Liberty Plaza, 20th Floor, New York, NY 10006, USA

477 Williamstown Road, Port Melbourne, VIC 3207, Australia

314–321, 3rd Floor, Plot 3, Splendor Forum, Jasola District Centre, New Delhi – 110025, India

103 Penang Road, #05-06/07, Visioncrest Commercial, Singapore 238467

Cambridge University Press is part of Cambridge University Press & Assessment, a department of the University of Cambridge.

We share the University's mission to contribute to society through the pursuit of education, learning and research at the highest international levels of excellence.

www.cambridge.org
Information on this title: www.cambridge.org/9781316510575

DOI: 10.1017/9781009038157

© Cambridge University Press & Assessment 2023

This publication is in copyright. Subject to statutory exception and to the provisions of relevant collective licensing agreements, no reproduction of any part may take place without the written permission of Cambridge University Press & Assessment.

First published 2023

A catalogue record for this publication is available from the British Library.

Library of Congress Cataloging-in-Publication Data
NAMES: Baker, William, 1944– editor. | Nemesvari, Richard, editor.
Title: Wilkie Collins in context / edited by William Baker, Richard Nemesvari.
DESCRIPTION: Cambridge ; New York, NY : Cambridge University Press, 2023. | Includes bibliographical references and index.
IDENTIFIERS: LCCN 2023003486 (print) | LCCN 2023003487 (ebook) | ISBN 9781316510575 (hardback) | ISBN 9781009017619 (paperback) | ISBN 9781009038157 (epub)
SUBJECTS: LCSH: Collins, Wilkie, 1824–1889–Criticism and interpretation.
CLASSIFICATION: LCC PR4497 .W533 2023 (print) | LCC PR4497 (ebook) | DDC 823/.8–dc23/eng/20230405
LC record available at https://lccn.loc.gov/2023003486
LC ebook record available at https://lccn.loc.gov/2023003487

ISBN 978-1-316-51057-5 Hardback

Cambridge University Press & Assessment has no responsibility for the persistence or accuracy of URLs for external or third-party internet websites referred to in this publication and does not guarantee that any content on such websites is, or will remain, accurate or appropriate.

Contents

List of Illustrations	*page* viii
Notes on Contributors	ix
Preface	xvii
Chronology	xxii
List of Abbreviations	xxxiv

PART I LIFE AND WORKS

1	Life Melisa Klimaszewski	3
2	Letters William Baker, Andrew Gasson, Graham Law and Paul Lewis	11
3	Publishers and Editions Andrew Gasson	19
4	Early Novels Christopher Pittard	33
5	Middle Novels Tara MacDonald	41
6	Late Novels Maria K. Bachman	48
7	Shorter Fiction Graham Law	59
8	Journalism Deborah Wynne	69
9	Drama Caroline Radcliffe	77

v

PART II CRITICAL RESPONSE AND AFTERLIFE

10 Contemporary   89
    James Aaron Green

11 After Death to T. S. Eliot   97
    James Aaron Green

12 T. S. Eliot to 1990   105
    Richard Nemesvari

13 1990 to the Present   115
    Tim Dolin and Lucy Dougan

14 Modern Media Adaptations   130
    Alexis Weedon

15 Neo-Victorianism   138
    Jessica Cox

PART III CONTEXTS: LITERARY

16 Wilkie Collins's Library   147
    William Baker

17 Wilkie Collins and Serialisation   157
    Catherine Delafield

18 Wilkie Collins and Sensation Fiction   168
    Richard Nemesvari

19 Wilkie Collins and Scott   177
    Lizhen Chen

20 Wilkie Collins and Dickens   184
    Emily Bell

21 Wilkie Collins, Mary Braddon and Other Women Writers   190
    Jeanette Roberts Shumaker

PART IV CONTEXTS: CULTURAL AND SOCIAL

22 Money   201
    Paul Lewis

23	Gender *Tamara S. Wagner*	212
24	Science and Medicine *Laurence Talairach*	220
25	Language *Melissa Raines*	230
26	Collins and the Artists *Leonee Ormond*	238
27	Music *Allan W. Atlas*	245
28	Politics *Patricia Cove*	252
29	Law *Anne-Marie Beller*	262
30	Geography and Places *Susan R. Hanes*	271
31	Victorian Environments *Mark Frost*	282
32	Race and Empire *Melisa Klimaszewski*	291
33	Class Status and Social Identity *Jenny Bourne Taylor*	299
34	Disability *Heather Tilley*	309
35	Ethics *Biwu Shang*	318

Further Reading   324
Index   332

Illustrations

Frontispiece Men of the Day, No. 39, 'The Novelist who invented Sensation', *Vanity Fair* (3 February 1872)	*page* xxxvi
2.1 Number of letters by decade	12
2.2 Composition by day of the week	17
2.3 Major recipients of letters	17
17.1 Wilkie Collins and serialisation	158
22.1 Wilkie Collins – Income, 24 June 1871–23 June 1872	204
22.2 Wilkie Collins – Trip to Europe, 13 April–23 June 1863	205
22.3 Wilkie Collins – Spending, 1871–1872	207

Notes on Contributors

ALLAN W. ATLAS is Distinguished Professor of Music Emeritus at The Graduate Center of The City University of New York. His interests range from music of the fifteenth and sixteenth centuries – his *Renaissance Music* (1998) is the standard textbook on the subject – to the operas of Puccini, various aspects of Victorian music, the tangos of Astor Piazzolla and, most relevant today, the music of Ralph Vaughan Williams. His publications on Wilkie Collins include 'Wilkie Collins, Mr. Vanstone, and the Case of Beethoven's "No Name" Symphony', *Dickens Studies Annual* 33 (2003), and 'Wilkie Collins on Music and Musicians', *Journal of the Royal Musical Association* 124 (1999). Still another Collins publication, *A Wilkie Collins Songbook*, offers editions of thirty 'popular' songs cited in one or another of Collins's works; it will be published by A-R Editions in 2023. He has also served as Vice-President of the North American British Music Studies Association, of which he was recently made a lifetime honorary member.

MARIA K. BACHMAN was Professor of English at Middle Tennessee State University. She co-edited Wilkie Collins's *The Woman in White* (2006) and *Blind Love* (2003), as well as *Reality's Dark Light: The Sensational Wilkie Collins* (2003), *Fear, Loathing, and Victorian Xenophobia* (2013) and *The Socio-Literary Imaginary in 19th and 20th Century Britain: Victorian and Edwardian Inflections* (2019). She also served as co-editor of *Victorians Institute Journal*.

WILLIAM BAKER is Distinguished Professor, Emeritus, Northern Illinois University, Distinguished Chair Qiantang River Professor, Hangzhou Normal University, Hangzhou, PR China and Distinguished Professor, Emeritus, Norther Illinois University. He co-edits *The Year's Work in English Studies*, *Style* and *George Eliot-George Henry Lewes Studies*. Author or co-author of upwards of 175 articles in refereed journals and more than 25 books, his publications on Wilkie Collins include editing with Andrew Gasson, Graham Law and Paul Lewis, the four-volume *The Public Face of Wilkie Collins: The Collected Letters* (2005), and *Additional Wilkie Collins Letters* for the InteLex Full Text Humanities On-Line Databases (2019), http://pm.nlx.com.

EMILY BELL is Lecturer in Digital Humanities in the School of English at the University of Leeds. She has published on Charles Dickens, literary biography, periodicals and computational approaches to literature and history. Her most recent book is the edited collection *Dickens After Dickens* (2020), and she is writing a new biography of Dickens for Reaktion Books. Dr Bell is also editing Dickens's short fiction and *David Copperfield* for the Oxford Edition of Charles Dickens. She is co-editor of the *Curran Index* to nineteenth-century periodicals, co-editor of *Dickens Search* and Honorary Editor of *The Dickensian*.

ANNE-MARIE BELLER is Senior Lecturer in Victorian Literature at Loughborough University. She has published widely on the sensation novel and contributed chapters to *A Companion to Sensation Fiction* (ed. Pamela K. Gilbert, 2011) and *The Cambridge Companion to Sensation Fiction* (ed. Andrew Mangham, 2013). Recent research includes an article on the sensation short story for *Victoriographies* (2022), a chapter on disability and race in the work of Mary Elizabeth Braddon and Wilkie Collins for *Nineteenth-Century Literature in Transition: The 1860s* (forthcoming), and a translation and critical edition of a French serial by Braddon for *Le Figaro* (forthcoming).

LIZHEN CHEN is Professor of English Literature at the School of International Studies and research fellow at the Literary Criticism Institute of Hangzhou Normal University. His research interests focus on the circulation of literary discourses, comparative literature and ethical literary criticism. He is the author of *Ethical Perspectives in the Narratives of Regency Novels* (2020), *The Angel and the Dove* (2018) and *Victorianism in the Novels of Elizabeth Gaskell* (2015), as well as dozens of articles in journals including *Studies in Theatre and Performance*, *Style*, *Interdisciplinary Studies of Literature* and *Foreign Literature Review*.

PATRICIA COVE is an English Instructor at Dalhousie University, Canada, and the author of *Italian Politics and Nineteenth-Century British Literature and Culture* (2019), which she completed as a Social Sciences and Humanities Research Council of Canada Postdoctoral Fellow. Her research appears in *Journal of Victorian Culture*, *Nineteenth-Century Contexts*, *Victorian Literature and Culture*,

Romanticism and Victorianism on the Net, *Gothic Studies* and *European Romantic Review*. She is currently researching internationalism, citizenship and nineteenth-century poetry.

JESSICA COX is a Reader in English Literature at Brunel University London. She is the author of *Neo-Victorianism and Sensation Fiction* (2019) and *Victorian Sensation Fiction* (Readers' Guides to Essential Criticism, 2019), as well as numerous chapters and articles on Victorian popular literature, including several on Wilkie Collins. Her current research focuses on maternity in nineteenth-century Britain.

CATHERINE DELAFIELD is the author of *Women's Diaries as Narrative in the Nineteenth-Century Novel* (2009) and *Serialization and the Novel in Mid-Victorian Magazines* (2015). She has published articles on Collins's serialisations of *The Law and the Lady* and *Armadale*, as well as the serial writing of Elizabeth Gaskell and Dinah Craik, and on women's personal writings. Following on from the publication of *Women's Letters as Life Writing, 1840–1885* (2020), her biography of Jane Austen (2023) appears in Wiley Blackwell's 'Life of the Author' series.

TIM DOLIN is Professor Emeritus, Literary Studies at Curtin University, Australia. He is General Editor (with Christine Alexander) of the Cambridge Edition of the Novels and Poems of the Brontës, and a member of the editorial board of the Cambridge Edition of the Novels and Stories of Thomas Hardy, for which he edited *The Return of the Native* (2021). He has written books on Hardy and George Eliot, as well as essays and chapters on other nineteenth-century novelists including Wilkie Collins, Charles Dickens, Charlotte Brontë and Elizabeth Gaskell.

LUCY DOUGAN is a widely published and award-winning Australian poet, and an independent literary studies academic. She is co-author with Tim Dolin of 'Fatal Newness: *Basil*, Art, and the Origins of Sensation Fiction' (2004). Her poetry collections include *White Clay* (2007) and *The Guardians* (2015). She is also co-editor of the *Collected Poems of Fay Zwicky* (2017). Her research interests and publications include work on women's writing, and particularly on women's poetry. Her own poetry has been the recipient of the Mary Gilmore Award, the Alec Bolton Award and the Western Australian Premier's Award for poetry (2016).

MARK FROST is Principal Lecturer in English Literature at the University of Portsmouth and specialises in literature, culture and environment in the nineteenth century. His first monograph, *The Lost Companions and*

John Ruskin's Guild of St George: A Revisionary History (2014), will be followed by *Pastoral in Early Victorian Fiction: Environment and Modernity* (forthcoming). He is currently working on *Environments and Ecology in the Long Nineteenth Century*, a four-volume anthology (2022–4), and he has edited a new edition of Richard Jefferies's *After London* (2017). Trees are his favourite organisms.

ANDREW GASSON is the author of *Wilkie Collins: An Illustrated Guide* (1998), co-editor of *The Public Face of Wilkie Collins: The Collected Letters* (2005), of the Collins volume, with William Baker, of *Lives of Victorian Literary Figures* (2007) and, with Caroline Radcliffe, the first modern publication of Collins's dramas *The Lighthouse* and *The Red Vial* (both 2013). He has also contributed numerous other bibliographical and biographical essays on Collins. He is co-founder and Chairman of the Wilkie Collins Society and is currently working on a bibliography of Collins. He has been a collector of Collins books and related ephemera for over forty years.

JAMES AARON GREEN is an APART-GSK Postdoctoral Research Fellow at the University of Vienna, Austria, funded by the Österreichische Akademie der Wissenschaften (ÖAW). He specialises in the intersections of nineteenth-century popular fiction and science, and holds additional interests in game studies. His work in these areas has been published in *Gothic Studies*, *Victorian Network* and the *Journal of Victorian Culture*. His first monograph, *Sensation Fiction and Modernity*, is forthcoming with Palgrave Macmillan.

SUSAN R. HANES retired from the library profession after a diverse career in academic, public and special libraries. She is a writer, photographer and independent scholar and has published a range of material on Wilkie Collins, including *Wilkie Collins's American Tour, 1873–4* (2008) for the Pickering & Chatto 'History of the Book' series; 'The Persistent Phantom: Wilkie Collins and Dorothy L. Sayers', *Wilkie Collins Society Journal* (2000); and 'In Search of Wilkie Collins', *Book Magazine* (1999). Her book, *Hearts: Timeless, Universal, Transcendent* (2013, 2020) features her photographic images from around the world.

MELISA KLIMASZEWSKI is Professor of English and Director of Women's and Gender Studies at Drake University, Iowa, where in addition to Victorian studies she specialises in South African literature and critical race studies. She has authored brief biographies of Wilkie Collins and Charles Dickens for Hesperus Press and has edited nine of Dickens's collaborative works for publication. Her most recent book, *Collaborative*

Dickens (2019), examines all eighteen of Dickens's collaborative Christmas numbers in their entirety and argues for a conversational model of collaboration. She is currently researching representations of multiracial characters in Victorian literature.

GRAHAM LAW is Professor in Media History at Waseda University, Tokyo. His books include *Serializing Fiction in the Victorian Press* (2000) and (with Andrew Maunder) *Wilkie Collins: A Literary Life* (2008). With William Baker, Paul Lewis and Andrew Gasson, he is an editor of the letters of Wilkie Collins. He is currently working on a monograph analysing the nineteenth-century British media system under the title *The Periodical Revolution* and, with Jenny Bourne Taylor, an edition of the journalistic writings of E. S. Dallas.

PAUL LEWIS is one of the editors of *The Collected Letters of Wilkie Collins* (InteLex, 2019) and *The Public Face of Wilkie Collins* (2005) and a contributor to *The Dickensian* and other journals. He is an award-winning financial journalist and uses his skills to keep the database of the more than 3,350 known letters of Wilkie Collins up to date and to analyse Collins's finances. He has been a student of Wilkie Collins and a collector of his work for twenty-five years and is secretary of the Wilkie Collins Society. He has degrees from Stirling University and honorary doctorates from the University of Essex and the University of Chester.

TARA MACDONALD is Associate Professor and Chair of the Department of English at the University of Idaho. She is the author of *The New Man, Masculinity, and Marriage in the Victorian Novel* (2015) and co-editor of *Rediscovering Victorian Women Sensation Writers: Beyond Braddon* (2014). She is completing a book on Victorian sensation fiction and historical theories of affect and has published widely on Victorian and neo-Victorian fiction.

RICHARD NEMESVARI is Professor of English and former Dean of Arts at Wilfrid Laurier University, Canada. He has published on sensation fiction as a genre and on the works of Thomas Hardy, Wilkie Collins, Mary Elizabeth Braddon and the Brontës. His monograph *Thomas Hardy, Sensationalism, and the Melodramatic Mode* was published by Palgrave Macmillan (2011), and he is currently General Editor of the Cambridge Edition of the Novels and Stories of Thomas Hardy. His scholarly edition of Hardy's *Desperate Remedies* was published in that series in 2019, and a second edition of his text of *Jane Eyre* for Broadview Press was published in 2022.

LEONEE ORMOND is Professor Emerita of Victorian Studies at King's College London. A number of her publications are concerned with those who were both writers and artists, and with book illustration. Her first book was a biography of George du Maurier, the *Punch* cartoonist and novelist, and more recently she has written on another cartoonist, Edward Linley Sambourne.

CHRISTOPHER PITTARD is Senior Lecturer in English Literature at the University of Portsmouth. He has published widely on Victorian popular culture in journals including *Victorian Periodicals Review*, *Studies in the Novel*, *Women: A Cultural Review*, *19: Interdisciplinary Studies in the Long Nineteenth Century*, and *Clues: A Journal of Detection*. His books include *Purity and Contamination in Late Victorian Detective Fiction* (2011), *The Cambridge Companion to Sherlock Holmes* (co-edited with Janice M. Allan, 2019), a critical edition of *The Return of Sherlock Holmes* (Oxford University Press, 2023) and the forthcoming *Literary Illusions: Performance Magic and Victorian Literature*.

CAROLINE RADCLIFFE is a Reader in Drama and Performance at the University of Birmingham. She has published widely on nineteenth-century drama and popular performance. Her scholarly editions of Wilkie Collins's dramas, *The Lighthouse* and *The Red Vial* (both co-edited with Andrew Gasson), are the first printed editions of these early plays. She is also a performer and her multimedia performance installation, *The Machinery*, uses a nineteenth-century dance form to examine the human relationship between labour and creativity. *The Machinery* has toured widely, exhibited in heritage sites, festivals and galleries, and has also featured on British TV and radio.

MELISSA RAINES is a Senior Lecturer in English Literature at the University of Liverpool. Her monograph *George Eliot's Grammar of Being* (2011) is a study of Eliot's manuscripts, syntax and writing process. She has also published on Anthony Trollope and Thomas Hardy, as well as on representations of psychopathy in crime fiction in adaptation. She is currently working on projects involving murder in the Victorian novel and trauma in contemporary horror films.

BIWU SHANG is Professor of English at Shanghai Jiao Tong University and editor-in-chief of the De Gruyter journal *Frontiers of Narrative Studies*. His research interests include contemporary fiction, narratology and ethical literary criticism. He is the author of *In Pursuit of Narrative Dynamics* (2011), *Contemporary Western Narratology: Postclassical*

Perspectives (2013), *Unnatural Narrative across Borders: Transnational and Comparative Perspectives* (2019) and *Ian McEwan* (2022). His work has appeared in *Comparative Literature Studies*, *Critique: Studies in Contemporary Fiction*, *Partial Answers*, *Neohelicon*, *Journal of Literary Semantics*, *Semiotica* and *Arcadia*, among other journals.

JEANETTE ROBERTS SHUMAKER is a Professor of English at San Diego State University, Imperial Valley, located five blocks from the Mexican border. She has published on Victorian novelists, modern Irish women writers and nineteenth- and twentieth-century Jewish writers from the UK. Currently she is writing a book on British and Irish novels set in Venice.

LAURENCE TALAIRACH is Professor of English Literature at the University of Toulouse-Jean Jaurès and associate researcher at the Centre Alexandre Koyré for the history of science and technology. Her research interests cover medicine, life sciences and English literature in the long nineteenth century. She is the author of five monographs, including *Gothic Remains: Corpses, Terror and Anatomical Culture, 1764–1897* (2019) and *Wilkie Collins, Medicine and the Gothic* (2009). She has also edited two novels by Mary Elizabeth Braddon: *Thou Art the Man* [1894] (2008) and *Dead Love Has Chains* [1907] (2014), as well as several collections of articles on the popularisation of science in the nineteenth century.

JENNY BOURNE TAYLOR is Professor Emerita of English at the University of Sussex. Her publications include *In the Secret Theatre of Home: Wilkie Collins, Sensation Narrative and Nineteenth-Century Psychology* (1988, 2018) and, as editor, *The Cambridge Companion to Wilkie Collins* (2006) and *The Oxford History of the Novel in English*, Vol. III: *1820–1880* (2012, with John Kucich). With Graham Law, she is currently editing a collection of E. S. Dallas's journalism and criticism in *The Times*.

HEATHER TILLEY held a lectureship in Victorian Literature at Queen Mary University of London and has been a British Academy Postdoctoral Fellow at Birkbeck, University of London. She has also worked in the gallery sector in various curatorial roles, including at the National Portrait Gallery. Her research explores the representation of embodied experience and disability in nineteenth-century literature and visual and material culture, and has focused extensively on the history of visual disability. Her book *Blindness and Writing: From Wordsworth to Gissing* was published in 2017, and her work has appeared in journals including the *Journal of Victorian Culture*, *Disability Studies Quarterly* and the *Journal of Literary & Cultural Disability Studies*.

TAMARA S. WAGNER is Associate Professor at Nanyang Technological University, Singapore. Her books include *The Victorian Baby in Print: Infancy, Infant Care, and Nineteenth-Century Popular Culture* (2020), *Victorian Narratives of Failed Emigration: Settlers, Returnees, and Nineteenth-Century Literature in English* (2016), *Financial Speculation in Victorian Fiction* (2010) and *Longing: Narratives of Nostalgia in the British Novel, 1740–1890* (2004). She has also edited the collections *Domestic Fiction in Colonial Australia and New Zealand* (2014), *Victorian Settler Narratives* (2011) and *Antifeminism and the Victorian Novel: Rereading Nineteenth-Century Women Writers* (2009). Her research has appeared in several academic journals and collections of essays.

ALEXIS WEEDON is Professor of Publishing Studies at the University of Bedfordshire. She is author of *The Origins of Transmedia Storytelling in Early Twentieth Century Adaptation* (2021) and *Victorian Publishing: The Economics of Book Production for a Mass Market, 1836–1916* (2003), and co-author of *Elinor Glyn as Novelist, Moviemaker, Glamour Icon and Businesswoman* (2014). She has collaboratively edited books on a range of cultural and new media subjects, including *Fiction and 'The Woman Question' from 1850 to 1930* (2020), *Developing a Sense of Place* (2020), *Retelling Cinderella: Cultural and Creative Transformations* (2020) and *The History of the Book in the West, 1800–1914* (2010), as well as the journal *Convergence* (1993–2016).

DEBORAH WYNNE is Professor of Nineteenth-Century Literature at the University of Chester. Her publications include *The Sensation Novel and the Victorian Family Magazine* (2001), *Women and Personal Property in the Victorian Novel* (2010), *Charlotte Brontë: Legacies and Afterlives* (2017, co-edited with Amber Regis), and *Victorian Manufactured Things* (2022, co-edited with Louisa Yates).

Preface

This volume of essays marks the 200th anniversary of the birth of Wilkie Collins, an author whose literary legacy provides a conspicuous example of the advantages, and pitfalls, of extreme popular success. The phenomenal impact of his novels *The Woman in White* and *The Moonstone* on Victorian readers, and on the period's wider culture, ensured his place in the history of nineteenth-century fiction. The continued focus on these two works, however, also resulted in a narrowing of attention that it has taken some time to rectify. This constriction of interest was exacerbated by the legitimate, but still limiting, establishment of Collins's central place in the debate over sensation novels that burst onto the pages of prominent literary journals during the 1860s, generating vehement arguments about the proper subject matter, tone, audience and purpose of prose fiction. The resulting legitimisation of realism, in contrast to an ostensibly improper, commoditised, and therefore dismissible sensationalism, meant that Collins's writing could be constructed by reviewers as admirable of its kind – a condescending assessment that recognised his impressive sales while relegating his books to second-class status. The different treatment accorded his good friend Charles Dickens is revealing because Dickens's career as a novelist began early enough that by the 1860s he could largely escape being tarred with the sensationalist brush, although some reviewers did make the effort. Nonetheless, despite his often equally sensational narratives, the older author's novels could retroactively be made to fit into what an even later author, Thomas Hardy, would designate (in an effort to downplay his own use of sensational elements) 'novels of character and environment'. The exploration of psychological states and the detailed evocation of setting is placed against 'mere' complicated plots and melodramatic events, with the first type of fiction worthy of canonisation (Dickens, George Eliot, Hardy) and the second not (Collins, Mary Elizabeth Braddon, Ellen Wood, Charles Reade). The resulting relegation of Collins to the status of one-dimensional purveyor of a niche and ephemeral genre, although no longer as dominant as it once was, is unfair on multiple levels, as the contributors to this collection emphatically reveal.

The thirty-five essays gathered here reveal the multifaceted quality of Wilkie Collins's genius that goes far beyond the focus on *The Woman in White* and *The Moonstone*. Given scholarly interest in the treatment of women, 'insanity', legal abuses and colonialism in Victorian literature, these well-known works have experienced a revival in critical attention. Yet the broad range of Collins's interests remains unrecognised. For example, his connection to painting is the subject of Leonee Ormond's incisive discussion of artists in his work. It should not be forgotten that Wilkie Collins's first published book was his *Memoirs of the Life of William Collins, Esq., R.A.: With Selections from His Journals and Correspondence*, published in 1848. This account of his father the painter, and his early struggles, illuminates Collins's own early years in addition to his father's friendships by drawing on journals, correspondence and notes. Although the young Collins glosses over his father's excessive religiosity, this is, in the words of a later advocate of Collins's work, Walter de la Mare, 'a remarkable book ... for its enduring loyalty and affection, its modesty, insight, judgment, dignity, and quiet and sedate style'. It should not be forgotten too that Wilkie's brother Charles Allston Collins was a highly accomplished painter associated with the Pre-Raphaelite movement. His complicated emotional instability led to an early death, and several of the contributors to this volume point to the rich and complex psychological depiction of the artistic temperament in Wilkie Collins's work. In terms of his own biography and correspondence, it is noticeable that Collins's friendships were extensive in the mid-Victorian artistic community and included, amongst others, William Holman Hunt, the best man at his brother's wedding; John Everett Millais, who drew the frontispieces for several of Collins's novels; and William Powell Frith, with whom Collins took part in amateur theatricals, shared a mutual friendship with Dickens and travelled to Italy. Melisa Klimaszewski provides the context for these relationships through her succinct account of Collins's life that opens this volume.

Collins's, and for that matter Dickens's, love of the theatre is also often elided in considering their lives and works. Contributions to this volume attempt to address this neglect. They draw attention to Collins's love of acting and to his overlooked dramatic work and collaborations. As Caroline Radcliffe notes in her essay, 'Wilkie Collins achieved considerable success as a dramatist in Britain and the United States, with plays such as *Man and Wife* and *The New Magdalen* enjoying long and successful runs.' Contributors also discuss the dramatic adaptations of his fiction, the unchecked piracy with which he was continually plagued, and the issue of melodrama, now unfashionable, but in Collins's day a dominant Victorian theatrical mode. As Jenny Bourne Taylor observes in her essay on 'Class Status and Social Identity', Collins's 'reworking of Gothic and melodramatic tropes in contemporary settings gave his work a subversive currency'.

Collins's correspondence is yet another facet of his work which, until the present volume, has not received the attention it deserves, and which constitutes an important part of its author's oeuvre. His letters reveal not only his family relationships, especially his closeness to his mother Harriet, his friendships and personal preoccupations, but also his connections to broader Victorian literary concerns, such as serialisation, newspaper syndication and copyrights. Collins reveals a continuous attention to detail in dealing with publishers and literary agents. Dependent for his living upon his writing and the income he received from it – a subject fully explored by Paul Lewis in his essay 'Money', which presents some hard facts and revelations – the correspondence shows that Collins was exceedingly worldly wise and shrewd in his dealings with publishers on both sides of the Atlantic, on the European continent and elsewhere. He was most anxious to protect his rights as an author, participating in attempts to form what today we would refer to as a writers' union or guild in which he took an active part – attending dinners, giving speeches and writing articles advocating the rights and responsibilities of authorship. Social issues and injustices such as the incarceration of women in lunatic asylums, legal inequity, inheritance, sanitation, poverty and urban deprivation continually engaged his creative attention. A further subject which occurs in his correspondence and in his novels is that of physical and mental disabilities, as Heather Tilley points out in her essay.

Other areas explored in this volume include Collins's presentation of and concern with social relations and didacticism, marriage laws, gender issues, inheritance laws and vivisection. Laurence Talairach extensively treats Collins's interest in, and creative transformation of, 'Science and Medicine', while Mark Frost draws attention to Collins's exploration of what is now referred to as Victorian ecology. Specific topics covered also encompass Allan W. Atlas's analysis of the music in Collins's writing, his musical awareness, as well as the close personal relationships that shaped his extensive musical engagement.

Collins's relationship to Dickens is the concern of Emily Bell, while Jeanette Roberts Shumaker discusses his relationship to Mary Elizabeth Braddon and other women writers. Lizhen Chen examines the author Collins considered the greatest of all novelists, Sir Walter Scott. William

Baker, in his discussion of the books owned by Collins, draws attention to the extensive collection of Scott's works found in his library following his death. Anne-Marie Beller writes on the significance and importance of law to Collins and his work. Collins's relevance today is revealed by Alexis Weedon's contribution, 'Modern Media Adaptations'; consideration of the issue of 'Ethics' is explored by Biwu Shang; as are critical responses to Collins amongst his Victorian contemporaries, during the twentieth century and more recently, by James Aaron Green, Richard Nemesvari, and Tim Dolin and Lucy Dougan. Patricia Cove addresses Collins's engagement with politics and Melisa Klimaszewski discusses colonialism and race.

Wilkie Collins in Context is divided into four sections. Part I is devoted to essays on his 'Life and Works' with treatment of his biography, letters, publishers and editions, while the fiction is divided into the consideration of the early novels, the middle novels, the later novels, then the shorter fiction. This first section concludes with essays on Collins's prolific journalism and his largely neglected drama. The first four essays of Part II, 'Critical Response and Afterlife', treat the broad canvas of reactions to his life and writings. The final two contributions to this section deal with media adaptations and Collins's impact upon contemporary neo-Victorian fiction. Part III, 'Contexts: Literary', also has six contributions. These include considerations of the author's library, the impact and importance of serialisation when considering Collins's work, and Collins's foundational association with sensation fiction. It also includes discussions of Collins's relationships with Scott, Dickens and Braddon.

Part IV, the longest section, with fourteen essays, treats the diversity of 'Contexts: Cultural and Social', including a consideration of Collins's style and language, his treatment of gender, his relationship with, on a personal level and in his work, artists, music, politics, law, science and medicine, the environment, class status and social identity, disability, ethics, race and empire, and geography and places. These topics are not meant to be exhaustive but intended rather to generate further discussion of Collins's diversity and to suggest additional areas of exploration in Collins studies.

This volume was compiled during the time of the Covid-19 pandemic. Both of the general editors are grateful to the contributors for their immediate responses during a most difficult period: some indeed even had Covid themselves or had to cope with those close to them becoming ill, yet still managed to contribute and submit on time. We cannot but repeat how grateful we are to them, and we are sure that Wilkie Collins would have been so too. William Baker was especially fortunate in his co-editor, Richard Nemesvari, and his savvy: in addition to jointly editing this volume, we also enjoyed when we could our mutual observations on the fortunes of English football teams – an area of course not covered in our subject's work. Baker would also like to thank the following for their assistance and responses to questions: Emily Bell, Andrew Gasson, Maxwell Hoover, Graham Law, Paul Lewis, Patrick Scott and Ken Womack.

We are likewise grateful to Bethany Thomas, Commissioning Editor (Literature) at Cambridge University Press, who suggested this volume, and to her colleagues at the Press for their advice and assistance. In particular we would like to thank Rose Bell, whose exemplary work as copy editor for the book impressed us both. Richard Nemesvari wishes to thank the Office of the Provost and Vice-President: Academic at Wilfrid Laurier University for its funding support, and (as always) Jane Strickler, whose comments on his writing never fail to improve its clarity. He would also like to note that it was a pleasure editing this collection with William Baker, who generously shared his wide-ranging expertise on the life and work of Wilkie Collins.

Chronology

1824
8 January — William Wilkie Collins is born at 11 New Cavendish Street, Marylebone

1826
— Family moves to Pond Street, Hampstead Green

1828
25 January — Brother, Charles Allston Collins is born

1829
Summer — Family visits Boulogne
September — Family moves to Hampstead Square

1830
— Family moves to Porchester Terrace, Bayswater

1835
January — Collins begins to attend Maida Hill Academy

1836
September — Family visits France and Italy (until August 1838)
[Dickens, *The Posthumous Papers of the Pickwick Club*]

1838
— Family moves to 20 Avenue Road, Regent's Park
Collins boards at Henry Cole's school, Highbury
[Dickens, *Oliver Twist*]

1840	
	Family moves to 85 Oxford Terrace, Bayswater
1841	
January	Leaves Cole's school; apprenticed to Antrobus & Co., tea merchants
	[Dickens, *The Old Curiosity Shop*, *Barnaby Rudge*]
1842	
June–July	Visits Scotland with his father
1843	
	Family moves to 1 Davenport Street, Hyde Park Gardens
July	'Volpurno; or, The Student' published in *The Albion* (first signed publication)
August	'The Last Stage Coachman' published in *The Illuminated Magazine*
	[Dickens, *A Christmas Carol*]
1844	
	Visits France with Charles Ward
1845	
January	Finishes *Ioláni; or, Tahíti as it Was*; rejected by Longman and Chapman & Hall
September–October	Visits Paris alone
1846	
April	Begins writing *Antonina; or, The Fall of Rome*
18 May	Enters Lincoln's Inn
July	Visits Belgium with Charles Ward
1847	
17 February	Death of William Collins; Collins begins writing his father's memoir
August	To France again with Charles Ward
	[Charlotte Brontë, *Jane Eyre*; Emily Brontë, *Wuthering Heights*; Anne Brontë, *Agnes Grey*]

1848

Autumn	Family moves to 38 Blandford Square, Marylebone
November	*Memoirs of the Life of William Collins* published by Longman (Collins's first published book)
	[Dickens, *Dombey and Son*; Thackeray, *Vanity Fair*; Gaskell, *Mary Barton*; Kingsley, *Yeast*]

1849

19 June	Amateur production of Goldsmith's *The Good Natur'd Man* at Blandford Square
Summer	Exhibits *The Smuggler's Retreat* at Royal Academy
	[Charlotte Brontë, *Shirley*]

1850

26 February	Charity performance of *A Court Duel* at the Soho Theatre
28 February	*Antonina* published by Bentley (Collins's first published novel)
July–August	Walking tour of Cornwall with Henry Brandling
August	Family moves to 17 Hanover Terrace, Regent's Park
	[Dickens, *David Copperfield*; Thackeray, *Pendennis*]

1851

30 January	*Rambles Beyond Railways* published by Bentley
March	'The Twin Sisters' published in *Bentley's Miscellany*
12 March	Meets Dickens for the first time at the house of John Forster
16 March	Acts with Dickens in Bulwer-Lytton's *Not so Bad as We Seem, or, Many Sides to a Character*
27 September	'A Plea for Sunday Reform' published in *The Leader*
21 November	Called to the Bar
23 December	Christmas book *Mr Wray's Cash-Box* published by Bentley

1852

24 April	'The Traveller's Story of a Terribly Strange Bed' published in *Household Words*
August	'Nine O'Clock' published in *Bentley's Magazine*
September	Stays with Dickens in Dover
16 November	*Basil: A Story of Modern Life* published by Bentley
December	'A Passage in the Life of Mr Perugino Potts' published in *Bentley's Miscellany*

1853

July–September	Stays with Dickens in Boulogne
October–December	Tours Switzerland and Italy with Dickens and Augustus Egg
	[Dickens, *Bleak House*; Gaskell, *Ruth*]

1854

6 June	*Hide and Seek* published by Bentley
December	'The Lawyer's Story of a Stolen Letter' published in *The Seven Poor Travellers*, Christmas number of *Household Words*
	[Dickens, *Hard Times*]

1855

11–21 February	Illness during trip to Paris with Dickens
16 June	*The Lighthouse* performed at Dickens's home, Tavistock House
July–September	Stays with Dickens at Folkestone
September	Sails with Edward Pigott to the Scilly Isles
November–December	'The Monktons of Wincot Abbey' published in *Fraser's Magazine*
22 December	'The Cruise of the *Tomtit*' published in *Household Words*
	[Gaskell, *North and South*; Thackeray, *The Newcomes*; Trollope, *The Warden*]

1856

	Begins to sign himself 'Wilkie Collins'
February	*After Dark* published by Smith, Elder (first collection of stories)
February–April	Visits Paris with Dickens
March	*A Rogue's Life* serialised in *Household Words* (first serialised novel)

April	Takes lodgings at 22 Howland Street, off Tottenham Court Road
June–July	Sails along the South Coast and to Cherbourg with Pigott
June	Family moves to 2 Harley Place, Marylebone Road
August–September	Visits Boulogne with Dickens
13 September	'To Think or Be Thought For' published in *Household Words*
October	Joins permanent staff of *Household Words*

1857

3 January	*The Dead Secret* begins in *Household Words*
6 January	*The Frozen Deep* performed at Tavistock House
24 January	*The Dead Secret* begins in *Harper's Weekly* (first authorised American serialisation)
June	*The Dead Secret* published by Bradbury & Evans
10 August	*The Lighthouse* produced at Royal Olympic Theatre (first professional production)
21 August	*The Frozen Deep* produced in Manchester
7 September	Leaves with Dickens for a walking tour in Cumberland
3–31 October	*The Lazy Tour of Two Idle Apprentices* (with Dickens) published in *Household Words*
December	*The Perils of Certain English Prisoners* (with Dickens) published in Christmas number of *Household Words*
	[Dickens, *Little Dorrit*; Hughes, *Tom Brown's School Days*]

1858

April	'Who is the Thief?' ('The Biter Bit') published in *The Atlantic Monthly*
June	Sailing trip to Wales
July–August	First visit to Broadstairs, Kent
25 August	'The Unknown Public' published in *Household Words*
September	Resigns from the Garrick Club in support of Edmund Yates
11 October	*The Red Vial* opens at the Olympic Theatre [Eliot, *Scenes of Clerical Life*]

1859

January	By now living with Caroline Graves, at 124 Albany Street, Regent's Park
April	Moves to 2a Cavendish Street with Caroline Graves
30 April	'Sure to be Healthy, Wealthy and Wise' published in *All the Year Round* (first contribution in first issue)
August–September	Stays at Church Hill Cottage, Broadstairs
October	*The Queen of Hearts* published by Hurst & Blackett
26 November	*The Woman in White* starts serialisation in *All the Year Round* and *Harper's Weekly* [Dickens, *A Tale of Two Cities*; Eliot, *Adam Bede*; Meredith, *The Ordeal of Richard Feverel*]

1860

17 July	Charles Collins marries Kate Dickens
15 August	*The Woman in White* published by Sampson Low and Harper & Brothers
September	Sailing trip to Newport, Wales
3 November	Unauthorised production of *The Woman in White* opens at the Surrey Theatre [Eliot, *The Mill on the Floss*]

1861

January	Leases copyrights to Sampson Low; resigns from *All the Year Round*
April	Single-volume edition of *The Woman in White* published by Sampson Low [Dickens, *Great Expectations*; Reade, *The Cloister and the Hearth*; Wood, *East Lynne*]

1862

15 March	*No Name* begins serialisation in *All the Year Round* and *Harper's Weekly*
August	Visits Whitby with Caroline Graves
31 December	*No Name* published by Sampson Low [dated 1863] [Braddon, *Lady Audley's Secret*]

1863

January	Severe attack of gout in both feet
April–June	Visits Aix-la-Chapelle and Wildbad for the waters
August–September	Visits Isle of Man with Caroline Graves and her daughter Carrie
October	Visits Italy for four months with Caroline Graves and Carrie
November	*My Miscellanies* published by Sampson Low [Braddon, *Aurora Floyd*]

1864

April	Begins writing *Armadale*
August	Visits Great Yarmouth; meets Martha Rudd (?)
November	*Armadale* begins serialisation in *The Cornhill Magazine*
December	Moves to 9 Melcombe Place, Dorset Square; *Armadale* begins serialisation in *Harper's Weekly* [Trollope, *Can You Forgive Her?*]

1865

	Smith, Elder acquires Collins's copyrights from Sampson Low
27 February	Visits Paris for a week
10 March	Resigns again from the Garrick Club for blackballing of W. H. Wills

1866

12 April	Completes writing of *Armadale*
April	Visits Paris with Frederick Lehmann
October	*Armadale* published by Smith, Elder; *The Frozen Deep* produced at the Olympic Theatre
October–December	Visits Italy with Pigott

1867

August	Moves to 90 Gloucester Place, Portman Square
September–October	Stays with Dickens at Gad's Hill

December	*No Thoroughfare* (with Dickens) published as the Christmas number of *All the Year Round*
26 December	*No Thoroughfare* produced at the Adelphi Theatre
	[Trollope, *The Last Chronicle of Barset*]
1868	
	Martha Rudd established at 33 Bolsover Street as 'Mrs Dawson'
4 January	*The Moonstone* begins serialisation in *All the Year Round* and *Harper's Weekly*
22 February	Taken ill with gout in Gloucester Place
19 March	Death of Harriet Collins, Collins's mother
July	*The Moonstone* published by Tinsley Brothers
August–September	Visits Switzerland with Frederick Lehmann
29 October	Witnesses the marriage of Caroline Graves and Joseph Clow
1869	
29 March	*Black and White* produced at the Adelphi Theatre
4 July	First child, Marian Dawson, born to Collins and Martha Rudd
20 November	*Man and Wife* begins serialisation in *Cassell's Magazine*
1870	
12 February	'A National Wrong' (with James Payn) published in *Chambers's Journal*
9 June	Death of Charles Dickens
27 June	*Man and Wife* published by F. S. Ellis & Co.
1871	
April (?)	Caroline Graves returns to Gloucester Place
14 May	Second daughter, Harriet Dawson, born to Collins and Martha Rudd
2 September	*Poor Miss Finch* begins serialisation in *Cassell's Magazine*
9 October	*The Woman in White* produced at the Olympic Theatre
25 December	*Miss or Mrs?* published in *The Graphic* Christmas number
	[Hardy, *Desperate Remedies*]

1872

26 January	*Poor Miss Finch* published by Bentley
October	*The New Magdalen* begins serialisation in *Temple Bar* and *Harper's Weekly*
	[Eliot, *Middlemarch*; Hardy, *Under the Greenwood Tree*]

1873

January	*Miss or Mrs? and Other Stories in Outline* published by Bentley
22 February	*Man and Wife* produced at the Prince of Wales Theatre
9 April	Death of Charles Collins
17 May	*The New Magdalen* published by Bentley
19 May	*The New Magdalen* produced at the Olympic Theatre
July	Visits Boulogne and Paris
13 September	Sails from Liverpool for reading tour of North America
25 September	Arrives in New York
22 October	Breakfast banquet at Union Club, New York, given by William Seaver
10 November	*The New Magdalen* produced at the Broadway Theatre, New York, with Collins in attendance

1874

	The Dead Alive published by Shepard & Gill
7 March	Leaves Boston for return trip to England
18 March	Arrives at Liverpool
April?	Moves Martha Rudd to Taunton Place
August	*The Frozen Deep* begins serialisation in *Temple Bar*
26 September	*The Law and the Lady* begins serialisation in *The Graphic*
2 November	*The Frozen Deep and Other Stories* published by Bentley
19 November	Leases copyrights to Chatto & Windus, now his main British publisher
25 December	Son, William Charles Collins Dawson, born to Collins and Martha Rudd
	Readings in America and *The Dead Alive* published by Hunter, Rose & Co.
	[Hardy, *Far from the Madding Crowd*]

1875

	Alicia Warlock and Other Stories published by William Gill
February	*The Law and the Lady* published by Chatto & Windus
October–November	Travels to Brussels and Antwerp
9 December	*Miss Gwilt* begins production at the Alexandra Theatre
25 December	*The Two Destinies* begins serialisation in *Harper's Bazar*
	[James, *Roderick Hudson*]

1876

January	*The Two Destinies* begins serialisation in *Temple Bar*
August	*The Two Destinies* published by Chatto & Windus
October	Visits Paris with Caroline Graves and Carrie (?)
	[Eliot, *Daniel Deronda*]

1877

August[?]	*Percy and the Prophet* published in Harper's Half-Hour Series
29 August	*The Dead Secret* produced at the Lyceum Theatre
17 September	*The Moonstone* produced at the Olympic Theatre
September–December	Travels to Brussels, the Tyrol and northern Italy
December	*My Lady's Money* published in *The Illustrated London News*
	[James, *The American*]

1878

	My Lady's Money published in Harper's Half-Hour Series
12 March	Marriage of Carrie Graves and Harry Barley
June	*The Haunted Hotel* begins serialisation in *Belgravia*
	[Hardy, *The Return of the Native*]

1879

1 January	*The Fallen Leaves* begins serialisation in *The World*
7 April	*A Rogue's Life* published by Bentley
July	*The Fallen Leaves* published by Chatto & Windus
13 September	*Jezebel's Daughter* begins newspaper syndication (W. F. Tillotson)
November	*The Haunted Hotel* published by Chatto & Windus

1880

March	*Jezebel's Daughter* published by Chatto & Windus
June	'Consideration on the Copyright Question' published in the *International Review*
2 October	*The Black Robe* begins newspaper syndication (*The Leader*)

1881

April	*The Black Robe* published by Chatto & Windus
5 December	Approaches A. P. Watt, who becomes his literary agent [James, *The Portrait of a Lady*]

1882

22 March	Collins makes his final will
22 July	*Heart and Science* begins newspaper syndication (A. P. Watt)
August	*Heart and Science* begins serialisation in *Belgravia*

1883

16 April	*Heart and Science* published by Chatto & Windus
9 June	*Rank and Riches* produced at the Adelphi Theatre
22 December	*'I Say No'* begins newspaper syndication (A. P. Watt); also in *Harper's Weekly*

1884

January	*'I Say No'* begins serialisation in *London Society*
11 April	Death of Charles Reade
October	*'I Say No'* published by Chatto & Windus

1885

October (?)	*The Ghost's Touch and Other Stories* published in Harper's Handy Series
30 October	*The Evil Genius* produced at the Vaudeville Theatre
11 December	*The Evil Genius* begins newspaper syndication (W. F. Tillotson)

1886

19 August	*Victims of Circumstances* begins serialisation in *Youth's Companion*
September	*The Evil Genius* published by Chatto & Windus
15 November	*The Guilty River* appears in *Arrowsmith's Christmas Annual* and in Harper's Handy Series [Hardy, *The Mayor of Casterbridge*]

1887

May	*Little Novels* published by Chatto & Windus
24 December	'The First Officer's Confession' published in *Spirit of the Times* [Hardy, *The Woodlanders*]

1888

17 February	*The Legacy of Cain* begins newspaper syndication (W. F. Tillotson)
23 March	Moves from Gloucester Place to 82 Wimpole Street
November	*The Legacy of Cain* published by Chatto & Windus [dated 1889]

1889

19 January	Collins shaken by a cab accident
30 June	Collins suffers a stroke
6 July	*Blind Love* begins serialisation in the *Illustrated London News*
23 September	Death of Wilkie Collins at 82 Wimpole Street
27 September	Funeral at Kensal Green

1890

January	*Blind Love* published by Chatto & Windus
August	*The Lazy Tour of Two Idle Apprentices* published by Chatto & Windus

Abbreviations

Novels

An	*Antonina* (1850)
A	*Armadale* (1866)
B	*Basil* (1852)
BL	*Blind Love* (1890)
BR	*The Black Robe* (1881)
DS	*The Dead Secret* (1857)
EG	*The Evil Genius* (1886)
FL	*The Fallen Leaves* (1879)
GR	*The Guilty River* (1886)
HH	*The Haunted Hotel* (1879)
HS	*Heart and Science* (1883)
H&S	*Hide and Seek* (1854)
ISN	*'I Say No'* (1884)
JD	*Jezebel's Daughter* (1880)
LL	*The Law and the Lady* (1875)
LC	*The Legacy of Cain* (1888)
M&W	*Man and Wife* (1870)
M	*The Moonstone* (1868)
MM	*Miss or Mrs?* (1873)
NM	*The New Magdalen* (1873)
NN	*No Name* (1863)
PMF	*Poor Miss Finch* (1872)
RL	*A Rogue's Life* (1879)
TD	*The Two Destinies* (1876)
WW	*The Woman in White* (1860)

Plays

B&W	*Black and White: A Love Story in Three Acts* (1869)
FD	*The Frozen Deep* (1857)
MG	*Miss Gwilt: A Drama in Five Acts, Altered from the Novel* (1875)
NMDS	*The New Magdalen: A Dramatic Story in a Prologue and Three Acts* (1873)
NT	*No Thoroughfare: A Drama in Five Acts* (1867)
RV	*The Red Vial* (1858)
WWD	*The Woman in White: A Drama, in a Prologue and Five Acts* (1871)

Secondary Sources

AYR	*All the Year Round*
B&C	*The Letters of Wilkie Collins*, ed. William Baker and William M. Clarke, 2 vols. (London: Macmillan, 1999)
BGLL	*The Public Face of Wilkie Collins: The Collected Letters*, ed. William Baker, Andrew Gasson, Graham Law and Paul Lewis, 4 vols. (London: Pickering & Chatto, 2005); digital edition (Charlottesville, VA: InteLex, 2019)
HW	*Household Words*
Library	William Baker, *Wilkie Collins's Library: A Reconstruction* (Westport, CT, and London: Greenwood, 2002)
Page	Norman Page (ed.), *Wilkie Collins: The Critical Heritage* (London and New York: Routledge, 1974)
Pilgrim	*The Letters of Charles Dickens* (Pilgrim Edition), ed. Madeline House, Graham Storey and Kathleen Tillotson, 12 vols. (Oxford: Clarendon Press, 1965–2002)

Frontispiece Men of the Day, No. 39, 'The Novelist who invented Sensation', *Vanity Fair* (3 February 1872)

PART I

Life and Works

CHAPTER I

Life

Melisa Klimaszewski

Wilkie Collins lived what appears to have been a full, exciting and satisfying life. He enjoyed good food and drink, travelled, nurtured close family relationships, sustained decades-long friendships and distinguished himself as a novelist and playwright. Limited by health problems, including gout attacks that were sometimes disabling, Collins attempted to balance physical rest with professional obligations and a ceaseless desire to live a stimulating, unconventional life.

Biographical work is more critically interpretive than archeologically factual. As Rosemarie Bodenheimer puts it, 'everything we know is on a written page', which means that reconstructing a sense of a person's life is always an act of textual interpretation.[1] We can never know what it was like to sit in a pub with Collins or laugh at a joke he told, but we can know that he enjoyed dining out and had a sparkling wit. Fortunately, many of the letters Collins wrote have survived, as have the papers of many of his correspondents. Studying these documents, his publications and other historical records, we can begin to understand some of the details that shaped Collins's life.

Harriet Collins gave birth to William Wilkie Collins on 8 January 1824 in London. Called 'Willie' in childhood then simply Wilkie from young manhood onward, Collins was an intellectually stimulated youth. His father, William Collins, was a painter and member of the Royal Academy of Arts, and the close-knit, churchgoing, Tory family welcomed another son, Charles Allston Collins, four years later. Wilkie and Charley remained close throughout their adult lives; Charley was the more physically attractive – tall with eye-catching red hair – but was always weaker and more sickly than his older brother. Wilkie Collins grew a long beard, wore small spectacles, chose colourful clothing, and often relied on a walking stick. The most prominent feature of his physique was a forehead bulge that had been present since birth and that he never attempted to hide. Many acquaintances commented on the shape of his head, but those accounts quickly shift to descriptions of his vivacious personality. Short in stature, with hands and feet small enough to require the purchasing of ladies'-sized or even children's gloves and footwear, Collins was not an imposing person physically, but his zest for parties and debauchery could infuse a room with energy.

A formative experience for Collins was a two-year residence in Italy that commenced when he was twelve years old. William Collins's painting kept him at work in studios around Rome while his sons studied with tutors and learned about Italian culture while receiving language lessons. Living in Rome and spending significant time in France on the journey impressed European tastes upon Collins's young character that enabled him to question some English ways of doing things. His appreciation of good wine and fine foods was also influenced by this period of youthful travel, which led to a lifelong willingness to leave England for pleasure trips or to visit continental convalescent destinations.

In his twenties, Collins partied without shame or apology, boasting of drunken nights out in letters to his mother and 'dissipating fearfully' with Charles Ward in Paris so satisfactorily that they repeated the holiday antics in Europe every summer for five years.[2] He loved to shop in Paris, dine extravagantly, attend performances and cavort with women, activities his parents were loath to fund. Collins worked at Antrobus & Co. tea merchants but did not take the position seriously, rejected a career as a clergyman, and spent his time at Lincoln's Inn focused on fiction writing and pleasant dinners rather than actual study of law.

Collins's earliest published work, a short story from the summer of 1843, draws upon his travel experiences, as 'Volpurno' tells the story of a haunted Venetian groom going mad on his wedding day. His first proper book was a well-reviewed biography of his father published in 1848, a year after William Collins's death, which was followed by *Antonina* (1850), another work set in Italy. Collins also published *Rambles Beyond Railways* (1851), a travel narrative based on a hiking tour of Cornwall that featured the tinted lithographs of fellow traveller Henry Brandling. *Basil* (1852), *Hide and Seek* (1854) and *The Dead Secret* (1857), all novels, show Collins at the forefront of the emergence of sensation fiction as he also continued to write non-fiction journalism. Wilkie and Charley continued to share a home with Harriet, and the house was a place full of amateur theatricals, lively dinners and artistic production. In multiple genres, Collins developed his storytelling skills throughout the 1850s as his career ascended. Some of his early work was translated into Dutch, French, German and Russian, and his personal relationships thrived as he nurtured old friendships while beginning a crucial new one with Charles Dickens, whose literary celebrity was well established.

Shared theatrical interests led Augustus Egg to suggest that Charles Dickens ask Collins to join Dickens's amateur production of Bulwer-Lytton's *Not so Bad as We Seem* in 1851. The men quickly became close friends and would remain so until Dickens's death in 1870. The two collaborated with each other more closely and frequently than they ever collaborated with other writers, and Collins even joined W. H. Wills in standing in for Dickens as editor of *All the Year Round* when Dickens went to the United States in 1867. Collins's other close friends included Nina (née Chambers) and Frederick Lehmann; Charles and Jane Ward; Frances Dickinson, whose divorces educated Collins on the marriage laws that many of his novels interrogate; and Edward Pigott. With Charles Dickens, however, Collins could share personal and professional passions simultaneously. Dickens secured Collins as a contracted staff writer for *Household Words*, and Collins secured his name in print in the journal's pages as the author of *The Dead Secret* – an impressive arrangement, given that no other pieces carried by-lines. The men travelled to Europe, co-wrote plays and stories, socialised respectably at the Garrick Club and enjoyed less respectable nights on the town. Dickens would invite Collins to join him in 'amiable dissipation and unbounded license' as casually as he would ask Collins to work on a Christmas collaboration (understanding, ironically, that Collins detested the holiday).[3] In the autumn of 1857, they travelled to Cumberland to follow Ellen Ternan, a young actress with whom Dickens was enamoured and for whom he would later separate from his wife, then published a fictionalised account of their trip as 'The Lazy Tour of Two Idle Apprentices' in *Household Words*. A quirky travel narrative in which the men lampoon themselves in the alter-egos of Thomas Idle (Collins) and Francis Goodchild (Dickens), 'The Lazy Tour' showcases the humour and jousting wits that underpinned the friendship.

In contrast to his father's religious conservatism, which Charley had internalised, Wilkie's social life is just one realm in which he exhibited behaviour showing that his beliefs were far from traditional. In a series of letters to George Henry Lewes published in *The Leader* in 1852, Collins attempted to generate respect for mesmerism and clairvoyance. The hypocrisies and unthinking bureaucracy of organised religions disgusted Collins, but he respected humble, unostentatious demonstrations of faith even if he did not share a particular belief system. The most fundamental way in which he rejected dominant practice was in his domestic and sexual arrangements.

In the mid-1850s, Collins met and began a romantic relationship with Caroline Graves, a widowed shopkeeper, and by 1858, they were living together. Collins effectively adopted Caroline's young daughter Carrie but never expressed any interest in marrying Caroline or anyone else, despite his mother's disapproval. Sometimes, the couple would refer to Caroline as Mrs Collins or as his housekeeper, but they were honest with friends about their unmarried life. The critiques of marriage laws that surface in Collins's fiction and drive many of his plots align with his personal opposition to the absurdity of patriarchy in practice. 'Bold Words by a Bachelor', a non-fiction piece, rails against marriage, and Collins was comfortable with polyamory.[4] In the mid-1860s, he met Martha Rudd, twenty-one years his junior, and began a long-term relationship with her. They had three children and, to live as peacefully as possible, took the names Mr and Mrs Dawson while Collins also continued to maintain a separate household with Caroline and Carrie. When Caroline left for two years and married Joseph Clow, Collins did not object and was present at the wedding, but that marriage failed quickly, and Caroline returned to Collins. There is no evidence that Caroline and Martha socialised, but it appears that the families coexisted calmly, and for the last two decades of his life, his children with Martha and grandchildren from Carrie surrounded him.

Collins was certainly not the only major Victorian literary figure to live outside of traditional marriage. George Eliot (Mary Ann Evans) and Charles Dickens both lived with partners to whom they were not wed. Dickens chose to attempt to keep his relationship with Ellen Ternan secret, causing pain to many others as he abruptly separated from his wife and treated her unkindly, whereas Eliot/Evans and George Henry Lewes were quite open about their choice to live together in partnership while his wife resided in an asylum. Collins struck something of a middle path, never apologising for his choices, treating both Caroline and Martha with respect and assuming married names to minimise any social shame the children might feel. He supported both households financially and took care to ensure that all of the children were provided for after his death. Above all, Collins remained true to his beliefs about love, intimacy, family and life partnership.

The most successful period of Collins's career was the decade of the 1860s. *The Woman in White*, published weekly in *All the Year Round* from November 1859 to August 1860, was a massive hit. Featuring a masterfully narrated, suspenseful plot, the text broke new novelistic ground that not only propelled Collins into celebrity but also secured him financially. The book, inspiring dances and themed merchandise, was so popular that it reached an eighth edition in volume form by November 1860. Collins enjoyed fame and took no rest, publishing *No Name* (1862–3) and *Armadale* (1864–6) in quick succession. The reading public purchased copies eagerly, and although critical reviews were not as enthusiastic as those for *The Woman in White*, the publication of *The Moonstone* (1868) once again resulted in near-universal praise and excitement. Recognised as the first detective novel in English, *The Moonstone* is narrated through documents, and it established many of the most recognisable traits – including bumbling local investigators, a quirky professional detective, amateur detective figures and false initial leads – of the genre.

In alignment with Collins's unconventional lifestyle and non-traditional beliefs, throughout his oeuvre one finds sympathy for typically maligned or ignored people and situations. Individuals with physical disabilities, multiracial characters and strong women characters appear in a wide range of roles. His plots also consistently recognise the legitimacy of non-biological family bonds. Although some of these depictions indulge problematic stereotypes, they are also often sympathetic in tone, and the psychological depth of such multi-layered characters establishes full humanity. These characters are not uniformly righteous or villainous; rather, they are as complex and unpredictable as the more conventional characters. Collins's playwriting tended towards melodrama, sometimes exhibiting less complex characterisation, and his success in that field was inconsistent. *The Frozen Deep* (1856), a collaboration with Dickens, was done so well that, following Queen Victoria's attendance at a private benefit performance on 4 July 1857, Dickens received notice that 'her Majesty particularly wishes that Her high approval should be conveyed to Mr. Wilkie Collins'.[5] The first professional stage production of Collins's work was *The Lighthouse* in August 1857, and he never lost his passion for playwriting, sometimes publishing a dramatised version of a story before the serial run of the same novel was finished in order to protect copyright. Some productions, like *The Red Vial* of 1858, were such flops that Collins took pains to destroy all copies of the script, but others, like his adaptation of *The Woman in White* (1871) and *Man and Wife* (1873) were unqualified triumphs.

Through all this success and a life full of social, bodily and sensual pleasures, Collins also suffered tremendously. He was plagued by severe gout, a condition his father had also managed. The first acute episode seems to have occurred in early 1853, at just twenty-nine years of age, and it took Collins several months to recover strength in his lower body. Leg and foot pain would trouble him intermittently for the rest of his life, as would extreme ocular inflammation that sometimes required bandaging of his eyes. Some of these symptoms are more characteristic of venereal disease than gout or rheumatism, and it is likely that multiple conditions led to Collins's periods of illness. He used laudanum (opium dissolved in alcohol) to manage pain since at least the early 1860s, and he understood addiction as a consequence. Having tried other methods of pain relief, such as potassium and quinine, Collins turned to laudanum – widely available and marketed in small doses for infants – as the only option that actually provided comfort. His addiction was severe, and as his tolerance rose, the high doses he took would have killed most people. When nightmares, hallucinations and ongoing pain made the situation intolerable, Collins and Caroline visited sulphur spas in Germany, but those treatments provided only temporary relief. At times, in addition to limited mobility, he was unable to read or write and would rely on Carrie to act as amanuensis. In 1867, he was so ill that he could not attend his beloved mother's funeral. Astoundingly, he was able to compose a masterwork like *The Moonstone* and enjoy its success in the midst of such challenges.

The final period of Collins's life included a trip to the United States and Canada in 1873–4. The public readings in America received mixed reviews, with many commentators noting that his performative talents were far inferior to his writerly ones. He continued to battle sometimes poor health, and difficulties with tour managers resulted in an unpredictable reading schedule. In his correspondence, Collins ignored bad reviews, noticing instead the kindness and sincerity of American people as he revelled at impressive dinners with hosts and came home with experiences that informed some of his future works.[6] The novels and plays that followed were of uneven quality, including passages that seem to validate more restrictive views of femininity and disability at odds with the nuances of Collins's earlier works. Still, *The Law and the Lady* (1874–5) features a pregnant British woman in a detective role fearlessly taking herself into one of the nineteenth-century Spanish civil wars – a depiction that outraged conservative respondents. *The Black Robe* (1880–1) is a fast-paced, humorous novel full of homoeroticism that uses documents strategically for narration and includes a critique of Catholicism, all demonstrating that Collins had not lost all of the talents that characterised his work in the 1860s. Collins also distinguished himself in 1884 as a founding member of the Society of Authors, an advocacy group that argued for more effective copyright laws and that remains active today.

At the end of his life, Collins could not host the lavish dinner parties he and Caroline so enjoyed because his health was so often poor. His letters describe near-constant pain or discomfort, but he still tried to take short walks, visit friends when possible, and take comfort in the presence of his children and grandchildren. Just after his sixty-fifth birthday, Collins was in a terrible cab crash and was thrown from the vehicle but, shockingly, was not seriously injured. Later that year, a serious stroke left him severely impaired, but he rallied briefly and was able to write some letters of farewell before he died on 23 September 1889. Collins was aware of death's approach and realised that he would die before finishing *Blind Love*, so he left detailed plans and arranged for Walter Besant to complete the final seven weekly parts. Collins's last will and testament named and provided for Caroline, Carrie, Martha and all of his known biological children. Unfortunately, Carrie's husband Henry Bartley had been mismanaging Collins's affairs, which left much less of an estate for the family to inherit than one would expect. Collins's gravestone stands in London's Kensal Green Cemetery with the inscription he wrote. Caroline is buried with him, but her name does not appear on the white stone marker that reads simply (under a white cross): 'In Memory of Wilkie Collins, Author of The Woman in White and Other Works of Fiction'.

The legacy of Wilkie Collins, as forecasted on that gravestone, stems from his path-breaking work. His name is no longer recognised instantly the world over, nor do adaptations of his works flood cinema screens. Yet Collins's influence remains ubiquitous. The serialised storytelling, suspenseful cliffhangers and crime plots of today's fiction in all forms, whether in print or visually streaming, continue to use techniques and styles that Collins innovated or prefigured. Netflix detectives may not share Sergeant Cuff's penchant for roses, but the presence of their individual quirks remains indebted to a tradition that began in the imaginations of Collins and his contemporaries. The life Collins led was path-breaking in literary circles as well as social ones. He insisted upon experiencing his romantic and sexual love unconventionally, consistently abiding by his principles and caring for others. Although Collins was hardly the only person rejecting patriarchal marriage traditions in the mid-nineteenth century, to openly and publicly eschew monogamy as a famous author was no small risk. Collins took that risk with a smile, loved his families and continued to dream up fiction that entertains 150 years after its publication. Understanding such a life not only helps establish the biographical context for Collins's literary works but also enhances our understanding of the Victorians more generally.

Notes

1. R. Bodenheimer, *Knowing Dickens* (Ithaca, NY: Cornell University Press, 2007), p. 16.
2. Wilkie Collins to Harriet Collins, 4 September 1844, in W. Baker and W. M. Clarke (eds.), *The Letters of Wilkie Collins*, Vol. 1: *1838–1865* (London: Macmillan, 1999), p. 22.
3. Charles Dickens to Wilkie Collins, 12 July 1854, in G. Storey, K. Tillotson and A. Easson (eds.), *The Letters of Charles Dickens* (Pilgrim Edition), Vol. VII: *1853–1855* (Oxford: Clarendon Press, 1993), p. 366. Hereafter cited as Pilgrim.
4. W. Collins, 'Bold Words by a Bachelor', *Household Words* 14 (13 December 1856), pp. 505–7.
5. Col. Charles Beaumont Phipps to Charles Dickens, 5 July 1857. Pilgrim, Vol. VIII, p. 366.
6. See S. R. Hanes, *Wilkie Collins's American Tour, 1873–4*, The History of the Book, No. 3 (London: Pickering & Chatto, 2008).

CHAPTER 2

Letters

William Baker, Andrew Gasson, Graham Law and Paul Lewis

There are essentially three versions of Wilkie Collins's collected correspondence. The recent InteLex digital edition of the *Collected Letters of Wilkie Collins* (2019) incorporates and updates two earlier series by the same editors, listed in alphabetical order (William Baker, Andrew Gasson, Graham Law and Paul Lewis), although the bulk of the work for the digital edition was conducted by the last two named: the upwards of 3,000 letters included in the four volumes of *The Public Face of Wilkie Collins: The Collected Letters* (Pickering & Chatto, 2005); and the nearly 400 letters gradually added between 2005 and 2020 in the thirteen numbers of *The Collected Letters of Wilkie Collins: Addenda and Corrigenda* issued by the Wilkie Collins Society, initially in the pages of the *Wilkie Collins Society Journal*. The process of updating includes making a large number of corrections and revisions to both the letter transcripts and the accompanying editorial material, including in not a few cases changes involving the recipient and/or the dating. This is particularly so with the selection of nearly 600 letters initially published some twenty years ago in *The Letters of Wilkie Collins* (2 vols.; Macmillan, 1999), edited by William Baker and William M. Clarke. With few exceptions, these appeared in *The Public Face of Wilkie Collins* only in summary form, but in the electronic edition all appear complete within the sequence, while both the transcriptions and annotations have now been thoroughly revised. However, the electronic edition in the 'Past Masters' InteLex digital series of editions of the correspondence of major British writers is unfortunately not widely available; indeed, only educational establishments are permitted to buy the 'campus wide license' to access it and only a very few have been sold, and those only to American university libraries including Columbia and Princeton.

In Baker and Clarke's two-volume Macmillan edition (1999) there was a conscious decision to give less priority to 'business letters' or 'notes to his publishers' than to correspondence revealing 'details of his personal or

Table 2.1 *Number of letters by decade*

Decade	Extant Letters	Average Per Annum
1831*–39	9	1.0
1840–49	65	6.5
1850–59	273	27.3
1860–69	703	70.3
1870–79	1093	109.3
1880–89	1224	122.4
1830–89**	3367	57.1

* 1831 was his first known letter
** He died on 23 September 1889

artistic life'.[1] Thus, the Macmillan edition features the lion's share of the letters to his mother, Harriet Collins, and lifelong friend and financial adviser Charles Ward, but passes over the bulk of the correspondence to A. P. Watt, his literary agent, the solicitor William Tindell and publisher Andrew Chatto – to take only the top five identified recipients listed in Table 2.3. As a consequence – to use the formula of Collins's sixty letter-writing years presented in Table 2.1 – the Baker and Clarke selection includes the majority of the letters surviving from the author's earlier decades, but excludes all but a small proportion of those from the later ones.

While new letters continue to surface, the preparation of the digital edition demonstrates that just short of 3,350 items of correspondence have thus far been located in one form or another: at the time of writing, May 2021, there were 3,362 letters with five more waiting in the wings. While this remains only a fraction of the more than 14,000 extant letters written by Dickens, it still represents a substantial body of evidence concerning the hopes and fears of a key Victorian novelist at work and at leisure.

As a collection, Collins's surviving correspondence ranges from the seven-year-old child's letter to his mother away at Brighton (17 October 1831 [0001]) to the dying man's desperate appeal to Francis Carr Beard, his longstanding doctor and friend (21 September 1889 [2972]).[2] The correspondents themselves are active in an extraordinary range of cultural and social activities, and represent a wide variety of backgrounds and outlooks. The tone veers from the brisk and business-like – as in Collins's tart response to a review of *The Queen of Hearts* in the *Athenaeum* (26 October 1859 [0316]), to the painfully private – as in the note of commiseration to his cousin Annie Linsell (née Clunes) on the death of her mother (14 September 1888 [2890]).

For a sample of the range of the charm and wit of his correspondence at its best, here are examples of Wilkie Collins on wine. This offers an anthology of the author's characteristic attitudes: the precocious young man, the cavalier bohemian, the worldly socialite, the gourmet connoisseur, the unconventional traveller, the racy raconteur, the slightly seedy lady's man, the worn and weary man of letters. At the same time, it celebrates the cheerful inventiveness of Collins's self-deception, suggesting that one of his most enduring fictions – almost as elaborate and complex as *No Name* or *Armadale*, and sustained over many more instalments – was the denial of any causal connection between his atrocious diet and appalling health. Few letters from 1863 onwards seem to be entirely free of the spectre of what he prefers to call 'rheumatic gout'.

> The *parties* have knocked me up – I've made two *speeches* at supper and drunk so much of the juice of the grape that (to use the impassioned language of Elihu the Buzzite a comforter of Job) – 'My belly is as wine'. To Harriet Collins, 13 January 1844 [0018]

> How I shall be able to stand the tea & coffee breakfasts at home I don't know! ... I take to the déjeuner à la fourchette regularly – Oyster and Chablis – omlettes and radishes ... afraid I shall be as fat as a pig if I stay here much longer – do nothing but eat and drink – very wrong I know – shall repent upon leg of mutton and rice-pudding when I get home. To Harriet Collins, 21 September 1844 [0023]

> What a night! What speeches! What songs! I carried away much claret and am rather a seedy barrister this morning. I think it must have been the *oaths* that disagreed with me! To Edward Pigott, 22 November 1851 [0095]

> I have begun the great reformation. Observe the hour above [*10 minutes to 9*], and know that I am dressed, and *waiting* for the breakfast bell – a position I never remember to have been placed in before in the whole course of my life ... I feel better already – I take no beer – and I stop short at my three glasses of wine. To Harriet Collins, 7 July 1853 [0148]

> At this moment I don't know where I am going to be in August. My last idea of the Isle of Man has been discouraged by competent authorities who tell me I should be starved there if I went into lodgings and poisoned with execrable wine if I try the Hotels. To Charles Ward, 19 July 1859 [0307]

> The doctor ... proposes no medicine. He is a jolly German with a huge pair of gold spectacles, and a face like an apple – and he smokes his cigar with me every morning after breakfast, like a man who thoroughly enjoys his

tobacco. He allows of *all* wines, provided they are of the best vintages ... all cookery provided it is thoroughly good. To Charles Collins, 22 April 1863 [0535]

The hotel ... contains a cellar of the best Hock and Moselle wines I ever tasted – and possesses a Parisian cook who encourages my natural gluttony by a continuous succession of entrées which are to be eaten but not described. To Nina Lehmann, 29 April 1863 [0536]

If I am alive, it is needless to say how gladly I shall take my place at your table. If I am *not* alive, be so good as to look towards the conservatory, when the butler comes round for the first time with the Champagne. You will perceive a Luminous Appearance – with an empty glass in one hand. To Lady Louisa Goldsmid, 15 May 1865 or 1866 [0677]

Dry champagne is good for your arm. To William Tindell, 16 November 1871 [1163]

Try some good wine – and beware of whisky and water (the last fashionable delusion of the doctors!) To Charles Reade, 21 March 1879 [1832]

The wedding was a triumph – and we were all the better for it. I look back on it with but two subjects for regret. First, the bridesmaids' petticoats were too short. Secondly, I was medically forbidden to drink Champagne. To Jane Ward, 6 January 1882 [1998]

Come with the ducks, next time – receive my thanks in person – and let us drink one more bottle of Old Champagne, with 'gout staring us in the face', and you and I staring back again at the gout with defiant eyes and resolute stomachs. To Sebastian Schlesinger, 27 January 1885 [2398]

The pints of champagne have disappeared. Will you send me six dozen more of the same 'Vin Brut' in half bottles? The sherry also is reported to be on its last legs. Please let me have a three-dozen case (as before) – and send another three-dozen case, address to | Mrs. Dawson | 10 Taunton Place | Park Road, Regents Park. To Beecheno, Yaxley & Co., 12 January 1886 [2515]

Being onboard 'La Champagne', I venture to suggest an amusement for you. Wait till dinner time, and then ask everybody at the table ... if he, she, and they know who invented Champagne? ... Unless I am very much mistaken, you will be the one distinguished person who has heard of that benefactor to his species. His name was Perignon – he was a Benedictine Monk – and he officiated as cellarman in a monastery, when he made his immortal discovery in 1688. To Jane Bigelow, 5 October 1887 [2758]

There are also significant gaps and blind spots. For example, there is only a single letter in draft form to the house of Longman (8 March 1845, [2999]), which published Wilkie Collins's first book, the life of his father, the artist William Collins, though several of Wilkie's letters soliciting subscriptions from his father's distinguished friends and patrons have been preserved. No letters to the Pre-Raphaelites William Holman Hunt and John Millais before the 1860s have surfaced, though we know that Collins was intimate with both from the late 1840s. With the possible exception of [1378], a farewell telegram as Collins set sail for North America on 14 September 1873, still no letters have surfaced to Wilkie's two partners, Caroline Graves and Martha Rudd, or to his and Martha's three children, although there is evidence that a number were still in existence well after the author's death.

The most significant gap is that only a handful of letters to Dickens himself have been preserved ([0091], [0364], [0293], [0593], [3001–3003]), most in fragmentary form. The rest – and altogether there must have been at least somewhere in the region of the 165 from Dickens to Collins that are recorded in the Pilgrim edition – were presumably among the mountains of correspondence destroyed by Dickens at a stroke in September 1860 and piecemeal thereafter.

As for the blind spots, it must be admitted that Collins, unlike George Eliot for instance, can make no claim to be a great intellectual force and there is little in the way of sustained engagement with contemporary debates in religion and science, philosophy or politics. Not infrequently we see him gamely riding hobby horses – for the rights of authors or married women, against the cult of athleticism or the practice of vivisection – but he is never in the vanguard of the active political movement in question. Of course, Collins is always *au fait* with what is 'in the news'. There are, for example, early passing references to the Exposition Universelle in Paris or war in the Crimea; around the 1860s to the American Civil War, or the Persian famine (1870–1), or, in his final decade, to the dispatch of troops to Egypt or the death of Queen Victoria's Highland servant, John Brown. We gather from his correspondence that he is a regular reader of the *Times*, subscribes to the *Evening Echo*, and passes on literary weeklies like the *Athenaeum* and literary monthlies like the *Cornhill* to his aged mother. But he consistently avoids the heavy quarterly reviews, whether the Whig *Edinburgh*, the Tory *Quarterly* or the radical *Westminster*. He smugly advises his mother: 'Whatever the critics may say, readers are certainly grateful for a story that interests them. So don't mind what the Quarterly Review, or any Review says. Or rather, do as I do – don't waste your time in reading them' (18 June 1863, [0539]). Thus we look in vain in the letters for impassioned discussions of Mill or Carlyle, Darwin or Spencer, Newman or Huxley, Arnold or Morris, never mind Comte and Marx. For all that, what we do have is evidence – measured in scores of letters – of a sustained dialogue with family members and relatives, with the companions made in youth (and often later with their partners and children), with new friends acquired on trips to continental Europe or North America, with novelists, poets and painters, with playwrights, actors and theatre managers, with doctors, solicitors and wine merchants, with publishers, editors, printers, copyists and literary agents. Predictably, surviving correspondence with this last group is especially prominent. In addition, there are hundreds of cases where there are only one or two letters to a single correspondent. Occasionally – as with Dickens – these are merely the fragments of a substantial relationship. More typically they bear witness to the growing fame of a writer who struggles to respond to an army of society hostesses, critical cranks, devoted readers and autograph hunters. Together these documents chart the gradual changes in a specific Victorian social and literary milieu.

What then is the overall significance of Wilkie Collins's letters? They provide insight into his compositional methodology, his friendships, whom he knew and his personal relationships, especially, for instance, with his mother. They reveal many facets of his personality: the shrewd businessman; his warmth and generosity; the obsessive worker; a man of complex personal relationships; his international connections over several continents; his pastimes such as yachting, love of cigars and champagne; his health. They throw light on the Victorian novel, theatre and publishing worlds. In short, his letters illuminate a rich tapestry of Victorian life and letters.

Tabular Data

Table 2.1 indicates that, inevitably, the bulk of the extant letters date from Collins's later decades: on average, we have rather over one letter per week for the whole of Collins's letter-writing life, but this figure disguises a spread from less than one a year in his first decade to more than two a week in his last.

Table 2.2 shows little variation from Monday through Thursday but a decline towards the weekend, with under 5 per cent of letters written on Sunday when no mail was delivered.

Table 2.2 *Composition by day of the week*

Day of the Week	No. of Letters	%*
Monday	528	15.7
Tuesday	543	16.1
Wednesday	511	15.2
Thursday	530	15.7
Friday	472	14.0
Saturday	420	12.5
Sunday	160	4.8
Unknown	203	6.0
TOTAL	3,367	100

* Sum may not add up due to round up.

Table 2.3 *Major recipients of letters*

Rank	Correspondent	Letters
1	A. P. Watt	294
2	Harriet Collins	171
3	Unidentified	162
4	William F. Tindell	126
5	Andrew Chatto	113
6	Charles Ward	110
7	George Bentley	107
8	Chatto & Windus	63
9	Edward Pigott	59
10	Charles Kent	56
11	Harper & Brothers	54
12	Hunter, Ross & Co.	46
13	Sebastian Schlesinger	43
14	Cassell, Petter & Galpin	35
15	George Smith	35
16	Richard Bentley	32
17	Frank Archer	31
18	William Holman Hunt	31
19	Anne Wynne	30
20	Nina Lehmann	28
21	Frederick Lehmann	27

Table 2.3 reveals that of the most numerous recipients of identified extant letters, five were publishing houses and their representatives

(Harper, Hunter, Cassell, George Smith, George Bentley), three were women (Harriet Collins, Nina Lehmann, Anne Wynne), seven were close male friends (Charles Ward, Edward Pigott, Charles Kent, Frank Archer, Sebastian Schlesinger, William Holman Hunt, Frederick Lehmann) and none were fellow novelists.

Notes

1. William Baker and W. M. Clarke (eds.), *The Letters of Wilkie Collins*, 2 vols. (London: Macmillan, 1999), vol. 1, p. xii.
2. Throughout, the four-digit numbers in square brackets refer to the unique permanent numbers allocated to each letter in the InteLex edition. In the data tables above, Collins's correspondents not yet mentioned include Edward Pigott, editor of *The Leader* and Collins's sailing companion; Collins's brother Charles; Nina Lehmann, Lady Louisa Goldsmid, Jane Ward and Jane Bigelow, all close friends; the author Charles Reade; Sebastian Schlesinger, subsequently one of the executors of Collins's will; and the wine merchants Beecheno, Yaxley & Co.

CHAPTER 3

Publishers and Editions

Andrew Gasson

During his writing career Collins used nine English publishers for first editions in book form, starting with Longman (1848) for the biography of his father and ending with Chatto & Windus, which ultimately took over twenty-nine of his copyrights. Collins was a firm but fair negotiator but particularly so when he was established as an author, when he would frequently change publishers in order to secure the most advantageous financial arrangement.

English Editions

Single titles were published by: Longman, *Memoirs of the Life of William Collins, Esq., R.A.* (1848); Hurst & Blackett, *The Queen of Hearts* (1859); Tinsley, *The Moonstone* (1868); F. S. Ellis & Co., *Man and Wife* (1870); and Arrowsmith, *The Guilty River* (1886).

Multiple titles were issued by Bentley, Sampson Low, Smith, Elder and Chatto & Windus.

Despite the partial collections issued by these firms, there is no complete edition of Collins's works. Their series might be termed 'cumulative editions', as new titles were added as they were written or their copyrights acquired.

Richard Bentley & Son

Richard Bentley published ten first editions:

Antonina (1850)
Rambles Beyond Railways (1851)
Mr Wray's Cash-Box (1852)
Basil (1852)
Hide and Seek (1854)

Poor Miss Finch (1872)
Miss or Mrs? and Other Stories in Outline (1873)
The New Magdalen (1873)
The Frozen Deep (1874)
A Rogue's Life (1879)

Collins's connection with Richard Bentley began with the publication of *Antonina* (27 February 1850). It was followed by *Rambles Beyond Railways* (30 January 1851), *Mr Wray's Cash-Box* (December 1851 [book dated 1852]), which included John Everett Millais's first book illustration, *Basil* (16 November 1852) and *Hide and Seek* (6 June 1854). Collins also made several contributions to *Bentley's Miscellany*.

Basil subsequently appeared in Bentley's Railroad Library (Bentley's Shilling Series) during 1854 before the title was bought by James Blackwood in 1856.

During the early 1860s Bentley made various overtures to Collins, which he politely declined, to renew their 'former literary connection'.[1] There was, in fact, an interval of eighteen years before their association was re-established with the publication of *Poor Miss Finch* in January 1872. Collins's negotiations with the firm had always involved hard bargaining, but in this instance he showed great fairness. The novel was still running in *Cassell's Magazine* when it was offered to the lending libraries Mudie and W. H. Smith. Smith, in particular, realised that the title would soon be available much more cheaply as a bound volume from Cassell, and placed a negligible order for the three-volume edition. Collins immediately proposed to adjust the terms of his contract so that Bentley would not lose by the transaction: this offer, however, was declined.[2]

Bentley next published a one-volume collection of short stories, *Miss or Mrs? and Other Stories in Outline* (1873). George Bentley was at this time editing *Temple Bar* magazine, and *The New Magdalen* (October 1872–July 1873) was the first of Collins's novels to appear in the monthly publication, followed by *The Frozen Deep* (August–September 1874). *Poor Miss Finch* (1872) and *The New Magdalen* (1873) were issued respectively in three and two volumes and subsequently in Bentley's Favourite Novels at 6s.

Collins also began negotiations with Bentley to issue *The Woman in White* in a 6s edition because of the poor proceeds from Smith, Elder's cheap 2s series. Ultimately, however, he accepted a better offer from Chatto & Windus in November 1874 for all of his available copyrights together with his next novel, *The Law and The Lady*. *The Two Destinies*, however, was serialised in *Temple Bar* (January–September 1876), together with the Christmas story 'The Mystery of Marmaduke' (January 1879). Collins also gave Bentley the first refusal to publish the three-volume edition of *The Fallen Leaves*, although this was eventually issued by Chatto & Windus.

Bentley's final Collins publication came in 1879 with *A Rogue's Life*. This slim volume appeared as number VII in Bentley's Half-crown Empire Library which consisted of sixteen titles issued between 1878 and 1881.³

Sampson Low

Sampson Low published three first editions:

The Woman in White (1860)
No Name (1862 [dated 1863])
My Miscellanies (1863)

Following the success of *The Woman in White*, Sampson Low during 1861–2 began to issue The Novels and Romances of Wilkie Collins in a 'cheap and uniform edition' of six titles, priced at either 5s or 6s. Each had a vignette frontispiece, by H. K. Browne for *Antonina* and by John Gilbert for *Basil*, *Hide and Seek*, *The Dead Secret*, *The Queen of Hearts* and *The Woman in White*. Low added a one-volume edition of *No Name* in 1864, illustrated by Millais and priced at 6s. The series was subsequently advertised as both Low's Favourite Library of Popular Books and Low's Popular Library of Favourite Books.

The original six titles in this uniform edition were published in 1861 and 1862 in purple or magenta cloth. There were several reissues, and copies bound in green cloth were usually but not invariably of later date. With the exception of *Basil*, these are the first one-volume editions:

Antonina (1861); with a new Preface dated November 1860 and frontispiece by H. K. Browne, 5s. Reissued in 1863 and 1864, and in pictorial boards in 1865 at 2s 6d.

The Dead Secret (1861); with a new Preface dated January 1861, advertisements dated 1 August 1861 and frontispiece by John Gilbert, 5s. Later issues in 1862 and 1863.

The Woman in White (1861); with a new Preface dated February 1861, frontispiece by John Gilbert and a photographic portrait of the author, 6s. Published in April 1861. Later issues in 1862 and 1863; and with the same binding by Smith, Elder in 1868. Also issued in pictorial boards in September 1865 at 2s 6d.⁴

Hide and Seek (1861); with a new Preface dated September 1861 and frontispiece by John Gilbert, 5s. A later issue in 1863.

The Queen of Hearts (1862); with advertisements dated February 1862 and frontispiece by John Gilbert, 5s. This title has a different pattern from the rest of the series for the blocking on the front and rear boards. A later issue in 1863. Issued in pictorial boards in 1865 at 2s 6d.

Basil (1862); with a new 'Letter of Dedication' dated July 1862, advertisements dated January 1862 and frontispiece by John Gilbert, 5s. A later issue in 1863.

No Name (1864); Preface dated November 1862 (from the first edition in three volumes) and frontispiece by J. E. Millais, 6s.

Sampson Low sold the copyrights of these seven titles to Smith, Elder in 1865. Chatto & Windus subsequently bought the copyrights to *Antonina*, *The Dead Secret*, *Hide and Seek* and *The Woman in White* in 1874 and *After Dark* and *No Name* in 1890.

Smith, Elder & Co.

Smith, Elder published two first editions:

After Dark (1856)
Armadale (1866)

George Smith issued *After Dark* in 1856 followed by one-volume editions at 2s 6d between 1859 and 1863 in limp orange cloth as part of their Cheap Editions of Standard Works, plus a one-volume illustrated edition at 5s in 1862.

Smith always regretted missing *The Woman in White* and was also unsuccessful in obtaining *No Name*, managing only to push up the price paid by Low to £3,000. Still determined to publish Collins, he secured *Armadale* for *The Cornhill Magazine* with an offer of £5,000, the largest sum at that time paid to any novelist except Dickens. Smith, Elder also published for Collins his dramatic version of *Armadale* (1866) in an edition of twenty-five copies.

In 1865, Smith, Elder took over the publishing rights from Sampson Low for their six one-volume titles issued from 1861 to 1862: *Antonina*, *Basil*, *The Dead Secret*, *Hide and Seek*, *The Queen of Hearts* and *The Woman in White*, plus the 1864 one-volume edition of *No Name*. These were issued as 'Cheap editions of Mr. Wilkie Collins's Novels. In Fancy

Boards. Fcap. 8vo. 2s. 6d. each.' These were similar in style to yellowbacks but in orange-brown boards lettered and decorated in black on front and back covers.⁵

Smith, Elder also advertised *After Dark* in their 'Cheap editions of Standard Works, well printed on good paper, and strongly bound in cloth', at 2s 6d. *Armadale*, which had been serialised in monthly parts in *The Cornhill Magazine*, was subsequently issued in book form from 1866, and Smith, Elder issued the nine titles in a variety of uniform editions:

1. Pictorial Boards at 2s, from 1871.
2. Limp green cloth at 2s 6d, between 1870 and 1889.
3. Bright red pebble-grain cloth, between 1871 and 1874.

Also, from 1871, Smith, Elder issued in 5s editions *The Moonstone* (originally in three volumes from Tinsley in 1868) and *Man and Wife* (originally in three volumes from F. S. Ellis in 1870).

In 1874 Chatto & Windus purchased the copyrights of all Collins's titles except *After Dark*, *Armadale* and *No Name*. Smith, Elder continued to issue these three titles until they were sold to Chatto in November 1890. They were included in Smith, Elder & Co.'s Popular Library of Cheap Editions of Standard Works, foolscap octavo at 2s 6d, as well as other editions at 3s 6d and 2s.

Chatto & Windus

Chatto & Windus published twelve first English editions (‡). By November 1890, they had issued in various formats twenty-nine titles, including the three (†) which had been retained until then by Smith, Elder and *A Rogue's Life* from Bentley, which was also first issued by Chatto in 1890. Those marked (*) were originally issued in the New Illustrated Library Edition during 1875:

Antonina
Basil
Hide and Seek
†*After Dark*
The Dead Secret
The Queen of Hearts
The Woman in White
†*No Name*
My Miscellanies

†*Armadale*
*The Moonstone
*Man and Wife
*Poor Miss Finch
*The New Magdalen
**Miss or Mrs?: and Other Stories in Outline*
**The Frozen Deep: and Other Stories*
‡**The Law and the Lady* (1875)
‡*The Two Destinies* (1876)
‡*The Haunted Hotel* (1879)
‡*The Fallen Leaves* (1879)
† *A Rogue's Life*
‡*Jezebel's Daughter* (1880)
‡*The Black Robe* (1881)
‡*Heart and Science* (1883)
‡*'I Say No'* (1884)
‡*The Evil Genius* (1886)
‡*Little Novels* (1887)
‡*The Legacy of Cain* (1888 [dated 1889])
‡*Blind Love* (1890)

Chatto & Windus became Collins's main publishers, commencing in 1875 with *The Law and the Lady*. *The Haunted Hotel* (1879) and *Heart and Science* (1883) first appeared in *Belgravia* magazine.

Collins had always been keen to see his books in cheap editions to appeal to the widest possible range of readers. He had previously suggested the idea to Smith, Elder which felt it would not be in their joint interests, and to Bentley who was prepared to proceed. Ultimately, however, Collins reached agreement in November 1874 with Andrew Chatto for an inclusive payment of £2,000 for a seven-year lease of the thirteen available copyrights for his earlier works.[6]

The first new work to be published by Chatto was *The Law and the Lady*. The contract was signed on 9 September 1874 for a lease on the copyright, for which Collins was to receive £1,500. Chatto & Windus issued thirteen titles (*) from 1875 in 6s and 2s editions. The three copyrights retained by Smith, Elder were excluded. *After Dark*, *No Name* and *Armadale* (†) together with Bentley's *A Rogue's Life*, did not appear in Chatto's advertisements until November 1890. They then listed twenty-nine titles which were published in various formats well into the twentieth century, at least partly dispelling the myth that Collins's popularity declined after his death in 1889.

In March 1883 Collins considered the sale of the copyrights of nineteen titles – the original thirteen plus the first six published by Chatto between 1875 and 1881 – but in the event he declined the sum of £2,500.[7] In April 1889, however, he was obliged to accept £1,800 for the then available twenty-four works, excluding his last novel, *Blind Love*, which was subject to a separate agreement.[8]

New Illustrated Library Edition

The first cheap editions from Chatto were issued in the New Illustrated Library Edition priced at 6s. Collins was one of the few exceptions to the series design which was uniform for the majority of authors, where each was assigned a different coloured cloth. For example, Walter Besant had light blue, James Payn dark blue, Hall Caine olive green and Charles Reade red. Chatto seemed to have experimented with various trial bindings for Collins, so that early examples from 1875 and 1876 are occasionally found in green, blue and red, although his final colour became green – which Collins observed to Chatto was his favourite colour.[9] He also had a different and more elegant cover design when compared with those of his contemporaries. The size was approximately 18 × 12.5 cm with various shades of plain yellow endpapers and frequently without a rear publisher's catalogue. There were fourteen titles (*), the thirteen previously issued by Sampson Low, Smith, Elder and Bentley, plus the recently published *The Law and the Lady*. They used the same stereo plates and frontispiece engravings, with further illustrations added by artists such as Alfred Concanen, George du Maurier, F. A. Fraser, A. B. Houghton and M. F. Mahoney. The New Illustrated Library Edition lasted until mid-1876, when the series became the Piccadilly Novels.

The Piccadilly Novels

The Piccadilly Novels became Chatto's superior collected edition for all authors. Titles were originally priced at the same 6s until around May 1880, after which they were advertised at the lower price of 3s 6d. Most issues can be dated from the title page and usually carried a publisher's catalogue bound in at the end, but this date is frequently unreliable. The page size was approximately 19 × 12.5 cm in crown octavo format, always in green cloth with the same consistent cover design for all titles. The endpapers are occasionally found in black but usually carried a fern or floral design which changed with time. Previously published titles continued to use the same stereo plates. Ultimately all Collins's twenty-nine titles were published in the Piccadilly Novels until about 1895. From the 1890s Chatto advertisements began to refer to Piccadilly Novels as a 'Library Edition'. A few of the early titles were reset and badly worn plates were sold on to cheap publishers such as R. E. King.

The New Illustrated Library Edition and Piccadilly Novels were illustrated up until the issue of *The Two Destinies* (1876). This and later titles were unillustrated, except for *The Haunted Hotel* and *Blind Love*, where illustrations were taken from their previous serialisation. With *Antonina*, *The Dead Secret* and *My Miscellanies*, the illustrations from their 1875 publication were dropped by 1889, 1890 and 1895 respectively, although frontispieces were retained.

Library Edition

The Piccadilly Novels were superseded by the Library Edition, designated thus on the title page, and published in dark maroon vertical fine-ribbed cloth in crown octavo at 3s 6d. The first titles appeared about 1890, and continued to be issued well into the twentieth century, eventually including all twenty-nine Chatto titles. There were hybrid editions such as *The Legacy of Cain* in 1891 and *A Rogue's Life* in 1894, with the title page and format of the Piccadilly Novels but using the maroon binding of the Library Edition. Some Library Edition titles are seen as late as 1925. Several titles dropped the illustrations but continued to use the same stereo plates throughout: seven were advertised as 'reset in new type, in uniform style':

Antonina
Basil
Hide and Seek
The Dead Secret
The Woman in White
The Moonstone
Man and Wife

From the 1920s some were issued in dust wrappers which advertised the following seven titles in the New Piccadilly Library while retaining 'Library Edition' on the title page:

The Dead Secret
The Woman in White
The Moonstone

Man and Wife
No Name
Armadale
The Legacy of Cain

Popular Edition

After publication in the Piccadilly Novels, titles were issued from 1877 in Chatto's small-format Popular Edition in limp green cloth at 2s 6d. Ultimately, all twenty-nine titles appeared in this format, with several issued into the early twentieth century. They used the same stereo plates as the Piccadilly Novels but generally did not include illustrations. The page size varied from approximately 17 × 11.5 cm to 18.5 × 12.5 cm, with front covers lettered and decorated in black.

The earlier issues had undated title pages with rear advertisements dated between 1877 and 1885 and the rear covers blocked in blind with a publisher's medallion device. Later issues mostly had dated title pages. Between about 1885 and 1895, rear covers were blocked in blind with a floral decoration; copies with dates between 1893 and 1911 had plain rear covers.

Pictorial Boards (Yellowbacks)

Copies in pictorial boards were advertised as 'Cheap editions of popular novels post 8vo, illustrated boards, 2s. each'. Ultimately, all twenty-nine Chatto titles were issued in this format into the early twentieth century. They carried a front cover illustration taken from the New Illustrated Library or Piccadilly Novels, mainly with typical yellow boards. Some issues of *The Woman in White* and *Blind Love* had, unusually, white boards. Yellowbacks were first issued from 1877, and up to about 1881 had undated title pages with spine titles printed on a pale blue or pale green background above a design incorporating a circle. Chatto also used this design for other authors. From about 1882 onwards, most issues had dated title pages and spine titles printed on a yellow background above a purely rectangular design.[10] The approximate page size of yellowback volumes was 17 × 11 cm.

Sixpenny and Shilling Editions

Six titles advertised as 'Popular Sixpenny Editions in medium 8vo' were issued in tan or buff paper wrappers printed in black or dark blue with an approximate size of 22 × 15 cm. They were published between about 1894 and 1907, dated on the front cover and with the text printed in double columns. Of the six titles, the first three, and possibly others, were also issued in boards at 1s with the wrappers bound in. There was also a combined edition of *The Woman in White* and *The Moonstone* in red boards in 1895:

The Woman in White
The Moonstone
The Dead Secret
Antonina
The New Magdalen
Man and Wife

There are also references in advertisements around 1910 to *The Haunted Hotel* and *Poor Miss Finch* in this format.[11]

Other Editions

The Woman in White was issued in 1902 as part of the St Martin's Library in a large-type fine-paper edition, post octavo; in cloth at 2s or in leather at 3s. This was subsequently reissued by Albert & Charles Boni from 1925.

The Frozen Deep was issued in a large-type foolscap octavo edition in cloth at 1s; and in a small format Popular Edition in both red boards and leather dated 1905 and reprinted in 1917.

The Legacy of Cain was issued in 1915 in brown cloth as part of Chatto's Khaki Library 'For Soldiers and Sweethearts' priced at 1s 6d.

Heart and Science was issued in purple cloth with yellow lettering in 1917.

Overseas Editions: Harper's

In the United States, Collins's main publishers were Harper's. They first published Collins in 1850, paying £15 for early proofs of *Antonina*. *The Dead Secret* appeared anonymously in *Harper's Weekly* in 1857, although not published by them in book form until 1873. In 1858, Harper's made a five-year agreement for Collins's books in the US for which they paid royalties of 5 per cent. With his increasing success, they later paid £750 for both *The Moonstone* (1868) and *Man and Wife* (1870). Harper's were generally reluctant to issue collections of short stories as they found them unremunerative.

Harper's liberally entertained Collins during his reading tour of North America, and from 1873 issued a uniform, illustrated library edition of his works to commemorate his visit. Relations remained extremely cordial until 1878 when there was a temporary falling out. Harper's declined to take *The Haunted Hotel* because of the activities of pirate publishers and changes in international copyright, which allowed Canadian imprints to be sold in the USA. Relations were restored by 1884 for the publication of *'I Say No'*. Collin's novels and short stories appeared in several Harper's series.

Harper's Illustrated Editions

The first book editions of eight serialisations from *Harper's Weekly* were printed in double columns, using the same type and illustrations. They were in demy octavo format and issued simultaneously in cloth and paper wrappers. *Antonina* and *The New Magdalen*, using the same format, were numbered as part of Harper's Library of Select Novels. The dates and prices given are those of first issue:

Antonina (1850), No. 141, only in tan paper wrappers at 37½ cents; and reissued in 1864 at 50 cents.
The Woman in White (1860), in paper wrappers at 75 cents and cloth at $1.25.
No Name (1863), in paper wrappers at $1.25 and cloth at $1.50.
Armadale (1866), in paper wrappers at $1.60 and cloth at $2.00.
The Moonstone (1868), in paper wrappers at $1.50 and cloth at $2.00.
Man and Wife (1870), in paper wrappers at $1.00 and cloth at $1.50.
Poor Miss Finch (1872), in paper wrappers at $1.00 and cloth at $1.50.
The New Magdalen (1873), No. 395) only in paper wrappers at 50 cents.
The Law and the Lady (1875), only in paper wrappers at 75 cents.
The Two Destinies (1876), only in paper wrappers at 50 cents.

Harper's Illustrated Library Edition

This is the most complete edition from Harpers, with seventeen titles in 12mo green cloth issued between 1873 and 1902. This series was issued to coincide with Collins's reading tour of North America and contains a facsimile inscription in Collins's hand: 'I gratefully dedicate this collected edition of my works, to the American People'.

The books were first issued from 1873 at $1.50. Later issues from about 1874 were priced at $1.25 and the edition was reissued until early in the twentieth century. Beginning about 1893, Harper's issued titles in the Moonstone Edition in dark blue cloth:

After Dark and Other Stories
Antonina
Armadale
Basil
Hide and Seek
'I Say No'
Man and Wife
My Miscellanies
No Name
Poor Miss Finch
The Dead Secret
The Law and the Lady
The Moonstone
The New Magdalen
The Queen of Hearts
The Two Destinies
The Woman in White

No Name and *The Woman in White* were issued in the same format as part of The People's Library in 100 Volumes, designated thus on the front cover and spine.

Other Harper's Series

Harper's Handy Series
The Ghost's Touch and Other Stories (1885), No. 30.
The Evil Genius [1886], No. 72, first book publication.
The Guilty River (1886), No. 105.

Harper's Half-Hour Series
Percy and the Prophet (1877), No. 25, first separate edition.
My Lady's Money (1877), No. 45, first separate edition.

Franklin Square Library

A cheap series started in 1878 to compete with pirated editions from other publishers. Harper's paid an honorarium to British authors and generally did not use the series for new books:

Man and Wife (1879), No 38, in paper wrappers at 15 cents.
'I Say No' (1884), No. 385 at 20 cents.

Other North American Publishers

Other legitimate US publishers included D. Appleton & Co. (New York; *Basil*, 1853 and *Blind Love*, 1890); Miller & Curtis (New York; *The Dead Secret*, 1857); and William Gill (Boston; *The Frozen Deep*, 1874 and *Alicia Warlock and Other Stories*, 1875). In Toronto, works were issued by Hunter, Rose & Company (*The New Magdalen*, 1873, *Readings in America*, 1874, *The Dead Alive*, 1874, *The Law and the Lady*, 1875, and *The Two Destinies*, 1876); Rose-Belford Publishing Company (*The Haunted Hotel*, 1878, and *The Fallen Leaves*, 1879); and Rose Publishing Company (*The Black Robe*, 1881).

Collier (New York) published a thirty-volume collected edition in 1900. This does not include all of Collins's works since it omits *The Guilty River*, *Mr Wray's Cash-Box* and the non-fiction.

Many of Collins's titles were issued in pirated, unauthorised editions, the most comprehensive of which were the Seaside Library (Munro, New York) and those issued by T. B. Peterson (Philadelphia). The many other inter-related pirates included Belford, Clarke, the Federal Book Company, the International Book Company, J. W. Lovell and F. M. Lupton.

Other Overseas Publishers

Tauchnitz (Leipzig) in English issued twenty-eight titles in fifty volumes. Fifteen French translations were published by Hachette (Paris) and four by Hetzel (Paris). Dutch translations were issued by Belinfante Brothers and works in Italian by Fratelli Treves. There were translations into German, Russian, Spanish, Danish and Swedish, amongst other European languages.

Notes

1. W. Collins to Richard Bentley, 5 January 1863, in W. Baker, A. Gasson, G. Law and P. Lewis (eds.), *The Public Face of Wilkie Collins: The Collected Letters*, 4 vols. (New York: Routledge, 2005), vol. I, p. 287. Hereafter cited as BGLL.
2. W. Collins to George Bentley, 22 March 1872. BGLL, vol. II, pp. 34–5.
3. M. Sadleir, *XIX Century Fiction: A Bibliographical Record Based on His Own Collection*, 2 vols. (New York: Cooper Square Publishers, Inc., 1969), vol. II, p. 91.
4. C. W. Topp, *Victorian Yellowbacks & Paperbacks, 1849–1905*, 9 vols. (Denver, CO: Hermitage Antiquarian Bookshop, 1999), vol. IV, p. 282.
5. G. Hargreaves, 'Wilkie Collins in Smith, Elder Boards 1865–66', *Studies in Bibliography* 59.1 (December 2015), pp. 269–80.
6. W. Collins to Andrew Chatto, 8 February 1875, Notes 2 and 3. BGLL, vol. III, pp. 70–7.
7. W. Collins to Andrew Chatto, 28 March 1883, Note 3. BGLL, vol. III, pp. 392–3.
8. W. Collins to Andrew Chatto, 2 April 1889. BGLL, vol. IV, pp. 369–70.
9. W. Collins to Andrew Chatto, 29 April 1887. BGLL, vol. IV, p. 249.
10. Topp refers to this as a 'special Collins spine', in *Victorian Yellowbacks*, vol. III, p. 92.
11. All eight titles together with *Armadale*, *No Name*, *Poor Miss Finch*, *The Legacy of Cain* and *The Law and the Lady* are illustrated in *Sixpenny Wonderfuls: 6d Gems from the Past* (London: Chatto & Windus/Hogarth Press, 1985). They are undated but shown with bright pictorial wrappers, priced on the cover at 6d.

CHAPTER 4

Early Novels

Christopher Pittard

Early in his writing career, Wilkie Collins appeared anxious that wider cultural contexts might not only inform his works, but bury them. His first published work was not a novel but *Memoirs of the Life of William Collins, Esq., R.A.* (1848), a biography of his artist father. In a letter to the writer R. H. Dana, of 15 November 1848, Collins cautiously notes: 'What chances of success can be predicted for a book devoted to so peaceful a subject as the Art, amid the vital and varied interests of home politics and foreign revolutions now attracting everybody's attention in England, it is impossible to say.'[1] Similar concerns resurface in his correspondence about the novel usually seen as closing his early period, *Hide and Seek* (1854), published at the outset of the Crimean War. He tells his mother that half of the first edition has been sold, 'Not so bad in War times', but more pessimistically speculates to his publisher Richard Bentley that 'If this war continues, the prospects of Fiction are likely to be very uncertain.'[2] Collins was equally capable of harnessing topical events to promote his writing, but his first four novels – the initially unpublished *Ioláni*, *Antonina* (1850), *Basil* (1852) and *Hide and Seek* – are particularly concerned with the place of the individual in broader historical contexts, and the position of the artist/novelist in the marketplace.

The conflict between art and commerce was especially vivid for Collins in writing his first novel, *Ioláni; or, Tahíti as it Was*, since he drafted it while working at the tea merchant Antrobus & Co. The novel attempted to capitalise on the early nineteenth-century fascination with Polynesia in texts such as Mary Russell Mitford's *Christina, the Maid of the South Seas* (1811), Harriet Martineau's *Dawn Island* (1845), and most famously Herman Melville's *Typee* (1846). This fascination was, in part, the inheritance of eighteenth-century explorations of the South Pacific by James Cook, Captain Bligh and the *Bounty* mutineers, and various missionary trips between the 1760s and 1830s. The most influential of these was William Ellis's 1816–24 expedition, an account of which was published as

Narrative of a Tour through Hawaii (1825) and expanded into the four-volume *Polynesian Researches* (1831–3). Ellis's Christian depiction of the Polynesians as immoral and simultaneously violent and indolent shaped Collins's plot, in which the titular villainous priest fathers a child with Idía, who (with her companion Aimáta) absconds with the child to protect it from the religiously decreed fate of ritual infanticide. Ioláni's personal pursuit of Idía becomes entwined with politics when his power is threatened by the rebel leader Mahine, an ally of Idía's who eventually marries Aimáta. As Ira Nadel notes, Collins's names are all borrowed from existing Tahitian figures portrayed in Ellis's book, though the personalities of Collins's characters do not exactly correspond to their originals.[3]

For modern readers *Ioláni* is an atypical Collins novel, partly because the manuscript was unpublished until 1999. Longman accepted the book in 1845 on condition that William Collins pay for the publishing costs; he declined. Chapman & Hall rejected the submission outright, a disappointment to Collins who had bet on the novel's success when asking his mother for a loan to cover travel expenses: 'Could you not send me £100 upon the strength of my M.S. and Chapman and Hall?'[4] Yet the novel anticipates the centrality of memory and shock to Collins's later work. In one scene, Ioláni pursues Idía through the forests, but the hunt is interrupted by his sudden encounter with a solitary savage figure among the trees, illuminated by lightning. Transfixed by the sight, Ioláni later finds that he involuntarily replays the image in his memory:

> More and more vivid grew the ghastly repetition of the scene. A darkness gathered over his eyes, and again, in his imagination, did the thunder howl forth, the lightening [sic] flash and the thick, fierce rain pour around him. It was too terrible to be borne ... It seemed as if the thousand imaginary fears – the many assaults of irresolution, that had been spared him during the commission of former crimes, had arisen, at the signal of his present iniquity, to heap on him, in one short hour, the torments of years on years; and then to resolve themselves ... into a single recollection – a simple remembrance of a terrible and unwelcome sight. But even in this, lay a mystery mortal penetration could not fathom. It was a memory unlike other memories.[5]

A 'memory unlike other memories' provides a succinct summary of the kinds of psychological shock Collins would go on to explore, drawing on the mid-Victorian psychological research of William Carpenter on unconscious processes and John Elliotson on mesmerism and its therapeutic uses. *Tahiti as it Was*, then, is influenced by 1840s models of the mind.

Collins began work on a second historical novel, *Antonina; or, The Fall of Rome*, but the work was interrupted by the death of his father in 1847, and by Collins's subsequent writing of William's *Memoirs*, a text of double significance. Firstly, its vivid depiction of the social world of early nineteenth-century visual art finds echoes in the subsequent fiction, with William providing the model for the titular artist of the short story 'A Passage in the Life of Perugino Potts' (1852) and potentially for the artist Valentine Blyth in *Hide and Seek*, though more recent criticism disagrees on the extent of this influence. The second point of significance of the *Memoirs* is their representation of the artist as reconciling the demands of creative vision with the artistic marketplace. Collins portrays his father as an artist who achieves commercial success through the development of a speciality (in this case, images of the kind of bright domestic scenes that his son would later demonstrate were underwritten by Gothic darkness). From an early stage of his career Collins was acutely aware of a disjuncture between his version of artistic truth and a more commercial readership (particularly in the revised preface to *Basil*), but at this stage he had not yet discovered his own niche.

Collins returned to *Antonina* in July 1847. Like *Ioláni* it relied heavily on textual sources, including Edward Bulwer-Lytton's *The Last Days of Pompeii* (1834), Edward Gibbon's narrative of the Goth Alaric's conquest of Rome in 410 CE, and Jean Charles Léonard de Sismondi's *Histoire de la chute de l'Empire romain* (1835). But unlike Tahiti, the imperial Roman setting had more immediate political and personal relevance. The novel was published shortly after the 1848–9 upheaval in Rome prompted by the assassination of Pellegrino Rossi and the French siege of the city, resisted by Garibaldi. Collins, ever alert to marketing opportunities, enquired on 30 August 1849 whether Bentley might be interested in the book 'while recent occurrences continue to direct public attention particularly on Roman affairs'.[6] Collins had in mind the earlier rejection of the manuscript by Smith, Elder, on the basis that George Smith did not want a historical novel. The appeal to contemporary events worked, and Bentley published the novel the following February. But the Roman setting also had personal resonance for Collins; between 1836 and 1838 William had taken his family to Italy on an extended tour, passing through Rome twice. Wilkie later mythologised the experience; returning to the city with Dickens in 1853, he told Dickens that his first trip involved a love intrigue with an older woman in which (in Dickens's phrase) 'he came out quite a pagan Jupiter in the business'.[7] Even if the details of this story were mostly fantasised (the biographical record is unclear on the question), the tale demonstrates the considerable emotional import of Rome for Collins.

Dickens's description of the teenage Collins as a 'pagan Jupiter' neatly recalls *Antonina*'s revisitation of the dominant themes of *Ioláni*: the political power of religious extremists and the manner in which women resist these forces. Religious conflict in the novel is represented in the antagonism of the Christian fundamentalist Numerian and the Pagan priest Ulpius (a reworking of Ioláni), who seeks to reinstate the older religion. Ulpius's scheme is twofold: initially planning to undermine Numerian by encouraging the seduction of his daughter Antonina by Vetranio, a more powerful opportunity emerges when the Goths besiege the city and Ulpius plots to betray Rome in return for their assistance in restoring paganism. A second strand concerns the Goth Goisvintha, whose hatred of the Romans after the death of her children at the siege of Aquileia becomes all-consuming, to the extent that when she discovers that her brother Hermanric has fallen in love with Antonina, she attempts to kill them both. Political insurrection is thus paralleled with psychological disturbance, and critical attention to *Antonina* reads it in the contexts of British insurrections of the 1840s (in particular, agitations surrounding the delivery of the third Chartist petition to Westminster in 1848) and the mid-Victorian psychology of Jean-Etienne Esquirol and Forbes Winslow that drew connections between insanity and insurrection.[8]

The narratorial form of *Antonina* facilitates these connections between imperial Rome and 1840s Britain. At the time of publication Collins had worried that the fifth-century setting was too remote to find a readership, yet the narrator is nevertheless of the nineteenth century.[9] The beginning of chapter 2 snaps the Victorian reader back into the present day with references to 'the ordinary track of tourists in modern Italy'; in the novel's most remarkable chapter, describing Vetranio's Gothic 'banquet of famine', the slaves who have prepared the orgy then flee the house 'like engineers who had fired a train, and were escaping ere the explosion burst forth'.[10] Collins's preoccupation with visual metaphor is likewise deployed anachronistically when the trio of Hermanric, Antonina and Goisvintha is described as 'a picture executed by the hand of Rembrandt and imagined by the mind of Raphael' (An: 139). The novel's various biblical quotations are, unavoidably, from the King James Version. Any easy division between Collins's earlier historical novels and his narratives of Victorian modernity is not quite as secure as it seems; unsurprisingly given its personal context, *Antonina* is a touristic novel, narrated by a spectral Victorian observer.

Early Novels

Nevertheless, Collins saw his next novel, *Basil*, as a break with historical fiction, emphasising in his letter of dedication that the novel was one of urban realism (scenes include 'the most ordinary street sounds – sounds that could be heard', and the initial meeting of Basil and Margaret Sherwin on a bus takes place 'in the very last place and under the very last circumstances which the artifices of sentimental writing would sanction').[11] The early pages of the novel tempt the reader into aligning Basil with Collins himself: the opening sentence of the novel 'What now am I about to write?' is as much Collins's question, having decided to shift genre.[12] Basil, too, is drafting a historical novel set on the continent. But it rapidly becomes clear that Basil's interpretive skills are some way from Collins's; his historical novel goes unfinished and he fails to read the signs and clues of a darker plot in the agreement to keep his marriage to Margaret unconsummated for a year (ostensibly to allow Basil's aristocratic father to accept a daughter-in-law from the world of trade). The clerk Robert Mannion presents Basil with 'an utter void. Never had I before seen any human face which baffled all inquiry like his. No mask could have been made expressionless enough to resemble it; and yet it looked like a mask' (B: 110). Mannion's blankness is really an error of Basil's perception, a twist facilitated by the novel's first-person narration; on trailing Mannion and Margaret to a hotel, Basil overhears evidence of her infidelity. The enraged Basil brutally attacks Mannion and disfigures him, and the two men become locked in a destructive mutual obsession, although Mannion's hatred of Basil is revealed to have deeper roots. Their climactic confrontation occurs on the cliffs near Land's End, with Collins's depiction of Cornwall heavily influenced by his visit there in the summer of 1850 that formed the basis for the travelogue *Rambles Beyond Railways* (1851).

Despite Collins's claims that *Basil* marks a move to urban modernity and realism, its foregrounding of obsession, psychosexual desire (another text Basil fails to interpret correctly is his own prophetic dream) and the Gothic doubling of fatally intertwined characters is a continuation from *Antonina*. The Gothic excesses of the earlier novel are reworked in *Basil*'s oft-cited debt to Mary Shelley's *Frankenstein* (1818), with Mannion as the disfigured creation of Basil, and where each complements the other's monstrosity. What is less often noted, however, is the manner in which both novels turn on the shoddiness of built environments: the crumbling and hollow city wall plays a vital part in *Antonina*, while Basil hears his wife's infidelity through a hotel's flimsy partition ('It's only boards papered over') (B: 160). The wall contrasts with the solidity of the pavement, 'newly mended with granite', into which Basil fatefully grinds his rival's face, but the trajectory of the novel decomposes the stones of the road into the unmined granite of the Cornish cliffs (B: 164).

Stylistically, then, there is a greater break between *Basil* and Collins's next novel, *Hide and Seek*, centred on the mystery of the young girl Madonna's true parentage after her adoption by Valentine Blyth. The novel introduces two features which would characterise Collins's subsequent work: a more comedic sensibility (drawn from Dickens, the novel's dedicatee) and the sympathetic representation of disability, which would be developed further in *The Moonstone* (1868), *Poor Miss Finch* (1872), *The Law and the Lady* (1875) and *The Two Destinies* (1876). The prologue's depiction of a dull Sunday in which the young Zack Thorpe (Blyth's artistic protégé) resists his father's authoritarian Christianity recalls Dickens's 1836 pamphlet 'Sunday Under Three Heads', arguing that prohibitions on Sunday opening would restrict the access of the working class to leisure facilities. The comedic heart of the novel is Blyth's private exhibition of two new paintings with a pompous gloss on his theory of art, much to the bemusement of the gathered audience, including a pair of scornful critics (Collins here thinking back to the tension between artistic truth and commercial success). There are private jokes: Zack Thorpe complains of his father forcing him to work at a tea merchant's, a reference to Collins's own experience at Antrobus & Co. during the writing of *Ioláni*. Dickens himself commented that *Hide and Seek* was 'the cleverest novel I have ever seen written by a new hand', though he did not 'really recognise much imitation of myself'.[13]

The more significant innovation of *Hide and Seek*, however, lies in the character of Madonna herself. Injured as a child in a circus horse-riding accident, she is deaf and mute. In writing Madonna, Collins drew extensively on John Kitto's *The Lost Senses* (1845), a discussion of various forms of disability (including blindness), but which focused primarily on deafness and Kitto's own experience of losing his hearing after falling from a ladder. As a result, Collins's depiction of Madonna is markedly more sympathetic than accounts of deafness which equate loss of hearing with deterioration in mental faculties, or which deploy it for comedic effect (though *Hide and Seek* introduces humour into Collins's work, it is never at Madonna's expense). Collins presents *Hide and Seek* as following the opposite trajectory of Madonna's treatment at the circus, where she is gradually demoted from stunt performer and conjuror to something like a freak show exhibit: the circus posters proclaim her as 'THE MYSTERIOUS FOUNDLING! AGED TEN YEARS!! TOTALLY

DEAF AND DUMB!!!'[14] The emphasis on her use of sign language intervenes in the contemporary debate between proponents of sign language and 'oralists' who believed that the deaf should be encouraged to speak, since (in their analysis) the embodied nature of signing could not approach the intellectual complexity of verbal language. This debate is not merely a local historical detail but, as Jennifer Esmail argues, offers a challenge to criticism which unreflectively equates voice with power (and, conversely, silence with repression). As Esmail notes, 'in the context of nineteenth-century deaf history, and in the narrative of Madonna's life, the oppression of deaf people is located precisely in being forced to speak'.[15]

It is this issue of spoken dialogue (or its absence) which brackets the early section of Collins's novelistic career. For although the Victorian novel is intimately connected to dialogue, *Ioláni* attempts to break this connection: the novel uses direct speech sparingly, and then mostly for declarative purposes, with very few passages of dialogue. It is difficult to read this as an oversight by an inexperienced novelist; rather, Collins's first attempt at fiction keeps dialogue to a minimum in order to foreground *Ioláni*'s more mythic narrative. Having failed to find a publisher for his first novel, in *Antonina* Collins slyly refers to readers' preference for voice, when at the start of chapter 3 the narrator assures the audience that they will not have to wade through pages of description in order 'to alight on the first oasis that may present itself, whether it be formed by a new division of the story, or suddenly indicated by the appearance of a dialogue' (An: 40). Collins's first four novels all deal with voice in strikingly different ways: rendering it almost absent (*Ioláni*), ventriloquising historical figures (*Antonina*), subsuming it within first-person confession (*Basil*), or promoting other linguistic forms (*Hide and Seek*). From these experiments grow the multi-voiced novels of the later 1850s and 1860s.

Notes

[1] W. Baker and W. M. Clarke (eds.), *The Letters of Wilkie Collins*, 2 vols. (Basingstoke: Palgrave Macmillan, 1999), vol. 1, p. 52. Hereafter cited as B&C.

[2] W. Collins to Richard Bentley, 10 July 1854. B&C, vol. 1, pp. 120, 122.

[3] I. B. Nadel, 'Introduction' to W. Collins, *Ioláni; Or, Tahíti as It Was: A Romance*, ed. I. B. Nadel (Princeton University Press, 1999), pp. ix–xxxix (p. xxiv).

[4] W. Collins to Harriet Collins, 13 September 1845. B&C, vol. 1, p. 28.

5. Collins, *Iolàni*, p. 61.
6. W. Collins to Richard Bentley, 30 August 1849. B&C, vol. I, pp. 56–7.
7. Quoted in C. Peters, *The King of Inventors: A Life of Wilkie Collins* (Princeton University Press, 1991), p. 41.
8. T. Heller, *Dead Secrets: Wilkie Collins and the Female Gothic* (New Haven, CT: Yale University Press, 1992); A. Mangham, 'Mental States: Political and Psychological Conflict in *Antonina*', in A. Mangham (ed.), *Wilkie Collins: Interdisciplinary Essays* (Newcastle: Cambridge Scholars Press, 2007), pp. 90–106.
9. W. Collins to R. H. Dana, 17 June 1850. B&C, vol. I, p. 62.
10. W. Collins, *Antonina; or, The Fall of Rome* (London: Chatto & Windus, 1875), pp. 18, 306. Hereafter cited in the text as An.
11. W. Collins, 'Letter of Dedication', in *Basil: A Story of Modern Life*, ed. D. Goldman (Oxford World's Classics, 1990), p. xl. Novel hereafter cited in the text as B.
12. Ibid., p. 1.
13. G. Storey, K. Tillotson and A. Easson (eds.), *The Letters of Charles Dickens* (Pilgrim Edition), Vol. VII: *1853–1855* (Oxford: Clarendon Press, 1993), p. 376.
14. W. Collins, *Hide and Seek*, ed. C. Peters (Oxford World's Classics, 1999), p. 56.
15. J. Esmail, '"I Listened with My Eyes": Writing Speech and Reading Deafness in the Fiction of Charles Dickens and Wilkie Collins', *ELH* 78.4 (2011), pp. 991–1020 (p. 1000).

CHAPTER 5

Middle Novels

Tara MacDonald

In Mary Elizabeth Braddon's popular sensation novel *Lady Audley's Secret* (1862), the dandy-turned-detective Robert Audley insists, 'I haven't read ... Wilkie Collins for nothing.'[1] Collins was already a byword for detective and sensation fiction by 1862, no doubt due to the success of *The Woman in White* (1860), as well as earlier novels like *Hide and Seek* (1854) and *The Dead Secret* (1857). Into the 1860s–70s, Collins continued to publish narratives that shaped the emergent form of sensationalism – as well as those that expanded the boundaries of realistic representation – with *No Name* (1862 [dated 1863]), *Armadale* (1866), *The Moonstone* (1868), *Man and Wife* (1870), *Poor Miss Finch* (1872), *The New Magdalen* (1873), *The Law and the Lady* (1875) and *The Two Destinies* (1876). *The Fallen Leaves* (1879), Collins's final novel from this period, may best be regarded as transitional, as it anticipates his later social problem novels. A key element that runs through these middle novels is an investment in the collective: these narratives question how collectives are formed (and who is excluded), how best to narrate collective experience, and how emotions shape bodies and collectives. In what follows, I use these questions to explore Collins's depiction of women and/as outcast figures, use of differing narrative modes and representation of shared feeling in his best-known novels of the 1860s–70s. What does it mean, these novels ask, to be a person affected by and affecting other people?

Collectives and Outcasts

While the plots and styles of narration in Collins's 1860s–70s novels differ, they all imagine worlds in which sensations move freely and spontaneously between people and spaces. And this affective world has very different stakes for men and women. The iconic moment in *The Woman in White* in which Walter Hartright is startled by the touch of Anne Catherick, dressed in white and on the road after midnight, is narrated by Walter and thus focuses on his reaction. D. A. Miller, in his influential reading of the novel, notes that this scene is above all about affective transmission, even as he also highlights its gender dynamics: 'Released from-and-with-the Woman, nervousness touches and enters the Man.'[2] Yet we might focus not merely on the *transference* of nervousness but ask why it originates in Anne's body in the first place. This moment exemplifies Victorian women's social and physical vulnerability, a concern to which Collins's work consistently returns, as critics such as Tamar Heller, Lyn Pykett and others have shown. Anne's speech shows how she must constantly assess the world around her and decide whether she wants to call in the help of a male stranger. She hopes that Walter will answer honestly when she asks, 'May I trust you?' and explains, 'I am very unfortunate in being here alone so late. . . . I heard you coming . . . and hid there to see what sort of man you were, before I risked speaking.'[3] Anne is aware that being a woman alone on the street at night makes her both suspicious and exposed. She must assess her own role in the larger collective ('I am very unfortunate'), as well as those she encounters ('what sort of man') as a means of survival.

Many of Collins's female figures in his middle novels are forced to cannily negotiate the world around them in this way, as they are marked as out of place or are displaced by others. To be an outcast is to be pushed out of the collective. To gain entry (back) into society, women like Magdalen Vanstone in *No Name*, Lydia Gwilt in *Armadale* and Valeria Woodville in *The Law and the Lady* don disguises, create secret identities, or enhance their appearance in an attempt to achieve their goals. Others remain outcasts: Rosanna Spearman in *The Moonstone* and Hester Dethridge in *Man and Wife* are so invisible as lower-class women that their stories of pain and trauma are ignored until they become important to the male characters in the novels. Their first-person accounts are examples of what Heller identifies as the trope of hidden feminine writing in Collins's fiction, an extension of the female Gothic. Collins's middle fiction unearths such writing – and such pain – and allows it to surface, so that outcast figures are often central to his narratives and plotlines. Hester Dethridge's confession tells her story of marital abuse; when she seeks help, she is told over and over that there is nothing that she can legally do. While she acknowledges that 'people . . . were almost always good to me', she also insists that when she wanted action and not merely kindness, she found others to be 'helpless as a flock of sheep'.[4] She takes matters into her own hands and murders her husband, a decision that not only renders her mute and haunted by ghostly visions but forever at the periphery of society. Collins's outcasts in these middle novels extend beyond lonely women to figures such as the 'half man, half chair'[5] Miserrimus Dexter and to racialised and effeminate men such as Ozias Midwinter and Ezra Jennings. These novels have been rich sources for scholars invested in the history of disability, race and queerness. As many have claimed, Collins's own unconventional life likely encouraged his attention to and sympathy towards those deemed unconventional in mid- to late Victorian society.

To be an outcast, Collins's middle novels suggest, requires that characters form collectives on their own terms. These chosen collectives are frequently brought together as a means of survival. Laura Hartright's half-sisters, Anne and Marian, both attempt to protect her from a painful future; this is especially remarkable not only because the villainous male characters actively attempt to separate them but also because they must reject any sense of jealousy of Laura's wealth and social position, advantages denied to them. Just as these women resist models of rivalry and competition, so too do many of Collins's male characters: Allan Armadale and Ozias Midwinter instantly possess 'mysterious sympathies' for one another, and their more gentle models of masculinity work to eventually repair their fathers' murderous rivalry in *Armadale*.[6] In *Man and Wife*, a multi-generational and mixed-gendered cast of characters work to rescue Anne Glenarm from her abusive husband, permitting her a future very different from that of Hester Dethridge.

Narrating Collectives

Collectives are also formed via the act of writing in these novels: Walter Hartright and Franklin Blake draw from a wide range of people to edit their collective narratives, narratives that admittedly aim to protect the purity of the white, middle-class women that they love, but which nonetheless rely upon accounts by servants, foreigners and other women. Indeed, in his middle novels, Collins experiments with a range of styles, including single-character narration, multiple-character narration and omniscient narration, the latter often incorporating letters, diaries and advertisements. His most innovative narrative style is his use of collective narration. In his 1860 preface to *The Woman in White*, Collins explained that his 'experiment' of having the narrative 'told throughout by the characters of the book' worked to move the story forward but also 'afforded my characters a new opportunity of expressing themselves'.[7] This style can appear almost postmodern in its seeming acceptance that truth is subjective. Jenny Bourne Taylor, attempting to characterise Collins's 'dialogic and self-reflexive' writing style, refers to him as 'one of the most "modern" (even postmodern) of nineteenth-century novelists'.[8] Yet Collins's 'self-reflexive' style is also very much *of* his time. While it may indeed anticipate postmodern narration, as well as late Victorian novels like Bram Stoker's *Dracula* (1897), his use of multiple narrators is incredibly effective for mystery fiction and serial fiction published in periodicals alongside various other first-person accounts, both fictional and real. We see, in these collectively narrated texts, a writer successfully finding a form that works to trace both 'the influence of circumstances upon character' *and* 'the influence of character upon circumstances'.[9]

Yet even in Collins's third-person narrated novels from this period, including *Armadale*, *No Name* and *The Law and the Lady*, letters and diaries are prominently incorporated, such as Lydia's diary in *Armadale*. Lydia tells her eventual husband a story of her life drawn from 'the common-place rubbish of the circulating libraries' (A: 594). Yet Lydia's actual diary, her 'second self', is a rich, genre-bending narrative filled with humour, anger and self-reflection (A: 659. In this lengthy novel with a huge cast of characters, it is striking for the reader to access one character's rich interiority in this manner. What emerges is not only insight into Lydia's mind but an awareness that what she presents to the world often differs from what she actually feels. Though she appears calm, she admits to being filled up with 'terrible excitement' (A: 589). Collins certainly utilises letters and diary entries for plot development and suspense, but they also function as reminders that it is difficult to truly know what another is thinking or feeling. Collins's first-person accounts thus develop what would eventually be called Theory of Mind or mind reading, a concept coined by cognitive psychologists in the twentieth century to describe our ability to assign states of mind, feelings and beliefs to others. We take part in mind reading when 'we ascribe to a person a certain mental state on the basis of her observable action'.[10] Cognitive narrative theorists suggest that mind reading allows readers to understand fictional characters in the same way, and Collins's characters are also adept mind readers. Maria Bachman has suggested that *The Woman in White* 'engages its readers in a kind of [Theory of Mind] marathon', and, in fact, all of Collins's middle novels are attentive to the ways in which characters intuit others' states of mind.[11] Captain Wragge notes Magdalen's 'extraordinary talent as a mimic' in *No Name*, a comment that attests not only to her acting skills but also to her canny ability to read others' bodies for meaning.[12]

Sharing Feeling

Mind reading is significant in these novels beyond the function of letters and diaries since they are filled with emotive characters but also with characters desperate to hide their bodily affects. Bodies in these novels are so often anxious that Collins's middle novels may be said to be studies in this distinctly modern emotional state. Mr Fairlie's pronouncement that 'I am nothing but a bundle of nerves dressed up to look like a man' is funny, but Collins's narratives earnestly explore anxiety as a shared feeling (WW: 356). In *Man and Wife*, one character proclaims, 'Anxiety is one of the civilized emotions. Man in his savage state is incapable of feeling it' (M&W: 177). In this novel, one of the warning signs about the abusive Geoffrey Delamayn is that he feels no 'disinterested anxiety for the welfare of another person' (M&W: 191). In *The Law and the Lady*, Valeria experiences anxiety – 'the irritable condition of my nerves' – which is exacerbated when she meets Miserrimus Dexter and his cousin, Ariel (LL: 23). After interviewing Dexter, she records that she can only process her feelings some time later: he 'had disturbed me far more seriously than I suspected at the time. It was not until some hours after I had left him, that I really began to feel how my nerves had been tried by all that I had seen and heard during my visit at his house' (LL: 261). Dexter himself has 'delicate nerves', although he insists, cruelly, 'Ariel has no nerves' (LL: 327). For Dexter, Ariel's supposed lack of nerves is less a sign of her strength than it is of her brutishness or her 'savage state' – one of the ways in which he validates his abuse. Evolutionary thinking was crucial to how emotions were understood after Darwin, and Dexter's language relies on principles of degeneration and recidivism. In the case of Delamayn, however, Collins ironically employs such assumptions to critique the very character in the novel celebrated by the public as a perfect specimen of English manhood.

These examples show that Collins's middle novels theorise the ways in which emotions shape and make bodies. Feelings work to form collectives but also to draw lines between them. Take cousins Allan and Ozias, for instance: while Allan is a white Englishman, Ozias, whose mother was of 'mixed blood of the European and the African race', is said to possesses 'hot Creole blood' (A: 23, 479). In *The Moonstone*, Collins's novel from this period that most explicitly deals with Britain's colonial past and present, Gabriel Betteredge confidently asserts that 'the Hindoo people' are clever 'in concealing their feelings' (M: 71). He does not seem to connect the dots when he locates similar tendencies in servants, himself included: 'People in high life have ... the luxury of indulging their feelings. People in low life have no such privilege. ... We learn to put our feelings back into ourselves, and to jog on with our duties' (M: 159). This emphasis on controlled emotion in racialised and lower-class individuals may seem surprising given the rhetoric surrounding 'civilized emotions' and colonialism in this period. Further complicating things, Betteredge's narrative is preceded by a prologue, '*Extracted from a family paper*', that describes the 1799 siege of Seringapatam, the victory that positioned the British with their stronghold in India (M: 1). For contemporary readers, it may have called to mind the Indian Rebellion of 1857, the largest threat to English imperial rule in the nineteenth century. Collins's account of the 1799 siege, however, notes both the terrible slaughter that the colonial troops encounter as well as British soldier John Herncastle's 'fiery temper ... exasperated to a kind of frenzy' (M: 4). He is, the anonymous author notes, 'very unfit, in my opinion, to perform the duty that had been entrusted to him' (M: 4). This is just one example of the way in which Collins's novels both rely upon and work to upend expectations about emotion – and thus about gender, race, class and disability.

It would seem an oversight to discuss shared feelings in Collins's middle fiction without mentioning the playful ways in which readers are encouraged to share the feelings of characters in these novels. The engaging, if judgmental, narrator of *Poor Miss Finch*, Madame Pratolungo, employs the second person and refers to her readership as 'my friends'.[13] In *The Moonstone*, Betteredge commands his reader to

> [p]ay attention ... or you will be all abroad, when we get deeper into the story. Clear your mind of the children, or the dinner, or the new bonnet, or what not. Try if you can't forget politics, horses, prices in the City, and grievances at the club. I hope you won't take this freedom on my part amiss; it's only a way I have of appealing to the gentle reader. (M: 29)

Collins's narrators invite 'the gentle reader' to be immersed in their stories and to feel along with them. His middle novels often refer to 'public opinion' and 'public feeling', too, suggesting that Collins himself did not just imagine a single reader but a reading public when writing novels at the height of his popularity (M: 217; M&W: 210). In fact, these asides have much in common with Collins's prefaces in which he foregrounds his narrative experiments. In the preface to *No Name*, he admits that the novel's only secret will be revealed not at the end but midway in the first volume. His object in trying this new design is 'to enlarge the range of my studies in the art of writing fiction, and to vary the form in which I make my appeal to the reader'.[14] Collins's consistent experimentation with character, form and emotional appeal in these middle novels make them significant not just within Collins's own oeuvre but in the history of the English novel and the relationship between fiction and feeling.

Notes

1. M. E. Braddon, *Lady Audley's Secret*, ed. L. Pykett (Oxford World's Classics, 2012), p. 342.
2. D. A. Miller, '*Cage Aux Folles*: Sensation and Gender in Wilkie Collins's *The Woman in White*', *Representations* 14 (1986), pp. 107–36 (pp. 110–11).
3. W. Collins, *The Woman in White*, ed. J. Sutherland (Oxford World's Classics, 1998), pp. 21, 22. Hereafter cited in the text as WW.
4. W. Collins, *Man and Wife*, ed. N. Page (Oxford World's Classics, 2008), pp. 594, 589. Hereafter cited in the text as M&W.
5. W. Collins, *The Law and the Lady*, ed. J. Bourne Taylor (Oxford World's Classics, 1992), p. 206. Hereafter cited in the text as LL.
6. W. Collins, *Armadale*, ed. C. Peters (Oxford World's Classics, 2008), p. 164. Hereafter cited in the text as A.
7. W. Collins, 1860 Preface, in *The Woman in White*, ed. Sutherland, p. 644.
8. J. Bourne Taylor, *In the Secret Theatre of Home: Wilkie Collins, Sensation Narrative, and Nineteenth-Century Psychology* (London and New York: Routledge, 1988), p. 1.
9. W. Collins, Preface to *The Moonstone*, ed. F. O'Gorman (Oxford World's Classics, 2008), p. liii. Hereafter cited in the text as M.
10. L. Zunshine, *Why We Read Fiction: Theory of Mind and the Novel* (Ohio State University Press, 2006), p. 6.
11. M. K. Bachman, 'Concealing Minds and the Case of *The Woman in White*', in A. Pionke and D. Tischler Millstein (eds.), *Victorian Secrecy: Economies of Knowledge and Concealment* (Farnham: Ashgate, 2010), pp. 75–94 (p. 94).
12. W. Collins, *No Name*, ed. V. Blain (Oxford World's Classics, 1998), p. 236.
13. W. Collins, *Poor Miss Finch*, ed. C. Peters (Oxford World's Classics, 2008), p. 427.
14. Collins, Preface to *No Name*, ed. Blain, p. 6.

CHAPTER 6

Late Novels

Maria K. Bachman

> Who among us knows the capacity for wickedness that lies dormant in our natures?[1]

In the prefaces to almost every one of his novels, Wilkie Collins explained his aesthetic vision in terms of reshaping and expanding the contours of nineteenth-century literary realism. In his preface to *No Name* (1863) he wrote, 'My one object in following a new course, is to enlarge the range of my studies in the art of writing fiction, and to vary the form in which I make my appeal to the reader, as attractively as I can.'[2] Collins's late novels well demonstrate that commitment as they span a variety of genres ranging from the Gothic melodrama *Jezebel's Daughter* (1880), to the domestic realism of *The Evil Genius* (1886), to the political sensationalism of *Blind Love* (1889). Though these novels mark a clear departure from the shocking effects and labyrinthine plotting of his earlier sensation novels, there is much that can be seen as an expansion of Collins's realist vision. In the novels of the 1880s, Collins continues to engage with contemporary social and scientific debates, such as treatment of the insane (*Jezebel's Daughter*), vivisection (*Heart and Science*), Scottish divorce laws (*The Evil Genius*), hereditary behaviour (*The Legacy of Cain*) and Irish Home Rule (*Blind Love*). Moreover, these late novels reframe certain familiar themes and tropes, such as madness and incarceration, transgressive femininity, the crisis of masculinity, questions of identity and legitimacy, fear of the foreign, and anxieties over experimental science.

While Collins endeavoured to present characters 'as recognisable realities' throughout his literary career,[3] the 'chief effort' or *mission* of his later novels was to draw characters 'with a vigour and breadth of treatment, derived from the nearest and truest view that [he] could get of the one model, Nature'.[4] Collins particularly sought to create more psychologically nuanced characters who embodied the 'inherent inconsistencies and self-contradictions' and 'intricate mixture of good and evil' in human nature.[5]

This evolving project is perhaps most fully realised in the novels of the 1880s where Collins draws attention to the complexities of 'human motives and human actions' (PMF: xxxiii) and considers what underlying factors – environmental, inherited, or innate – drive his characters toward various acts of criminal and social villainy.

While female characters who defy convention are a hallmark of Collins's fiction, in *Jezebel's Daughter*, *Heart and Science*, *The Legacy of Cain* and '*I Say No*', Collins is particularly focused on the motivations that drive seemingly respectable women to commit heinous acts. In *Jezebel's Daughter*, Madame Fontaine, the German widow of an experimental chemist, is one such example. In a devious scheme to ensure her daughter's marriage to Fritz Keller, she poisons his father, who is opposed to the match on account of Madame Fontaine's unpaid debts and reputation for scandal. It is not her intention to kill Mr Keller, but rather to make him seriously ill so that she can nurse him back to health by administering a mystery antidote and thus obtain his undying gratitude and blessing for Fritz and Minna's union. With neither guilt nor remorse, Madame Fontaine justifies her actions as motivated by her unwavering commitment to her daughter's happiness. In actuality, she desperately needs Minna to marry Fritz in order to secure her own financial solvency and 'return' to respectability, though her devotion to her daughter is her excuse for falling into debt in the first place.

Despite Madame Fontaine's imputation as the 'Jezebel' of the novel, Collins shows an individual who, in the context of Victorian psychological discourse, displays symptoms of moral insanity – someone who does not possess a 'wholly corrupted heart', but whose 'perverted mind' slowly loses ground in the 'struggle between good and evil' (JD: 78). In his *Treatise on Insanity* (1835), James Cowles Prichard introduced the term *moral insanity* to describe a form of mental derangement that affected ethical behaviour and feelings, but not the intellect or understanding. Moral insanity could be ascribed to an individual who knew right from wrong, but went ahead and acted without any regard for moral consequences.[6] Indeed, Madame Fontaine is fully cognisant of her actions – she loses neither her self-awareness nor her power of reason – but rather slips into a moral decline as her need for social respectability and the power she believes it confers becomes pathological. In another desperate attempt to keep up appearances, Madame Fontaine steals a large sum of money from Mr Keller's firm. When she is discovered, Madame Fontaine poisons her accuser, which ironically results in her own death, much like the thwarted designs of her fictional predecessor, Lydia Gwilt, in *Armadale*. Ultimately, Collins suggests that Madame Fontaine's moral degradation is not necessarily evidence of innate evil, but rather triggered out of circumstantial desperation.

In *Heart and Science* (1883), Mrs Gallilee's moral decline is similarly motivated by financial need and a desire for social acceptance. Though the novel has received considerable attention for its engagement in the vivisection debates of the 1880s,[7] the main plot is focused on Mrs Gallilee's sinister machinations to prevent her orphaned niece, Carmina, from marrying Ovid Vere (her son from another marriage) so that she can claim Carmina's inheritance. With Ovid out of the country (recovering from nervous exhaustion) and the departure of her old Italian nurse Teresa, the physically and emotionally frail Carmina is left completely isolated, a helpless victim of her aunt's absolute authority and unrelenting emotional abuse, which results in the further deterioration of Carmina's health.

Throughout the novel, Mrs Gallilee, a social climber and amateur scientist, is described as 'dangerous' and 'cruel' with an 'inbred capacity for deceit' (HS: 76). Yet Collins suggests that her moral (and maternal) sense has been corrupted by her 'scientific education' (HS: 67) – an endeavour which 'deliberately starved her imagination, and emptied her heart of any tenderness of feeling which it might have once possessed' (HS: 67) – and her obsession with social success at all costs. Indeed, Mrs Gallilee's motivation for pursuing a 'glorious career' (HS: 71) in science was jealousy and social affirmation – to best her younger sister who had married a wealthy nobleman.[8] As the narrator observes, 'Vanity wants nothing but the motive power to develop into absolute wickedness' (HS: 204). Thus, much like Madame Fontaine, Mrs Gallilee's 'pecuniary liabilities' (HS: 143) have all been incurred to maintain an extravagant lifestyle that she is unable to afford.

When her malicious schemes and 'cold-blooded cruelty' (HS: 249) towards her niece are exposed, including the false accusation that Carmina is the illegitimate child of an adulteress, Mrs Gallilee begins to unravel. After suffering a nervous breakdown, she is committed to a private asylum and supposedly restored to mental health several months later, 'as sane a woman as ever', with the exception of one lingering 'unfavourable symptom' – her preoccupation with scientific subjects (HS: 311). Ironically, the novel's final picture of Mrs Gallilee shows her glorying in the success of her 'at home' scientific soirées, 'at last ... a happy woman' (HS: 327). Here Collins seems to express some measure of scepticism over the efficacy of moral management, particularly when the patient's mania is rooted in the need for social approbation.

The extent to which environment and upbringing influence an individual's moral development is broached in *'I Say No'* (1884) and then further complicated in *The Legacy of Cain* (1888). Like *The Law and the Lady* (1875), the mystery plot of *'I Say No'* unfolds through the discovery of a suicide. The novel chronicles Emily Brown's quest to uncover the mystery of her father's supposed murder, which has been covered up by overprotective family and friends. In addition to Emily's sleuthing, the story also concerns the treacherous designs of Francine de Sor, a nineteen-year-old heiress from the West Indies who attempts to unravel the mystery for her own selfish and spiteful ends. When she arrives at Emily's boarding school, Francine receives no warm welcome, but is instead treated with disdain by her fellow students, excluded from participating in their activities and even snubbed at one point by Emily. The daughter of unloving parents and the victim of a neglected education, Francine is, by her own admission, 'ignorant, and superstitious, and foreign, and rich', and it is her outsider status and sensitivity to exclusion and rejection (both real and perceived) that serve as provocations for her 'cold-blooded cruelty'.[9]

Though the novel emphasises her exoticism, Francine's 'heartless and wicked' (ISN: 511) disposition is not rooted in any kind of foreign or hereditary 'taint'. Francine is actually of European descent – her father is a Spanish gentleman and her mother is English. Collins instead presents a villainess, however unsympathetic, whose formative life experiences may be a contributing factor to her arrested moral development. Despite her proud nature, she seeks love and acceptance, and when those desires are disappointed, she lashes out with anger, hostility and malice. At the same time, Collins does not dismiss the notion that every person has certain innate characteristics – in Francine's case it may very well be her irascibility – that, when provoked, become uncontrollable.[10] Indeed, Francine's bitter resentment and jealousy of Emily, 'the irresistible little creature whom everyone likes', ignite her 'meanest instincts' and 'capacities for wickedness' (ISN: 338–9). Francine first schemes to steal the heart of Alban Morris, who is in love with Emily. When she realises that Morris's adoration of Emily is unwavering, her 'wounded vanity' (ISN: 259) and passion for revenge drive her to sabotage that relationship. In pursuit of that goal, Francine, much like Mrs Gallilee in *Heart and Science*, takes a sadistic pleasure in controlling and terrorising others. When she intuits that her new maid, Mrs Ellmother (the former servant of Emily's aunt Letitia) knows more about the circumstances surrounding James Brown's death than she is willing to admit, Mrs Ellmother becomes victim to Francine's merciless psychological persecution. Francine's 'curiosity and self-esteem' (ISN: 293) are gratified when she discovers not only the secret of James Brown's death, but also that this truth must never be revealed to Emily. Revelling in her newfound knowledge and power, Francine strategically bides her time before cruelly informing the victim of her 'jealous hatred' (ISN: 337) that her father was murdered. Francine's vindictiveness is amplified even further when she fails to win the affections of the 'popular preacher' (ISN: 154) Miles Mirabel, who is also in love with Emily. When she is rebuffed by Mirabel, her bitterness and malice are again fully unleashed.

The Legacy of Cain is perhaps Collins's most sustained investigation into individual morality and the 'struggle between Good and Evil' as it engages in and complicates the nature versus nurture debate. The novel tells the story of Helena and Eunice Gracedieu, two sisters who are raised in a middle-class religious home; one of the sisters is actually the daughter of a murderess, who was adopted by the Reverend Abel Gracedieu, while the other sister is the biological child of the minister. Echoing debates on the role that biology and environment play in shaping human behaviour, the prison doctor suggests that if one of the sisters can be provoked to murder, it most certainly will be the daughter of the murderess. Reverend Gracedieu, however, counters this speculation of 'inherited evil' with 'inculcated good': he maintains that religious instruction and his modelling of righteousness will develop 'the brightest and best in the nature' of his adopted child.[11] When Eunice discovers that she has been betrayed by her sister and her lover (the rich and handsome Philip Dunboyne), she confesses the need to distract herself from her evil thoughts for fear of going mad. In a drug-induced sleep, the spirit of her mother (the murderess) appears to her to entice her to kill her sister, thus suggesting that Eunice possesses the 'poisonous hereditary taint' (LC: 34). Despite Eunice's acknowledgement of her 'new evil self', she resists such impulses for 'vengeance and death' (LC: 216). In this way, she bears some resemblance to Magdalen Vanstone in *No Name*, who possesses an 'inborn nobility' (NN: 212) and is able to resist her propensity for 'Evil' (NN: 197).

Instead, it is Helena, the minister's own daughter, who emerges as the novel's mentally unbalanced villainess who succumbs to the monomaniacal delusion that she is 'destined' to steal Philip from her sister. Though her 'fatal passion' promises to be 'the utter destruction of everything that is good' in her (LC: 171), Helena wonders whether it is pride or envy or jealousy – (indeed, those same 'excessive passions' that afflict Francine de Sor in *'I Say No'*) – that sparked 'the new flame' burning within her 'wicked heart' (LC: 173). Helena succeeds in winning Philip's affections, but her cunning and malevolence are given full rein when she later finds herself the spurned lover. Consumed with jealousy and rage over his rejection, Helena embarks on a calculated plan of revenge and murder, inspired by actual cases of female poisoners. Though Philip comes dangerously close to death, he recovers, and Helena is arrested and imprisoned for two years for her crime. Ultimately, the novel suggests that an individual's behaviour and actions are not solely determined by parental inheritance (the prevailing causal theory of psychopathology) or by upbringing, but instead may be directed by innate moral qualities: 'There are virtues that exalt us, and vices that degrade us, whose mysterious origin is, not in our parents, but in ourselves' (LC: 479).

Portraits of unbridled passion and ambition are not limited solely to Collins's female characters. In *Heart and Science*, *The Evil Genius*, *The Guilty River* (1886) and *Blind Love* (1890), Collins presents a spectrum of male characters who struggle between their obsessions and their better natures.

In *The Guilty River*, Collins draws in part on Victorian anxieties about the hereditary transmission of behaviour, a concern which he takes up more fully in *The Legacy of Cain*, as noted above. The drama focuses on the misanthropic deaf 'Lodger' and his rivalry with Gerard Roylake, the heir of a large estate, over the affections of Cristel Toller, the miller's daughter. Early in the novel, we learn of the mixed-race Lodger's ancestral history: his English grandfather was a murderer, his uncle, a cheating gambler, and his own father, a shameless womaniser. The discovery of his family's transgressions and crimes, along with his deafness from a midlife illness, have taken a toll on his mental state. He is convinced of the 'inherited evil lying dormant', and he also suffers from paranoia, believing that people are mocking his 'infirmity'.[12] At the same time, the Lodger wonders if his deafness may have caused the 'hardening' of his nature: 'Is there a moral sense that suffers when a bodily sense is lost?' (GR: 269).[13] As in the case of Francine de Sor, Collins suggests that personal circumstances may adversely affect an individual's moral temperament. The Lodger develops a fatal attraction for the miller's daughter, and despite the fact that Cristel has given the Lodger no encouragement, he becomes monomaniacal in his pursuit of her. When he discovers that Roylake has also fallen in love with Cristel, the Lodger becomes increasingly unhinged and plots to poison Roylake. However, despite the Lodger's ruse of friendship, Cristel knows that he possesses a 'hatred that never forgives and never forgets' (GR: 302) and successfully thwarts his deadly plan and saves Roylake's life.

In *Heart and Science*, Collins explores the link between professional ambition and moral insanity in the novel's male villain, the sadistic Dr Nathan Benjulia. Benjulia is consumed with his research on nervous disease, though the nature of his work – medical experiments on live animals – is shrouded in mystery. He possesses a 'mania for experiments in chemistry' such that he 'work[s] incessantly' and 'never leav[es] his laboratory' (HS: 97). The blurred line between such single-mindedness of purpose and pathological obsession is, of course, a common feature of the quintessential 'mad scientist'.[14] Benjulia exhibits, moreover, the same kind of extreme egocentrism and obsessive behaviour that Henry Maudsley associated with the morally insane individual.[15] Benjulia's fervour to discover a cure for nervous disease is not to serve 'the medical interests of humanity' (HS: 190), but rather for his own vainglorious ends. Ironically, this quest will be the cause of his own demise.

While *Heart and Science* does draw on anxieties surrounding animal experimentation, Collins explained that he was interested specifically in 'the moral influence of those [laboratory] cruelties on the nature of the man who practices them'.[16] His psychological study presents 'a man *not* originally wicked and cruel', but whose experiments on animals have resulted in the 'inevitable hardening of the heart [and] the fatal stupefying of all the fine sensibilities' (HS: 446–7).[17] Benjulia's monomania, however, crosses over into psychopathy as his Faustian quest for knowledge 'sanctifies cruelty' (HS: 190) to not only animals, but humans as well. This is evidenced in his deliberate neglect of Carmina following her nervous collapse. Viewing her as nothing more than a convenient research specimen, Benjulia allows the incompetent Dr Null to serve as the attending physician so that he can observe Carmina's deterioration and place her 'along with the other animals, in his note-book of experiments' (HS: 280).

In his final novel, *Blind Love*, Collins explores the ways in which love and fervent nationalism contribute to cases of moral insanity and monomania. The novel opens in rural Ireland, focusing on the 'Irish blackguard'[18] Lord Harry Norland and his lawless activities with a secret society of political assassins, and Iris Henley, a high-spirited English woman, who finds herself compulsively drawn to the devilish Lord Harry, eventually marrying him. Harry's criminal behaviour throughout the novel, along with the inexplicable 'blind love' (BL: 273, 363) that Iris has for the 'wild Irish' lord (BL: 206), suggest the perceived madness behind the movements for Irish independence as well as the apparent madness of English sympathisers who displayed a misplaced but obsessive blind love for the Celts.

It is Harry's fatal wilfulness that causes him to vacillate wildly from his fervent allegiance to a Fenian terrorist group, to his avowed vengeance against those political assassins, to suicidal despair over losing both Iris and his money, to his desperate involvement in fraud, conspiracy and murder, and, finally, to his ultimate act of self-destruction. It is this 'fatal purpose' (BL: 158) or mania, which also enables the volatile and reckless Irish lord to falsely rationalise his participation in deceit, bloodshed, murder and treachery, never quite acknowledging his actions for what they are. He admits that his alliance with the political assassins was 'inexcusably rash and wicked' (BL: 107), yet after his cousin Arthur Mountjoy is 'foully assassinated' (BL: 157), Harry vows a 'merciless resolution of revenge' (BL: 166). Like a textbook example of Prichard's morally insane, Harry's justification of his plan attests to his grandiose delusions – (he compares himself to two historical assassins) – and to his inability to see his own intended actions in their proper moral proportions: 'Is a mere modern murderer beneath my vengeance, by comparison with two classical tyrants who did their murders by deputy?' (BL: 165).

Moreover, Iris Henley's 'blind love' for her militant Irish nationalist husband can also be seen as a type of partial insanity. Iris is blinded to Harry's faults because she is not 'in her right senses' (BL: 118). She believes (much like Helena Gracedieu in *The Legacy of Cain*) in a 'fatality' (BL: 108) that keeps drawing her back to Lord Harry, and, just as Harry's passions have impaired his judgment, so too is Iris's moral deterioration caused by a 'blind passion' (BL: 371). Refusing to listen to warnings that she will 'lose [her] sense of right and wrong' (BL: 194), Iris soon finds herself caught up as an accomplice and co-conspirator in Harry's criminal activities.

Despite its focus on the scandalous topics of adultery, divorce and child custody, *The Evil Genius* features 'no very wicked people'; indeed, there are no sinister male villains with 'unholy aims' nor are there any malicious 'golden-haired deceivers'.[19] In fact, it is the only novel of the 1880s that eschews violence of any kind – there are no murders, suicides or poisonings. Yet Collins's aim to present the 'inherent inconsistencies and self-contradictions' (PMF: xxxiii) of human nature is at the very centre of this tale of moral weakness and marital infidelity. While the novel has been lauded for its sympathetic portrayals of both the wronged wife and the naive mistress, the character on which the entire plot hinges is the husband who gives in to his unregulated passions. Herbert Linley is a wealthy, respectable man, happily married, and an affectionate and doting father who suffers from what Prichard would describe as a 'want of self-control'

(EG: 47) when he seduces Sydney Westerfield, the naive and attractive young governess he had rescued from the oppression of her aunt's school.

As a result of his mother-in-law's suspicious meddling (the supposed 'evil genius' of the novel), Herbert's 'guilty passion' (EG: 159) for Sydney is made known to his devoted wife Catherine and the young governess is removed from the household. However, when he unexpectedly encounters Sydney, 'the maddening fascination of her presence' (EG: 124) again renders him powerless to 'honourably restrain himself' (EG: 170). Catherine discovers them and orders Herbert to leave the house with his mistress. Though the lovers live together for some time, it becomes clear that Herbert's reckless infatuation – the derangement of his moral will – was a temporary transgression. Even after his divorce is finalised, he is not inclined to marry the woman for whom his passion has waned, but instead reconciles with his wife.

Collins does not exactly absolve Herbert of what many would see as a temporary moral lapse. Though Herbert acknowledges that he is at fault for his behaviour – 'What a scoundrel I am!' (EG: 125) – he nonetheless proceeds to lead the vulnerable governess into an affair. Herbert Linley, however, is not intended to be a contemptible character; rather, his internal moral struggle is illustrative of Collins's belief that no one is 'above the reach of temptation to do ill' (EG: 324), and also an implicit challenge to the so-called power of self-control that was such a prominent feature of Victorian thought.[20]

While Collins has been credited with introducing in his sensation novels 'the most mysterious of mysteries, the mysteries which are at our own door',[21] the overarching goal of his later fiction was to uncover the mysteries and 'inconsistencies' of the human mind. In carrying out this mission, Collins 'required for his purposes', as Andrew Lang observed, 'character[s] of only occasional sanity'.[22] Indeed, just as Prichard saw that a disposition to moral insanity was part of human nature and could be detected in a wide variety of people, so too did Collins want his readers 'to take a look at humanity from a wider and truer point of view' and see that 'humanity, in general, is neither perfectly good nor perfectly wicked' (BL: 119).

Notes

[1] W. Collins, *Jezebel's Daughter*, ed. J. D. Hall (Oxford World's Classics, 2016), p. 75. Novel hereafter cited parenthetically in the text as JD.

[2] W. Collins, Preface to *No Name*, ed. V. Blain (Oxford World's Classics, 1990), n.p. Novel hereafter cited parenthetically in the text as NN.

3. W. Collins, 1860 Preface to *The Woman in White*, ed. M. K. Bachman and D. R. Cox, 2nd ed. (Peterborough, ON: Broadview Press, 2006), p. 620.
4. W. Collins, Preface to *Heart and Science: A Story of the Present Time*, ed. S. Farmer (Peterborough, ON: Broadview Press, 1996), p. 37. Novel hereafter cited parenthetically in the text as HS.
5. W. Collins, Preface to *Poor Miss Finch*, ed. C. Peters (Oxford World's Classics, 1995), p. xxxiii. Novel hereafter cited parenthetically in the text as PMF.
6. According to Prichard, moral insanity is characterised by a 'morbid perversion of the natural feelings, affections, inclinations, temper, habits, moral dispositions, and natural impulses without any remarkable disorder or defect of the intellect or knowing or reasoning faculties' and with no other apparent symptoms of mental impairments, such as delusions and hallucinations. See J. C. Prichard, *A Treatise on Insanity and Other Disorders Affecting the Mind* (London: Sherwood, Gilbert & Piper, 1835), p. 6.
7. See Farmer, 'Introduction' and Appendix B, in Collins, *Heart and Science*, pp. 13–19, 339–68.
8. Mrs Gallilee is described as a woman who possessed 'more than her fair share of the jealous, envious, and money-loving propensities of humanity' (HS: 48).
9. W. Collins, *'I Say No'* (New York: Peter Fenelon Collier, 1900), pp. 13, 394. Hereafter cited parenthetically in the text as ISN.
10. Prichard suggested that moral insanity could be triggered by 'the excessive intensity of any passion', such as anger, jealousy, revenge and hatred (*Treatise on Insanity*, p. 24).
11. W. Collins, *The Legacy of Cain* (New York: Peter Fenelon Collier, 1900), p. 46. Hereafter cited parenthetically in the text as LC.
12. W. Collins, *The Guilty River*, in *Miss or Mrs?, The Haunted Hotel, The Guilty River*, ed. N. Page and T. Sasaki (Oxford World's Classics, 1999), p. 266. Hereafter cited parenthetically in the text as GR.
13. Collins first addressed the ways in which heredity and circumstance may determine behaviour in *Basil* (1852).
14. *The Spectator* found Benjulia to be a 'curiously interesting psychological study': 'Nothing could be truer to human nature than this picture of a man in whom the lust of knowledge has become as purely selfish and degrading as the lust for gold.' See [Unsigned review], 'An Anti-Vivisection Novel', *Spectator* 56 (26 May 1883), pp. 679–81, reproduced in W. Collins, *The Evil Genius: A Domestic Story*, ed. G. Law (Peterborough, ON: Broadview Press, 1994), p. 334. Novel hereafter cited parenthetically in the text as EG.
15. According to Henry Maudsley, the morally insane individual has 'no capacity for true moral feeling; all his impulses and desires … are egoistic, his conduct appears to be governed by immoral motives' (*Responsibility in Mental Disease*, 2nd ed. [London: Henry S. King, 1876], pp. 171–2).
16. W. Collins to Francis Power Cobbe, 23 June 1882, in W. Baker and W. M. Clarke (eds.), *The Letters of Wilkie Collins*, Vol. II: *1866–1889* (New York: St Martin's Press, 1990), pp. 446–7.

[17] In the preface to the novel, Collins similarly explained to readers that his aim was not to focus on 'the hideous secrets of Vivisection', but rather to trace how the 'habitual practice of cruelty' results in the 'fatally deteriorating nature of man' (HS: 38).

[18] W. Collins, *Blind Love*, ed. M. K. Bachman and D. R. Cox (Peterborough, ON: Broadview Press, 2004), p. 152. Hereafter cited parenthetically in the text as BL.

[19] [Unsigned review], '*The Evil Genius*', *Saturday Review* 62 (9 October 1886), pp. 487–78, and [Unsigned review], '*The Evil Genius*', *Athenaeum* 3073 (18 September 1886), p. 367. Both reproduced in Collins, *The Evil Genius*, pp. 355, 354.

[20] See, for instance, John Barlow's popular text, *On Man's Power Over Himself to Prevent or Control Insanity* (London: W. Pickering, 1843).

[21] H. James, 'Miss Braddon', *The Nation* (9 November 1865), p. 594.

[22] A. Lang, 'Mr. Wilkie Collin's Novels', *Contemporary Review* 57 (January 1890), pp. 20–8, reprinted in N. Page (ed.), *Wilkie Collins: The Critical Heritage* (London and New York: Routledge & Kegan Paul, 1974), p. 266.

CHAPTER 7

Shorter Fiction

Graham Law

In Lieu of a List

Over a literary career of nearly half a century, Collins produced well over fifty fictional works of less than novel length, including the thirty shorter stories, each typically less than 15,000 words, collected in *After Dark* (1856), *The Queen of Hearts* (1859) and *Little Novels* (1887), as well as four longer stories of up to 50,000 words or so issued complete at Christmas time, *Mr Wray's Cash-Box* (1851), *Miss or Mrs?* (1871), *My Lady's Money* (1877) and *The Guilty River* (1886). Although it would be useful to provide a definitive listing, this is impossible for three reasons. First, there are a couple of journals, *The Leader* and *All the Year Round*, for which the author was for a while a regular staff writer but where uncertainties remain concerning what precisely he contributed, while recent discoveries suggest that others may remain to be unearthed in less accessible locations.[1] Second, there are issues of definition making it difficult to draw a line between fiction and non-fiction among the shorter compositions firmly attributed to Collins. With Dickens's encouragement to adopt a personalised style, Collins's journalistic pieces are less likely to take the form of the discursive third-person essay of review or criticism, than that of social satire in the guise of comic monologue. The line is especially difficult to maintain with the twenty-five articles reprinted from Dickens's weeklies in *My Miscellanies* (1863), which Collins grouped under seven generic headings. For example, all three 'Cases Worth Looking At', but no others, are included in Julian Thompson's edition of the author's shorter fiction,[2] while the Dickens Journals Online (DJO) project flags a further seven pieces by Collins as works of fiction, including all those labelled 'Sketches of Character'.[3] Third, Collins's shorter fiction includes collaborations where it is impossible to disentangle his contribution from that of others, most notably Dickens himself. This would include material in several special Christmas numbers of *Household Words* and *All the Year Round*, where Dickens and his apprentice shared the editorial role.

Publishing Format and Literary Form

Here, I avoid the terms 'short story' and 'novella', because they did not acquire their current generic meaning until late in the century, when, under American influence, they became associated with the aesthetics of early modernism with its preference for realism, irony and compression.[4] Yet there was no dearth of British shorter fiction earlier in the Victorian era, especially in general periodicals aimed at a family audience, where briefer narratives tended to function as fillers between the runs of serial novels, while longer stories were typically given priority in the special numbers and annuals that flourished around Christmas. Then the term 'tale' was preferred for such self-contained stories which typically mimicked a traditional mode of oral delivery, balancing a Gothic fear of the uncanny with the comforts of hearth and home. As the century wore on, however, the pleasures of romantic comedy began to outweigh those of sensational melodrama. Tales of the supernatural told around the fireside at night are perhaps naturally associated with the midwinter period, though there are also powerful cultural and economic reasons for the association between Victorian tales and Christmas as a merry domestic festival.[5] When authors wished subsequently to gather such shorter fiction together for re-publication in volume form, they typically had a choice between appending generic titles like *XXX, and Other Tales*, where XXX represented the longest and/or best known, and creating a narrative framework to connect the stories, often in a form reminiscent of Dickens's collaborative Christmas numbers.

These general tendencies regarding literary form and publishing format are apparent in Collins's evolving engagement with shorter fiction. From the recently recovered 'Volpurno; or, The Student', a story of the uncanny from mid-1843,[6] to 'The First Officer's Confession', a comic love story from late 1887, virtually all of Collins's tales were issued initially in periodicals of various kinds, while at least a dozen remained uncollected at the author's death, including the two just mentioned. Perhaps the most striking development is a gap in the middle of the author's career, covering most of the 1860s, the decade when Collins issued his most successful sensation novels, but produced little by way of tales. And on account of this gap, the contrast between the predominance of melodrama in the earlier period and of social comedy in the later appears even more marked.

The exceptions that secure the rule are Collins's earliest longer tale, *Mr Wray's Cash-Box*, a Christmas story in jovial comic style, and his last Christmas annual, *The Guilty River* a dark romance with Gothic elements. Yet the two early story collections, *After Dark* and *The Queen of Hearts*, are both made up predominantly of tales with melodramatic leanings previously published in *Household Words*. The former, with these tendencies declared in the title, is constructed as by the wife of a travelling portrait-painter from tales typically told by her husband's sitters. The latter uses the Sheherazade-like conceit of an elderly lawyer spinning stories with his brothers to detain his beautiful young ward, so that his son will have time to return from Crimea to claim her heart. Following his reading tour of North America, Collins resumed writing shorter fiction in earnest but in a rather different vein. In addition to other yuletide stories for British journals, for twelve consecutive years, from 1876 to 1887, he composed a seasonal tale specifically for the popular New York sports-and-theatre paper, *The Spirit of the Times*, with whose editor he had become friendly. These stories, typically culminating in marital union and lighter in tone than those for Dickens's Christmas numbers, formed the core of Collins's final collection of shorter fiction, *Little Novels*. Here, though there was no frame narrative, the titles were reworked into a common pattern ('Mr Cosway and the Landlady'; 'Miss Morris and the Stranger'), reflecting the reliance on various modes of romantic comedy.

The title chosen for his final collection suggests the importance of Collins's own use of terminology relating to shorter fiction. The term 'short story' is found only occasionally in letters to editors and publishers, consistently with reference to relative quantity of text rather than generic form,[7] while 'novella' does not seem to occur at all. In the preface to *After Dark*, Collins alternates between 'stories' and 'tales', while in that to *My Miscellanies* he prefers 'papers' and 'contributions'. There is no preface commenting on the title of *Little Novels*, though a letter to his publisher shows that, only a day before the final decision was made, the author's preference was for 'Mrs Zant and the Ghost: and Other Stories', giving priority to the tale heading the collection.[8] His longer 1871 Christmas story was reprinted in a single volume as *Miss or Mrs?: and Other Stories in Outline* (1873), with a preface explaining that the subtitle referred to the fact that '[i]n their original form of publication, the stories ... were restricted within limits which alike precluded elaborate development of character and subtle handing of events'.[9] The most instructive case, however, concerns Collins's first longer tale, *Mr Wray's Cash-Box; or, The Mask and the Mystery*, where the author made major changes to the title page and other preliminary matter between the first edition of mid-December 1851 and the second a few weeks later. Apart from obliging his friend the Pre-Raphaelite artist John Everett Millais, who had provided the vignette for the frontispiece, the main purpose was to replace the original two-page Introduction, due to its clumsily divulging the secret signalled in the subtitle, with a much briefer Advertisement. But at the same time, the author not only changed the generic description on the title page from 'A Christmas Sketch' (the holiday season was already over) to 'A Modern Story' (the setting is contemporary), but also added a quotation from Shakespeare, explicated in the new preface: 'I have endeavoured, in writing my little book, to keep the spirit of its title-page motto in view, and tell my "honest tale" as "plainly" as I could – or, in other words, as plainly as if I were only relating it to an audience of friends at my own fireside.'[10]

Now we need to come to cases, beginning with *Mr Wray's Cash-Box* itself and 'My Lady's Money', as earlier and later examples respectively of Collins's longer Christmas stories, followed by 'Gabriel's Marriage' and 'Mrs Zant and the Ghost' as similarly representative shorter tales not linked to the holiday season.

Exemplary Longer Tales

When Collins was called to the Bar in November 1851, his direction as a writer was still uncertain. He had published only a single novel, *Antonina* (1850), a florid historical affair following Edward Bulwer-Lytton, but two works of non-fiction, the memoirs of his father and a travel book on a Cornish walking tour. He had already joined Dickens's circle as an amateur performer but had not yet contributed to *Household Words*, though since the spring he had been writing fairly regularly for *Bentley's Miscellany*, from the publishers of *Antonina*. These, though, were mainly journalistic pieces concerning the art world, and there was only a single work of fiction, 'The Twin Sisters', a shorter tale of dark romance. In the autumn, however, he began to provide articles for the literary 'Portfolio' section of the radical political paper, *The Leader*, then owned by Edward Pigott, his fellow student at Lincoln's Inn. 'The New Dragon of Wantley', a recently identified early effort for the Christmas issue of the paper, was probably his first attempt at a Dickensian comic monologue.[11] The enjoyment the author clearly derived from composing this piece was perhaps one of the factors underlying his sudden decision to write his one and only Christmas Book in Dickens's style. Consisting of just over

30,000 words written hastily in about a fortnight, *Mr Wray's Cash-Box* was first issued before Christmas 1851 in a slim volume from Richard Bentley.

The story is set at midwinter in Tidbury-on-the-Marsh, a Dickensian 'genteel provincial residence',¹² with the conclusion a fireside Christmas dinner complete with old port wine and plum-pudding. The domestic heroes are an aging Shakespearean actor, his diminutive, fairylike granddaughter, her kind but clumsy giant carpenter lover, and the paternal local squire who protects the family and supplies the port and pudding. The villains are an ugly pair of burglars who covet the cash-box of the title, though the plot revolves around the fact that it contains not money but Mr Wray's most prized possession, a mask cast from a statue of the Bard, which, to his great distress, is destroyed during the robbery scene but marvellously restored at the climax. Despite the author's worries about the preface, there is little in the way of mystery and suspense, and almost no hint of the supernatural; rather the tone is dominated by robust sentimental comedy culminating in the happy betrothal of the young lovers, celebrated in Millais's charming vignette of the giant bending forward in front of the fireplace to have his new neckcloth tied by the fairy in her apron. All the same, the book was not markedly successful and there was to be no repetition.¹³

Two decades later, Collins composed two longer tales for the special Christmas issues of rival pictorial papers, *The Graphic* in 1871 and *The Illustrated London News* in 1877. The first ('Miss or Mrs?: A Christmas Story in Twelve Scenes') was of a length with *Mr Wray*, but more melodramatic in form and darker in tone, the oppressed heroine of the title being a girl of only fifteen, with the violent motives of the villain obscured for much of the narrative. The second ('My Lady's Money: An Episode in the Life of a Young Girl') is divided into two sections entitled 'The Disappearance' and 'The Recovery', centring in turn on the commission and detection of a domestic crime, the theft of a banknote inserted in an unsealed letter. Nevertheless, the dominant tone is one of romantic comedy, and the story ends with the happy marriage of the endearing heroine, the orphaned Isabel Miller, on whom suspicion had initially fallen. At something over 50,000 words, with four elegant full-page illustrations supplied by Fred Barnard, then engaged on the Household Edition of Dickens's novels, the lengthy narrative extended the *Illustrated London News* number from the standard thirty-two to forty pages. The only other copy was the usual dozen pages devoted to festive illustrations, typically focused on children.

While Collins's narrative itself does not feature adolescents, much of the sentimental interest as well as one of Barnard's illustrations focuses on the household's pet, the naughty Scotch terrier Tommie, the reactions to whose illness in the opening scenes help distinguish between heroes and villains, and who in the closing scenes recovers the banknote and helps to identify the criminal. In the tale's farewell to its characters, the author makes it clear the pet exists beyond the fiction, since he 'gave Tommie his dinner not half an hour since, and is too fond of him to say good-bye'.[14] On the heroine's side are the frumpy Lady Lydiard who has adopted the orphan, the long-serving steward Moody, whose faithful service to Tommie and his mistress eventually persuades Isabel to accept his suit, and the dishevelled detective Old Sharon, who is captured by Barnard with his own scruffy pug-dog on his lap, thus assuring his moral probity. Against her are Sweetsir and Hardyman, two selfish swells with different designs on Isabel's honour who both prove to be implicated in the theft, as well as her punctilious aunt Miss Pink, proprietor of a Young Ladies' Academy. In stark contrast to Lady Lydiard, she regards Tommie as a brute and tries to force Isabel to refuse the honest and accept the wealthy suitor. 'My Lady's Money' was the author's last attempt at a longer romantic comedy for the holiday season, since *The Guilty River*, his 1886 *Arrowsmith's Christmas Annual*, a series devoted to the modern thriller, was a tale of sexual jealousy foregrounding the psychological effects of physical handicap.

Exemplary Shorter Tales

Of the six shorter Gothic tales constituting *After Dark*, four are set abroad, with 'Gabriel's Marriage' and 'Sister Rose' both taking place mainly in provincial France during the Revolution. With the exception of 'The Lady of Glenwith Grange', written specifically for the collection, all had appeared initially in *Household Words*. The main textual revisions were the inclusion of the narrator's status in the story titles, and creating within the wife's frame narrative a lengthy prologue introducing the circumstances surrounding each tale, plus a brief epilogue drawing a conclusion, both in the voice of the portrait-painter himself. The story in question here became 'The Nun's Story of Gabriel's Marriage', with the added prologue and epilogue set in the parlour of a convent, where the painter copies a Holy Family by Correggio accompanied by a middle-aged sister who tells her tale while overseeing his work. This serves to extend the story by over 2,000 words from the 16,000-word version issued in Dickens's journal in two instalments in April 1853. Moreover, though the main story was initially issued in parts of equal length, with the break occurring at a significant crux in the narrative, the volume version was subdivided into five shorter chapters, thus further downplaying the suspense created at the serial break. The earlier part is dominated by the deathly fear deriving from ancient pagan superstition, while in the later part this is gradually overwhelmed by the Christian hope brought through contrition and forgiveness. In the volume version, this development is reinforced by the change of heart that the painter experiences regarding the wooden cross hanging in the parlour.

The scene opens after dark in the cottage of the Sarzeau family on the Breton coast during a sudden, violent storm, with the bedridden grandfather raving about the certain death of the father and younger son who are out at sea fishing, while the older son, Gabriel, and his fiancée Perrine struggle to calm him. When it becomes clear that the old man himself is about to pass away, with no chance of summoning a priest, he has no choice but to make his confession to his grandson. Here, he reveals that, ten years before, Gabriel's father had been guilty of the robbery and murder of a wealthy stranger who had sought shelter in the cottage, hiding the corpse beneath a nearby Druid monument. But before the old man expires, unexpectedly the son and grandson return safe from the storm and the old man disavows his confession, though Gabriel's doubts lead to a deep rift with his father – this despite the son later convincing himself that his father is innocent, when he fails to find the skeleton. The second part centres on the wedding of Gabriel and Perrine which takes place during the incursion into Brittany of the revolutionaries, persecuting believers and destroying their sacred sites. The Church responds by sending Father Paul on a mission to support the faithful by holding services on a ship at sea, where the young lovers arrange to be united. Before the ceremony Gabriel tells the priest of his grandfather's confession, whereon it is abruptly revealed that, having survived the murderous attack though still bearing the scar, the priest and the wealthy stranger are one and the same. Father Paul offers full forgiveness, and the now contrite father devotes the rest of his brief life to restoring the wayside wooden crosses laid waste by the revolutionaries, of which the parlour crucifix is revealed to be one. In ideological terms, in establishing communion between the Catholic nun and the Protestant painter, the story espouses ecumenical values unusual for the author, who more typically tends both to attack the corruption of the papacy and to mock evangelicals like his own painter father.

Of the fourteen shorter tales collected in *Little Novels*, only three were not published initially as yuletide entertainments, and, among those, 'Mrs Zant and the Ghost', despite its apparently happy ending with marriage on the horizon, is the least imbued with the spirit of romantic comedy. Originally entitled 'The Ghost's Touch', the tale was commissioned by W. F. Tillotson, the Lancashire newspaper syndicator. It was written over a few weeks in spring 1885: in mid-March the author had reported himself hard at work 'frightening myself, and trying to frighten the British reader' with a new ghost story, and at the end of April the completed manuscript was forwarded to Bolton.[15] With a lengthy new scene added to the proofs in mid-May, the story amounted to around 13,500 words divided into fourteen unequal chapters. In mid-June, in his flirtatious correspondence with twelve-year-old 'Nannie' Wynne, Collins described the story as especially 'written ... for you', and apologised when publication was delayed to the autumn by Tillotson.[16] The tale appeared in three instalments in around a dozen weeklies, with the most readable version found in the Dublin penny story paper the *Irish Fireside*, which supplied its own illustrations.[17]

These focus on the heavily bearded John Zant, the villainous brother-in-law of the eponymous heroine. The middle-aged hero, Rayburn, is a solitary widower devoted to his adolescent daughter Lucy; in the opening, the two encounter by chance the recently widowed but still youthful Mrs Zant, who herself has no children but finds comfort in her little dog. Despite the endearing presence of this creature, the story seems an unsuitable one to dedicate to a fatherless girl like Nannie Wynne. Not only is the intrusion of the deceased husband's ghost recounted in disturbing detail, but also sexual jealousy and harassment lie at the psychological heart of the narrative. The tale is set when parliament was debating the 1835 Marriage Act, which, throughout the Victorian era, prohibited marriage with a deceased wife's sister. Zant is revealed to be illicitly obsessed with his sister-in-law, employing psychological pressure, chemical stimulants, and even brute force to make her accept him, so that her 'guardian spirit' is finally forced to intervene corporeally, leaving the villain permanently paralysed. Even those on the side of the heroine are not without carnal interests: John Zant's housekeeper is shown repelling Mrs Zant because of her own passion for her master, while it is soon clear to the reader, if not to Rayburn himself, that he is motivated in his desire to protect the widow by something more than kindness. Lucy's role is particularly unsettling, as when, on first meeting the villain, she bluntly refuses to be kissed or to sit on his knee ('I'm not a fairy ... I'm a child'),[18] or in the final scene, where her father's reticence forces her to propose (successfully) to Mrs Zant that she should become her new stepmother.

As *Little Novels* lacks a frame narrative, no substantive changes were necessary in the collected stories aside from the new titles, although the author took pains to revise each tale for style. With 'The Ghost's Touch', the main change was the deletion of an entire scene at the beginning of chapter 11 (probably that added to the proofs), where Rayburn bumps into an old scientific acquaintance who warns of Zant's obsession with drugs affecting 'the mind through the body'.[19] Probably this cut was because the passage upset the desired balance between natural and supernatural explanations of events. This intention is flagged by the authorial voice, especially when Rayburn is asked to read Mrs Zant's account of the first intrusion of her husband's ghost and decide whether she is 'the object of a supernatural revelation' or 'fit for imprisonment in a mad-house'.[20] Here, the writer suggests, his hero wishes to avoid taking sides in this crucial question, though the conclusion of the tale suggests, of course, that Rayburn finally decides in favour of the former proposition.

In Lieu of a Summary

Two conclusions: first, Collins's explorations of shorter fiction are best seen as subject to the influence of a combination of preferred formal (generic) literary elements and the (material) constraints of dominant publishing formats; and second, despite his use of the terms 'little novels' and 'novels in outline' to describe shorter and longer tales respectively, it seems inadequate to regard such fiction as no more than a laboratory to tinker with themes and forms to be fully developed only in the novels.

Notes

[1] Concerning *The Leader*, see my introduction to Wilkie Collins, '"The New Dragon of Wantley: A Social Revelation", A Lost Tale', ed. G. Law (London: Wilkie Collins Society, 2007), pp. 1–7. Doubts about contributors also remain despite the recent location of an office copy of *All the Year Round*. See J. Parrott, 'The Skeleton out of the Closet: Authorship Identification in Dickens's *All the Year Round*', *Victorian Periodicals Review* 48.4 (Winter 2015), pp. 557–68.

[2] *Wilkie Collins: The Complete Shorter Fiction*, ed. J. Thompson (London: Constable Robinson, 1995).

[3] Dickens Journals Online, dir. J. Drew, www.djo.org.uk/

4 See G. Law, 'A Tale of Two Authors: The Shorter Fiction of Gaskell and Collins', *Wilkie Collins Society Journal NS* 9 (December 2006), pp. 43–52 (pp. 47–8).
5 See J. Plunkett on the role of the press in melding bourgeois family and nation state, in *Queen Victoria: First Media Monarch* (Oxford University Press, 2003), pp. 1–12; and S. Eliot on the emergence of the Christmas period as the climax of the publishing year, in *Some Patterns and Trends in British Publishing, 1800–1919* (London: Bibliographical Society, 1994), pp. 26–42.
6 See D. Hack, 'Volpurno – Or the Student: A Forgotten Tale of Madness by Wilkie Collins', *Times Literary Supplement* (2 January 2009), pp. 14–15.
7 See, for example, W. Collins to Harper & Brothers, 28 May 1872, referring to the two-volume novel *The New Magdalen* as 'my forthcoming short story'; in W. Baker, A. Gasson, G. Law and P. Lewis (eds.), *Collected Letters of Wilkie Collins* (Charlottesville, VA: InteLex, 2019), [1238]. Hereafter cited as BGLL.
8 See W. Collins to Andrew Chatto, 22 March 1887. BGLL, [2694].
9 W. Collins, Preface to *Miss or Mrs?: And Other Stories in Outline* (London: Richard Bentley, 1873), p. v.
10 W. Collins, 'Advertisement', *Mr Wray's Cash-Box; or The Mask and the Mystery. A Modern Story*, 2nd ed. (London: Richard Bentley, 1852), p. v; see Shakespeare, *Richard III*, IV.iv.359: 'An honest tale speeds best being plainly told.'
11 See Collins, 'The New Dragon of Wantley', pp. 7–12.
12 Collins, *Mr Wray's Cash-Box*, p. 1.
13 Remaindered copies were still available in the summer of 1855. See W. Collins to Charles Ward, 20 August 1855. BGLL, [0219].
14 W. Collins, 'My Lady's Money: An Episode in the Life of a Young Girl', *The Illustrated London News* 71.2005–6 (Christmas Number, December 1877), p. 34.
15 See W. Collins to Mary Anderson, 11 March 1885, and to A. P. Watt, 28 April 1885. BGLL, [2407] and [2419], respectively.
16 See W. Collins to Anne Wynne, 12 June and 15 September 1885. BGLL, [2432] and [2465] respectively.
17 W. Collins, 'The Ghost's Touch', *Irish Fireside* 5.119–21 (30 September–14 October 1885).
18 W. Collins, 'Mrs Zant and the Ghost', in *Little Novels*, 3 vols. (London: Chatto & Windus, 1887), vol. 1, p. 62.
19 Collins, 'The Ghosts's Touch', *Irish Fireside* 5.121, p. 258.
20 Collins, 'Mrs Zant and the Ghost', vol. 1, p. 34.

CHAPTER 8

Journalism

Deborah Wynne

Wilkie Collins's work as a journalist, which began when he was a young man, proved to be a valuable apprenticeship for his later career as a novelist. Indeed, journalism offered opportunities for would-be Victorian novelists to enter the professional world of letters, for most novelists wrote for magazines at some point in their careers, while others, such as Dickens and Thackeray, became editors of periodicals.[1] In 1841, as an unpaid apprentice to his father's friend Edward Antrobus, a tea importer, Collins found himself based in the Strand, London, near the offices of newly established periodicals including *Punch* (established in 1841) and *The Illustrated London News* (established in 1842), while the publishing firm Chapman & Hall was also close by.[2] Ostensibly training to be a tea importer, Collins actually focused on becoming a writer, and although he later referred to his five years at Antrobus & Co. as being trapped in his 'prison on the Strand', there were distinct benefits for him, as he was able to devote considerable time to writing stories and articles for magazine publication through the 1840s and 1850s.[3]

It was while he trained as an importer that Collins's earliest publications appeared in print, the first of which was the 'The Last Stage Coachman', published in *The Illuminated Magazine* (also based in the Strand) in 1843, a fantasy story focusing on the effects of the social transition from stage-coach to railway travel. This story set the tone for much of his subsequent non-fiction journalism, being a combination of social commentary and semi-autobiographical humour. Indeed, Collins became skilled in blending fact and fiction to develop his characteristic anecdotal style of journalism.[4] In the 1840s, the number of magazines on the market carrying fiction increased significantly and Collins swiftly saw the potential of the periodical press to broaden the literary culture and attract new readers. Journalism thus offered him an excellent opportunity to enter the world of letters.

In his 1863 collection of journalism, *My Miscellanies*, Collins, by now a well-known novelist, reflected on his early writing for periodicals, explaining that as a young journalist he had set out 'to present what I had observed ... in the lightest and least pretentious form; to address the public (if I could) with something of the ease of letter writing, and something of the familiarity of friendly talk'.[5] He added that by gently poking fun at 'some of the lighter eccentricities of character, and some of the more palpable absurdities of custom – without any unfair perversion of truth, or any needless descent to the lower regions of vulgarity and caricature', he avoided preaching to his readers.[6] The symbiotic relationship between publishing houses, periodicals and novels benefited Collins considerably, his willingness to provide editors with what they wanted proving an excellent foundation for his subsequent career as a writer of books. For example, in 1851, when Richard Bentley became editor of the family magazine *Bentley's Miscellany*, to which Collins contributed essays and reviews, Bentley's publishing house accepted his travel book, *Rambles Beyond Railways* (1851).

At this time Collins also contributed to a rather different periodical, *The Leader*, a weekly newspaper focusing on news items. *The Leader* offered lengthy reviews of literature and the arts, as well as sketches based on topical subjects.[7] Collins's first essay in *The Leader*, 'A Plea for Sunday Reform', appeared on 27 September 1851, signed 'WWC' (William Wilkie Collins), calling for more entertainment venues, such as art galleries and concert halls, to open on Sundays to cater to working people. *The Leader*, established by George Henry Lewes and Thornton Hunt in 1850 as a radical socialist weekly newspaper, was instrumental in helping Collins to develop confidence as a journalist.[8] When Collins's close friend Edward Pigott became editor of *The Leader* in 1851, Collins became a regular contributor. Collins showed his acumen as a journalist when he advised adapting the structure of *The Leader* by using subheadings to help readers navigate through the domestic and overseas news.[9] Collins did not contribute news items himself, however; most of his features appeared in the 'Portfolio' section, which focused mainly on discussions of art and culture. His most notable contribution was a series of letters he exchanged with Lewes (who commissioned this feature) called 'Magnetic Evenings at Home', where Collins proposed the validity of supernatural occurrences, such as clairvoyance and mesmerism, while Lewes counteracted with letters written from a rational, scientific standpoint, which dismissed the idea of the supernatural.

Collins's relationship with *The Leader* soured in 1852, however, following the publication of what he considered to be an inappropriate article. In February of that year, he wrote to Pigott:

> Nothing will ever persuade me that a system which permits the introduction of the private religious, or irreligious, or heterodoxical opinions of contributors to a newspaper into the articles on politics or general news which they write for it, is a wise or good system ... I hate controversies on paper almost more than I hate controversies in talk.[10]

The resulting disagreement led to the cooling of his friendship with Pigott and for two years Collins refused to contribute to the paper, despite this work being his main source of income at the time.[11] Nevertheless, he returned to *The Leader* two years later as a regular reviewer of literature, the arts and theatre, and in 1855 he temporarily took over Pigott's editorial duties when the latter was ill and away from London. These early experiences proved helpful in preparing Collins for the next stage of his career as a protégé of Dickens, the latter having established his popular weekly magazine *Household Words* in 1850.

By 1856 Collins was, then, an experienced journalist and writer of short fiction. In this year he gained a considerable advance in his prospects when he was appointed to the staff of *Household Words*, to which he had already contributed several features. As Anthea Trodd has argued, this was not an unequivocal benefit, for Collins feared 'that he would be submerging his distinct identity as a writer in the journal's collective personality'.[12] Dickens exercised complete editorial control over the magazine. Its tone was light and liberal, with issues related to reform and social justice presented in a lively register.[13] Dickens was particularly keen to employ Collins, writing to his subeditor, W. H. Wills, to praise his friend as 'industrious and reliable' and, more importantly, 'suggestive and exceedingly quick to take my notions'.[14] Collins soon joined Dickens's select band of protégés, a small number of promising young journalists who came to be known as Dickens's 'young men', a group that included George Augustus Sala and Edmund Yates.[15] Dickens had developed a 'house style' for his magazine, which Sue Lonoff characterises as 'the art of pleasing digression' and Collins, already skilled in this style of journalism, was able to provide essays which suited Dickens's requirements.[16] Occasionally, however, Collins used his platform to attack middle-class mores, a tendency which Dickens attempted to check. For the most part, though, the two men developed a smooth working relationship. The income Collins received as a staff member of *Household Words* was crucial to him until the success of *The Woman in White*, which was serialised in Dickens's successor magazine, *All the Year Round*, from 1859 to 1860.[17]

Dickens and Collins's professional relationship was strengthened by a series of collaborations in *Household Words*, the first of which was 'The Wreck of the Golden Mary', a story which appeared in the Christmas 1856 issue of the periodical. In 1857, the two writers published in *Household Words* a semi-autobiographical account of a tour they had taken together in the north of England in September that year. As Paul Schlicke notes, 'The Lazy Tour of Two Idle Apprentices' offers a 'journalistic account of a holiday in unfamiliar locations … infused with a whiff of surrealism', a blending of both writers' styles to create a tone of whimsical banter.[18] Appearing in October 1857 in five instalments it displays the fluid style of journalism that both authors favoured, a combination of fact and fiction which spun 'an amusing series out of scanty material'.[19] Despite Collins's initial anxieties about asserting his own voice as a *Household Words* contributor, working with Dickens proved beneficial for the younger writer; as Trodd contends, it was 'in the collaborations that the Collins of the 1860s novels developed'.[20] The spinning out of an entertaining essay, part personal account and part journalism, was typical of Collins's non-fiction work for *Household Words*, yet non-fiction essays were, for him, always subordinated to his writing of novels, and the tightly plotted economy of his best fiction is certainly missing from the digressive tendency of his journalism.

In August 1858, two years after joining the staff of *Household Words*, Collins published his best-known article, 'The Unknown Public'. Appearing on the front page of the 21 August issue of *Household Words*, it offered an overview of the current state of the popular periodical press and its readers, where Collins expressed his opinion of the market for cheap publications aimed at working-class readers. Graham Law sees 'The Unknown Public' as Collins's 'most widely cited' piece of journalism, while Andrew King and John Plunkett consider it as 'perhaps the most widely read article today on nineteenth-century mass-market writing'.[21] 'The Unknown Public' has in recent years become a matter of controversy, with scholars pointing out the ideological imperatives underpinning Collins's ridicule of the 'penny bloods' (sometimes called 'penny dreadfuls'), weekly periodicals catering to working-class readers. King and Plunkett warn against the 'many falsifications' hidden beneath the article's 'seductive readability'.[22] Lorna Huett sees 'The Unknown Public' as characterised by an 'inherent ambivalence' and riven by 'contradictions' related to Collins's own relationship with Dickens's *Household Words*, which at this time was 'an oddity: a cheap publication welcomed into the drawing rooms of the middle classes'.[23] Nevertheless, despite its flaws, the article offers an interesting snapshot of the sale and consumption of cheap periodicals in the late 1850s, drawing attention to the millions of 'unknown' readers – 'unknown', that is, by the respectable middle-class publishing houses and editors. These working-class readers avidly consumed 'penny weeklies', attracted to their apparently addictive sensational serialised novels.[24]

In 'The Unknown Public' Collins presents himself in the role of investigative journalist, describing his undercover visits to drab tobacconists' shops in 'second and third rate neighbourhoods' in London and beyond, where he finds myriad penny weekly papers on sale.[25] He examines a selection of these, reading some instalments which he condemns as trash, and is particularly scathing about the 'Answers to Correspondents' columns, whereby readers write to the paper with questions they would like to have answered, thus exposing their ignorance and inadequate education. Nevertheless, Collins reflects on the millions of semi-literate readers who consume the serialised stories of the penny weeklies, believing that they may in time demand better quality literature:

> The largest audience for periodical literature, in this age of periodicals, must obey the universal law of progress, and must, sooner or later, learn to discriminate. When that period comes, the readers who rank by millions, will be the readers who give the widest reputations, who return the richest rewards, and who will, therefore, command the service of the best writers of their time. A great, and unparalleled prospect awaits, perhaps, the upcoming generation of English novelists.[26]

It is possible that Collins's contemplation of this untapped readership stimulated him to focus on developing his own sensational mystery story for serialisation, which borrowed some of the features of the penny bloods, for in 1859 *The Woman in White* appeared in short weekly instalments in Dickens's *All the Year Round*.[27]

Between 1856 and 1860 Collins produced over fifty essays for *Household Words* and *All the Year Round*, some of which he collected in his two-volume *My Miscellanies*. While many of Collins's pieces for *Household Words* use fictional narrators to discuss contemporary issues, a few conform to more established standards of Victorian journalism. One of these is 'The Unknown Public', and another is 'To Think or Be Thought For', which appeared in the 13 September 1856 issue and discusses what Collins calls the 'Cant of Criticism' that afflicts visitors to

British art galleries. Collins complains that 'the public mind' is 'hopeless [ly] dependen[t] on arbitrary rules and critical opinions in the matter of Art. ... Why do people want to look at guide-books, before they can make up their minds about an old picture?'[28] Collins urges these visitors 'to trust entirely to their own common sense ... to express their opinions boldly, without the slightest reference to any precedent whatever'.[29] This is one of the small number of essays where Collins eschews the use of a fictionalised narrator who dramatises his subject. It is also an example of his hostility towards the middle classes, which Dickens often attempted to curtail, for he condemns them as 'indolent' and dominated by convention.[30]

Collins's most frequent technique as a journalist, however, was to fictionalise his subject by adopting a first-person narrator to strike an intimate personal note. Often a 'personal' anecdote is recounted as a way of opening the discussion, and a typical example of this is in 'A National Wrong', published in *Chambers's Journal* in 1870. Although this unsigned article was co-authored with James Payn, it is typical of Collins's style, which directly addresses readers in a personal way. The 'national wrong' of the title is the 'shameful omission in the law [of copyright] between countries calling themselves civilised',[31] which resulted in American publishers pirating the work of British authors. The article opens with an analogy, addressing a 'dear Materfamilias' who, having 'cut out a dress for [her] child ... devised the pattern' and made up the garment, believes the pattern to be her 'own private property'. The authors explain that the mother is quite rightly 'riled' when she finds an American woman stealing the pattern, because 'the law permits [her] to take it'.[32] There follows a discussion of the iniquities of Americans 'import[ing] the works of our most popular writers for nothing', and gives the example of Collins's own novel, *Man and Wife*, being subject to piracy.[33] The article reprints Collins's letters to an overseas publisher in which he demands, without success, proper remuneration for this work.[34]

Once Collins had established his reputation as a leading novelist in the early 1860s, his production of non-fiction journalism for periodical publication declined dramatically, suggesting that his labour as a journalist was expedient, rather than a pleasure. Nevertheless, the publication of his collected journalism in *My Miscellanies* in 1863 indicates that he valued his early work for periodicals and found a new market for his non-fiction essays. Indeed, many of his essays continue to be readable and engaging today, their value lying in the unique insight Collins presents on aspects of the culture and social mores of the mid-Victorian period.

Notes

1. G. Law, 'The Professionalization of Authorship', in J. Bourne Taylor and J. Kucich (eds.), *The Oxford History of the Novel in English*, Vol. III: *The Nineteenth-Century Novel, 1820–1880* (Oxford University Press, 2012), pp. 37–55 (p. 44).
2. C. Peters, *The King of Inventors: A Life of Wilkie Collins* (London: Minerva Press, 1992), p. 55; L. Pykett, *Authors in Context: Wilkie Collins* (Oxford University Press, 2005), p. 7; W. Baker and W. M. Clarke (eds.), *The Letters of Wilkie Collins*, 2 vols. (London: Macmillan, 1999), vol. 1, p. 16, n. 4. Hereafter cited as B&C.
3. Quoted in W. M. Clarke, *The Secret Life of Wilkie Collins* (Stroud: Alan Sutton Publishing, 1996), p. 44.
4. G. Law and A. Maunder, *Wilkie Collins: A Literary Life* (Basingstoke: Palgrave Macmillan, 2008), p. 47.
5. W. Collins, *My Miscellanies*, 2 vols. (London: Sampson Low, 1863), vol. 1, pp. v–vi.
6. Ibid., vol. 1, p. vi.
7. Law and Maunder, *Wilkie Collins*, p. 49.
8. K. H. Beetz, 'Wilkie Collins and *The Leader*', *Victorian Periodicals Review* 15.1 (Spring 1982), pp. 20–9 (p. 20).
9. Ibid., p. 22.
10. B&C, vol. 1, p. 82.
11. Beetz, 'Wilkie Collins and *The Leader*', p. 23.
12. A. Trodd, 'The Early Writing', in J. Bourne Taylor (ed.), *The Cambridge Companion to Wilkie Collins* (Cambridge University Press, 2007), pp. 23–36 (p. 29).
13. D. Wynne, *The Sensation Novel and the Victorian Family Magazine* (Basingstoke: Palgrave Macmillan, 2001), p. 23.
14. G. Storey and K. Tillotson (eds.), *The Letters of Charles Dickens* (Pilgrim Edition), Vol. VIII: *1856–1858* (Oxford: Clarendon Press, 1995), p. 188.
15. See P. D. Edwards, *Dickens's 'Young Men': George Augustus Sala, Edmund Yates and the World of Victorian Journalism* (London: Routledge, 1997).
16. S. Lonoff, *Wilkie Collins and His Victorian Readers: A Study in the Rhetoric of Authorship* (New York: AMS Press, 1982), pp. 50–1.
17. Pykett, *Authors in Context*, p. 98.
18. P. Schlicke (ed.), *Oxford Reader's Companion to Dickens* (Oxford University Press, 1999), p. 323.
19. Peters, *The King of Inventors*, p. 180.
20. Trodd, 'The Early Writing', p. 31.
21. G. Law, 'Wilkie Collins and the Discovery of an "Unknown Public"', in J. Shattock (ed.), *Journalism and the Periodical Press in Nineteenth-Century Britain* (Cambridge University Press, 2017), pp. 328–40 (p. 328); A. King and J. Plunkett (eds.), *Victorian Print Media: A Reader* (Oxford University Press, 2005), p. 168.

[22] King and Plunkett, *Victorian Print Media*, p. 168.
[23] L. Huett, 'Among the Unknown Public: *Household Words, All the Year Round* and the Mass-Market Weekly Periodical in the Mid-Nineteenth Century', *Victorian Periodicals Review* 38.1 (Spring 2005), pp. 61–82 (pp. 61, 64, 70).
[24] See Wynne, *The Sensation Novel*, pp. 10–14.
[25] W. Collins, 'The Unknown Public', *Household Words* 18 (21 August 1858), p. 217.
[26] Ibid., p. 222.
[27] Wynne, *The Sensation Novel*, p. 15.
[28] W. Collins, 'To Think or Be Thought For', *Household Words* 14 (13 September 1856), pp. 193–4.
[29] Ibid., p. 194.
[30] Ibid., p. 193.
[31] W. Collins and J. Payn, 'A National Wrong', *Chambers's Journal* 47.320 (12 February 1870), p. 110.
[32] Ibid., p. 107.
[33] Ibid., p. 107.
[34] Ibid., p. 108.

CHAPTER 9

Drama

Caroline Radcliffe

Although better known for his novels and short stories, Wilkie Collins achieved considerable success as a dramatist in Britain and the United States, with plays such as *Man and Wife* and *The New Magdalen* enjoying long and successful runs. Translations of his plays were performed throughout Europe and the many pirated theatrical adaptations of his novels are a testimony to the dramatic potential and far-reaching popularity of his work. His plays were produced in important theatres, renowned for advances in what could be described as a proto-naturalist acting style within a wider realist movement. Collins's dramas were sought after and staged by important, forward-thinking managers and actor-managers – Sir Squire Bancroft and Lady Marie Effie Bancroft, Benjamin Webster and W. S. Emden in London, François-Joseph Régnier and Charles Fechter in Paris and Augustin Daly in New York – and were acted by some of the best actors of the time, including Frederick Robson, Fanny Stirling, George and Frederick Vining, Carlotta Leclercq, Henry Neville, Charles Fechter, Ada Cavendish and George Alexander.

It is the purpose of this chapter to look at some of the factors that Collins had to contend with as a playwright that undoubtedly shaped his dramatic output. Collins's drive for a really progressive realist theatre upset critics and audiences, preventing him from fully realising his dramatic vision. This was further compounded by the dramatic licensing, censorship and copyright regulations of the time which influenced his decisions to either stage his dramas or withhold them from being performed.

Overview of the Dramatic Works

Collins wrote fifteen dramas which fall into two clearly definable categories covering the years 1850–69 and 1870–85 respectively.[1] The early period represents Collins's evolution as a dramatist, during which he wrote both single-authored and collaborative works. The second period comprises single-authored, original adaptations of his novels. It is notable that the periods identified align with the time before and after Dickens's death, with whom he had worked so closely.

Collins's first staged drama was *A Court Duel* (adapted from a French play by Lockroy and Badon first performed 1850);[2] it was followed by *The Lighthouse* (originally titled *The Storm at the Lighthouse* and written in consultation with Dickens, 1855); *The Frozen Deep* (conceived by Dickens, written and revised in collaboration with Dickens, first performed in 1857, later revised by Collins for the 1866 production); *The Red Vial* (1858); *Armadale* (in collaboration with the French actor, Régnier, 1866, but never staged, later revised by Collins as *Miss Gwilt*, 1875); *No Thoroughfare* (the stage version written by Collins, based on a story published simultaneously in collaboration with Dickens, 1867); and *Black and White* (written by Collins from an idea proposed by the Anglo-French actor Fechter, 1869). During this period Collins also co-authored a dramatic synopsis for *A Message from the Sea* with Dickens (1861) based on their collaborative Christmas story. In all of the collaborative plays, Collins authored the major part of the final texts, but his early career as a dramatist was inevitably eclipsed by Dickens. Until very recently his dramas were mentioned only in relation to scholarship on Dickens, with the major part of Collins's work on *The Lighthouse*, *The Frozen Deep* and *No Thoroughfare* frequently accredited to Dickens. After Dickens's death, Collins began a series of single-authored dramas, some adapted from his own novels: *No Name* (written in 1870 but never produced), *The Woman in White* (1871), *Man and Wife* (1873), *The New Magdalen* (1873), *Miss Gwilt* (1875), *The Moonstone* (1877), *Rank and Riches* (1883) and *The Evil Genius* (1885). Existing manuscripts, letters and notes reveal further ideas and plots for dramas that never materialised.

The State of the British Drama

In Jim Davis's excellent introduction to Collins and the theatre, he attributes Collins's relatively cautious approach to dramatisation to the 'low status of the dramatist as compared with the novelist and the comparatively poor financial returns',[3] and in a frequently cited account of his life and writings, from a letter to the Parisian journalist and scholar, Alfred-Auguste Ernouf, Collins states that if it had not been for the poor standards of British theatre, he would have dramatised all of his works:

> If I had been a Frenchman – with such a public to write for, such rewards to win, and such actors to interpret me, as the French Stage presents – all the stories I have written from 'Antonina' to 'The Woman in White' would have been told in the dramatic form. Whether their success as plays would have been equal to their success as novels, it is not for me to decide; But if I know anything of my own faculty, it is a dramatic one.[4]

The influence of French drama was central to his work as a dramatist and provided a comparative model of theatre that had fewer of the restrictions he was subject to as a British playwright. Frequently visiting the Parisian theatres, Collins and Dickens considered French theatre to have far higher professional standards than the British, in part due to a more established system of actor training, less restrictive censorship, better conditions for playwrights in terms of copyright protection and commensurate financial reward which, in turn, prevented poor, pirated versions from being written or performed and, lastly, audiences and critics who were open to more innovative and challenging dramas. The restrictive conditions of the British theatre discouraged Collins from staging many of his novels and from writing any more new dramas. This explanation is reinforced in a further response to Ernouf:

> In the present degraded state of the drama in England – degraded, I mean, in the literary sense – I have refused all proposals to publish them, or to allow them to be acted after the period of their first stage appearance. I mean to keep them till better times come – and if no better times come, I will turn them into Novels.[5]

Collins continued to wait for the 'better times' when his more controversial dramas might have been better received. In a holograph in which he lists the copyrights of his novels and dramas, he notes bitterly that the publication of his later novel, *Jezebel's Daughter* (1880), based on the play *The Red Vial*, 'which was damned at the Olympic', might serve to improve its reception in any revival.[6] Collins was not alone in his distrust of the British theatre. Dickens also refused to stage or adapt his works in a theatre that could not uphold his literary ideals. Dickens's amateur theatre company was created in order that he might have total control over any production, with him taking the roles of author, actor and what we would now recognise as the director and producer in the modern sense. Collins, similarly, took an active role in matters such as casting, scenographic decisions, read-throughs and rehearsals, working closely with the theatres that staged his works.

Collins's novella, *Mr Wray's Cash-Box*, was conceived during the provincial tour of *Not so Bad as We Seem*, by Edward Bulwer-Lytton, in 1851, the first of many 'theatricals' he performed in with Dickens, and embodies their shared views on acting and drama.[7] Dickens and Bulwer-Lytton were among the many literary authors who decried the state of British drama; Bulwer-Lytton had been instrumental in proposing dramatic reform in 1832. Using the story as a means to criticise the 'hack' writers of the contemporary theatre, Collins attacks the copyright laws that worked in their favour. Furthermore, he satirises 'the British drama', distancing himself from the formal, oratorical style of John Philip Kemble and encouraging a move towards the emotionally driven style of acting exemplified by Edmund Kean and Dickens himself.

Despite the poor state of British drama, as it was disparagingly characterised, throughout the 1850s and 1860s a strongly articulated British, realist-theatre movement was emerging, influenced by French dramatists, actors and the school of acting pioneered by the leading French comic actor of the day, François-Joseph Régnier, with whom Collins collaborated on the dramatic versions in French of *The Woman in White*, *Armadale* and *The New Magdalen*. Collins targeted his dramatic works at the increasingly conscientious circle of actors and actor-managers who were seeking to implement these realist practices, notably at the Olympic, the St James's and the Prince of Wales theatres. Determined to break the mould of bad dramatic writing, Collins offered serious dramas that challenged both theatrical and moral conventions. Although theatre managers and actors were ready for change and prepared to take risks, audiences were not. Collins frequently lamented the British public's inability to value drama that was unbroken by the elements of popular performance such as singing, comedy and dancing that were once integral to the minor theatres' performances of melodrama. In response to the news that his revised production of *The Frozen Deep* at the Olympic was not attracting audiences, Collins attributed this to the public's levity, writing ironically to Nina Lehmann that:

> The play is (I am told – for I have not yet had the courage to go and see it) beautifully got up, and very well acted. But the enlightened British Public declares it to be 'slow'. There is'nt [sic] an atom of slang or vulgarity in the whole piece from beginning to end – no female legs are shown in it – Richard Wardour does'nt get up after dying and sing a comic song – sailors are represented in the Arctic regions, and there is no hornpipe danced, and no sudden arrival of 'the pets of the ballet' to join the dance in the costume of Esquimaux maidens – finally, all the men on the stage don't marry all the women on the stage, at the end – and nobody addresses the audience, and

says: – 'If our kind friends here to-night will only encourage us by their applause, there are brave hearts among us which will dare the perils for many a night yet, of – The Frozen Deep!'[8]

Tim Dolin and Janice M. Allan have examined the relationship between Collins's career and realism in the visual arts and literature respectively, and it is helpful to apply this understanding of a realist aesthetic to Collins's dramas.[9] His unique position in the literary and artistic circles of the mid-nineteenth century led him to experiment with a style of drama that might be classified as 'sensational realism', influenced by his close association with the Pre-Raphaelite and Clique painters (two anti-Academy groups who actually opposed each other), and by his own pioneering development of sensation fiction.[10] Collins particularly combined these elements in *The Lighthouse*, *The Red Vial*, *The Frozen Deep* and *No Thoroughfare*, enhanced by an innate sense of theatricality, including the aural, the visual and the intermedial, to create a sensational realism that challenges a common trajectory in nineteenth-century theatre history.

Sensation literature came under frequent criticism and Collins's dramas were similarly attacked for their low morals and debased characters, with the characters' ability to oscillate *between* the mundane and the extraordinary areas of life – the 'dramatic' areas – the most disturbing to critics. With none of the binaries that melodrama conformed to, Collins's morally ambiguous characters challenged its neat categories of good or evil.

Dickens's somewhat dismissive appraisal of *The Lighthouse* as 'a regular old-style melodrama' failed to note Collins's startling focus on the human condition, with elements of the psychological and the environmental and a protagonist who is morally ambiguous – elements that would combine and manifest in the naturalist theatre of the late nineteenth century.[11] In *The Lighthouse*, the intense examination of a man's guilt for a crime that still haunts him challenges the claim that *The Bells* (by Leopold Lewis, 1871) in which Henry Irving played the murderer, Mathias, some sixteen years later, was the first psychological drama on the British stage. Similarly, in *The Red Vial*, a drama set in a German dead-house with a lunatic and a murderess as the protagonists, drawing overtly on the Gothic, Collins again broke with melodramatic convention, presenting a sensational realism that horrified audiences but was retrospectively viewed by some as a precedent for the dramatic naturalism of Emile Zola's 1873 drama, *Thérèse Raquin*, many years before the naturalist movement was recognised in Britain. Critics dismissed *The Red Vial* as a failure, yet it was defended by some of the most accomplished actors of the day as being ahead of its time.

Adaptation and the Later Dramas

After Dickens's death in 1870, Collins, liberated from Dickens's influence, took a freer direction in his later dramas, systematically adapting his major novels and writing more challenging 'new dramas' that increasingly reflected the concerns of his later novels. In an age in which a popular novel had hardly reached the printing press before it would appear on the stage, Collins might have profited from the success of novels such as *The Woman in White* and *The Moonstone* by adapting them immediately for the stage. Some were conceived and written originally as plays specifically for the theatre, and some lent themselves to simultaneous or later novelisation. In these later dramas, Collins renounced sensation in favour of more explicitly social plays, both coinciding with and anticipating rising theatrical movements.

In *Man and Wife* and *The New Magdalen*, Collins provocatively questioned prevailing ideologies of gender and religion. *The New Magdalen* was Collins's most successful drama, performed at the Olympic Theatre, and Ada Cavendish, who played the role of Mercy, went on to form her own production company touring the play throughout Britain and the USA. In *The New Magdalen* Collins provocatively subverted the trope of the fallen woman, anticipating George Bernard Shaw through his sympathetic representation of the prostitute, Mercy. Despite the controversy caused by the drama, it was an immense success. Collins's idealised masculinity in his representation of the religious minister, Julian Gray in *The New Magdalen*, contrasted strongly with the cultish athleticism of *Man and Wife*'s Geoffrey Delamayn.

It was perhaps due to the fact that both *The New Magdalen* and *Man and Wife* were originally conceived as dramas prior to their adaptation into novels that they worked so well on stage. Only by omitting many of the characters and subplots from his novels could the dramas conform to the stringent licensing requirements of the British stage. His dramatic adaptation of *No Name*, for instance, which was never performed, was viewed by Collins as 'not likely to succeed if it is produced on the stage',[12] yet his adaptation of *Man and Wife* which, like *No Name*, challenges and exposes marriage and inheritance laws, raising questions about women's agency, proved an extraordinary success. Critically, Collins omitted one of the key characters of the novel from the dramatisation, Hester Dethridge, the abused wife of a violent, alcoholic husband, as he had done with Rosanna Spearman, the reformed thief from *The Moonstone*. Working with hindsight and a knowledge of the licensing restrictions likely to be applied, Collins must have known that these characters, while accepted in the novels, would not be tolerated onstage. Collins continued to challenge prevailing ideologies in *Rank and Riches*, which he wrote solely in its dramatic version, and in *The Evil Genius*, written simultaneously as both novel and play. Both plays demonstrate progressive sympathy for more liberal marriage, divorce and child custody laws for women, but *Rank and Riches* was badly received and the stage version of *The Evil Genius*, although extensively worked on by Collins, was only ever produced for one performance in order to establish dramatic copyright.

Beyond the practical considerations of censorship, Collins made a clear compositional distinction between the novel and the dramatic form, approaching adaptation as the means to create new dramatic works, taking the particular demands of theatre into account rather than attempting to replicate his novels onstage. *The Times* summarised this in 1873: '[Wilkie Collins] never dramatizes his own novels in the strict sense of the word, but he invents a story which is capable of both narrative and dramatic treatment, and in two distinct forms he successively presents it.'[13]

Collins's own advice to an aspiring dramatist who was seeking to adapt Gerald Griffin's book, *The Collegians*, into a play called *The Foster Brothers* was: '[i]f you do re-write "The Foster Brothers" try to forget that such a novel as "The Collegians" ever existed. When you have taken the idea of the story, you have taken all that the novel can give to the play.'[14]

Drama versus Metadrama

In this final section I address Collins's puzzling omission of the overtly theatrical characters in his novels from his dramas. Collins's subversion of standard nineteenth-century literary tropes in relation to alterity has been the focus of much scholarship. By placing characters perceived as 'other' through their race, class, gender, physical difference or neurodivergence at the centre of his narratives, Collins scandalised and shocked critics of sensation fiction whilst continuing to reject melodramatic binaries of good and evil by populating his fiction with characters who defy the 'conventionalities of sentimental fiction'.[15] Collins frequently uses theatre and the performance of identity as metaphors for alterity. By drawing on the peripheral social status of the actor as a paradigm of illegitimacy and otherness, he emphasises a character's ability to survive through their learned resourcefulness as performers and their readiness to breach social convention. In *Armadale*, for example, Ozias Midwinter ekes out a living as an itinerant child-performer in parallel to Lydia Gwilt's juvenile career as a touring exhibit with a quack doctor; both Lydia and Ozias are masterful at concealing their true identities. Mary Grice in *Hide and Seek* also earns her keep as a child circus-performer while her true identity is concealed. Furthering the connection between illegitimacy and performance, Collins turned closer to home to find his inspiration for the protagonist of *No Name*. *No Name* is Collins's most overtly theatrical novel, taking inspiration from his mother's experiences as an aspiring actor and his own experiences in amateur theatre. Like Dickens, Collins was influenced by the actor, Fanny Kelly, who started the first professional acting school in London, the Royal Dramatic School and Theatre, or more simply, 'Miss. Kelly's Theatre'. In the novel, Magdalen Vanstone is a consummate actress. In the impersonations and theatrical vignettes in which she appears, Collins draws on Kelly's solo performances, for which she represented a variety of characters in a series of 'Dramatic Recollections'. Like Lydia Gwilt, and later, Mercy Merrick in *The New Magdalen*, Magdalen is skilled at impersonation and the creation of false identities.

Given the importance that theatre is granted within the novel, it is surprising that Collins discards all of Magdalen's performances in his four-act drama; the loss of Magdalen the actress – intrinsic to her actions and indispensable to the novel's plot – could perhaps have contributed to Collins's pronouncement of *No Name* as unviable for the stage.

For an author who was so involved in theatre, fostering so many close relationships with actors and playwrights, it seems almost inconceivable that he should exclude *No Name* from the medium that most favoured its representation. I suggest that by rejecting the metadramatic potential of the novel, Collins consciously shed the dissembling nature of his character's theatricality, in line with the dramatic realism that he was seeking.

Collins, and the actors who supported a realist theatre, prioritised a believable and truthful representation of life, even when the life and characters represented onstage were beyond the audiences' own experiences. In the letter of dedication to the 1862 edition of his novel *Basil*, Collins wrote the often-quoted passage:

> Believing that the Novel and the Play are twin-sisters in the family of Fiction; that the one is a drama narrated, as the other is a drama acted; and that all the strong and deep emotions which the Play-writer is privileged to excite, the Novel-writer is privileged to excite also, I have not thought it either politic or necessary, while adhering to realities, to adhere to every-day realities only.[16]

Flying in the face of the everyday realities of the naturalist 'cup and saucer' dramas of his contemporary, Tom Robertson, influencing the problem plays of Arthur Pinero, and anticipating the radical nature of Shaw, Collins defied dramatic convention by insisting on the realistic representation of the extraordinary on the dramatic stage.

Notes

1. I am indebted to Andrew Gasson's and Paul Lewis's work in compiling information on and dates of Collins's dramas. See Gasson, *Wilkie Collins Information Pages*, 'The Plays of Wilkie Collins', www.wilkie-collins.info/plays_wilkie_collins.htm and Lewis, 'The Wilkie Collins Pages', www.wilkiecollins.com/
2. This and subsequent dates are for first performances.
3. J. Davis, 'Collins and the Theatre', in J. Bourne Taylor (ed.), *The Cambridge Companion to Wilkie Collins* (Cambridge University Press, 2006), pp. 168–80 (p. 178).
4. W. Collins to Alfred-Auguste Ernouf, 21 March 1862, in W. Baker, A. Gasson, G. Law and P. Lewis (eds.), *The Collected Letters of Wilkie Collins* (Charlottesville, VA: InteLex, 2019), [0462]. Hereafter cited as BGLL.
5. W. Collins to Ernouf, 7 May 1862. BGLL, [3024].
6. Ibid.
7. W. Collins, *Mr. Wray's Cash-Box; or, The Mask and the Mystery. A Christmas Sketch* (London: Richard Bentley, 1852).
8. W. Collins to Nina Lehmann, 9 December 1866. BGLL, [0714].
9. T. Dolin, 'Collins's Career and the Visual Arts', in Bourne Taylor (ed.), *The Cambridge Companion to Wilkie Collins*, pp. 7–22; J. M. Allan, 'Sensationalism Made Real: The Role of Realism in the Production of Sensational Affect', *Victorian Literature and Culture* 43.1 (2015), pp. 97–112, www.jstor.org/stable/24577272
10. See Allan's reference to 'sensational realism' in 'Sensationalism Made Real', p. 98.
11. Dickens to Clarkson Stanfield, 20 May 1855, in G. Storey and K. Tillotson (eds.), *The Letters of Charles Dickens* (Pilgrim Edition), Vol. VIII: *1856–1858* (Oxford: Clarendon Press, 1995), pp. 624–5.
12. W. Collins, 'Copy-right Novels which belong to me', p. 3, in the Henry W. and Albert A. Berg Collection of English and American Literature, New York Public Library, Holograph January 1882, *New York Public Library Digital Collections*, 1882-02, https://digitalcollections.nypl.org/items/a06be5f4-a6a7-914f-e040-e00a18062de9
13. *The Times* (20 December 1873), p. 10.

14 W. Collins to unidentified recipient, 16 February 1859. BGLL, [0294], cited in R. Pearson, *Victorian Writers and the Stage: The Plays of Dickens, Browning, Collins and Tennyson* (Basingstoke: Palgrave Macmillan, 2015), p. 152.
15 W. Collins, Letter of Dedication, *Basil* (London: Sampson Low, 1862), p. iv.
16 Ibid., p. v.

PART II

Critical Response and Afterlife

CHAPTER 10

Contemporary

James Aaron Green

As the 1850s drew to a close, a 35-year-old Wilkie Collins could reflect with some satisfaction on twelve years that had seen him carve out a reputation as a talented writer, and one of even greater promise. His writing career had begun with works that were misnomers of his future trajectory; yet the *Memoirs* (1848) of his late father, the painter William Collins, and the historical novel *Antonina; or, The Fall of Rome* (1850), each helped to establish his reputation. 'The first work of a new aspirant after fame in this class of literature, it [*Antonina*] is one sufficient in itself to entitle its author to a place in the foremost rank', was the effusive response of the *Gentleman's Magazine*.[1] Collins would not return to the 'classic romance', but *Antonina*'s reception prefigured some of the features for which his fiction would become acclaimed; the *New Monthly Magazine* highlighted the novel's 'great originality and boldness of conception' and, tellingly (in terms of his later renown for depicting 'fallen women'), how readers' interest was directed towards a marginal perspective – that of the 'barbarian invaders'.[2] *Basil: A Story of Modern Life* (1852) transplanted the sensational incidents of *Antonina* from the distant locale of Roman Italy to the streets of nineteenth-century London. This temporal shift – definitional to the sub-genre of 'sensation fiction' of which *Basil* was prototypical – led to a sharp rebuke from critics: whether the quality of the prose offset its brazen treatment of infidelity and violence (the 'aesthetics of the Old Bailey', as *The Athenaeum* branded it),[3] or only heightened its offence, was a major point of contention;[4] rare was a voice like that of *The Literary Gazette*, which saw the novel as attempting a flawed moral lesson.[5] The novel's unreality (or 'want [of] nature')[6] and fine plot construction were other aspects noted. Lyn Pykett rightly states that the 'tone of the nineteenth-century critical debate on Collins's work was set by the reviews to *Basil*'.[7] That said, one crucial difference between these and later reviews (including of his 1860s fiction) is that even the most censorious were tempered by the recognition that Collins was as yet a junior writer – there was time for him to amend and expunge coarse subjects from his work.

In his next novel, *Hide and Seek* (1854), the critics did not find the change they had hoped for; it was, as Collins himself said, only a 'fresh variation' on his prior writing.[8] Even so, it was hailed as a 'great improvement' upon *Basil*,[9] albeit without commercial success to match.[10] The inclusion of humour and a greater fidelity to 'nature' were singled out for praise; the story's naturalness was something on which Geraldine Jewsbury, a critic by no means predisposed to sensationalism, concurred; she moreover commends a facet that was to become increasingly definitional in Collins's future reception – his aptitude for 'construction':

> It [the plot of *Hide and Seek*] is skilfully and artfully worked out; there is not a single scene, or character, or incident, however trivial, that does not in some way tend to carry on the story and to bring on the *dénoûment*; there is nothing useless or extraneous introduced.[11]

The appearance of two assessments of Collins himself in the years after *Hide and Seek* signal the growing interest in his career. In an extended essay of 1855, 'enthusiastic though not uncritical' as Norman Page notes,[12] the editor of the *Revue des Deux Mondes*, E. D. Forgues, excludes him from the first rank of novelists only by a want of originality – the need to cultivate a 'public' beyond that already reading Edward Bulwer-Lytton, Charles Dickens, and William Makepeace Thackeray.[13] It was a prescient suggestion, given Collins's 'discovery', only a year before *The Woman in White* began its serialisation in 1859, of 'The Unknown Public' – the vast cohort of working-class fiction readers, unrecognised by middle-class writers and reviewers. Edmund Yates's 1857 perspective corroborates Jewsbury's reflection upon his skill as a plotter, but deems it a result of Collins's dedication to his craft; though he might not equal Dickens's 'pathos and humour', or the specialties of other contemporaries,[14] he had already crafted a niche in plot construction. (This picture of Collins-as-labourer was to be a recurrent one.) Dickens was among those who privately praised *Hide and Seek*, and it was in his magazine *Household Words* that much of the rest of the writer's late 1850s output was published. The short story collections *After Dark* (1856) and *The Queen of Hearts* (1859) were each admired, though there was criticism about a trade-off between plotting and characterisation; reviewing the last, *The Saturday Review* repudiates Collins's ideas about the role of the fiction writer: to follow his storytelling method is to ensure that 'a story ... becomes a well-managed puzzle', and 'we cannot agree with him that this art of setting and solving a puzzle is anything like the ideal of a novelist'. In their opinion, if Collins's success was to go beyond a 'small one', his finely tuned 'machinery' would need to be overseen by characters more appealing to readers' feelings.[15] The figure of the 'puzzle' – and the deprecation attached to it – was to cast a long shadow over Collins's critical reception.

On the cusp of the 1860s, Collins therefore seemed to promise a great deal. But even his most ardent admirers could not have anticipated the success of *The Woman in White* – if only for the fact that there was little precedent for it. Befitting its eventual designation as the work that formalised sensation fiction, the popular reaction to his first and arguably greatest bestseller was itself sensational. Its seizure of the public imagination in the form of the myriad clothing, perfumes and dances it inspired has itself become something of a legend, as has its grip upon various readers.[16] By attracting a 'public' that belonged as much to the kitchen as to the drawing-room, it more than fulfilled Forgues's hopes regarding Collins's expanded readership. The near-universal coverage it received, however, only made starker a long-in-the-making gap between readers' and reviewers' opinion of the author's writing. That said, it is easy to overstate the critics' lukewarm reception of the novel, as Collins himself fell prey to doing. Praise for *The Woman in White* was not difficult to find: 'it may justly claim a high rank amongst the light literature of the day' suggested one reviewer,[17] while another found it 'almost ... the best piece of story-telling in our language'.[18] Implicitly, though, even the positive reviews reignited an intractable question: was this the work of a novelist, a 'story-teller', or simply a puzzle maker?[19] The contrivances of plot and the quality of characterisation hence returned as central issues, but generic considerations arose with unprecedented urgency; *The Examiner*'s approving review ends, suggestively, by staging Collins's achievements within strict boundaries: 'upon *his own peculiar ground* he is already without a rival'.[20] It was only in the years following its serialisation that this 'ground' was definitively given as sensation fiction; when Margaret Oliphant and Henry James, among others, extolled the merits of *The Woman in White* during the 1860s, the novel occupied a paradoxical status as the sensation novel *tout court* but also *sui generis* – displaying all the defining characteristics of the sub-genre, yet somehow more ingenious, honest and thrilling than its brethren.[21] If the reviews of *Basil* set the tone for Collins's contemporary reception, as Pykett suggests, then those of *The Woman in White* fixed it firmly.

Buoyed by success, the early 1860s saw Collins stridently continue in the same vein and use his popularity as ammunition against the critics.

Concurrent with the release of his next novel, *No Name*, he chose 1862 as the time to reissue *Basil*, to which he appended a preface that stoked further division between the public and reviewers:

> On its appearance, it was condemned off-hand, by a certain class of readers, as an outrage on their sense of propriety ... I knew that 'Basil' [*sic*] had nothing to fear from pure-minded readers ... Slowly and surely, my story forced its way through all the adverse criticism, to a place in the public favour which it has never lost since.[22]

For him to risk this group's disfavour indicates Collins's growing surety of sales despite, or perhaps even assisted by, critical censure. The reception to *No Name* recognised such provocations, but was not obviously soured by them. Two issues already mentioned are conspicuous: the figure of the 'puzzle' and Collins's prodigious working habits. The visible labour that the author expended upon such fiction as *No Name* redeemed it from being 'mere[ly]' a puzzle, according to *The Saturday Review*, and instead allowed it some claim (as Collins asserted) to being 'art'.[23] *The Examiner* takes an alternate line on the 'puzzle' issue, deeming it anathema to the higher forms of art; yet they too perform an about-turn: 'we do not say that we would like better to have Mr. Wilkie Collins other than he is'.[24] Conversely, *The Reader* decries the 'first-rate sensation novel' as further proof of wasted talents; *No Name* 'rises to a height of eloquence and pathos' not yet seen in the author's fiction, indicating that it is more by choice than merit that he 'does not belong' to the same category as Thackeray, Dickens and George Eliot.[25] Meanwhile, the story's illegitimacy theme – personified in the wily young protagonist Magdalen Vanstone – was criticised as either actively corrupting or a flawed ethical position.[26] For H. L. Mansel, writing in 1863, issues of plotting were inconsequential when a sensation novel like *No Name* displayed and propagated moral depravity.[27] Such detractions show how, in the context of the 1860s sensation debate, Collins's fiction might rise within but not above the strictures of genre.

These criticisms did nothing to impede *No Name*'s commercial success or the price that Collins commanded for its follow-up, *Armadale*; it was the highest he had received in his career to date and likely higher than any received by his contemporaries, Dickens excluded.[28] But, though its serialisation in the *Cornhill* from 1864 began auspiciously, it proved unable to sustain the lofty ambitions of the editor George Smith through its near two-year release; the declining sales of the serial were a portent for disappointing sales of the volume release upon its eventual publication in

1866.²⁹ Its reception reiterated many of the points raised in discussing *No Name*; indeed, *The Athenaeum* frames the discussion well in finding *Armadale* a '"sensation novel" with a vengeance, – one, however, which could hardly fail to follow *No Name*', and in raising the idea that declining moral attitudes run in tandem with declining standards of fiction.³⁰ Amid outcry over the bigamous conduct of Lydia Gwilt – Collins's version of the fairground menagerie's 'big black baboon', according to one reviewer³¹ – *Armadale* earned some of the highest praise Collins's fiction had received: 'no ordinary novel [but] a work of real art, on which the artist has evidently bestowed very great care' and 'displaying talents of the highest order' were two such examples.³² For others (evoking the discourse around *Basil*), the 'masterly' way that Gwilt was drawn only enhanced the reprehensibility of the story;³³ *The Saturday Review* dismissed questions about the truthfulness or otherwise of the portraiture by declaring that 'the question is whether it is worth while [sic] drawing her'.³⁴ By the middle of the following year, Collins had begun his next novel and his last of the decade, *The Moonstone*; it was serialised from January to August 1868. Just as later scholars have hailed it as the originator of a new genre, that of the English detective novel, so too were contemporary critics alert to its distinction from *Armadale* and previous works. This difference – which arguably lay in its prioritisation of the puzzle element ('less a work of literature than ... an elaborate puzzle', as one reviewer found it)³⁵ – led to startlingly opposed verdicts; it was either 'the most ingenious, interesting, and many-sided of [Collins's] novels' or 'not worthy of Mr. Wilkie Collins's reputation as a novelist'.³⁶ Yet, overall, reflecting perhaps the comparative tameness of its major themes, its reception was favourable and it aroused fewer strong feelings or accusations of immorality than had *Armadale* or *No Name*. As *The Times* observed, those wanting 'ingenuity in the construction of plot ... should seek, and will find, it in [the novel]'.³⁷ For all its supposed distinctions from his prior fiction, therefore, there was still something quintessentially of Collins about his last novel of the 1860s.

In an admiring review of *The Moonstone*, the New York City's *Round Table* magazine rued its past encouragement that Collins cease writing sensation fiction after *Armadale*, believing it insurmountable: 'while he might be content to leave his new novel to stand as his masterpiece, it must also convince his admirers of the idleness of any apprehensions that his powers have reached their zenith and must next slant toward their nadir'.³⁸ Hindsight lends a certain irony to this verdict, for those 'apprehensions' were exactly the shape that the critical consensus began to assume: Page, writing in 1974, pays note to its enduring influence: 'one might suggest, with truth if not with gratitude, that if Collins … had died in 1870, his reputation would be in no significant respect different from what it is [today]'.[39] During the next almost twenty years of his 'later period' – in fact, nearly half his career – he was not to recapture the runaway success of his 1860s novels, but the so-called decline and fall narrative is one that has been shown repeatedly to be untrue.[40] *Man and Wife* (1870), the immediate successor to *The Moonstone*, displayed no signs of diminishing powers – it lifted the circulation of *Cassell's Magazine* to new heights and was received in no different terms than his previous fiction: the critics found it a page-turner, albeit several deemed its social message to be misplaced.[41] Whilst the more than a dozen novels and shorter fiction published after *Man and Wife* received their fair share of criticism, including negative comparisons to his earlier output, this was, as has been shown, not a new development but a feature of Collins's reception since its beginning.[42] The considerable sales of *The Evil Genius* (1885–6) and *The Guilty River* (1886), meanwhile, indicate an enduring popularity with readers until his final years, as do the attestations of fellow writers, readers' polls, and periodical pieces trading in familiarity with his name.[43] To *The Academy*, writing in 1886, Collins remained the 'greatest living master of narrative, pure and simple';[44] and though his greater emphasis upon writing 'with a purpose' – the explicit tackling of some social problem – did not always receive acclaim, neither was it universally deplored.[45] If no living contemporary could match him on his own territory, however, his past achievements formed their own yardstick; his final completed novel, *The Legacy of Cain* (1888), elicited a telling remark from *The Spectator*: it was a '*comparative* failure … for absolute failure [by the author] is all but impossible'.[46]

By 1889, it had been over forty years since the release of Collins's first published novel, *Antonina*; he had forged a career longer than Eliot, Thackeray and Dickens. Yet, even though he continued to write, be read and be reviewed more than two decades after the period in which his most revered works had appeared, there was a sense in which he still belonged to the 1860s; Collins himself teased *Heart and Science* (1883) as a return to *The Woman in White*, and a never-to-be written work as 'another "Moonstone"', giving real cause to the critics' claims of self-parody and repetition in the novels of his later period.[47] It was an unfitting end to a career that had for so many years inspired reviewers to high praise and sharp rebuke, but almost never apathy.

Notes

1. 'Antonina; or, The Fall of Rome', *The Gentleman's Magazine* 33 (April 1850), p. 408.
2. 'Antonina', *New Monthly Magazine* 88.352 (April 1850), p. 560.
3. 'Basil: A Story of Modern Life', *The Athenaeum* 1310 (4 December 1852), p. 1323.
4. 'Basil: A Story of Modern Life', *The New Quarterly Review* 2.5 (January 1853), p. 96; 'Basil: A Story of Modern Life', *The Examiner* 2339 (27 November 1852), p. 757.
5. 'Basil: A Story of Modern Life', *The Literary Gazette* 1871 (27 November 1852), p. 872.
6. *The New Quarterly Review* 2.5 (1853), p. 96.
7. L. Pykett, *Authors in Context: Wilkie Collins* (Oxford University Press, 2005), p. 105.
8. G. Law and A. Maunder, *Wilkie Collins: A Literary Life* (Basingstoke: Palgrave Macmillan, 2008), p. 71.
9. N. Page (ed.), *Wilkie Collins: The Critical Heritage* (London: Routledge, 1974), p. 54. Hereafter cited as Page.
10. Page, p. 8.
11. [G. Jewsbury], 'Hide and Seek', *The Athenaeum* 1391 (24 June 1854), p. 775.
12. Page, p. 12.
13. E. D. Forgues, 'Études sur le roman anglaise: William Wilkie Collins', *Revue des Deux Mondes* 12.4 (1855), p. 848.
14. Page, p. 68.
15. 'The Queen of Hearts', *The Saturday Review* 8.208 (22 October 1859), pp. 487, 488.
16. Page, p. 13.
17. 'The Woman in White', *The London Review* 10 (8 September 1860), p. 233.
18. 'The Woman in White', *The Examiner* 2774 (1 September 1860), p. 549.
19. 'The Woman in White', *The Saturday Review* 10.252 (25 August 1860), p. 249.
20. *The Examiner* 2774 (1860), p. 549. Emphasis added.
21. Page, pp. 108, 110–20, 122–3.
22. Cited in Pykett, *Authors in Context*, p. 104.
23. 'No Name and Thalatta', *The Saturday Review* 15.377 (17 January 1863), pp. 84–5.
24. 'No Name', *The Examiner* 2869 (24 January 1863), pp. 54–5.
25. 'No Name', *The Reader* 1.1 (3 January 1863), p. 15.
26. Page, p. 143.
27. Pykett, *Authors in Context*, p. 108.
28. Page, p. 17.
29. Law and Maunder, *Wilkie Collins*, p. 93.

30 'Armadale', *The Athenaeum* 2014 (2 June 1866), p. 732.
31 'Belles Lettres', *Westminster Review* 30.1 (July 1866), p. 270.
32 'Armadale', *The London Review* 12.311 (16 June 1866), p. 680; 'Armadale', *The Reader* 7.179 (2 June 1866), p. 539.
33 Page, p. 156.
34 'Armadale', *The Saturday Review* 21.555 (16 June 1866), p. 727.
35 'The Moonstone', *The London Review* 17.421 (25 July 1868), p. 115.
36 'The Moonstone', *The Round Table* 188 (29 August 1868), p. 138; 'The Moonstone', *The Spectator* 41.2091 (25 July 1868), p. 881.
37 Page, p. 178.
38 *The Round Table* 188 (1868), p. 138.
39 Page, p. 20.
40 R. P. Ashley, 'Wilkie Collins Reconsidered', *Nineteenth-Century Fiction* 4.4 (1950), pp. 265–73 (pp. 265–8); Page, pp. 20–30; Pykett, *Authors in Context*, pp. 109–10.
41 Pykett, *Authors in Context*, p. 109.
42 Ibid., p. 110.
43 Page, p. 24.
44 Page, p. 29.
45 Page, p. 26.
46 Page, p. 222. Emphasis added.
47 Cited in Law and Maunder, *Wilkie Collins*, p. 178.

CHAPTER 11

After Death to T. S. Eliot

James Aaron Green

As the end of the 1880s approached, the assessment of Wilkie Collins's legacy had begun to assume the tone of the prematurely posthumous. In his article 'A Living Story-Teller' (April 1888), the critic and writer Harry Quilter sought to remind readers that in their midst was 'the last of that group of great novelists whose works will make the Victorian era for ever famous'. Despite its title – which Collins was duly obliging by a relentless writing schedule that saw *The Legacy of Cain* begin its serialisation in 1888 and *Blind Love* soon follow – the article paints him as an overlooked elder whose 'ancient quiet claim' to the public's attention is liable to be lost among the 'louder and fresher voices' of the day. Less from an inclination to prophesise than from cognisance of the author's declining health, Quilter positions himself as a sort of executor of Collins's literary legacy: the first to summarise and interpret his contributions as a whole. It is, he writes, a case of doing justice to a neglected author in their 'last years', in which circumstances it would not do to wait until his death.[1] Lyn Pykett's notice of the 'somewhat obituary tone' of the piece is right,[2] perhaps even understating the case, and, in Quilter's reminder that 'this article is professedly an *eulogium*', readers would be forgiven for conjuring the funerary associations of that word.[3] Striving to 'show something of the nature ... and extent of Mr. Wilkie Collins' genius', Quilter traces his career from *Antonina* through his novels of the 1860s to conclude with *The Moonstone*.[4] In a verdict that was to be at odds with the critical consensus for some time, he singles out *No Name* and *Armadale* as the 'most fascinating' and 'important' of Collins's novels, respectively.[5] But of his entire corpus, Quilter's praise is unstinting, and the conceit of the article's title is revealed: Collins is the storyteller par excellence: 'this author has told stories better than they have ever been told ... and probably better than they ever will be told again'.[6] The piece ends with an appeal for the author to be given his warranted praise antemortem, while it is 'not too late'.[7] Only eighteen months afterwards, on 23 September 1889, Collins died at the age of sixty-five from complications following a stroke.

Collins's death ensured that his name was once again on the lips of critics. A slew of obituaries appeared in the literary magazines, to be followed by more extended reflections a few months later. Something approaching a critical consensus on Collins's legacy is already visible in these early pieces, between which there are numerous points of commonality; such a coalescing of opinion was to stand relatively undiminished for nearly forty years. Even the most permissive critics admitted that Collins's most fecund period, and the basis of his reputation, was the 1860s – a decade that saw the release of *The Woman in White* (1860), *No Name* (1862), *Armadale* (1866) and *The Moonstone* (1868).[8] The trajectory of Collins's career was generally conceived of in spatial terms as a steep ascent from his earliest works such as *Antonina* (1850) and *Basil* (1852) to the heights of this middle period, with an equally sharp descent to his later works. 'What has worst served his fame is, doubtless, the flood of later novels, in which he so decidedly fell below his own standard', writes Andrew Lang. 'But these will be forgotten, while his earlier books may long retain their very wide and deserved popularity.'[9] Others were more sympathetic: A. C. Swinburne, while agreeing on the stark qualitative difference between the middle years and everything else, nonetheless deems his later work to contain 'real and great merit' at its best – more 'to his credit than to his discredit'.[10] Unbridled praise was given to *The Woman in White* and *The Moonstone* from every quarter, between which it was a two-horse race for the title of *magnum opus*. 'It must have been a hard task to follow that masterpiece of sensational fiction', opines H. Chartres for *London Society*; 'only the historian of *The Moonstone* could have done it with success'.[11] There was much more debate about the placement of his other works of the same period: *No Name* was either only a 'less excellent example' of his talents than the two aforementioned,[12] or it was not amongst the novels to which he would owe his future fame;[13] *Armadale*, equally, represented either a continuation of the talents displayed in *The Woman in White* or a precipitous (albeit only temporary) descent.[14] By substituting *The New Magdalen* (1873) for *No Name*, and *Man and Wife* (1870) for *Armadale*, in their assessment of Collins's best fiction, *The Academy* and *The Spectator* demonstrated that the concept of his 'four great novels' was yet to be firmly established – its constituent parts still up for debate, even if its numbers were not.[15] Here, posthumous opinion anticipates the widening of focus in late twentieth- and early twenty-first-century studies of Collins, as scholars and then publishers turned to consider those works that had made less immediate impact.

The discussion was framed in no small degree by generic and chronological considerations. Like Quilter, the critics located Collins as the last representative of a coterie of mid-century novelists that included William Makepeace Thackeray, Charles Reade, George Eliot, Anthony Trollope and, most conspicuously, Charles Dickens.[16] Comparison to these writers would elevate and deprecate him in equal measure. On the one hand, to have 'become prominent even in this company' during the 1860s was, so *The Saturday Review* concluded (in an otherwise uncomplimentary verdict on Collins), to his considerable credit.[17] In evidence of his talent, *The Scots Observer* pointed to his having 'enjoyed the inestimable praise of Dickens and the high honour of collaborating with the Master'.[18] Comparisons between Dickens and Collins were almost ubiquitous, but far from universally one-sided; *Temple Bar* posed the two authors as inversions of each other – one who had no trouble in creating memorable characters, but who 'longed to shine as an elaborator of plots, inspired no doubt by admiration for his friend's genius', versus 'Collins, the past master of the plot', who sought Dickens's aptitude for characterisation.[19] *The Academy*, equally, viewed theirs as a relationship of complementary talents, though by declaring Collins the 'disciple' it strove nonetheless to uphold a categorical difference in their posthumous esteem.[20] But being in the company of these fellow writers also provided a basis for less ennobling comparisons. For Lang, it meant that any praise must be decidedly relative: 'As to the best [of his work], one cannot equal it with the excellence of Dickens, of Thackeray, of George Eliot, of Charles Reade, or even of Anthony Trollope.'[21] The sentiment was one corroborated by *The Spectator*'s obituary: though they admitted to the enduring popularity of Collins's work, they denied that his place was among the 'front rank of English novelists'.[22] Moreover, the quarter of a century between the period of these writers' best work and the situation in 1889, with Collins's death, had for some commentators only accentuated the differences within the coterie; *The Saturday Review* ends its assessment by casting doubt on his ability to attract future readerships 'grown accustomed to more artistic workmanship'.[23] Collins may have remained popular, but would the alleged anachronism of his style deny his fiction longevity?

Such questions of workmanship and of genre were the second frame within which Collins's legacy was debated by critics after his death. The popularity and esteem of his 1860s output ensured that it was as a writer of 'sensational novels', rather than as a writer of 'didactic' novels – or, an even more distant prospect, as a dramatist – that he was hailed. (Swinburne, notoriously, went so far as to pen a couplet in which didacticism is ascribed as fatal to Collins's later fiction, with the notable exception of *Man and Wife*; it was not an isolated opinion).[24] Even the strictest of the critics deemed him unrivalled in cultivating incident, suspense and thrill: the hallmarks of sensation fiction. 'Collins stands at the head of sensational novelists', declares *The Academy*'s reviewer.[25] It was further to his credit, for many, that this distinction was earned by so-called 'legitimate' means; the passage of time, and the types of fiction produced in those intervening years, had served to tame the original heterodox quality of Collins's novels and to produce a fairly remarkable inversion: they were now praised for delivering sensation without resorting to the vulgarity of excess violence or horror.[26] More than this, in tones starkly different to the initial outcry that anticipated *The Woman in White* in 1859 (such novels being said then to produce 'mental dissipation' not unlike 'dram-drinking'),[27] his fictions were now declared to be, in their own way, *moral* productions.[28] Far from being a corrupter of public morals and tastes, Collins in the posthumous verdict emerges as someone who had honourably – and for many years despite ill health – discharged a duty to excite his readers.

But categorising Collins as the superlative *sensational* novelist was also a case of damning by qualified praise, for it relegated him to a lesser status within the hierarchy that saw literary fiction as a 'higher' form than its popular counterpart. It was this generic placement that made plausible Lang's denial of even his best work as being comparable to that of Eliot, Thackeray and others: 'The *genre* of novel to which Mr. Collins devoted himself was lower than theirs.'[29] Such a sentiment was not always quite so plainly expressed, but it suffused the obituaries nonetheless; in his *London Society* article of November 1889, for instance, Chartres attempts a partial rebuttal:

> The modern critic has never quite forgiven Wilkie Collins for being a sensational novelist. It may not be the highest type of novel – our author was himself conscious of that; but at its best it is a very good thing. Nothing is probably easier than to write a bad sensational story, and nothing harder than to write a good one.[30]

The dictates of a contemporary opinion that deprecated melodrama and sensation formed as yet, however, an insurmountable barrier for those wishing to elevate Collins into the first rank of English novelists; arguably, it was not until T. S. Eliot's intervention in 1927 that it began, gradually, to be dismantled.[31] Hence, even among the most generous assessments of his legacy, as in that by Swinburne, generic considerations are an all-determining qualifier: 'it will be admitted that Wilkie Collins was *in his way* a genuine artist'.[32] It was a point that Quilter, who returned to the discussion in October 1889 to admonish the 'chorus of critical censure' and 'faint deprecation' of the obituaries, felt compelled to tackle directly. '"A sensation novelist only." Yes, if you will have it so', he admits, before elucidating the didactic purposes to which Collins put those 'sensations'.[33] But it was a charge against which the enduring popularity of the author's fiction could serve as no defence; instead, this only fuelled the suspicions that, crowd-pleasing though his works surely were, 'high art' they were not.

The longer effect of such a verdict is apparent in an article published in 1904, fifteen years after Collins's death. After a rambling entry onto the topic of popular novels, and of those of Collins in particular, via the case of *Armadale*, 'Sensationalism of Yesterday and To-Day' finds the writer G. K. Chesterton broaching and then tackling a topic that he deems inexplicable: 'I cannot understand why nobody has to all appearance grasped the inestimable value of these novels. In these days it is the fashion to re-discover: why has nobody seriously re-discovered Wilkie Collins?'[34] It is the refrain of the late Victorian critics writ anew: Collins's talents and artistry become starkly apparent, in Chesterton's view, by juxtaposing the 'feeble modern' imitations of the sensational novel with those 'good old [ones]' he wrote; his do not rely on the 'vulgar', but have some real substance to them.[35] Distinctly – and although these comparisons are admittedly *within* the popular genre rather than between it and something else – there is nothing here of the critical deprecation of sensationalism that was so apparent in the posthumous assessments. But the question that Chesterton refuses to be drawn on is this: is the 'inestimable value' of Collins's novels absolute or relative? Only in comparison to his pale imitators in sensation, or to his contemporaries, 'popular' and otherwise? Two years later, Chesterton added his own contribution to the Edwardian 'fashion to re-discover' with the publication of *Charles Dickens: A Critical Study* (1906). The rediscovery of that author's collaborator and friend would have longer to wait.

Such a defence of Collins as that given by Chesterton was rare, and the beginning of the 1910s found the writer in sore critical neglect. In 1912, Arthur Compton-Rickett was compelled to pen an 'apologia' for him, citing 'the disfavour into which he has fallen' and 'the general neglect and detraction' that he faced.[36] Compton-Rickett's piece is a spirited defence and examination of Collins's career, rehabilitating even those aspects of his fiction that had previously been derided. His ingenuity for plot construction and 'sensational effects' are emphasised again, but his characterisation is also affirmed; it was Compton-Rickett's view that Collins was sensibly aware that his characters existed to serve the story and not vice versa, and yet, despite this, they exhibited a palpable vigour – 'they are *alive*'.[37] Like Chesterton's, however, his was an isolated voice. Collins's absence from the 'English Men of Letters' series of literary biographies edited by John Morley, which was published from 1878 to 1892 and then again from 1902 to 1919, was a telling sign of his relative obscurity. He did appear in the *Cambridge History of English Literature*, though his receipt of less coverage than Reade and Trollope within a section entitled 'Lesser Novelists' speaks to the same neglect.[38] But the turn of the 1920s saw an incipient revival of critical interest that was to culminate in more momentous developments. First, Walter C. Phillips's *Dickens, Reade, and Collins: Sensation Novelists* (1919) saw him share top billing with a writer whose reputation was several stages more established. Some of the classic accusations against his works are retrodden by Phillips – that characterisation and plotting are engaged in a zero-sum game, for instance[39] – but the essential development that gave scope for Collins to receive greater appreciation was serious attention to sensationalism; a more accurate gauging of its pervasiveness and utility as a mode of mid-century writing was to put Collins on a more equal footing with his fellow writers. It was again alongside Reade and Dickens that he was discussed in the second volume of Oliver Elton's *A Survey of English Literature, 1830–1880* (1920), which bestowed greatest praise upon *The Moonstone*.[40] These aspects of Phillips's and Elton's work were to be elaborated upon seven years later by the poet and critic T. S. Eliot. In his essay 'Wilkie Collins and Dickens', published in *The Times Literary Supplement* in 1927, Eliot made strident claims for the validity of melodrama and Collins's sizeable contributions to the form. It was an intervention that, in retrospect, would mark the beginning of a favourable turn in his critical fortunes.

   The posthumous assessment of Wilkie Collins only clarified the diminished and uneasy status that the writer had held for some time, particularly given the relatively unfavourable opinion towards the output of his later period. For the next nearly forty years, defenders of his work could only take rearguard action against critical obscurity – they were too isolated and intermittent to set his legacy on a more solid footing. But the more generous assessment of sensationalism that began to emerge by the end of the 1920s simultaneously gave space for the 're-discovery' of his fiction within criticism. The intervention of such an established voice as that of T. S. Eliot in 1927 signalled a new phase in Collins's critical reception.

Notes

1. H. Quilter, 'A Living Story-Teller (Mr. Wilkie Collins)', *The Contemporary Review* 53 (April 1888), pp. 572–93 (p. 572).
2. L. Pykett, *Authors in Context: Wilkie Collins* (Oxford University Press, 2005), p. 214.
3. Quilter, 'A Living Story-Teller', p. 573. Emphasis added.
4. Ibid., p. 593.
5. Ibid., p. 588.
6. Ibid., p. 573.
7. Ibid., p. 593.
8. 'Wilkie Collins', *The Academy* 908 (28 September 1889), p. 203.
9. A. Lang, 'Mr. Wilkie Collins's Novels', *The Contemporary Review* 57 (January 1890), pp. 20–8 (p. 22).
10. A. C. Swinburne, 'Wilkie Collins', *The Fortnightly Review* 46.275 (November 1889), pp. 589–99 (p. 594).
11. H. Chartres, 'Wilkie Collins', *London Society* 56.335 (November 1889), pp. 515–23 (p. 515).
12. Swinburne, 'Wilkie Collins', p. 593.
13. 'Wilkie Collins', *The Academy* 908 (1889), p. 203.
14. 'The Novels of Wilkie Collins', *Temple Bar* 89.357 (August 1890), p. 530; 'Mr. Wilkie Collins', *The Athenaeum* 3231 (28 September 1889), p. 418; Lang, 'Mr. Wilkie Collins's Novels', pp. 26–7.
15. M. Klimaszewski, *Brief Lives: Wilkie Collins* (London: Hesperus Press, 2011), p. 67; Wilkie Collins, 'Preface' to *No Name*, ed. M. Ford (New York: Penguin Books, 2004), pp. xxvii–xxviii.
16. 'The Novels of Wilkie Collins', *Temple Bar* 89.357 (1890), p. 528; 'Wilkie Collins', *The Academy* 908 (1889), p. 203.
17. 'Mr. Wilkie Collins', *The Saturday Review* 68.1770 (28 September 1889), p. 343.
18. 'Wilkie Collins', *The Scots Observer* 2.45 (28 September 1889), p. 512.
19. 'The Novels of Wilkie Collins', *Temple Bar* 89.357 (1890), p. 529.
20. 'Wilkie Collins', *The Academy* 908 (1889), p. 203.
21. Lang, 'Mr. Wilkie Collins's Novels', p. 28.
22. [M. W. Townsend], 'Wilkie Collins', *The Spectator* 63 (28 September 1889), p. 12.
23. 'Mr. Wilkie Collins', *The Saturday Review* 68.1770 (1889), p. 343.
24. Swinburne, 'Wilkie Collins', p. 598; 'The Novels of Wilkie Collins', *Temple Bar* 89.357 (1890), p. 529.
25. 'Wilkie Collins', *The Academy* 908 (1889), p. 203.
26. Chartres, 'Wilkie Collins', p. 522.
27. 'Novels, Novel Readers, and Novel Writers', *The Scottish Review* (July 1859), p. 240.
28. 'The Novels of Wilkie Collins', *Temple Bar* 89.357 (1890), p. 532.
29. Lang, 'Mr. Wilkie Collins's Novels', p. 28. Original emphasis.

[30] Chartres, 'Wilkie Collins', p. 517.
[31] Pykett, *Authors in Context*, pp. 217–18.
[32] Swinburne, 'Wilkie Collins', p. 591. Emphasis added.
[33] H. Quilter, 'In Memoriam Amici (Wilkie Collins)', *The Universal Review* 5.18 (October 1889), pp. 208, 225.
[34] G. K. Chesterton, 'With the Long Bow: Sensationalism of Yesterday and To-Day', *The Bystander* 2.15 (16 March 1904), p. 91.
[35] Ibid., p. 91.
[36] A. Compton-Rickett, 'The Reader. Wilkie Collins', *The Bookman* 42.249 (June 1912), pp. 107–22 (pp. 114, 107).
[37] Ibid., p. 114. Original emphasis.
[38] A. W. Ward and A. R. Waller (eds.), *The Cambridge History of English Literature*, Vol. XIII (New York: G. P. Putnam's Sons, 1917), pp. 486–7.
[39] W. C. Phillips, *Dickens, Reade, and Collins: Sensation Novelists* (New York: Columbia University Press, 1919), p. 186.
[40] O. Elton, *A Survey of English Literature, 1830–1880*, 2 vols. (London: Edward Arnold, 1920), vol. II, p. 21.

CHAPTER 12

T. S. Eliot to 1990
Richard Nemesvari

Robert P. Ashley, Jr., begins his 1950 essay 'Wilkie Collins Reconsidered' aggressively:

> Perhaps no other English novelist of comparable stature has been the victim of such misrepresentation and slipshod scholarship as Wilkie Collins, chiefly because until recently no one had made him the object of a major investigation. The earlier studies of Collins were, without exception, brief and were usually conducted by scholars and writers who had stumbled on Collins in the course of investigating someone else, usually Dickens.[1]

Ashley is equally assertive in his repudiation of the '"decline and fall legend"' in which 'Collins not only died forgotten, but remained forgotten until T. S. Eliot's essay in the *Times Literary Supplement* exhumed him in 1927.'[2] Certainly Eliot's article 'Wilkie Collins and Dickens' had a significant influence on subsequent approaches to Collins's fiction. Essays linking Collins to Charles Dickens and other authors as a way of understanding his work became common, at least partly as attempts to bolster a reputation that appeared in need of support. The close friendship with Dickens led to an interest in Collins's biography, which had several mysteries of its own that needed solving; biographical elements were often introduced into essays discussing his novels and stories, which in turn led to biographical studies of varying detail. Additionally, Eliot championed *The Moonstone* as a foundational text in the development of English detective fiction, as did Dorothy L. Sayers, whose fascination with Collins and this newly burgeoning genre was connected to her own role as a mystery writer. Finally, the discourses invoked by detection generated specific theoretical approaches, most often expressed through psychological and feminist criticism, although examples of postcolonial and poststructuralist readings of Collins also occur. His texts therefore became available for debate within what D. A. Miller called 'the "subversion hypothesis" of . . . literary studies'.[3] By 1990 Collins was in no danger of inadequate critical notice or treatment.

Nonetheless, at the time of Eliot's essay in the *TLS* this was not a foregone conclusion. His overall intention is clearly to provide Collins with credit for his achievements, but Eliot's underlying acceptance of Dickens's superiority undercuts his argument. This is made overt when Eliot suggests the reader compare the deaths of Rosanna Spearman in *The Moonstone* and Steerforth in *David Copperfield* (1850): 'We may say "There is no comparison!" but there *is* a comparison; and however unfavourable to Collins, it must increase our estimate of his skill', which illustrates the hierarchy established throughout his essay.[4] This being the case, it is unsurprising that Eliot says of Collins's *Armadale* (1866) that '[i]t has no merit beyond melodrama, and it has every merit that melodrama can have'.[5] Melodrama's inferiority due to its emphasis on thrilling plots over character development was a given at this cultural moment, and thus, while Eliot does treat Collins's work seriously, his article creates problematics that will echo into the future.

Walter de la Mare, in his 'The Early Novels of Wilkie Collins' (1932), shares Eliot's perspective. Discussing the collaboration between Collins and Dickens on *No Thoroughfare* (1867), he observes that '[t]he one writer, a sedulous and gifted craftsman, works with the pains and sobriety of a Dutch painter.... The other, a man of genius ... usually *seems* to be following his nose.'[6] There is no insult in comparing Collins to a 'Dutch painter', but the distinction between 'craftsman' and 'genius' is telling. Still, de la Mare recognises the attractions of Collins's devices. After listing the '"properties"' of the early novels, the critic observes that '[a]s a catalogue it is absurd, the machinery of melodrama. But in judicious doses how telling!'[7] Yet his conclusion is ambivalent: 'So admirable indeed is that "best" [of Collins's work] ... that one can hardly avoid speculating ... how far it falls short ... of what Collins himself in other circumstances might have attempted.'[8] This disappointment over an implied wasted potential retains the sense that Collins's writing results in a second class of fiction.

In 'Wilkie Collins and *A Tale of Two Cities*' and '*The Eustace Diamonds* and *The Moonstone*', both published in 1939, Henry J. W. Milley traces Collins's impact on Dickens and then Anthony Trollope, although he reads the expression of that influence very differently. He argues that *A Tale of Two Cities* (1859) demonstrates 'a shift in emphasis from characterization to narrative, together with a new interest in construction, as the means for achieving the quality of breathless interest'.[9] Crucially, this is not seen as a weakening of Dickens's writing, but as a reasonable recognition of Collins's achievement. For Trollope, Milley's main point is different: he sees the narrative parallels between *The Eustace Diamonds* (1872) and *The Moonstone* (1868) as parody. In particular, the police attempting to solve the theft of Lizzie Eustace's diamonds 'gain[s] considerably in comic value if their buffoonery were intended as a burlesque of the methods employed by Sergeant Cuff'.[10] Since acts of detection often drive Collins's plots, Trollope's choosing to mock this technique serves as a wider critique, unlike Dickens's complimentary emulation. Yet such a satire 'affords another example of the considerable influence of Wilkie Collins on the mid-Victorian novel, even in unlikely places'.[11] A little over a decade after Eliot's essay, then, critics began to recognise that Collins's significance extends beyond being a protégé of Dickens.

This critical predisposition to view Collins's work through the lens of biography and connections to established authors shaped the work of S. M. Ellis in *Wilkie Collins, Le Fanu and Others* (1931) and Clyde K. Hyder in 'Wilkie Collins and *The Woman in White*' (1939), culminating in the first comprehensive study of Collins's life, Kenneth Robinson's *Wilkie Collins: A Biography*, published in 1951. Although Robinson acknowledges both Ellis and Hyder, his research is much more in-depth, including quotations from letters that were unpublished at the time, and archival work that had not been previously undertaken. Individual chapters are dedicated to *The Woman in White* (1860), *No Name* (1863), *Armadale* and *The Moonstone*, with discussions of various lengths on Collins's other writings, so Robinson's study can claim the status of full critical biography. A chapter entitled 'Caroline' expands significantly on previous information concerning Caroline Graves, with Robinson observing that '[m]ost of the details which enable us to trace the course of this relationship have come to light within the last ten or fifteen years; some of them appear for the first time here'.[12] Specific information about Martha Rudd, however, eludes Robinson, who provides very few details about her. This mystery in Collins's biography would take another thirty-seven years to solve.

The title *The Secret Life of Wilkie Collins* (1988) clearly identifies William M. Clarke's purpose: not 'a full, rounded biography covering an assessment of Collins as a writer: rather a simple account of Collins, the man, and the women in his life'.[13] The archival investigations are impressive, encompassing banking accounts, birth certificates, death certificates, marriage certificates, census information, London street guides, rate books and the Post Office Street Directory. With comprehensive details about Martha Rudd, and much more specific information about Caroline Graves, the mysteries of Collins's domestic relationships with his mistresses were largely solved.

The link between the mysteries of biography and the solving of mysteries in Collins's novels is Dorothy Sayers. By 1931 she had prepared five chapters of a life of Collins before abandoning the project, but it was her championing of *The Moonstone* as detective fiction that was most significant. In the Introduction to *The Omnibus of Crime* (1929) she observes that 'Nothing human is perfect, but *The Moonstone* comes about as near perfection as anything of its kind can be',[14] while her Introduction to the Everyman edition of the novel declares '*The Moonstone* is impeccable. What has happened, in fact, is that *The Moonstone* set the standard, and that it has taken us all this time to recognise it.'[15] Such testimonials were reinforced by Eliot through his widely quoted comment that '*The Moonstone* is the first, the longest, and the best of modern English detective novels.'[16] These endorsements, linking Collins to a rising form of literature, helped create new directions for criticism.

The 'brief summary of the Freudian theory of aesthetics' provided by Lewis A. Lawson in 'Wilkie Collins and *The Moonstone*' (1963) provides one such new approach.[17] Using dream psychology as a way to explore what he describes as the wish-fulfilment of both the characters and the author he argues that '[t]he pattern of symbols in *The Moonstone* [reveals] ... a residual sexual layer in the novel lying beneath the consciously censored literal level', and that the novel 'is, then, with artistically induced modifications and amplifications, based upon the Oedipal wish phantasy of its author's unconscious'.[18] These classic Freudian formulations are challenged by Albert D. Hutter in 'Dreams, Transformations, and Literature: The Implications of Detective Fiction' (1975), which asserts that 'newer theories of dreaming allow us to incorporate into literary criticism changes in analytic theory based on a reappraisal of language and its significance for the psychoanalytic process'.[19] For Hutter, Jacques Lacan's rereading of Freud demonstrates that '[t]he wish-fulfillment model commits us to oversimplification and distortion',[20] and that this is particularly true of *The Moonstone* because it requires a concentration on content, when in fact '[l]atent structure, not latent content, is the critical interpretive issue'.[21] The multiple narrative perspectives of the novel mimic the requirements of psychoanalytic dream analysis, so that '[t]he resolution of the mystery is never as important as ... building a more complete account from an incomplete vision or fragment'.[22] These two readings of *The Moonstone*, in some ways complementary and in some ways conflicting, use detection to move Collins away from the formalist modes that can only position him as not achieving the goals of literary realism.

Winifred Hughes, in her chapter 'Wilkie Collins: The Triumph of the Detective' in *The Maniac in the Cellar: Sensation Novels of the 1860s*, and Mark M. Hennelly, Jr., in 'Reading Detection in *The Woman in White*' (both 1980), broaden the discussion of detective tropes in Collins. For Hughes the use of detection in *The Woman in White*, *No Name* and *Armadale* reveals that the 'real conflict ... is not between good and evil, as in authentic melodrama, but between two sets of more or less unscrupulous characters', and that 'conventional categories of good and evil are simply irrelevant to the action that takes place and even to the motives of the participants'.[23] The compromises required by Walter Hartright, the sympathy generated for Magdalen Vanstone and Lydia Gwilt, the subversive attractiveness of Count Fosco, even the roguish charm of Captain Wragg, undercut the ethical certainties of 'genuine melodrama'.[24] What is revealed by the overdetermined resolutions of Collins's plots is 'a hypocritical and venal society, in which the traditional moral categories have utterly lost their meaning', so it is little wonder that many of Collins's Victorian readers were left feeling uncomfortable.[25] Hennelly generates a somewhat similar perspective through his invocation of Wolfgang Iser and the employment of reader-response criticism. For him, Hartright's problematic acts of detection in *The Woman in White* are 'paradoxically double-edged for the identifying, trapped reader since he detects that there always are mysteries in extratextual life which he can never detect'.[26] Successful detection in Collins for these critics does not end in self-satisfied closure, but rather in irresolution and continuing questions.

Moving beyond a focus on detection, John R. Reed opens his seminal postcolonial essay, 'English Imperialism and the Unacknowledged Crime of *The Moonstone*' (1973), by stating that '[f]ar from being merely a classic detective tale, [it] ... is a novel of serious social criticism ... the theme of wilful and unwilled alienation penetrates to the centre of an oppressive society that Collins could not approve'.[27] In his analysis the novel's subtextual sympathy lies with the reprobated colonial Other, rather than the main British characters. The resulting subversion of the imperial project repudiates the racist assumptions upon which it rests. A text whose primary narrative concentrates on determining guilt and innocence suddenly expands beyond its fictional boundaries.

Similarly focused on Collins's discourse of disruption, U. C. Knoepflmacher's 'The Counterworld of Victorian Fiction and *The Woman in White*' (1975) asserts that 'beneath the moralism ... invoked by most Victorian novelists ... lurks a vital "counterworld" that is asocial and amoral, unbound by the restraints of the socialized superego', and that

Collins's novel is 'a unique instance ... in which the author openly acknowledges an anarchic and asocial counterworld as a powerfully attractive alternative to the ordered, civilized world of conventional beliefs'.[28] Knoepflmacher calls into question the hero's supposed objectivity, arguing that 'Collins skillfully encourages the reader to regard [Marian Halcombe and Fosco] as the true protagonists of his novel, far more deserving of our sympathy and interest than Hartright and his insipid Laura.'[29] Although Marian is finally aligned with social conventions, and Fosco is driven from England and killed, the supposed triumph of order is severely compromised, since 'Collins ... forces the reader to admit the justice of Fosco's anarchic belief in the fragility of our social identies.'[30] Collins's construction as a subversive author was thus well established by the time discussions of his examination of gender arose in the 1980s.

In *Corrupt Relations: Dickens, Thackeray, Trollope, Collins, and the Victorian Sexual System* (1982), Richard Barickman, Susan MacDonald and Myra Stark detect a certain ambivalence in the novels, asserting that 'Collins does assail certain inequities in the marriage laws and at least acknowledges the constraints on women's economic roles; but the issues he raises are often curiously peripheral to the major cause of economic and social oppression of women'.[31] Nonetheless, of the four authors examined, Collins is presented as the most resistant to social norms. His evocations of melodrama are no longer treated dismissively, so that although his plots have 'often been called, disparagingly, melodramatic .... [there] is little different [in them] from the obsessive nature of Shakespearian tragic figures: the "mad" obsession proves true as the facade of ordinary social relations is stripped away'.[32] The melodramatic mode of excess becomes a way for him to challenge complacency and expose what decorum would rather conceal, especially in matters of sexuality. While he cannot escape his cultural conditioning, he 'can so fuse the outlaw and heroine as to deeply trouble his middle-class public with [the] vivid image of his own ambivalent desires about women', and through a character such as Lydia Gwilt he 'presents the outsider, the outlaw, the deviant as the only sane role in a totally corrupt sexual system'.[33] In this reading, Collins's improper subject matter and non-realist approach serve to create a complexly radical resistance to the nineteenth-century status quo.

Jenny Bourne Taylor's single-author study *In the Secret Theatre of Home: Wilkie Collins, Sensation Narrative, and Nineteenth-Century Psychology* (1988) does something similar, but from a very different angle. Her exploration of nascent Victorian psychology, and especially the concept of 'moral management' that was revolutionising the structure of asylums and the treatment of madness, illustrates how it

> might promote the belief that a stable, sane identity could be built up by proper training and self-regulation, yet at the same time it could also tacitly suggest the very fragility of the identity that it aimed to sustain .... supplying a dominant model within which narrative authority and meaningful identity are formed, yet at the same time offering a means of overturning that authority, revealing its mechanisms of manipulation, its sources of power.[34]

But because moral management was given a particular resonance as a way of confronting female 'hysteria', it also takes on a specifically gendered focus. Thus 'the figure of middle-class feminine domestic virtue becomes the epitome of rationality and self-management .... yet the key sign of that social identity is now receptivity .... the fit between the pliant female asylum inmate and the dutiful wife is apparent'.[35] For Bourne Taylor the ambiguity of this type of boundary is reflected in Collins's recurring narrative style. She argues that his fiction is 'labyrinthine ... dialogic and self-reflexive', with the result that 'who narrates, who appropriates and represents others' testimony and evidence as history, which the story constructs as truth – is often bound up with both the undermining and the affirmation of a gendered, middle-class subjectivity'.[36] Her analysis combines psychology, narratology and feminist criticism in order to demonstrate that Collin's challenge to his society's values is destabilised and protean. Whatever elements of subversion Collins provides, they are not expressed simplistically.

Given this trajectory of Collins criticism it is perhaps not surprising that a book published in the same year as Bourne Taylor's should claim that Collins is not subversive at all. D. A. Miller's influential *The Novel and the Police* (1988) includes two essays on Collins – 'From *roman policier* to *romain-police*: Wilkie Collins and *The Moonstone*' and '*Cage aux folles*: Sensation and Gender in Wilkie Collins's *The Woman in White*' – originally published in 1980 and 1986, respectively. Miller's poststructuralist approach is driven by Michel Foucault's theories of disciplinary power, so that 'the discretion of social discipline in the Novel seems to rely on a strategy of *disavowing the police* .... Rendered discreet by disavowal, discipline is thereby rendered more effective.'[37] *The Moonstone* provides an especially prominent example of this. Sergeant Cuff's failures in detection are not a simple plot device, but rather a rejection of external 'policing' so that the society of the novel can more effectively police itself. In a quintessentially Foucauldian construction, Miller asserts:

> The community does not mobilize in a concerted scheme of police action, and yet things turn out as though it did. *The Moonstone* satisfies a double exigency: how to keep the everyday world entirely outside a network of police power and at the same time to preserve the effects of such power within it . . . . It cannot be decried as an intervention because it is already everywhere . . . it cannot ever be seen, for it is a power that never passes as such; therein lies its power.[38]

For Miller, *The Moonstone* merely *appears* to be multivocal; instead, it presents a fully unified ideological position that supports a monological exercise of power. *The Woman in White* is analysed as achieving the same effect through its seeming subversion of gender roles. The construction of Marian as masculine and Fosco as feminine might appear to question such socially assigned designations, but 'we must not conceive of this inversion standing in opposition to what it inverts . . . . Not less than that of the woman-in-the-man, the motif of the man-in-the-woman is a function of the novel's anxious male imperatives.'[39] Accordingly, any potential homoerotic desire is forcefully disciplined into heteronormative channels. For Miller, conflicted perspectives in these texts only serve to distract from the conservative maintenance of accepted power dynamics.

Ann Cvetkovich, in her 1989 article, 'Ghostlier Determinations: The Economy of Sensation and *The Woman in White*', agrees with Miller about the novel's 'somatic experience of sensation' but, rather than something to be dreaded, she asserts 'that it serves as a welcome screen and conduit for Walter Hartright's accession to power'.[40] Using a combination of psychological and materialist theory she argues that Hartright's repeated expressions of nervousness and anxiety as he battles for the return of Laura's identity are a way of repressing what he does not wish to consciously acknowledge – that 'saving' her will lift him out of his low-status social position, and that this is 'a form of mystification that turns the woman's body into a fetish object in both the Freudian and the Marxist sense'.[41] Hartright's determination to solve the mysteries surrounding Laura creates a psychic fixation that, once resolved, will remove the male hysteria threatening to overwhelm him, while at the same time Laura becomes a type of commodity fetish because 'Laura, even as a body, is a figure for something else. This in fact is the implication of Marx's description of the commodity; if correctly perceived it stands as a sign of social relations, and is perhaps the only way they are made tangible or visible.'[42] For Cvetkovich, *The Woman in White* exposes how this discourse works, but whether the novel endorses it or rejects it cannot be easily determined. The way is therefore prepared for future analyses of Collins which eschew the subversive/reactionary binary by recognising that such rigid dichotomies are rarely sustainable.

Notes

1. R. P. Ashley, Jr., 'Wilkie Collins Reconsidered', *Nineteenth-Century Fiction* 4.4 (March 1950), pp. 265–73 (p. 265).
2. Ibid., p. 267.
3. D. A. Miller, *The Novel and the Police* (Berkeley and Los Angeles: University of California Press, 1988), p. xi.
4. T. S. Eliot, 'Wilkie Collins and Dickens', in F. Dickey, J. Formichelli and R. Schuchard (eds.), *The Complete Prose of T. S. Eliot: The Critical Edition*: Vol. III: *Literature, Politics, Belief, 1927–1929* (Baltimore, MD: Johns Hopkins University Press, 2015), pp. 164–74 (p. 164).
5. Ibid., p. 170.
6. W. de la Mare, 'The Early Novels of Wilkie Collins', in J. Drinkwater (ed.), *The Eighteen-Sixties: Essays by Fellows of the Royal Society of Literature* (Cambridge University Press, 1932), pp. 51–101 (p. 63).
7. Ibid., p. 96–7.
8. Ibid., p. 100.
9. H. J. W. Milley, 'Wilkie Collins and *A Tale of Two Cities*', *The Modern Language Review* 34.4 (October 1939), pp. 525–34 (p. 528).
10. H. J. W. Milley, '*The Eustace Diamonds* and *The Moonstone*', *Studies in Philology* 36.4 (October 1939), pp. 651–63 (p. 658).
11. Ibid., p. 663.
12. K. Robinson, *Wilkie Collins: A Biography* (New York: Macmillan, 1952), p. 130.
13. W. M. Clarke, *The Secret Life of Wilkie Collins* (London: W. H. Allen & Co., 1988), p. xiii.
14. D. L. Sayers (ed.), *The Omnibus of Crime* (New York: Payson & Clarke Ltd., 1929), p. 25.
15. Quoted in Robinson, *Wilkie Collins*, p. 218.
16. T. S. Eliot, 'Introduction' to Wilkie Collins, *The Moonstone* (London: Oxford University Press, 1928), p. [v].
17. L. A. Lawson, 'Wilkie Collins and *The Moonstone*', *American Imago* 20.1 (Spring 1963), pp. 61–79 (p. 71).
18. Ibid., pp. 71, 75.
19. A. D. Hutter, 'Dreams, Transformations, and Literature: The Implications of Detective Fiction', *Victorian Studies* 19.2 (December 1975), pp. 181–209 (p. 181).
20. Ibid., p. 203.
21. Ibid., p. 207.
22. Ibid., p. 208.
23. W. Hughes, 'Wilkie Collins: The Triumph of the Detective', in *The Maniac in the Cellar: Sensation Novels of the 1860s* (Princeton University Press, 1980), pp. 137–65 (pp. 145, 148).
24. Ibid., p. 159.
25. Ibid., p. 150.

26 M. M. Hennelly, Jr., 'Reading Detection in *The Woman in White*', *Texas Studies in Literature and Language* 22.4 (Winter 1980), pp. 449–67.
27 J. R. Reed, 'English Imperialism and the Unacknowledged Crime of *The Moonstone*', *Clio* 2 (June 1973), pp. 281–90 (p. 281).
28 U. C. Knoepflmacher, 'The Counterworld of Victorian Fiction and *The Woman in White*', in J. H. Buckley (ed.), *The Worlds of Victorian Fiction* (Cambridge, MA: Harvard University Press, 1975), pp. 351–71 (pp. 352, 353).
29 Ibid., p. 366.
30 Ibid., p. 368.
31 R. Barickman, S. MacDonald and M. Stark, *Corrupt Relations: Dickens, Thackeray, Trollope, Collins, and the Victorian Sexual System* (New York: Columbia University Press, 1982), p. 5.
32 Ibid., p. 26.
33 Ibid., pp. 114, 133.
34 J. Bourne Taylor, *In the Secret Theatre of Home: Wilkie Collins, Sensation Narrative, and Nineteenth-Century Psychology* (New York: Routledge, 1988; Brighton: Victorian Secrets Ltd, 2018), p. 46.
35 Ibid., pp. 52–3.
36 Ibid., pp. 9, 33.
37 Miller, *The Novel and the Police*, p. 16.
38 Ibid., p. 50.
39 Ibid., p. 176.
40 A. Cvetkovich, 'Ghostlier Determinations: The Economy of Sensation and *The Woman in White*', *NOVEL: A Forum on Fiction* 23.1 (Autumn 1989), pp. 24–43 (p. 27, n. 5).
41 Ibid., p. 34.
42 Ibid., p. 41.

CHAPTER 13

1990 to the Present

Tim Dolin and Lucy Dougan

Collins studies has boomed since 1990.[1] As readers of the previous chapter will know, Collins's critical reputation was well established by the end of the 1980s, thanks to upheavals in literary studies which had broadened the canon to admit popular culture and genre fiction and exposed them to sophisticated reading techniques previously reserved for traditional forms of literature.[2] Only *The Woman in White* (1860) and *The Moonstone* (1868) really benefited from these conditions, however, and while these two novels still account for most criticism, much of Collins's other fiction, drama and journalism has emerged from obscurity over the past three decades – again, in lockstep with a discipline becoming progressively more inclusive, politically fractured and ethically oriented, and more focused on the unique perspectives of specific social groups and the new critical interventions they make possible. The three primary identity categories of the theory-and-history heyday (class, gender and race) have been subjected to re-examination and contention as successive generations of new political actors come to the fore. Apparently settled theoretical approaches – versions and hybrids of Marxism, feminism, poststructuralism, historicism, psychoanalysis, reader theory and others – have been opened to revision, revitalisation, subdivision and realignment. Postcolonialisms and critical race theories, feminisms, ecocriticisms, queer theories, theories of disability, posthumanisms, affect theories, new materialisms: these and other approaches have multiplied, splintered, intersected and regrouped.

Collins has held out through this volatile process at least partly because our ever-changing concerns so often turn out to be his concerns: with social power and disempowerment; secrecy and corruption; symbolic, sexual, legal, state and ethnic violence; faith in and mistrust of science and medicine; and social and psychic crisis. We continue, too, to be attracted to Collins's unconventional life, his progressive, critical views of domestic and imperial Britain, and his willingness to address inequality openly in his fiction. We admire his empathy with suffering, human and non-human, and especially the cruelty inflicted on anyone physically, mentally or socially different or marginal; and admire, too, that these characters are not always confined to the colourful sidelines of his plots.

Yet Collins entered the 1990s with his credentials as a social radical and subversive novelist looking dubious, as many (but by no means all) critics followed the lead of D. A. Miller's Foucault-inspired readings in *The Novel and the Police* (1988).[3] Far from damaging Collins's standing, however, the ascent of symptomatic reading turned him into something of a poster boy for the hermeneutics of suspicion. The 'turn from Freudian to Foucauldian readings', as Susan Zieger terms it, unlocked new readings of Collins's fiction, where 'power, rather than negating or repressing rebellious impulses[,] … operates through a diffuse, insidiously ordinary mode of policing'.[4] So dominant had this particular brand of critique become in Collins studies by the early 2000s that Anna Maria Jones in *Problem Novels* (2007) redubbed it the 'hermeneutics of sensation'.[5] Critics write themselves 'into the role of the detective who has discovered a crime',[6] Jones found, and are driven to call out suspect motives, pleasures or politics, turning the narrative logics of sensation and detective fiction back onto the texts by revealing unpalatable truths hiding in plain sight.

Such readings now and then inclined to parody, displaying ingenuities and dazzling peripeteias worthy of Collins's early novels, if not also a prolixity and missionary zeal worthy of his later ones. Yet over time playful postmodern ironies have given way to the moral seriousness and trenchant defensiveness of an increasingly embattled discipline. Most notably, long-running debates in Victorian studies about the political effectivity of narrative fiction itself,[7] debates that often recruited Collins, revealed associated anxieties about the role of the critical humanities in the modern university. This can be seen as early as 1992, in *Mixed Feelings*, where Ann Cvetkovich applied Foucault's work on disciplinarity and sexuality to an analysis of the then-contemporary politics of sensationalism and affect, when the AIDS epidemic was inspiring new forms of political activism. Casting doubt on an article of feminist faith – that affective expression was a political act and strategy – Cvetkovich countered that it originated in 'a nineteenth-century discourse that made affect meaningful'.[8] Sensation novels represented social problems as affective dilemmas, she argued, and represented in the sensationalised woman 'the relation between femininity and affect crucial to the middle-class domestic ideology that both grants and denies power to women'.[9] The sensational woman attracts to herself the nervous, sympathetic hero who 'consolidates his position all the more firmly because of the invisibility of his aspirations', mobilising a discourse of masculine affect that covertly reimposes domination.[10]

For scholars obliged to stand up for the relevance of academic literary study, the time-honoured moves of calling out Collins in this way, or rallying in defence of him, make less and less sense. It is now more often asserted or implied that old novels, whatever their silences or self-contradictions, continue to matter because identities continue to be formed, and deformed, by institutions, discourses and practices that derive their power from the stories we tell. This is why Collins remains such a reliable ally of literary studies in hard times. A fellow traveller with both radical bohemians and members of the cultural establishment, and a self-professed fellow outcast with the socially marginalised and poor, he is an appealing figure in a discipline that has always thrived on crises of identity, a compulsion to self-problematisation and, more often than not, an ethical calling. As John Kucich astutely observed in 1994, Collins saw himself as one of a new class of cultural intellectuals, the class he represented in the 'drawing masters, writers, actresses, amateur painters and philosophers' that take leading roles in his fiction.[11] These intellectuals, as Kucich describes them, now look a bit like literary critics before their time. Both share 'affinities with transgressive moral sophistication', a 'skillful suspicion' and forms of social insecurity that authorise them to subject 'the dynamic of insider and outsider to a more corrosive scrutiny'.[12]

The transgression and erosion of identity boundaries have always contributed to the allure of sensation fiction, and since 1990, critics have been drawn to the genre's predilection for messing with binaries: past and present; material and ideal; body and mind; surface and depth; self and other; legitimate and illegitimate; domestic and foreign. Thus, whilst valuable studies of the contingency and volatility of gender and class identities are still produced (studies of servants, for example)[13] they are fewer and farther between. And Collins's fiction, if it 'destabilises social categories, treating identity as fluid and obscuring differences in class, race and gender', also destabilises disciplinary categories, encouraging, even requiring, interdisciplinary approaches.[14]

This is evident in studies of science and technology, for example, which are often obliged to incorporate readings of law, gender, the body and medicine, or empire whilst they pursue Collins's interests in psychology and neurology (especially the 'magnetic sciences', mesmerism and clairvoyance),[15] or evolutionary biology and physiology; or examine Victorian debates and controversies over scientific method and the figure of the scientist.[16] Thus, Nicholas Daly, inspired by the Victorians' own neurophysiological tropes for society, analyses the way sensation fiction like railway travel 'synchronizes its readers with industrial modernity' by 'wiring' them into 'a new mode of temporality' in which consciousness of time 'would be recast as pleasurable suspense'.[17] In a similar vein, Jessica Straley characterises sensation fiction as 'the aesthetic counterpart to vivisection', since vivisectors 'exposed the brains of immobilized animals, boiled their skins, and galvanized their spinal cords, while Sensation writers stood likewise accused of "Harrowing the Mind, making the Flesh Creep … [and] Giving Shocks to the Nervous System" of the captive reader'.[18] And unlike his Gothic predecessors, argues Lillian Nayder, the scientist in sensation fiction 'experiments in a laboratory adjacent to, or indistinguishable from, his home. He uses physiology, vivisection and chemistry – their techniques, powers and elixirs – to test, defend and/or transform domestic relations.'[19] As Kucich observes, 'scientific professionals of various kinds are on trial' in the Victorian novel generally, and in sensation fiction particularly, because of prevalent Victorian anxieties about 'the conjunction of scientific knowledge and social power'.[20] Nowhere is this more evident than in the representation of medical science in Collins,[21] and in the figure of the forensic scientist, whose techniques, 'however scientifically represented, often prove to have a political genealogy', as Ronald Thomas shows.[22]

The same could be said of other dominant forms of Victorian knowledge and power, which invariably impinge on domestic relations in Collins's fiction. With his interest in the secret manipulations and misuses of the law and its institutions to seize control of property and identity, and the abuses that follow, Collins has become a prominent figure in Victorian studies in law and literature since 1990. Sensation fiction arose with the reform of English marriage laws beginning in the 1850s (especially the secularisation of divorce and the struggle for married women's property rights), and appealed to readers already *au fait* with the sensationalised reporting of real-life cases. Marlene Tromp's *The Private Rod* (2000) provides original insights on the new light Collins and other sensation novelists threw on marital violence, shattering the illusion, created by the debates surrounding the 1857 Divorce and Matrimonial Causes Act, that only poor women suffered violence at their husbands' hands.[23] If sensation novels offered an 'alternative discourse' to that of 'the scripted social text' of the law, as Tromp avers, Lisa Surridge responds that they were by no means the first to do so. It was divorce court journalism, Surridge shows, that played the really critical role in exposing marital violence outside the working classes.[24]

Collins's interest in and knowledge of law and the nature, practices and proceedings of the legal system also had a profound influence on the direction of his narrative experimentation and the epistemological and political questions driving it. In the 1861 preface to *The Woman in White* he revealed that he had taken his innovative multi-narratorial technique from the practice of witness testimony in the criminal courtroom, and some of the most interesting criticism since 1990 has been at the busy intersection of jurisprudence, legal history, literary history and narrative discourse. Alexander Welsh's *Strong Representations* (1992) assesses Collins's ambivalent place in a tradition of fictions 'that openly distrust testimony, insist on submitting witnesses to the test of corroborating circumstances, and claim to know many things without anyone's having seen them at all'.[25] Despite its schematic and summative consideration of Collins, Welsh's book has been significant for subsequent studies. In *Common Precedents* (2013), for example, Ayelet Ben-Yishai extends Welsh's method to narrative and the common law doctrine of precedent, seeing both as resources for shared meaning-making. Precedent was rediscovered in the nineteenth century, she argues, 'as a source of authority, ... a stabilizing element in an increasingly volatile legal system', showing that 'precedential thinking' was 'a culturally dominant way of relating to, representing, and incorporating the past'.[26]

How Collins's fiction relates to, represents and incorporates the past is a concern of Nicholas Dames's *Amnesiac Selves* (2001), which investigates how nostalgia is used to mobilise cultural forgetting as a strategy of containment. Collins's pathological amnesiacs, for whom forgetting is the nervous system's reaction to extreme shock, are likened to his readers: 'amnesiac compulsives' who absorb and forget plot after plot, novel after novel.[27] Thus Dames asserts 'the pivotal, even dominant, role of the novel in constructing and propagating the mnemonic strategies of Victorian life', and the role of those strategies in amnesia, noting all the while 'our occasionally uncanny complicity' with the Victorians, 'our continued pleasure in the nostalgic memories they so often present'.[28] Literature may have taught us 'the cultural habit of nostalgia,' but our elegiac feelings for it may also be a forewarning: we are beginning to forget it.[29] No wonder, then, that Collins, who can sometimes feel more like a neo-Victorian than a Victorian novelist, has inspired many neo-Victorian novels and been an important figure in the field of neo-Victorian studies.[30]

Sensation fiction's own past was the subject of Tamar Heller's groundbreaking, influential *Dead Secrets* (1992). For Heller, Collins represents in the recurrent image of buried writing both social and textual marginality and the subversiveness beneath the surface of social and literary conventions.[31] Heller traces a narrative pattern in Collins – the pattern was first identified by feminist critics of nineteenth-century women's writing – in which social powerlessness creates the conditions for narrative transgression. In Heller's hands, Collins's use of Gothic to tell a story about female victimisation becomes a plot of female subversion,[32] and at the same time a self-reflexive commentary about the influence on his work of one of the major nineteenth-century genres associated with women writers.[33] Heller's point – an already familiar one, as we have seen – is that 'Collins' novels ... are often paradoxically Gothic plots that end with the containment of the Gothic as the site of subversion and literary marginality.'[34]

Heller's argument about 'the relation of Collins' generic choices to his position as a male writer in the Victorian literary marketplace'[35] has been challenged in recent decades by newly available biographical and bibliographical resources and more nuanced accounts of the Victorian literary field.[36] In fashioning himself as a 'humanistic professional',[37] Collins was at pains to set himself apart: from the culture of ruling-class patronage that had shaped his father's practice as a painter; from other rising professional classes; and most of all from dominant constructions of professional authorship produced by the economics of fiction production.[38] In Daniel Hack's *The Material Interests of the Victorian Novel* (2005) Collins is one of four novelists coming to terms with the limits of their artistic autonomy in industrial print culture. In a deft reading of the confidence trickster Captain Wragge in *No Name* (1863), Hack demonstrates 'the kinship of begging letters and begging-letter writers with ostensibly more legitimate forms of writing and kinds of writers, in particular novels and novelists'.[39] At stake is the question of cultural labour: is it productive? Can novels convert readerly sympathy into action? In the end, Hack finds, affective indulgence is 'an end in itself, detached from the question of action (which is to say, the question of ethics)'.[40]

Collins learned his profession from Dickens, and if he successfully forged his own professional identity in the 1860s, he remained in Dickens's shadow for a long time. An essay collection of 1995, *Wilkie Collins to the Forefront: Some Reassessments*, signalled that he was at last coming into his own, but its title also implied that Collins has never been a writer able to set the terms of his own reputation.[41] Since 1990, he has been joined at the front by, or brought back into the throng with, Mary Elizabeth Braddon, Charles Reade, Ellen Wood and many other sensation novelists.[42] Meanwhile there has been no shaking off Dickens. Their complex relationship is the subject of Lillian Nayder's *Unequal Partners*

(2002), as well as essays by Anthea Trodd.[43] Nayder acknowledges the mutual indebtedness of Collins and Dickens, and examines Collins's increasing resistance to his mentor's authority and exploitation and Dickens's increasing discomfort with Collins's unorthodox personal life and radical opinions.[44] Considering their collaborative writings in the context of Victorian publishing and the wider context of Victorian labour disputes and political unrest, Nayder concludes that Collins, genuinely 'troubled by his perception of working-class injuries, gender inequities, and imperial wrongdoing', was forced in his collaborations to collude with Dickens whilst adopting covert strategies that counterpointed or subverted the latter's politics.[45]

Once again Nayder projects into interpersonal dynamics the all too familiar tension, or compromise, in Collins's work between subversion and containment. Yet – and Heller was among the first to register this[46] – as Collins broke away from Dickens and those strategies became less covert, he returned some of his socially marginalised characters to the centre of his plots and in the process found himself increasingly aesthetically marginalised.[47] Some of the best work on Collins since 1990 has engaged with multiple intersecting forms of social and cultural inequality and marginality from the perspectives of disability studies, queer theory, critical race theory and their hybrids. Disability rights activism emerged in the 1980s, and since the mid-1990s interdisciplinary (and intersectional) disability studies have thrived, questioning social and medical models of disability and their impact on human rights, social policy and quality of life. Collins, who has been claimed as a leading proponent of the social model of disability before his time, has taken an important place in literary disability studies.[48] As early as 2003, in the important essay collection *Reality's Dark Light*, Martha Stoddard Holmes examined the significance of disability and its pathologisation in Collins.[49] His empathy with the lives of his disabled characters, and his deep engagement with popular culture – the melodramatic stage, cheap literature, sensational newspaper reportage, popular medico-social narratives, sideshows – encouraged him to include and represent disabled characters in complex, empathetic and non-pathologised ways that run against the grain of his time. Collins's disabled female protagonists are not always barred from the marriage plot, for example, but integrated into conventional plots of romance, sex, marriage and childbearing.[50] In *Fictions of Affliction* (2004) and elsewhere,[51] Holmes extends her argument, showing how in contemporary society the melodramatisation of disability, with its origins in Victorian culture, has a profound impact on perceptions of disability and the formulation of public policy.[52]

For Clare Walker Gore, 'literary history has been written in such a way as to distort our sense of where disability is to be found in "the" nineteenth-century novel'.[53] Taking up Rosemarie Garland-Thomson's dictum that disability is 'not so much a property of bodies as a product of cultural rules about what bodies should be or do',[54] Gore argues that the political programme of disability activism – writing disability back into history – has led to a tendency to read literary works in ways that are not always critical.[55] Collins (again) 'destabilizes the categories by which we read bodies', she suggests, by 'representing disabled characters who are objects of admiration and love', alongside 'able-bodied characters who see themselves as deformed because their love is rejected, beautiful women with masculine intellects and women with massively powerful bodies and exaggeratedly feminine minds, aggressive men who cross-dress and conventionally handsome men with entirely feminine behaviour'.[56] Being attentive to these destabilisations inhibits any schematic account of plot in Collins's plot-driven fiction, Gore contends, because Collins exploits disability 'as an unreliable sign . . ., engaging the reader's preconceptions about a disabled character's relationship to plot so that he can perform sensational reversals at the novels' conclusions', eliciting sympathy along the way 'for their social and narrative exclusion'.[57]

The presence of disability in Collins's fiction is characteristic of a larger cultural engagement with the meaning of difference itself, as Mark Mossman has suggested.[58] For Richard Collins, Marian Halcombe in *The Woman in White* is a forerunner of 'our own "category crisis" of postmodern gender identity'.[59] It is repeatedly argued, indeed, that Collins provokes category crises that can never be completely resettled by narrative closure. This is because he creates characters that, to adapt Richard Nemesvari's words, deviate from normativity for the sensational possibilities offered by a range of alterities.[60] Referring to queer characters, Nemesvari concludes that there is always a 'disjunction between professed narrative/textual disapproval, and the pleasure . . . characters take in their constructed perversity, mak[ing] the machinations of plot required to suppress and punish them appear excessive and unconvincing, resulting not in the undercutting of the non-normative, but in a questioning of the normative instead'.[61]

Can this argument be sustained for the formidably entangled complex of prejudices and sympathies towards the British empire and its subjects in Collins's work? In 1993, Ashish Roy challenged *The Moonstone*'s then 'new career as an anti-imperialist text', arguing that 'by its special, detective programming of conventional ruptures like inside/outside, domestic/alien, sacred/profane, or familiar/uncanny in the intersection of its Indian and English plots, [the novel] produces a *mythos* entirely consonant with arguments for empire'.⁶² In response, Ian Duncan maintained that 'Collins's tale does not propound an anti-imperialist sympathy for oppressed colonial peoples, nor does it enthrone the imperialist subject-position, the proud seat of world-historical agency'.⁶³ Contrary to Roy, for whom the novel achieves a 'structural cohesion the imperial imagination aimed at but could never quite achieve',⁶⁴ Duncan concludes that it 'resists an ideologically closed justification of empire by grimly but far from mournfully depicting India as a powerful alien origin that constitutes the limit or end of English national historical identity'.⁶⁵

Jaya Mehta applied Edward Said's contrapuntal approach to Collins in 1995, arguing that 'imperial violence, originally wrought on the colony by the English, [and] subsequently represented as springing from the colony and invading English peace, ... paradoxically produces domestic pleasure, enjoyed in an armchair by the hearth'.⁶⁶ As many critics have since demonstrated, however, colonial violence also produces domestic violence. Nayder makes the important point that in Collins, and in other sensation novelists, imperial relations and domestic gender relations are interdependent. Each is

> often represented *as* the other, with courtship plots intertwined with plots of imperial conflict. In the 'marriage' that is British India, as sensation novelists sometimes represent the colony, the 'feminized' native is protected and exploited much like a Victorian wife, while the wife is subjected to the 'imperial rule' of her husband, her lack of property rights and legal autonomy similar to that of a subservient or rebellious native.⁶⁷

Should domestic cruelty, oppression and sexual violation therefore be read as symptoms of the 'traumatic inner damage' produced by slavery, colonial rule and colonial violence: as part of Collins's radical critique of imperialism?⁶⁸ Or are these pathologies caused by an 'ongoing internalised conflict between the forces of self-command and an intractable natural element' in civilised modern English life?⁶⁹ When we encounter the 'savage colonial other' in Collins, is it really 'a veiled encounter with strategically estranged aspects of the self'?⁷⁰

In her challenging, if sometimes obscure, 2012 study of the historical emergence of the phenomenon of 'racial sight', Irene Tucker sets aside 'discourses and institutional practices ... central to the conceptualizing of race – slavery and colonialism being the most salient', and asks instead 'why, in the final quarter of the eighteenth century, skin suddenly came to be privileged as the primary sign of racial identity'.[71] This approach sanctions Tucker to bypass the obvious Collins novels and focus solely on *The Woman in White*, where what race *does* – it produces, in her argument, 'the experience of immediate and self-evident knowing'[72] – is problematised by temporality: 'By insisting that to be known, bodies must be known over time, *The Woman in White* complicates any hard-and-fast distinction between the particularity of individual bodies and the bodily resemblances by which groups of people come to be understood as connected to one another.'[73]

Given her interest in the recurring plot device in Collins in which 'one character comes to be interchangeable with another',[74] it is surprising that Tucker should not refer to the one Collins novel where the moment of racial sight is overtly treated. *Poor Miss Finch* (1872), with its dark-blue hero and blind, melanophobic white heroine, has become an important text in contemporary Collins studies. Nayder relates it to Collins's interest in the phenomenon of racial passing, citing Mr Murthwaite in *The Moonstone* as an agent of empire whose ability to cross racial boundaries seems to be an English prerogative, denied to the three Hindu priests sent to reclaim the diamond.[75] This observation raises a question about historical prerogatives in English studies: is anyone working on Collins now free to move across identity boundaries unseen and unremarked? The question comes up in an essay published in *Victorian Studies* in 2020 on white and brown cousin kinship relations in *The Moonstone* and Colombian novelist Jorge Isaacs's *María* (1867). The authors frame their readings with a personalised narrative, positioning themselves as 'a queer Cherokee Latin Americanist and a Panjabi-American Romanticist wandering the grounds of Victorian studies'.[76] In this way they assert their kinship with the Hindu priests, but where the priests' kin relation is 'defined by its alterity to the normative white network that the novel restores' in the cousin marriage of Rachel Verinder and Franklin Blake, the authors define their own relation implicitly by its alterity to the normative white networks of academic literary studies.[77] Here again the dynamics of subversion and containment in Collins are turned on a fractured disciplinary moment, even if such moves risk the ideological doubleness they find in Collins's works by simultaneously attacking and reinstating the established social order.

Notes

[1] As a rough indicator, the MLA International Bibliography lists 167 items on Collins from 1926 to 1989, and 714 items since 1990.

2. L. Pykett, *Authors in Context: Wilkie Collins* (Oxford University Press, 2005), p. 221.
3. D. A. Miller, *The Novel and the Police* (Berkeley: University of California Press, 1988).
4. S. Zieger, 'Opium, Alcohol, and Tobacco: The Substances of Memory in *The Moonstone*', in P. K. Gilbert (ed.), *A Companion to Sensation Fiction* (Chichester: Wiley-Blackwell, 2011), pp. 208–29 (p. 208). For a Freudian reading of *The Moonstone*, see R. R. Thomas, *Dreams of Authority: Freud and the Fictions of the Unconscious* (Ithaca, NY: Cornell University Press, 1990).
5. A. M. Jones, *Problem Novels: Victorian Fiction Theorizes the Sensational Self* (Columbus: Ohio State University Press, 2007), p. 4.
6. Ibid., p. 8.
7. See, for example, M. Poovey, *Genres of the Credit Economy: Mediating Value in Eighteenth- and Nineteenth-Century Britain* (University of Chicago Press, 2008).
8. A. Cvetkovich, *Mixed Feelings: Feminism, Mass Culture, and Victorian Sensationalism* (New Brunswick, NJ: Rutgers University Press, 1992), p. 6.
9. Ibid., p. 2.
10. Ibid., p. 6. See also T. S. Wagner, '"Overpowering Vitality": Nostalgia and Men of Sensibility in the Fiction of Wilkie Collins', *MLQ: Modern Language Quarterly* 63.4 (2002), pp. 471–500. On the feminisation of literature and culture which began with Richardson and the sentimental novel in the eighteenth century, see L. Pykett, *The Sensation Novel: From The Woman in White to The Moonstone* (Plymouth: Northcote House with the British Council, 1994), p. 41. On male melancholia as a symptom of the feminisation of male identity in Collins, see J. Kucich, 'Collins and Victorian Masculinity', in J. Bourne Taylor (ed.), *The Cambridge Companion to Wilkie Collins* (Cambridge University Press, 2006), pp. 125–38.
11. J. Kucich, *The Power of Lies: Transgression in Victorian Fiction* (Ithaca, NY: Cornell University Press, 1994), pp. 81–2.
12. Ibid., pp. 118, 83.
13. See, for example, E. Steere, *The Female Servant and Sensation Fiction: 'Kitchen Literature'* (Basingstoke: Palgrave Macmillan, 2013); J. Gooch, *The Victorian Novel, Service Work, and the Nineteenth-Century Economy* (Basingstoke: Palgrave Macmillan, 2015).
14. L. Nayder, 'Science and Sensation', in A. Mangham (ed.), *The Cambridge Companion to Sensation Fiction* (Cambridge University Press, 2013), pp. 154–67 (p. 155).
15. J. Bourne Taylor, 'Psychology and Sensation: The Narrative of Moral Management in *The Woman in White*', *Critical Survey* 2.1 (1990), pp. 49–56; L. Garrison, *Science, Sexuality and Sensation Novels: Pleasures of the Senses* (Basingstoke: Palgrave Macmillan, 2011).
16. S. D. Bernstein, 'Ape Anxiety: Sensation Fiction, Evolution, and the Genre Question', *Journal of Victorian Culture* 6.2 (2001), pp. 250–71; N. Dames,

The Physiology of the Novel: Reading, Neural Science, and the Form of Victorian Fiction (Oxford University Press, 2007).

17. N. Daly, *Literature, Technology, and Modernity, 1860–2000* (Cambridge University Press, 2004), pp. 37, 49. See also N. Daly, *Sensation and Modernity in the 1860s* (Cambridge University Press, 2009).
18. J. Straley, 'Love and Vivisection: Wilkie Collins's Experiment in *Heart and Science*', *Nineteenth-Century Literature* 65.3 (2010), pp. 348–73 (pp. 351–2). See also S. Murphy, 'Heart, Science, and Regulation: Victorian Antivivisection Discourse and the Human', *Law and Literature* 26.3 (2014), pp. 365–87.
19. Nayder, 'Science and Sensation', p. 156. On Collins's indebtedness to and transformations of the Gothic, see A. Milbank, *Daughters of the House: Modes of the Gothic in Victorian Fiction* (Basingstoke: Macmillan, 1992); D. Wynne, *The Sensation Novel and the Victorian Family Magazine* (Basingstoke: Palgrave Macmillan, 2001); and H. Logan, *Sensational Deviance: Disability in Nineteenth-Century Sensation Fiction* (New York: Routledge, 2018). On Collins's updated Gothic in Victorian discourses of pathology, insanity, degeneracy and criminality, see L. Talairach-Vielmas, *Wilkie Collins, Medicine and the Gothic* (Cardiff: University of Wales Press, 2009).
20. J. Kucich, 'Scientific Ascendancy', in P. Brantlinger and W. B. Thesing (eds.), *A Companion to the Victorian Novel* (Malden, MA: Blackwell, 2002), pp. 119–36 (p. 134).
21. L. Penner and T. Sparks (eds.), *Victorian Medicine and Popular Culture* (London: Pickering & Chatto, 2015), p. 97. See also A. Mangham, *Violent Women and Sensation Fiction: Crime, Medicine and Victorian Popular Culture* (Basingstoke: Palgrave Macmillan, 2007), and Talairach-Vielmas, *Wilkie Collins*.
22. R. R. Thomas, '*The Moonstone*, Detective Fiction and Forensic Science', in Bourne Taylor (ed.), *The Cambridge Companion to Wilkie Collins*, pp. 65–78 (p. 77).
23. M. Tromp, *The Private Rod: Marital Violence, Sensation, and the Law in Victorian Britain* (Charlottesville and London: University Press of Virginia, 2000).
24. L. A. Surridge, *Bleak Houses: Marital Violence in Victorian Fiction* (Athens: Ohio University Press, 2005), p. 135.
25. A. Welsh, *Strong Representations: Narrative and Circumstantial Evidence in England* (Baltimore, MD: Johns Hopkins University Press, 1992), p. 8.
26. A. Ben-Yishai, *Common Precedents: The Presentness of the Past in Victorian Law and Fiction* (Oxford University Press, 2013), pp. 17, 82.
27. N. Dames, *Amnesiac Selves: Nostalgia, Forgetting, and British Fiction, 1810–1870* (Oxford University Press, 2001), p. 170.
28. Ibid., pp. 8, 18, 17.
29. Ibid., pp. 237, 42.
30. See J. Cox, *Neo-Victorianism and Sensation Fiction* (London: Palgrave Macmillan, 2019).

31 T. Heller, *Dead Secrets: Wilkie Collins and the Female Gothic* (New Haven, CT: Yale University Press, 1992), p. 1.
32 Ibid., p. 3.
33 Ibid., p. 4.
34 Ibid., p. 8.
35 Ibid., p. 4.
36 See, for example, C. Peters, *The King of Inventors: A Life of Wilkie Collins* (London: Secker & Warburg, 1991); G. Law and A. Maunder, *Wilkie Collins: A Literary Life* (Basingstoke: Palgrave Macmillan, 2008); W. Baker, A. Gasson, G. Law and P. Lewis (eds.), *The Public Face of Wilkie Collins: The Collected Letters*, 4 vols. (Abingdon: Routledge, 2016); G. Law, 'Yesterday's Sensations: Modes of Publication and Narrative Form in Collins's Late Novels', in M. K. Bachman and D. R. Cox (eds.), *Reality's Dark Light: The Sensational Wilkie Collins* (Knoxville: University of Tennessee Press, 2003), pp. 329–60; and G. Law, 'The Professional Writer and the Literary Marketplace', in BourneTaylor (ed.), *Cambridge Companion to Wilkie Collins*, pp. 97–111.
37 Kucich, 'Collins and Victorian Masculinity', p. 132.
38 See M. Costantini, 'Sensation, Class and the Rising Professionals', in Mangham (ed.), *The Cambridge Companion to Sensation Fiction*, pp. 99–112.
39 D. Hack, *The Material Interests of the Victorian Novel* (Charlottesville: University of Virginia Press, 2005), p. 104.
40 Ibid., p. 104.
41 N. C. Smith and R. C. Terry (eds.), *Wilkie Collins to the Forefront: Some Reassessments* (New York: AMS Press, 1995).
42 As evidenced, for example, in A. Maunder (ed.), *Varieties of Women's Sensation Fiction, 1855–1890* (New York: Routledge, 2004); Gilbert (ed.), *A Companion to Sensation Fiction*; Mangham (ed.), *The Cambridge Companion to Sensation Fiction*; and Wynne, *The Sensation Novel*.
43 L. Nayder, *Unequal Partners: Charles Dickens, Wilkie Collins, and Victorian Authorship* (Ithaca, NY: Cornell University Press, 2002); A. Trodd, 'Collaborating in Open Boats: Dickens, Collins, Franklin, and Bligh', *Victorian Studies* 42.2 (1999), pp. 201–25; and A. Trodd, 'Messages in Bottles and Collins's Seafaring Man', *Studies in English Literature, 1500–1900* 41.4 (2001), pp. 751–64.
44 Nayder, *Unequal Partners*, p. 4.
45 Ibid., pp. 5, 8.
46 Heller, *Dead Secrets*, pp. 5–6.
47 As he had done in the early *Hide and Seek* (1854).
48 On Collins as forerunner, see Logan, *Sensational Deviance*. For individual studies of epilepsy, blindness and deafness, see, respectively, G. Brophy, 'Fit and Counterfeit: The Volatile Values of Epilepsy in Wilkie Collins's *Poor Miss Finch*', *Journal of Victorian Culture* 24.4 (2019), pp. 535–50; M. A. O'Farrell, 'Blindness Envy: Victorians in the Parlors of the Blind', *PMLA* 127.3 (2012), pp. 512–25; and J. Esmail, '"I Listened With My Eyes": Writing Speech and

Reading Deafness in the Fiction of Charles Dickens and Wilkie Collins', *ELH* 78.4 (2011), pp. 991–1020.
49 M. S. Holmes, '"Bolder with Her Lover in the Dark": Collins and Disabled Women's Sexuality', in Bachman and Cox (eds.), *Reality's Dark Light*, pp. 59–93.
50 Ibid., pp. 81–2.
51 M. S. Holmes, *Fictions of Affliction: Physical Disability in Victorian Culture* (Ann Arbor: University of Michigan Press, 2004); M. S. Holmes and M. Mossman, 'Disability in Victorian Sensation Fiction', in Gilbert (ed.), *A Companion to Sensation Fiction*, pp. 493–506.
52 Holmes, *Fictions of Affliction*, pp. 2–4.
53 C. W. Gore, *Plotting Disability in the Nineteenth-Century Novel* (Edinburgh University Press, 2020), p. 14.
54 R. Garland-Thomson, *Extraordinary Bodies: Figuring Physical Disability in American Culture and Literature* (New York: Columbia University Press, 1997), pp. 6–7.
55 Gore, *Plotting Disability*, p. 6.
56 Ibid., pp. 77, 76.
57 Ibid., pp. 15–16.
58 M. Mossman, 'Representations of the Abnormal Body in *The Moonstone*', *Victorian Literature and Culture* 37.2 (2009), pp. 483–500 (p. 485).
59 R. Collins, 'Bearded Ladies, Hermaphrodites, and Intersexual Collage in *The Woman in White*', in Bachman and Cox (eds.), *Reality's Dark Light*, pp. 131–72 (p. 132).
60 R. Nemesvari, 'Queering the Sensation Novel', in Mangham (ed.), *The Cambridge Companion to Sensation Fiction*, pp. 70–84 (p. 71).
61 Ibid., p. 71.
62 A. Roy, 'The Fabulous Imperialist Semiotic of Wilkie Collin's *The Moonstone*', *New Literary History* 24.3 (1993), pp. 657–81 (p. 657).
63 I. Duncan, '*The Moonstone*, the Victorian Novel, and Imperialist Panic', *MLQ: Modern Language Quarterly* 55.3 (1994), pp. 297–319 (p. 300).
64 Roy, 'The Fabulous Imperialist Semiotic', p. 657.
65 Duncan, '*The Moonstone*', p. 319.
66 J. Mehta, 'English Romance; Indian Violence', *Centennial Review* 39.3 (1995), pp. 611–57 (p. 613).
67 L. Nayder, 'The Empire and Sensation', in Gilbert (ed.), *A Companion to Sensation Fiction*, pp. 442–54 (p. 445).
68 C. Herbert, *War of No Pity: The Indian Mutiny and Victorian Trauma* (Princeton University Press, 2008), p. 240.
69 T. L. Carens, 'Outlandish English Subjects in *The Moonstone*', in Bachman and Cox (eds.), *Reality's Dark Light*, pp. 239–65 (p. 244).
70 Ibid., p. 240.
71 I. Tucker, *The Moment of Racial Sight: A History* (University of Chicago Press, 2012), p. 7.
72 Ibid., p. 7.

73 Ibid., p. 78. Collins plays a small but significant role in another book-length study of bodies, surfaces and the culture of appearances: P. K. Gilbert, *Victorian Skin: Surface, Self, History* (Ithaca, NY: Cornell University Press, 2019). Gilbert is interested in the skin as a sensing and expressive surface, as a permeable membrane, as an alienable substance and as a possessor of intrinsic or inscribed properties (p. 8).
74 Tucker, *The Moment of Racial Sight*, p. 9.
75 L. Nayder, '"Blue Like Me": Collins, *Poor Miss Finch*, and the Construction of Racial Identity', in Bachman and Cox (eds.), *Reality's Dark Light*, pp. 266–82 (p. 268).
76 J. M. Pierce and M. S. Chander, 'Cousin Theory: Brown Kinship and the Nineteenth-Century Domestic Novel', *Victorian Studies* 62.3 (2020), p. 474–85 (p. 483).
77 Ibid., p. 478.

CHAPTER 14

Modern Media Adaptations

Alexis Weedon

'This is the story of what a Woman's patience can endure, and what a Man's resolution can achieve.' The opening line of Wilkie Collins's *The Woman in White* (1860) is one of the most famous of all novels. It establishes the story as one of heroic resolution, while also encapsulating the gender roles of Victorian society. Such a statement has roused later writers to reinterpret the tale in light of the injustices of their own age, and the many adaptations of Collins's novels and short stories show how his activism remains relevant to modern audiences.

Recent work in adaptation studies has moved the debate from arguments about fidelity to the original to focus on the processes of adaptation. Such scholarship explores how a familiar story is told on screen through the collaboration of the creative teams of writers, directors, actors and producers. The resulting screenplay addresses an audience who often already know the story and are familiar with the genre conventions of television drama and film. Karen Laird's historical work has explored the creation of early play and film adaptations of *The Woman in White* and their reception by knowing audiences with reference to the thrill-seeking of early film-goers.[1] Others have traced continuities between Collins's sensationalism and the emerging genre of neo-Victorian fiction in the works of Vera Caspary and the modern fiction of James Wilson in *The Dark Clue* (2001) and Sarah Waters in *Fingersmith* (2002).[2] This chapter adds to this work by focusing on media adaptations from the late twentieth century to today, exploring how writers have responded to the 'knowing audience' with allusions to other media forms, or to the original novel, and have updated the story with intertextual references to issues in the news. For instance, modern versions of Collins's two most adapted novels, *The Woman in White* and *The Moonstone* (1869), have demonstrated the stories' relevance to debates over gender identity, mental health and decolonisation in the twenty-first century.

Collins's box-office draw is less strong than that of Charles Dickens or Jane Austen, and there have been fewer classic films made from his work. Yet the range of media adaptations is broad, from unabridged readings of the stories on radio to audio dramatisations, daytime television miniseries and primetime TV movies, mostly British-made, but with his appeal extending beyond his home shores. There is a miniseries from Japan, a loose adaptation featuring a woman in white, called *Kiri ni sumu akuma* [Devil Living in a Fog] (Tokai Television Broadcast Company, 2011); a Moldova-film version, *Zhenshchina v belom* (Vadim Derbenyov, 1981); an Italian miniseries (RAI, 1980); as well as French and Russian versions. Elsewhere his shorter fiction has captured the adapter's interest, such as the German adaptation of *Poor Miss Finch* (1872), *Lucilla* (WDR, 1980), and his stories have been anthologised, as in 'The Dream Woman', in the notable Spanish TV series *El quinto jinete* (Thirteen Tales of Horror, TVE, 1975), and 'The Traveller's Story of a Terribly Strange Bed', in 'Orson Welles Great Mysteries' series on television (Anglia/ITV, 1974). In sum, Collins's tales have been adapted for television and radio consistently, if not frequently, since the invention of the media mostly by British and European companies.

As Linda Hutchinson points out in *A Theory of Adaptation* (2006), many adaptations of classic literature invite the audience to read the screenwork reciprocally with the book. Modern media adaptations of Wilkie Collins's work are period drama, but they have also been advertised as the forerunners of the country-house mystery or the psychological thriller. Making the argument that literary adaptations form a distinct genre, Thomas Leitch identifies four markers: a period setting; period music (not necessarily from the period of the setting); the foregrounding of authors, books and words in titles, intertitles and credits; and overt references to the time and place of the setting.[3] These elements appear in Collins's early films; for example, the 1934 first and only Hollywood film of *The Moonstone* opens with a hand taking a copy of *World's Best Known Mystery Stories* from a bookshelf and opening it to reveal the title page. A similar opening introduces the Warner Brothers 1948 adaptation of *The Woman in White*, which, in an overt piece of advertising, is placed among Olive Higgins Prouty's *Now, Voyager* (1941), Louise Randall Pierson's *Roughly Speaking* (1943) and Rachel Field's *All This, and Heaven Too* (1938), all novels that were made into films by the studio. In modern media adaptations, however, there is no expectation that the audience will have read the novel. *The Woman in White* (2018) television miniseries trailer simply advertises it as being 'Based on one of the world's most acclaimed mystery novels', and the 2014 film states it is 'from the classic novel by Wilkie Collins'.

Linda V. Troost draws a distinction between the Hollywood-style adaptation which takes liberties with the classic novel, the heritage British television productions which pride themselves on historical authenticity, and the mid-1990s fusion of the two, no longer wedded to fidelity, which appeals to a world market.[4] Yet Collins's modern adaptations also sit between genres and draw from the lineages of classic drama and of detective and mystery stories. Helen Wheatley adds another, arguing that the television drama adaptations on 'Hour of Mystery' (ABC, 1957) and 'Mystery and Imagination' (ABC/Thames TV, 1966–70) were part of the 'female Gothic'.[5] Collins's use of witness statements, investigative interviews and crime reconstruction in his narratives has enabled writers to draw upon screen narrative techniques created for true-life crime stories retold on television, and upon courtroom dramas. Their *mise en scène* owes much to the heritage of fictional mysteries from detective horror-thrillers to country-house whodunits.

The screenwriters of the 2016 adaptation of *The Moonstone* make this explicit. They wanted to reflect the epistolary structure of Collins's novel so took as their model *True Detective* (HBO, 2014). The television drama series had been a cultural phenomenon in 2014 with its gritty, absorbing narrative and the intensely drawn interaction of the two detectives. It ran two timelines and drip-fed clues to the audience, slowly unveiling the mystery across eight episodes. It attracted attention for its camera tracking of the characters from a distance as if they were being watched, and the dark lighting which created a tense, ominous atmosphere. Inspired by the series, Sasha Hails and Rachel Flowerday, co-writers of *The Moonstone*, decided to have two timelines in their adaptation with 'Franklin Blake interviewing, in the present day, the people who write their narratives in the book and flashing back to the earlier story they're discussing'.[6] Other features of the lighting and camerawork were also adopted. The adaptation illustrates two characteristics of modern media adaptation: the collaborative nature of screenwriting and how schedules affect both narrative and production values. Hails and Flowerday broke down the novel into the five episodes together, identifying the plot points and emotional beats for each, then wrote first drafts of each episode individually before exchanging their scripts and pitching their ideas to John Yorke, the producer. This BBC series of *The Moonstone* was commissioned for daytime TV and so had constraints on content as it had to adhere to guidance for daytime broadcasts and, in comparison to primetime, it had a more limited budget and a smaller staff. Financial constraints meant that filming took place in one location, Thornton Watlass Hall in Yorkshire, except for the Shivering Sands beach scenes.

Many early screen adaptations were based on stage plays. As film emerged as a medium, the studios bought performance rights that under copyright law were owned by the playwrights, which caused problems for some novelists. Early film scriptwriters and producers also benefited from studying the reactions of live audiences which guided them when selecting scenes for the script. Stage productions selected settings, broke down the story into emotional arcs through the acts of a play and selected dialogue to convey character. Collins's seventeen plays from 1850 to 1885 ensured he kept the revenue stream from stage productions (except any pirated ones such as J. M. Ware's unauthorised adaptation of *The Woman in White* in 1860). He was adept at creating socially meaningful yet popularly sensationalist moments on stage and added situations, as he said, which were 'of my own invention' and 'not in the novel'.[7] Over time, however, both the relevance of the social message and the susceptibility to sensation changed. Fatally for modern screenwriters, Collins's own play version of *The Moonstone* omitted, crucial to the postcolonial perspective, the mixed-race Ezra Jennings and the Brahmin Indians.[8] So modern adapters of Collins's works go back to the novels as the original source when adapting them for the stage and the screen.

The regular, if not frequent appearance of new versions of Collins's two most famous works for the stage from the 1950s to the 1990s has kept the tales alive for audiences of media adaptations. *The Moonstone* retains its relevancy: in Collins's novel, one character objects to her suitor's smoking habit, a key element in the plot, and another gives an angry anti-colonial critique of the treatment of the Brahmin priests and the pillaging of the stone from its ancient Indian statue. These themes were picked up in Kevin Elyot's play adaptation at the Swan Theatre, Worcester (1990) and brought him attention which led to a commission for a BBC screenplay for a two-part adaptation (1996). Prior to Elyot's work, Hugh Leonard's television adaptation in 1972 had opened with Herncastle's murderous theft of the jewel in India and the curse. In contrast, Elyot took the narrative back to the detective story, and began with Franklin Blake's arrival for Rachel Verinder's birthday and the mystery of a group of Indians appearing outside her house. Elyot and the director, Robert Bierman, gave the intelligent but flawed investigator Sergeant Cuff a deadpan humour linking him to later television detectives like Columbo. This shift from the genre of sensation to that of detection is characteristic of modern adaptations. Elyot went on to write scripts in the Poirot and Miss Marple series and co-wrote with the crime writer Ruth Rendell an adaptation of one of her own stories for television. Alasdair Steven said he combined 'a keen sense of the original with a sensitive understanding of the technicalities of modern television'.[9]

Going further, the 2018 version of *The Woman in White* caught the spirit of Wilkie Collins's activism. An agitator for women's legal rights in property and marriage, Collins deals with these issues in a story about abduction, incarceration and identity theft. The adaptation by Fiona Seres read this against the 2017 #MeToo social movement which unveiled the extent of sexual harassment in Hollywood and beyond, and sought to empower vulnerable women to speak out through solidarity with one another, spreading as a hashtag on social media. In Collins's novel, Sir Percival Glyde seeks to bully his wife, Laura Fairlie, into giving him her money and places his mentally disabled daughter, Anne Catherick, in an asylum. Both Anne and Laura are in his power, and it is only with the intervention of the men, Walter Hartright and Count Fosco, that his deceptions are uncovered. Nevertheless, Collins gives Laura stalwart support in her resourceful half-sister, Marian Halcombe, who risks her life to uncover Glyde's plot. And it is the relationship between Laura, Marian and Laura's lover Walter which is the emotional centre of the 2018 adaptation. The culottes, waistcoat and long military-style coat worn by Marian (played by Jessie Buckley) point to a later suffragette-style combative love, and the *mise en scène* contrast the lush Pre-Raphaelite interiors of Limmeridge against the chilling Georgian rooms of Blackwater Park. Such historical chiaroscuro made the series more relevant to contemporary debates without 'making it feel anachronistic and untrue to its period roots', as David M. Thompson, the executive producer, noted.[10]

Collins's novel was a popular success, drawing on public interest in the legal cases of Louisa Nottidge (1849, 1860), abducted and imprisoned by her male relatives, and the outcry against Rosina Bulwer-Lytton's detention in a lunatic asylum in 1858 by her husband. Screenwriter Fiona Seres drew on this heritage, saying the story 'explores how people behave, how we're driven to behave and when we step over the line'.[11] Seres invents another character, the sceptical Erasmus Nash, played by Art Malik, whom Marian persuades to investigate the disappearance of her sister. The narrative up to that point is relayed through his interviews with witnesses while the rest of the mystery moves forward in time. This flash-forward structure illuminates the transformative effect of the story on the listener, Nash, and is a comment on the healing power of a shared story. Malik's stern (and rather Dickensian) Nash keeps the viewer guessing, although at the end Nash's misery is dispelled and he goes off to be reconciled with his daughter.

Seres's invention gives her adaptation more pace and tension than either David Pirie's 1997 TV series, or Ray Jenkins's earlier televised version in 1982.[12] Pirie's adaptation makes the abuse of Anne the secret Sir Percival Glyde seeks to hide rather than his illegitimacy. The theme of trauma pervades this version; even the artist Walter Hartright is accused by a servant of trying to make them undress.[13] The prolific Ray Jenkins, who is named on the title of the miniseries of *The Woman in White* (1982), wrote many television police dramas as well as adapting *No Name* for radio (1989). The 1982 adaptation is a period melodrama rather than a heritage production. Family dysfunction is also at the heart of Radha Bharadwaj's 1998 film adaptation of the novel *Basil* (1852). Derek Jacobi plays the paterfamilias whose actions are brutal and unjust, and only at the end of the film are we given an explanation, which does little to justify his actions. For Bharadwaj, Collins's tale is a story of generational trauma, damaging secrets, disinheritance and revenge, figuratively expressed through imagery of masks and self-reflections.

Since the 1920s, Collins's stories have been aired on radio in readings and as dramatisations or discussed as books, as in the early broadcast of Eric N. Simons's 'Rambles Round a Library: The Frozen Deep by Wilkie Collins' (BBC, 7.40 p.m., 27 May 1926), possibly the earliest appearance of Collins's work on radio. Early radio plays were essentially broadcasts of stage productions, but as the medium spread scriptwriters found more effective ways of conveying suspense and horror. Audrey Lucas, playwright and novelist, adapted *The Woman in White* for radio in six parts for the BBC Home Service from 20 September 1943. Lucas, like Collins's adapter in the twenty-first century, Martyn Wade, adapted Dickens before coming to the novel and learned the dangers of over-narration in radio scripts. Paring back description, radio drama constructs ambiguity to unsettle the listener's mind, a skill which writers of radio thrillers and murder mysteries have brought to Collins's works. The scripts of Michael Robson, who adapted *Mad Monkton* in 1976, and Roger Danes, who has credits for Sherlock Holmes and *The Law and the Lady* (BBC, 2005), exemplify this. They use internal monologues and character points of view which are highly effective on radio. Playwright Doug Lucie's later adaptation of *The Moonstone* (2010) in four parts is told from the perspective of different characters: Gabriel Betteredge the butler, Sergeant Cuff, Miss Clack and Franklin Blake, the suitor. This gave each actor the opportunity to give depth to the character, so for instance through the eyes of Miss Clack we see how her obsession with good deeds and religion keeps her from perceiving what is going on in front of her.

In the heyday of the 1950s, music for radio drama was a separate occupation, but later writers for radio directed their own work. Many adapters worked across media and gained an understanding of what a foley soundscape (post-production background sound effects) and music can do to create atmosphere with and without visuals. Rod Beacham's adaptation of *The Haunted Hotel* (2012) is a good example, as he used the elements of radio horror, carefully deploying accents, music and foley. Beacham was a member of the BBC Radio Rep and had experience in television scriptwriting for police and detective series. In *The Haunted Hotel* he uses the power of music, monologue and dual timelines when Agnes Lockwood (played by Jasmine Hyde) recounts her experience of seeing the floating head above the prostrate form of Countess Narona (Adjoa Andoh). The radio adaptation very effectively dramatises her moment of breathless recoil and the inchoate scream as Gothic horror.

Arthur Conan Doyle was a great fan of Wilkie Collins, and the afterlife of their stories in transmedia adaptations has parallels. Frogwares's Sherlock Holmes game series has developed in the adventure game genre. and in a similar way Collins's novels have been adapted in video games (*Mystery Masterpiece: The Moonstone* and *Victorian Mysteries: Woman in White*; Big Fish Games, 2009 and 2010). Such adaptations are derivatives of the puzzle elements in the fiction while the story is reduced to a series of levels to play through. For readers of his books, the media adaptations on radio and screen are better at capturing the affective insight of Collins's genius for a modern audience.

Notes

[1] K. E. Laird, *The Art of Adapting Victorian Literature, 1848–1920: Dramatizing Jane Eyre, David Copperfield, and The Woman in White* (Farnham, Surrey: Ashgate, 2015).

[2] R. Malik, 'The Afterlife of Wilkie Collins', in J. Bourne Taylor (ed.), *The Cambridge Companion to Wilkie Collins* (Cambridge University Press, 2006), pp. 181–93; A. B. Emrys, *Wilkie Collins, Vera Caspary and the Evolution of the Casebook Novel* (Jefferson, NC, and London: McFarland, 2011).

[3] T. Leitch, 'Adaptation, the Genre', *Adaptation* 1.2 (2008), pp. 106–20.

[4] L. V. Troost, 'The Nineteenth-Century Novel on Film: Jane Austen', in D. Cartmell and I. Whelehan (eds.), *The Cambridge Companion to Literature on Screen* (Cambridge University Press, 2007), pp. 75–89.

5 H. Wheatley, 'Haunted Houses, Hidden Rooms: Women, Domesticity and the Female Gothic Adaptation on Television', in J. Bignell and S. Lacey (eds.), *Popular Television Drama: Critical Perspectives* (Manchester and New York: Manchester University Press, 2005), pp. 149–65 (pp. 150–1).
6 'The Moonstone: An Interview with Writers Sasha Hails and Rachel Flowerday', BBC Writers Room, Friday, 28 October 2016, 14:08, www.bbc.co.uk/blogs/writersroom/entries/c30e6661-776d-4f0e-b08d-4d5ab6724eb5
7 Quoted in Laird, *The Art of Adapting Victorian Literature*, p. 177.
8 See A. Gasson, *The Moonstone – A Dramatic Story in Three Acts*, www.wilkie-collins.info/play_moonstone.htm
9 A. Steven, 'Obituary: Kevin Elyot, Playwright', *The Scotsman* (11 June 2014).
10 'The Woman in White', BBC Media Centre, 16 April 2018, www.bbc.co.uk/mediacentre/mediapacks/the-woman-in-white
11 Ibid.
12 C. Salah, '"This Picture Always Haunted Me": Dramatic Adaptations of *The Woman in White*', *Neo-Victorian Studies* 3.2 (2010), pp. 32–55.
13 J. Cox, 'Narratives of Sexual Trauma in Contemporary Adaptations of Wilkie Collins's *The Woman in White*', in N. Boehm-Schnitker and S. Gruss (eds.), *Neo-Victorian Literature and Culture: Immersions and Revisitations* (New York: Routledge, 2014), pp. 137–50.

CHAPTER 15

Neo-Victorianism

Jessica Cox

An examination of Collins's work in relation to neo-Victorianism necessitates some explanation of the latter term. This is not necessarily straightforward, as it has been the subject of significant critical debate over the last twenty years or so. Broadly speaking, though, it refers to those works which engage with the Victorian period on some level, including both explicit adaptations and reworkings of specific nineteenth-century texts, and those productions which reference nineteenth-century history, literature and culture more generally. It includes – amongst other things – stage, screen and literary works, although as stage and screen adaptations of Collins's oeuvre are discussed elsewhere in this volume, this chapter will focus predominantly on literary reimaginings of Collins and his fiction. Collins's influence in this respect has been extensive, encompassing multiple genres, forms and periods. Inevitably, his two most successful novels – *The Woman in White* (1860) and *The Moonstone* (1868) – have exerted the most significant influence on later cultural productions, but his other works, as well as his life (and in particular his relationship with Charles Dickens), have also influenced later writers. The term 'neo-Victorian' cannot be understood as referring to a single, unified genre, but rather is an umbrella term that covers a wide range of texts which participate in a multitude of genres. The sense of unification comes from these works' engagement – at the level of setting, plot, character and/or intertextual influence – with the Victorian period and its literature. Some genres are, though, particularly popular with neo-Victorian writers, including the Gothic, crime and detective fiction – all of which are indebted more broadly to the Victorian sensation novels produced by Collins and his contemporaries. We might also identify within the wider field of neo-Victorian writing a sub-genre of neo-*sensation* fiction: those works which draw on (implicitly or explicitly) the conventions and characteristics of Victorian sensation fiction and echo their often-complicated plotting – frequently centred around mystery, crime and family secrets. Amongst the most popular neo-Victorian genres, then, there are strong echoes of Victorian sensation fiction more generally, and of Collins's novels in particular.

Critics have identified a number of prevalent trends and themes in neo-Victorian fiction – particularly in terms of the way in which the field 'writes back' to nineteenth-century literature and culture. These include a queering of the Victorian past; engagement with (personal and national/ historical) trauma (including the traumas of empire); a centring of marginalised figures; and an emphasis on the subject of inheritance – enabling an exploration of our own Victorian 'inheritance'. In some respects, then, neo-Victorian writing can be read as an attempt to return to and understand the past through what is largely *absent* in Victorian literature. Despite the lack of explicit reference to many of these issues in nineteenth-century writing, however, they do, in various ways, map onto the Victorian sensation novel, so it is unsurprising that they are clearly reflected in those neo-Victorian works which return to and reimagine Collins's life and fiction. In considering Collins's influence on neo-Victorianism, it is worth reflecting on the tension between 'literary' and 'popular' fiction – a tension evident in some of the nineteenth-century debates around the sensation novel and echoed in early critical constructions of the neo-Victorian canon. Collins was, first and foremost, an author of Victorian popular fiction – despite what may have been loftier ambitions and indeed later critical acclaim. Writing in 1861, one critic observed that 'a writer like George Eliot may look down from a very far height on such a dweller in the plains as he who wrote *The Woman in White*'.[1] Despite this, his work has exerted a significant influence on 'literary' neo-Victorian fiction, which, in contrast to Collins's oeuvre, was, initially at least, positioned as distinct from popular historical fiction by scholars who were keen to emphasise the postmodern aspects of the form and its 'self-conscious engagement' with the Victorian past. Although in recent years these critical hierarchies have begun to disintegrate, and as a scholarly field neo-Victorianism has begun to acknowledge and examine a wider range of texts and media, Collins's influence on neo-Victorian writing has always been more significant than that of Eliot and other 'highbrow' Victorian writers, and is evident in both 'literary' and popular incarnations of neo-Victorian fiction – though these distinctions are in themselves problematic and begin to crumble under close interrogation.

Mapping Collins's Influence: From the Victorian to the Neo-Victorian

Neo-Victorian critics initially focused their attention on works which had appeared since the 1960s, partly because the field was originally closely associated with postmodernism. In recent years, that focus has begun to shift, leading to various debates about the starting point for neo-Victorianism. The term implies, of course, that we cannot read Victorian productions as *neo*-Victorian, and yet in discussing the cultural afterlives of Collins and his work, it is worth returning to Collins himself, who was responsible for some of the earliest stage adaptations of his novels, as well as to some of his Victorian contemporaries whose work bears the hallmarks of Collins's influence. This overview, therefore, begins with a brief consideration of Victorian cultural productions which draw on Collins's fiction, before moving on to examine those works from the twentieth and twenty-first centuries which are more clearly identifiable as 'neo-Victorian'. It takes a broadly chronological approach in examining the extent of Collins's influence on later literary and cultural productions, whilst examining various trends which are evident in Collins's neo-Victorian afterlives. Although referencing a significant number of neo-Victorian works which position Collins's fiction (and indeed his life) as key intertexts, this is by no means an exhaustive bibliography. It does, however, provide evidence of the extent of the ongoing influence of Collins's life and work, as well as suggesting some of the possible reasons for this.

Collin's influence on other writers is evident almost from the start of his literary career, and certainly from the time of publication of his wildly successful work, *The Woman in White* in 1860. This novel remains closely associated with the emergence of Victorian sensation fiction – somewhat erroneously, as Collins's 1850s novels *Basil* (1852), *Hide and Seek* (1854) and *The Dead Secret* (1857) are also early examples of the form. Any account of Collins and adaptation must necessarily take into consideration his own dramatic reworkings of several of his novels, including *The Woman in White, No Name, Armadale, The Moonstone* and *Man and Wife*. These adaptations are not simply faithful transmutations of the novels from page to stage, but, like other reimaginings of his work, frequently introduce different emphases and plotlines. They demonstrate an awareness of the shift of medium and the implications of this, whilst also highlighting the parallels between stage fiction and melodrama – although Collins's stage productions arguably seek to aspire to something better than simply 'melodrama'. Whilst Collins was undoubtedly deeply interested in the theatre, his determination to adapt many of his own novels for the stage was in part linked to his concerns over copyright and his opposition to the multiple cheap productions which seemed to spring up in the wake of any moderately successful novel. The first (unauthorised) stage production of *The Woman in White*, for instance, appeared in the same year the novel was first published, and was quickly followed by various other attempts to produce the story for the Victorian theatre.

If dramatists were attempting to capitalise on Collins's success, the same could also be said of his fellow novelists, and in the years immediately following the publication of *The Woman in White*, several works appeared which draw on aspects of Collins's plot, and thus situate the novel as an important intertext. Significantly, these include the two novels most commonly cited alongside *The Woman in White* as the origin texts for Victorian sensation fiction: Ellen Wood's *East Lynne* (1861) and Mary Elizabeth Braddon's *Lady Audley's Secret* (1862). Both these works echo Collins's novel in terms of their sensational plotting and emphasis on the domestic Gothic, as well as in specific plot points: in all three novels, the heroine is presumed dead and reappears under a different identity. Like *The Woman in White*, both *East Lynne* and *Lady Audley's Secret* were hugely successful in the nineteenth century, although neither has exerted the same influence as Collins's work since then – a reflection, perhaps, of the greater credibility afforded Collins, as both a male writer and a close associate of Dickens. If they were not entirely responsible for the emergence of Victorian sensation fiction, these works did ensure its huge popularity in the 1860s and beyond, and consequently spawned numerous imitators – many of which also bear the hallmarks of Collins's influence. These works, whilst Victorian rather than neo-Victorian, evidence the continuing influence of Collins's fiction – and of *The Woman in White* in particular – on other writers since the time of its first publication.

Collins's next two novels, *No Name* (1863) and *Armadale* (1866), were also hugely popular with Victorian readers, but neither has exerted the same influence on later cultural productions as *The Woman in White* or his 1868 sensation-detective novel, *The Moonstone*. As with *The Woman in White*, the influence of this work is evident in several later Victorian novels, as well as in twentieth- and twenty-first-century works. Nineteenth-century fiction which exhibits the influence of *The Moonstone* includes Dickens's final, unfinished novel, *The Mystery of Edwin Drood* (1870), Anthony Trollope's *The Eustace Diamonds* (1872) and Arthur Conan Doyle's Sherlock Holmes story, *The Sign of Four* (1890). The significant influence of Collins's two most successful novels on other Victorian works anticipates his neo-Victorian legacy in the twentieth and twenty-first centuries, in which these two texts have attracted by far the most numerous cultural returns to his work.

    The sensation novel remained popular with readers throughout the nineteenth century, but by the early decades of the twentieth century, it had come to be viewed – somewhat erroneously – as an obscure sub-genre of the Victorian novel which had flourished for a short time in the 1860s. Certainly, it was deemed largely insignificant by literary scholars for the majority of the twentieth century, although Collins's fiction did attract some critical attention during this time. In reality, though, the sensation novel merely shifted into other guises, and its influence remains in evidence – particularly in popular fiction – into the twentieth century and beyond. There were several stage, screen and radio adaptations of Collins's work in the early decades of the twentieth century, including adaptations of works such as *Armadale* and *The New Magdalen* (1873), as well as the perennially popular *The Woman in White* and *The Moonstone*. His influence on fiction of this period is also evident – most notably in the detective fiction which flourished in this era, several examples of which explicitly reference Collins's novels, or rework his plots for a twentieth-century audience. Particularly influential in this regard are *The Moonstone* and his short story 'The Traveller's Story of a Terribly Strange Bed' (1852), which serve as important intertexts for the country-house and locked-room mysteries respectively. Collins also depicts the figure of the amateur detective in a number of his novels and short stories – a trend continued in the Golden Age of detective fiction with characters such as Agatha Christie's Miss Marple and G. K. Chesterton's Father Brown. Dorothy L. Sayers, author of over a dozen detective novels published in the 1920s and 1930s, was particularly influenced by Collins, and echoes of *The Moonstone* are found in her 1934 novel, *The Nine Tailors*.

    In the second half of the twentieth century, an increasing number of works of fiction adopted the Victorian setting – a trend which might be explained by the period's increasing historical distance as it moved beyond living memory. If we understand neo-Victorianism in relation to historical fiction (although some critics have been keen to emphasise the distinction between the two), then it is during this period that the neo-Victorian novel – separated from the Victorian age itself by some two generations or more – comes to fruition. This increasing distance between the Victorian past and the present creates – particularly within the popular imagination – a sense of nostalgia, and in some respects this is in evidence in popular reimaginings of Collins's work in this period. Whilst he continues to influence crime and detective fiction during this time, his work, along with Victorian sensation fiction more generally, exerts a significant influence on the popular genre of Gothic romance fiction, by authors including Victoria Holt and Mary Stewart. Holt (one of the various pseudonyms of Eleanor Hibbert) authored thirty-two works of historical fiction – primarily Gothic romances set in the nineteenth century. A number of these clearly reference the influence of Collins's fiction, including *The Shivering Sands* (1969) and *The India Fan* (1988), for both of which *The Moonstone* serves as a crucial intertext. The title of the former is taken directly from Collins's earlier work, and, like its predecessor, it depicts dangerous quicksand with an uncanny appearance which is responsible for the loss of life. *The India Fan* draws on the idea of the cursed Indian object (in Collins's novel a diamond; here a fan), and the name of the heroine – Drusilla – echoes that of the interfering spinster in *The Moonstone*, Drusilla Clack. Critical discussions of neo-Victorianism have only recently acknowledged the significance of the work of popular writers such as Holt, but in many respects, she was the natural descendant of the Victorian sensation novelists: producing popular fiction for a wide audience with an eye on commercial success rather than critical acclaim. Since the 1980s, Collins's influence on popular fiction has been evident in several Young Adult (YA) novels, including Philip Pullman's *The Ruby in the Smoke* (1985), which also draws on elements of *The Moonstone*, and contains echoes of *Armadale*. Other YA novels, such as Linda Newbery's *Set in Stone* (2006) and Jane Eagland's *Wildthorn* (2009), adapt the plot of *The Woman in White*. As with the Gothic romances of authors such as Holt, neo-Victorian criticism has only relatively recently begun to address the genre of YA fiction and its reimagining of Victorian literature and history.

Since the 1990s there have been several further fictional reworkings of *The Woman in White*, which fall into the category which we might, for want of a better term, label neo-Victorian 'literary' fiction – although such works might also accurately be described as neo-sensation fiction, drawing as they do on the conventions of the genre more broadly, as well as on the plot of Collins's novel in particular. They include Joanne Harris's *Sleep, Pale Sister* (1994), James Wilson's *The Dark Clue* (2001), Sarah Waters's (Booker-nominated) *Fingersmith* (2002), Diane Setterfield's *The Thirteenth Tale* (2006) and John Harwood's *The Asylum* (2013). All of these works draw on multiple nineteenth-century texts and histories, but all adapt the Laura Fairlie/Anne Catherick plot of Collins's novel in varying ways. They represent the type of fiction which neo-Victorianism initially foregrounded in its critical discourses, and all deal with several of the central concerns and themes of neo-Victorian writing. Several critics have examined Collins's Marian Halcombe as an example of the queer woman in nineteenth-century fiction, and works such as Waters's *Fingersmith* and Eagland's *Wildthorn* foreground this element of the text in their depiction of homosexual relationships in their reimagined versions of *The Woman in White*. Sexual abuse and the resulting trauma are rarely depicted in Victorian fiction (Collins's *Man and Wife* [1870], somewhat unusually, hints at the possibility of this in its depiction of the obviously traumatised character of Hester Dethridge), but this is a major concern in neo-Victorian writing, and this is reflected in several of those works which repurpose *The Woman in White*, including *The Dark Clue*, *The Thirteenth Tale* and *Set in Stone*. In some respects, Collins's original novel lends itself to this kind of reimagining given its focus on the abusive marriage of Laura Fairlie and Percival Glyde. *The Dark Clue* is also an example of bio-fiction (novels which adapt aspects of Victorian lives for a contemporary audience) – another key trend in neo-Victorian writing, although the subject of Wilson's work in this respect is the artist J. M. W. Turner, rather than Collins. However, Collins does appear as a character in several other neo-Victorian novels, including William J. Palmer's *The Detective and Mr Dickens* (1990) and Dan Simmons's *Drood* (2009), in both of which he is cast alongside a fictional Dickens – and in Simmons's novel as narrator. Michel Faber's epic neo-Victorian novel *The Crimson Petal and the White* (2002) also references Collins, and is undoubtedly indebted to his work as well as the life and fiction of Dickens.

It is perhaps inevitable that it is Collins's most successful novels, *The Woman in White* and *The Moonstone*, which continue to exert the most influence in terms of his neo-Victorian legacy. This, though, is not necessarily simply attributable to the initial popularity of these works. Many of the concerns of these two novels anticipate those of contemporary neo-Victorian writing. Neo-Victorian fictions might make more explicit their interrogation of identity, empire and sexuality, but, as the critical discourses around Collins's fiction indicate, these are issues with which Collins himself evinced a concern in his writing. His work shines a light on Victorian concerns and anxieties, and to this end proves a useful vehicle for neo-Victorian interrogations of the period. His woman in white haunted the Victorian cultural imaginary, and continues as a spectral presence in neo-Victorian returns to the period.

Notes

[1] [Unsigned review], 'Recent Popular Novels', *Dublin University Magazine* (February 1861), p. 200.

PART III

Contexts: Literary

CHAPTER 16

Wilkie Collins's Library
William Baker

Wilkie Collins's letters contain frequent references to his reading, to his searching for books, and, as he grew older, to thoughts on his favourite authors. Books and associated printed materials were important for him during the creative process. His notes, for example for *The Moonstone*, now at the Parrish Collection at Princeton University, contain lists of books to consult on India, Indian customs, and gems and their properties.[1]

There are characters in Collins's work whose fictional tastes are similar to those of their author. For example, Amelius Goldenheart of *The Fallen Leaves* (1879) has in his library the works of Sir Walter Scott. The reader is told that 'the writings of the one supreme genius who soars above all other novelists as Shakespeare soars above all other dramatists – the writings of Walter Scott – had their place of honour in his library'.[2] They were also in Collins's own library, and his letters attest to his profound admiration for Scott as a person and as a writer.[3]

Collins owned Scott's *The Miscellaneous Prose Works* (1834–6), Scott's edited five-volume *The Modern British Drama* (1811), the forty-eight volumes of *Waverley Novels* (1859) and, a year before he died, a twelve-volume *Poetical Works* (1888).

But how do we know that he owned these copies? The existence of two sale catalogues makes it possible to reconstruct the contents of his library. These catalogues also provide evidence of a neglected facet of his life and work: his intellectual interests. Biographies have focused too much attention on his complicated relationships with women. As absorbing as this side of his life may be, this emphasis neglects his life as a professional writer, as an intellectual and as somebody who needed books to exist.

Collins wrote for a living. He wrote to maintain himself and more than one family, and he depended upon books and printed materials as a central resource for his creative activities. Books were the tools of his trade. The volumes in his library reveal much about the man, the writer, his friendships, his associations and the sources for his creative inspiration.

Collins died on 23 September 1889. My *Wilkie Collins's Library: A Reconstruction* was published by Greenwood in 2002. It is partly based upon M. L. Bennett's *Caxton Head Catalogue 198: Books &c from the Library of the late Wilkie Collins*. This invaluable catalogue appeared in London in February 1890, and I am very much indebted to Catherine Peters, who sent me a copy. Wilkie Collins's sole living survivor, Faith, and her late husband, Bill Clarke, author of *The Secret Life of Wilkie Collins* (Alan Sutton, 1988), sent me the auctioneers' marked-up copy of the 20 January 1890 Puttick and Simpson's *Library of the Late Wilkie Collins Esq*. Collins's books and other objects, such as the paintings and artwork he owned, were sold at this auction, and the main buyer seems indeed to have been M. L. Bennett, who one month later attempted to sell the books bought at considerably higher prices.

The present audience may not be aware of Bernadette A. Meyler's 'Transparency and Textuality: Wilkie Collins' Law Books' (2007). This appeared as one of the Cornell Law School Legal Studies Research Paper series. Its focus is on the 1882 trial of Jessie Billings for the murder of his wife. Collins possessed a copy of a volume containing the arguments of the Albany prosecutor Nathaniel Moak. This became one of the chief sources for Collins's short story 'John Jago's Ghost; or, The Dead Alive, An American Story', originally published in the *Home Journal* (27 December 1873–4 February 1874). It was subsequently reprinted in book form under the title *The Dead Alive* (Boston, 1874). Incidentally, this story seems to have a particular fascination for eminent lawyers, as the text forms the foundation for Rob Warden's *Wilkie Collins's The Dead Alive: The Novel, the Case, and Wrongful Convictions*, published by the Northwestern University Press (2005). At the time, Warden was the executive director of the Center on Wrongful Convictions at the Northwestern University School of Law. There is a foreword by the eminent lawyer and novelist Scott Turow, who writes of *The Dead Alive*: 'gracefully written and artfully suspenseful, it is an early example of the popular novel as we know it now and an eerily prescient forerunner on much of the fiction about the legal process now so widely read in the United States and around the world'. Turow adds, 'More tellingly, its observations remain disturbingly accurate about the factors that can lead the criminal justice system to the wrong conclusions and to the ultimate moral mishap of condemning the innocent to death.'[4]

Following Collins's death, his executors, his son-in-law and solicitor Henry Powell Bartley, his doctor Frank Beard and a business advisor and close friend Sebastian Schlesinger, instructed that Collins's library and other possessions be sold at auction.⁵ Two catalogues survive. The first is an auction catalogue of books sold at the Puttick and Simpson auction rooms at 47 Leicester Square, London W.C. A venerable London auction house founded in 1794, it specialised in literary property and works of art. The catalogue comprised books grouped together by size described as 'Octavo et Infra' volumes and listed numerically as lots 1–246. Volumes of these sizes constitute most of the items listed and run from the first lot to 231. These are followed by seven lots under the 'Quarto' rubric and eight designated 'Folio' volumes.

The seven 'Conditions of Sale' listed at the start of the auction catalogue conform to standard London auction house practices at the time. Few lots attracted sums exceeding £3 (roughly £390 today). Volumes that commanded high prices included George Henry Borrow's six-volume compilation *Celebrated Trials, and Remarkable Cases of Criminal Jurisprudence, From the Earliest Records to the Year 1825* (1825: lot 43 – in my reconstruction), purchased by Nugent, who paid £8 7s 6d (roughly £1,066 today) for volumes possibly drawn upon by Collins for plotlines. Francis Edwards, the London booksellers, paid £19, the highest amount realised at the Puttick and Simpson auction (roughly £2,531 today), for lot 27. This has three items by John Forster, one of Dickens's executors, and the dedicatee of *Armadale* (1866): 'in affectionate remembrance of the friendship which is associated with some of the happiest years of my life'.⁶ One of the Forster items is a presentation copy of Forster's biography of Sir John Eliot (1592–1632), the staunch defender of parliamentary privilege imprisoned in the Tower of London by Charles I. There is a copy too of Forster's two-volume biography of the poet Walter Savage Landor, published in 1869. Collins wrote to Forster on 15 May 1869 thanking him for the copy that he 'shall read ... with no common interest and attention – first as coming from you; secondly as saying, what no one else could have said so well, in vindication of Landor's claims to a great place in English literature'.⁷ No copies of works by Landor are recorded amongst Collins's books. A presentation copy to Collins of Forster's *Debates on the Grand Remonstrance, November and December 1641: With an Introductory Essay on English Freedom under Plantagenet & Tudor Sovereigns* (1860) is the third item that Edwards paid such a relatively high amount for at the auction.

Other copies by Forster in the library found in the Puttick and Simpson catalogue are an undated presentation copy of Forster's *Land and Labour* purchased by 'Osborne' (lot 205) and a copy of the three-volume second edition of Forster's celebrated *Life of Dickens* (1872), containing Collins's signature on the title of the first volume and a few of his pencil notes (lot

206). This was purchased by the London booksellers Quaritch and was the subject of an effusive note of thanks from Collins to Forster on 16 November 1872. Collins tells him that he is 'devouring you at night', adding that that is 'the only time when I have any leisure hours at my disposal' (B&C 11: 356). Collins's marginalia in the volumes are of interest and have been described too.[8]

Another lot that reached a high price, also of £19, was paid by the London booksellers Maggs. The item that probably attracted such a price represents one of the earliest books of Collins's to have survived. This is the antiquary Joseph Ritson's *Robin Hood: A Collection of All the Ancient Poems, Songs, and Ballads, Now Extant Relative to That Celebrated English Outlaw: To Which are Prefixed Historical Anecdotes of His Life* (1820). According to Puttick and Simpson's catalogue, the volume has a 'woodcut on title painted, with signature "William Collins aged eight years 1832"' (lot 96). This lot also contains an inscribed copy from its translator, the Anglo-Irish Baronet Sir John Kingston James, of an English verse translation from the Italian of Tasso's *Jerusalem Delivered* (1865).

As noted, the main purchaser at the Puttick and Simpson auction was M. L. Bennett of the Caxton Head bookshop; at least forty-seven lots were knocked down to Bennett. Within a month of the auction, Bennett offered in his February 1890 *Catalogue 198: Books &c from the Library of the late Wilkie Collins, some with his Autograph Signature and many are Presentation copies from the respective Authors*. One hundred and thirty-three items are in this catalogue. Some of these consist of various volumes loosely grouped together under subject headings such as 'America' or 'Amatory'. The initial book listed is a copy of the two-volume reminiscences (1876) of the Liberal politician and soldier George Thomas Keppel, 6th Earl of Albemarle. The final item in Bennett's catalogue is another historical memoir, Sir Nathaniel William Wraxall's two-volume *Historical Memoirs of My Own Time* (1815). Wraxall served in the East India Company and also wrote about his European travels. His memoirs were of use to Collins, shown by his pencilled notes on the fly-leaf (*Library*: 162).

Bennett's listing and the Puttick and Simpson auction listing reveal an impressive working collection that covered a wide range of subjects and time periods and included many inscribed and presentation copies. These display Collins's capacity for friendship, his sociability and the influence of his writings upon so many of his contemporaries, many of whom were probably unknown to him. The two listings reveal fifty-six presentation copies. Some of these are not to Collins personally. For example, Edward

Fitzball's *The House to Let, with Other Poems* (1857) is a 'presentation copy to Charles Dickens from the author'. How it ended up in Collins's library (item 198) rather than Dickens's is something of a mystery, but perhaps a reflection of the close relationship between Dickens and Collins. A book that had personal associations for Collins and his family was Jeremy Taylor's *Holy Living and Holy Dying*. A two-volume copy dated 1824 and presented to his mother a year subsequently is found amongst his books and probably belonged to Collins's pious father. Charles, Collins's brother, insisted that Wilkie take a copy with him to Italy in 1853. Collins found it (item 482) very slow reading and commented in a letter to his mother dated 16 October 1853: 'I have read a little of Jeremy Taylor – in accordance with my promise: a *little* because my present course of life is not favourable to theological studies and hard to understand after days rolling over rough high roads in a travelling carriage' (B&C 1: 100).

Other inscribed copies of interest include a volume by Forbes Winslow, the physician and member of the Royal College of Surgeons, *Lettsomian Lectures on Insanity* (1854). This copy (item 519) was presented to the editor of *The Leader*, Edward Pigott, Collins's close friend with whom he went yachting. Collins contributed to *The Leader* from the autumn of 1851 until 1855. The 1861 second edition of Winslow's *On Obscure Diseases of the Brain* is inscribed to Collins (item 520). Both works relate to Collins's fictional explorations of the world of insanity and lunatic asylums in *The Woman in White* (1860). Winslow in 1847 'opened two private lunatic asylums' in the Hammersmith area that employed, for the time, more humane methods of treating the mentally disturbed, and Winslow 'did much to establish medical grounds for the plea of insanity in court cases'.[9]

A presentation copy that Collins probably drew upon for fictional purposes is the 1861 edition of *A Guide to Aldeburgh, With A Brief Description of Adjacent Places* (item 8). The Suffolk coastal town appears in *No Name* (1863), which Collins was writing between 1861 and 1862. He visited Aldeburgh, accompanied by Caroline Graves, in 1861, and his novel contains powerful coastal descriptions. Collins 'admired [George] Crabbe's poetry', which he frequently re-read, and 'reminded his readers that Aldeburgh was the poet's birthplace. His descriptions of the town, gradually being reclaimed by the sea, and the surrounding country are deliberately modelled on Crabbe's evocative backgrounds to his tales of rural violence and poverty.'[10] An eight-volume 1834 edition of *Crabbe's Poetical Works ... With His letters and Journals, and his Life* was Puttick and Simpson's lot 28 purchased by 'Withers'.

Charles Kent was a close friend and correspondent of Collins, especially in his later years. Kent's mother was the sister of a Roman Catholic bishop, both parents were Catholics, and Kent was educated at a Catholic school, Prior Park, Bath, and then at St Mary's College, Oscott. The presentation copy from Kent to Collins of his *Corona Catholica* (1880) was in Collins's library (item 284). There can be little doubt that Kent provided background material for Collins's *The Black Robe*, published the following year (1881), with its Catholic Jesuit setting. Collins probably also drew upon for this late novel Leopold von Ranke's *History of the Popes*. E. Foster's three-volume translation (1847) was in his library (item 407) as was a copy of another three-volume work, Andrew Steinmetz's *History of the Jesuits* (1848: item 458). These volumes contain numerous pencil markings by Collins. There is also a copy of Cardinal Wiseman's recollections of *The Last Four Popes and of Rome in their Times* (1858: item 530).

These are just a few examples of volumes in Collins's library that he drew upon. Other items of personal interest include his school 'presentation copy to "Master Collins 1st Prize Maida Hill Academy Xmas 1835"', purchased by 'Withers' (item 454), and Robert Southey's two-volume *Essays, Moral and Political First Collected* (1832). His mother's previously mentioned two-volume copy of Jeremy Taylor's *Holy Living* (1824: item 482) survived the two major moves of his later years: to 90 Gloucester Place in September 1867 and then, owing to high rent demands, to 82 Wimpole Street in March 1888. This move, as his letters reveal, was traumatic, and Collins seems to have lost a number of books in the process. He wrote to his friend Harry Quilter, the art critic, on 11 April 1888: 'I am sorry to trouble you, but I miss three books out of the library catalogue – Forster's Life of Goldsmith, and Lamb's Essays and Leigh Hunt's Essays. Do you think they have been stolen?' (B&C II: 555).

The specific titles in the Puttick and Simpson and M. L. Bennett listings do not represent all the volumes Collins possessed or consulted. To return to his sources for *The Moonstone*, none of the following that he lists in his notes for the novel are found in the catalogues, although they may have been present under the books that were grouped together. These include James Talboys Wheeler's *Madras in the Olden Time: Being a History of the Presidency from the First Foundation*, published in Madras for J. Higginbotham by Graves and Co. in 1861. Collins may have drawn too upon the first volume of Wheeler's four-volume *History of India*, published by N. Trübner between 1867 and 1881. Also listed are Theodore Hook's two-volume biography *The Life of General, the Right Honourable Sir David Baird, Bart* (London: Richard Bentley, 1832) and

C. W. King's *The Natural History, Ancient and Modern, of Precious Stones and Gems, and of the Precious Metals* (London: Bell & Daldy; Cambridge: Deighton, Bell & Co., 1865).

The evidence from the Puttick and Simpson and Bennett catalogues shows that Collins was not a bibliophile in the sense of amassing first editions, manuscripts or incunabula. Imprint date analysis demonstrates that he was not a collector of antiquarian or rare books. The highest percentage of publication dates in his library – just under 18 per cent, or 90 items – are the years 1871 to 1880. The final nine years of his life produced just under 16 per cent imprints, or 84 items. There are just over 13 per cent, or 71 items, with publication dates extending from 1861 to 1870. The previous decades provide little in the way of volumes; however, there are just over 6 per cent, or 34 items, with eighteenth-century imprints.

Subject analysis is a tricky business as subject categories are by no means exclusive, and duplication will inevitably arise. For example, a copy at Puttick and Simpson's auction of John Genest's ten-volume *Some Account of the English Stage from the Restoration in 1660 to 1830* (Bath, 1832), which had belonged to Robert Southey and contained his signature, and also that of Wilkie Collins, was purchased by 'Withers' (item 221). In addition to being a history of the English theatre covering a century and a half, it is also a work dealing with English literature and the English stage. To take one other example of the difficulties of pinning a subject down too narrowly: Walter Farquhar Hooks's *A Church Dictionary* (1843), listed in Bennett's catalogue but not in Puttick and Simpson's, belonged to Harriet Collins, Wilkie's mother. Her signature is on its title page (item 266) and belongs to two subject categories: religion and reference works.

Given this element of approximation, based on analysis of the volumes listed in the Puttick and Simpson and Bennett catalogues, English literature, including drama, represents 35 per cent, or 263 titles; French literature, 19 per cent with 146 titles; and history, 10 per cent and 75 titles. Of the first category, 46 titles are theatre related: dramatic histories, collections of plays, individual dramatists' works, biographies and memoirs. Yet there is a curious absence of the work of Collins's dramatic contemporaries and other nineteenth-century British dramatic writers. There are no plays, for instance, by the highly prolific Dion Boucicault or by Edward Fitzball, who churned out over 150 dramas. A copy of Fitzball's two-volume theatrical memoirs (1859) and a presentation copy to Charles Dickens of his poetry (1857) are recorded (item 198). The collection of plays includes Elizabeth Inchbald's two-volume edited *The*

British Theatre (1806–9: item 272), and the four-volume *London Stage: A Collection of the Most Reputed Tragedies, Comedies, Operas, Melodramas, Farces, and Interludes* (1824: item 318). Also present is Isaac Reed's twelve-volume *A Select Collection of Old Plays* from 1825 (item 412). The largest collection of theatrical works in Collins's library are copies of English dramatists from the Restoration and post-Restoration theatre. These include four volumes of plays by John Crowne (item 146); four of the five volumes of the dramatic works of Sir William D'Avenant (item 150); and two eighteenth-century editions of George Farquhar, one dated 1728 and the other dated 1760 (item 191). There is also a two-volume *Works of Mr. Thomas Otway* (item 381) with a 1712 imprint. There is a copy of the Anglo-Irish dramatist Thomas Southerne's *Sir Anthony Love or, The Rambling Lady: A Comedy* (1698: item 453). Unfortunately, there is no indication of marginal linings or annotations to indicate how much usage, if any, Collins made of these works.

Surprisingly, of Collins's contemporaries and fellow novelists, there is no Anthony Trollope, and only one George Eliot, an undated copy of *Scenes of Clerical Life*, her first novel (item 179). William Makepeace Thackeray is represented by *The Book of Snobs, The History of Pendennis, The Newcomes* and *Vanity Fair*; none is a first edition (items 484–7). There are fourteen volumes of William Harrison Ainsworth's works (item 6), an unspecified run of Charles Lever's novels (lot 311), and sixteen volumes of the works of Frederick Marryat (item 341).

There are fewer items than expected by Collins's collaborator and friend Charles Dickens. The eight items include a run of *Household Words* (item 161), and copies of three novels: *Great Expectations, The Pickwick Papers* and the uncompleted posthumous *The Mystery of Edwin Drood* (items 155–7). These are supplemented by Georgina Hogarth and Mary Dickens's three-volume edited *Letters of Charles Dickens* of 1880–2 (item 159) and there is a 22-volume library edition of Charles Dickens's works (item 162).

In conclusion, it should be asked how Collins's library compares with that of his contemporaries, such as Dickens or Eliot. Eliot's library is complicated as she jointly owned volumes with her partner, George Henry Lewes, so the items that we know of and that survive her in a way are heavily skewed towards Lewes's scientific and philosophical interests. However, a thorough collection of scholarly works and work that Eliot utilised is reflected in her volumes at the Dr Williams's non-conformist library housed in Gordon Square, London, and in inventories of her library.[11] Dickens's library, which was extensive at his house in

Rochester, has yet to be fully analysed. The twelve-volume Pilgrim edition of Dickens's *Letters*, as well as various attempts to reconstruct his Gad's Hill library, reveal that he, in common with Eliot and Collins, to name but two of his fellow Victorian writers, read extensively and drew upon external material for creative purposes.[12]

Collins's reading, as indicated by his library, contributed specifically to his strengths as a novelist. It shaped the intensity of his descriptive settings, his powerfully realistic evocations of cultural issues, and the dramatic interaction between his characters – in short, the things that made him popular with his Victorian audience and that continue to make him a significant figure in nineteenth-century fiction.

Notes

[1] See W. Baker, 'Wilkie Collins's Notes for "The Moonstone"', *Victorians Institute Journal* 31 (2003), pp. 187–205. Thanks are due to my co-editor, Richard Nemesvari, for his judicious observations on earlier drafts of this contribution.

[2] W. Collins, *The Fallen Leaves* (Stroud: Alan Sutton Publishing, 1994), p. 186.

[3] See W. Baker, A. Gasson, G. Law and P. Lewis (eds.), *The Public Face of Wilkie Collins: The Collected Letters*, 4 vols. (London: Pickering & Chatto, 2005), vol. IV, p. 442; and W. Baker, *Wilkie Collins's Library: A Reconstruction* (Westport, CT, and London: Greenwood, 2002), pp. 146–8 (hereafter cited as *Library*).

[4] R. Warden (ed.), *Wilkie Collins's The Dead Alive: The Novel, the Case, and Wrongful Convictions*, Foreword by S. Turow (Evanston, IL: Northwestern University Press, 2005), p. x.

[5] See W. M. Clarke, *The Secret Life of Wilkie Collins* (Stroud: Alan Sutton Publishing, 1996), p. 191.

[6] W. Collins, *Armadale*, ed. J. Sutherland (London: Penguin, 1995), p. iii.

[7] W. Baker and W. M. Clarke (eds.), *The Letters of Wilkie Collins*, 2 vols. (London: Macmillan, 1999), vol. II, pp. 322–3. Hereafter cited in the text as B&C.

[8] *Pall Mall Gazette* (20 January 1890), p. 3; and *Library*, pp. 108–9.

[9] J. Andrews, 'Winslow, Forbes Benignus (1810–1874)', *Oxford Dictionary of National Biography* (Oxford University Press, 2004). Online edition: https://doi.org/10.1093/ref:odnb/29752 (accessed 21 April 2021).

[10] C. Peters, *The King of Inventors: A Life of Wilkie Collins* (Princeton University Press, 1993), p. 238.

[11] See W. Baker, *The George Eliot-George Henry Lewes Library* (New York: Garland, 1977); W. Baker, *The Libraries of George Eliot and G. H. Lewes*, English Literary Studies Monographs 24 (Victoria, BC: University of Victoria, 1981); re-issued electronically (InteLex, 2003). Sadly, the Gordon Square,

London building where the Eliot and Lewes collection is housed is deteriorating and badly in need of repair: whether their books will survive is open to question.

[12] For Dickens's library, see K. J. Fielding, 'The Library of Dickens', in P. Schlicke (ed.), *The Oxford Reader's Companion to Dickens* (Oxford University Press, 1999), pp. 333–4.

CHAPTER 17

Wilkie Collins and Serialisation

Catherine Delafield

Serialised novels by Wilkie Collins occupied the pages of mid-Victorian newspapers and magazines for 475 weeks between January 1857 and December 1889. Collins did not publish his novels as part-works as Dickens largely did. From *The Dead Secret* (1857) onwards, all his novels were issued in serial format in a range of publications, mostly weekly, and both novel and periodical were influenced by the serialisation and the publication in parts. Collins explored assorted forms of periodical publication addressing a range of middle-class audiences for the journals and newspapers who paid him, his awareness of such audiences stemming from his belief in the potential of an 'Unknown Public' that expected 'a good pennworth'.[1]

In the course of his writing career, Collins moved from family weeklies to lighter metropolitan monthlies and weeklies before profiting from syndication in provincial newspapers facilitated by his agents A. P. Watt and Tindell. This is shown in Table 17.1, that gives also an indication of simultaneous publication in the United States or Canada and of the interaction with other serialised novels in the magazines. Collins began in Charles Dickens's twopenny-weeklies, their relationship punctuated by his income-driven excursion to the shilling-monthly *Cornhill Magazine*. Collins then turned to 'a new public' in the penny-weekly *Cassell's Magazine* before moving into the pricier metropolitan journals as well as the illustrated weekly newspaper *The Graphic*. After *Jezebel's Daughter* was syndicated in W. F. Tillotson's provincial newspapers in 1879, Collins's remaining novels used this format, sometimes in parallel with monthly publication of the cumulative weekly instalments. Any discussion of Collins and serialisation must account for the evolution in parts, the composition and context of the novel, and the commodification of the texts being produced.

Table 17.1 *Wilkie Collins and Serialisation*

SERIAL (Weekly unless M = Monthly)	PERIODICAL (Cost per issue)	SERIALISATION (No. Instalments)	FEATURES
The Dead Secret	*Household Words* (2d)#	3 January to 28 March 1857;	Occasional fiction e.g. *Hard Times* (1854: 20); *North and South* (1854–5: 22)
The Woman in White	*All the Year Round* (2d)#	11 April to 13 June 1857 (23) 26 November 1859 to 25 August 1860 (40)	Succeeds *A Tale of Two Cities* (31; overlapping No. 31); succeeded by *A Day's Ride* (15; overlapping Nos. 1–2 of 15); then by *Great Expectations* (36) and *A Strange Story* (31)
No Name	*All the Year Round* (2d)#	15 March 1862 to 17 January 1863 (45)	Succeeds *A Strange Story* (31); succeeded by *A Dark Night's Work* (9) and *Very Hard Cash* (40)
Armadale (M)	*Cornhill Magazine* (1s) [also *Harper's New Monthly*]	November 1864 to June 1866 (20)	Succeeds *Margaret Denzil's History* (12); with *Wives and Daughters* (Nos. 4–18 of 18); with *The Claverings* (Nos. 1–5 of 21)
The Moonstone	*All the Year Round* (2d)#	4 January to 8 August 1868 (32)	Runs with 'Holiday Romance' (4) and 'George Silverman's Explanation' (4) [intermittent]; *The Dear Girl* (Nos. 12–17 of 17)
Man and Wife	*Cassell's Magazine* (1d)#	20 November 1869 to 30 July 1870 (37)	
Poor Miss Finch	*Cassell's Magazine* (1d)#	2 September 1871 to 24 February 1872 (26)	Periodical edition published (as Volume 4 of magazine)
The New Magdalen (M)	*Temple Bar* (1s)#	October 1872 to July 1873 (10)	
The Law and the Lady	*The Graphic* (6d)	26 September 1874 to 13 March 1875 (25)	Succeeds 'The Village Surgeon' (6); 'Miss or Mrs?' in 1871 Christmas number
The Two Destinies (M)	*Temple Bar* (1s) [also *Harper's Bazaar*]	January to September 1876 (9)	

Title	Publication	Dates
The Haunted Hotel (M)	Belgravia (1s) [also Canadian Monthly]	June to November 1878 (6)
The Fallen Leaves	The World (6d) [also Canadian Monthly]	1 January to 23 July 1879 (30)
Jezebel's Daughter	Provincial newspapers	13 September 1879 to 31 January 1880* (20)
The Black Robe	Provincial newspapers [also Canadian Monthly]	2 October 1880 to 26 March 1881* (26)
Heart and Science	Provincial newspapers	22 July 1882 to 13 January 1883* (28)
Heart and Science (M)	Belgravia (1s)	August 1882 to June 1883 (11)
'I Say No'	Provincial newspapers	15 December 1883 to 12 July 1884* (30)
'I Say No' (M)	London Society (1s)#	January to December 1884 (12)
The Evil Genius	Provincial newspapers	11 December 1885 to 30 April 1886* (21)
The Legacy of Cain	Provincial newspapers	17 February to 6 July 1888* (21)
Blind Love	Illustrated London News (5d)	6 July to 28 December 1889 (26) Completed by Walter Besant

\# = Also *Harper's Weekly*; * = Dependent on day of issue

Evolution in Parts

As Table 17.1 indicates, Collins produced nineteen novels that were serialised in parts ranging in length from six weekly instalments (*The Haunted Hotel*) to forty-five (*No Name*). His novels often boosted sales of the magazines to which he contributed, with *Cassell's Magazine* achieving a circulation of 70,000 during the appearance of *Man and Wife*.[2] Critical responses were varied despite this popularity with audiences. Margaret Oliphant described '[t]he violent stimulant of weekly publication, with its necessity for frequent and rapid recurrence of piquant situation and startling incident' by comparison with Collins's 'delicate care and laborious reticence'.[3] *The Saturday Review*, which was frequently critical of Collins, found in *The Law and the Lady* 'the art of telling a secret at greater length than any one else', but the reviewer observed that this only worked in weekly parts; a sensible reader would otherwise just skip to the end.[4] Collins himself came to approach his role as a serialising novelist with a greater sense of his own importance conjoined with an assumption of increased earning potential. He argued with the proprietors of *Cassell's Magazine* that any voluntary abridgement of a serial was a contribution to the literary result.[5] They responded by producing *Poor Miss Finch* in a specially published volume edition of the periodical that undercut the official three-volume edition to be published by George Bentley in 1872. Other breaches were more public. When the short story 'Miss or Mrs?' appeared in the 1871 Christmas number of *The Graphic*, editor Frederick Locker was apparently able to ignore the sexualised depiction of its heroine. Three years later, however, Locker exercised his editorial privilege over a questionable passage in the serialisation of *The Law and the Lady* that Collins described as 'castrated' in a letter to his agent Tindell.[6] The passage was publicly restored but a damning disclaimer was printed in *The Graphic* in an adjacent column that would be read immediately in parallel with the novel's last instalment.[7]

Periodical serialisation combined economics with textuality. The publisher and author spread both risk and income over a given number of weeks or months while the novel evolved in conjunction with miscellaneous content and was read within a context. The novel was part of a reading whole at the same time as being engaged in the onward progression of the periodical series. The novel was also subject to review and possibly to revision in the course of serialisation. Thus, for instance, Collins's *Armadale* was given a less prominent place in *Cornhill Magazine* as a result of complaints about the diary of Lydia Gwilt. In Collins's case, the accompanying serials might also be adjusted. 'Margaret Denzil's History' was composed by *Cornhill* co-editor Frederick Greenwood to fill a gap in the delivery timescale of *Armadale*. Locker added his own 'The Village Surgeon' as a stopgap in *The Graphic* and Dickens wove two of his own short pieces into *All the Year Round* to counterbalance *The Moonstone*. Collins had originally been a co-worker in the fiction-driven launch of *All the Year Round*, but Dickens pronounced the construction of *The Moonstone* 'wearisome beyond endurance' in a letter to W. H. Wills, adding that the novel's 'vein of obstinate conceit ... makes enemies of readers'.[8]

In terms of periodical publication and repeat buying, it was vital to cultivate readers as friends united by their desire to acquire the next part of the story. At an earlier point in their association, Dickens praised *The Woman in White*, telling Collins 'it grips the difficulties of the weekly portion and throws them in a masterly style', but already suggesting that 'the great pains you take express themselves a trifle too much'.[9] Collins's fellow *Cornhill* contributor Anthony Trollope later observed that he could 'never lose the taste of the construction'.[10] Collins himself described his 'weekly race' to meet periodical deadlines,[11] and on 29 June 1872 he requested a longer first instalment for *The New Magdalen* in *Temple Bar* because he was 'obliged to "grip" the public at starting'.[12] To Cassell's proprietor T. D. Galpin he insisted, 'mine is the only hand which holds the threads of the story, and mine are the only eyes which see it as one complete whole – while others merely see it as a succession of parts'.[13] In the latter stages he complained to James Payn, the prolific novelist and admirer of *The Woman in White*, about rheumatism and the pressure of 'serial work', whilst confirming that he was working 'two months in advance of the Press'.[14] The serial was thus being devised in timed and textual parts to hold the attention of repeat buyers.

Composition and Context

Looking at context, it is surprising to discover that the famed opening sequence of *The Woman in White* does not open the issue of *All the Year Round* in which it appears. For the 26 November 1859 number of the magazine, Dickens contributed the closing chapter and thirty-first instalment of *A Tale of Two Cities*, set at the guillotine. This was a shorter instalment than usual and Collins's future bestseller was further prefaced in the magazine by the editor's prospectus for 'a continuous original work of fiction' to appear in the first 'station' of the magazine. The novel itself began with a 'Preamble' on the third page of the issue, but appeared below Dickens's statement a fifth of the way down the right-hand column. This opening promised 'more than one pen', like the content of the magazine itself, and introduced Walter Hartright at the bottom of the column. It was still a novel poised between the known and relatively unknown authors offered up to a public Dickens was courting in the wake of his damaging split from Bradbury & Evans. Collins later reported having rewritten the first chapter after the proofs were set up in type in order to set the scene for the mystery.[15] Having endured the best of times and the worst of times, the readers of *All the Year Round* were now presented with 'the story of what a Woman's patience can endure, and of what a Man's resolution can achieve'.[16]

Collins was invoked at the beginning of the Dickens serial project and it was to Collins that Dickens returned when sales of the magazine flagged. Dickens himself produced *Great Expectations* to rally his readers after the lacklustre performance of shorter novels by Charles Lever (*A Day's Ride*) and Edward Bulwer-Lytton (*A Strange Story*). Collins's follow-up to *The Woman in White* was trailed in the magazine at the end of *Great Expectations* with the promise of nine months of Collins that became *No Name*.[17] Collins was thus associated with the process of magazine serialisation itself and would return to *All the Year Round* with *The Moonstone* after periods of illness and the lucrative monthly publication of *Armadale*. In the case of *All the Year Round* and *Household Words* he was an employee, but acted as editor under supervision while Dickens was in the United States in 1867–8. He wrote to his mother Harriet on 26 November 1867, 'My very minutes are counted', because he was finishing *No Thoroughfare*, 'conducting All the Year Round – and correcting The Moonstone for its first appearance in London and New York'.[18] His editors Dickens, George Smith, Arthur Locker and the 'Cassell' proprietors were literally banking on him.

Collins would draw attention to serialisation in the prefaces to the volume editions of his novels, and 'the infernal periodical system'[19] that was both a burden and an advantage as he worked 'against the calendar'.[20] The manuscripts demonstrate the process of writing and cutting, but it also appears that seeing the proofs made a difference to the final serial in print. Collins engaged in foreplanning to create a puzzle that would extend 'from week to week', and in a letter to Harriet about a friend's illness he remarked, 'If she would only write a serial story, she would find it impossible to be ill long – the printers would not allow it!'[21]

The note attached to the manuscript of *The Woman in White* held in the J. Pierpont Morgan Library in New York gives important clues about

Collins's working methods and his approach to serialisation.[22] Collins notes that the story was begun at Broadstairs on 15 August 1859 and completed in Harley Street on 26 July 1860. He has moved from his research phase to a respectable metropolitan address. The publication of the novel in weekly parts began on 26 November 1859 three months after the beginning of composition, and by completion on 25 August 1860 Collins was only a few weeks ahead of his deadlines. Collins is quick to point out that parallel publication in *Harper's Weekly* was 'by special arrangement with me', indicating the ongoing struggle for copyright agency.[23] Collins also clarifies his plotting of the novel by referring to the rewriting of the first chapter and opening of the second after proofs were printed, and to the exigent writing of the section he entitles 'Miss Halcombe's Dream'. Despite the gruelling writing schedule reported in his letters, he preserves a sense of the fluency of plotting by declaring: 'The whole of the rest of the Mss was written for the press, once, and once only – exactly as it is here preserved.'[24]

The surviving manuscripts offer other insights into Collins's methods and his response to the duties and constraints of serialisation. As John Sutherland has explained, Collins was called upon for reasons unclear to provide two shorter parts, numbered 16 and 17, for *The Woman in White* in the 10 and 17 March 1860 issues of *All the Year Round*,[25] meaning that 'Miss Halcombe's Dream' was a forced addition, 'made, on the spur of the moment, upon the proofs'.[26] William Baker has examined the manuscript of *No Name* and observes that the form affected content and that Collins's practical instincts made him a master of that form.[27] In *No Name*, for instance, Baker notes that scenic passages are cut for part-publication and that the character of Captain Wragge is rendered more briefly, it having threatened to take over the story.[28] The serial was in a balance between its textual occupation of the columns within the magazine and the potential for one character to dominate. Length was a limitation and this degree of restraint within the evolving vehicle for fiction was an art practised by Collins after his experience of writing *The Woman in White*.

Commodification of Texts

In terms of its print commodity, the overall planned chapters and parts of the next novel, *Armadale*, could not finally be accommodated in the monthly issues of *Cornhill Magazine* and alignments become more ragged as the story progresses.[29] Despite their different styles, Dickens appears to have been happy to exploit Collins's ability to hook an audience, and

Collins therefore returned in 1868 to the weekly format that had given him success with its detailed plotting and breathless curtain lines. In fact, when *The Moonstone* began being serialised on 4 January 1868, *All the Year Round* was again labouring. Even with the prospect of publishing Percy Fitzgerald's *The Dear Girl*, Dickens was already advertising a 'NEW' unnamed 'SERIAL STORY by WILKIE COLLINS' on 5 October 1867, along with their collaboration, later entitled *No Thoroughfare*, to appear in the 'EXTRA DOUBLE NUMBER FOR CHRISTMAS written entirely BY CHARLES DICKENS AND WILKIE COLLINS'.[30] The originally contracted twenty-six parts of *The Moonstone* were perhaps thankfully extended to thirty-two to accommodate the labyrinthine conclusion of the novel in August 1868.[31] Collins then used his new preface to the Smith Elder 1871 edition of the novel to insist that 'the responsibility of the weekly publication of this story' had forced him to overcome illness and pain, and grief at the death of his mother;[32] serialisation was in part another drug that sustained him.

The serial as a periodical form thus influenced the composition, appearance and reception of Collins's novels in a number of significant ways. The family magazine context served to domesticate the sensation or Gothic subject matter. The evolution in parts contributed also to the suspense of this 'spasmodic form'.[33] The appearance of the magazine allowed an exploration of boundaries both textually and paratextually. The serial unfolded within a framework, whether 'conducted by Charles Dickens', set around the genial *Cornhill* table, or illustrated in lurid taste by William Small (*Man and Wife*). The subject matter of the novels was also derived from topics explored in the magazines. This operated in a direct context for examples such as the Road Murder of 1860 (*The Moonstone*) or the experience of the correspondent 'Without a Name' who emerges cured from Bethlehem Hospital during the serialisation of *The Woman in White*;[34] but also indirectly as when the female characters are careful to lock their doors in the same issue of *All the Year Round* as a poem called 'The Caged Lark',[35] or in *Poor Miss Finch* where the heroine is contrasted on the page with the sighted women illustrated in the body of the periodical.

Collins's use of narrative forms to impersonate his characters and their voices also interacted with the miscellaneous contents of the periodicals. During the composition of *The Moonstone*, Dickens described the serial to Wills as 'a series of "Narratives"', and the use of letters, newspaper cuttings, diaries and even a tombstone were part of the manipulation of texts that Collins employed in counterpoint or in competitive dialogue with the pages and columns of the periodicals.[36] Other critics expressed their scepticism about the approach. E. S. Dallas observed 'a miracle of art' in a review of *The Woman in White* when 'Miss Halcombe's diary exactly fits into all the little gaps of Mr Hartright's narrative.'[37] In this same review, Dallas described how a fortnight vital to the mechanics of Sir Percival's deception has been stolen from 'the almanac' in the weekly serialisation, a 'blunder' now replicated in the volume edition of the novel. Collins corrected the chronological error by re-dating the diary when the novel was reprinted in 1861. He then rose in *The Moonstone* to a new height of textual complexity. He refined the voices of his characters and their weekly interactions in such a way that the narrator himself does not know that he is the thief.

The novels in volume form retain traces of their serial production, and a contextual reading of the original serials reinforces an understanding of Collins's approach at the same time as confirming his place in the editorial framework of the magazine itself. In the enabling space of the periodical, the novels are moulded and enhanced by their visual appearance even when there are no illustrations. Collins was conscious of the commodification and materiality of his own texts, and his novels were mediated by the periodical format and by the collectivism of the writing and reading experience.

Collins's serials, their volume editions and the texts deployed for their narrative interrogate that 'gripping' of the portion or instalment identified by Dickens. Collins manipulates and monopolises the timeframe of the novel in ways that become less suspenseful in the volume form. The nineteenth instalment of *The Woman in White*, the seventh extract from Marian's diary, opens with an appeal to the reader in real time: 'The events of yesterday warned me to be ready, sooner or later, to meet the worst. To-day is not yet at an end; and the worst has come.'[38] In the more expansive form of the designedly monthly *Armadale*, where 'Books' operate within the serial and across the periodical, diarist Lydia runs out of paper at the end of 'Book the Fifth Chapter 3 continued' but the serial goes on without her.[39] The May 1866 portion migrates into 'Book the Last' and is instead 'gripped' by a vow from Midwinter at the end of 'Book the Last: Chapter 2': 'She has denied her husband to-night … She shall know her master tomorrow.'[40] Consciousness of the production process informs the reading of Collins's novels at this porous boundary between serial and periodical, narrative and narrative vehicle. His awareness of the material text was the driving force behind the serialisation that defined his career as a novelist.

Notes

1. [W. Collins], 'The Unknown Public', *Household Words* (21 August 1858), p. 219. Hereafter cited as *HW*.
2. W. Collins to Charles Ward, 19 January 1870, in W. Baker, A. Gasson, G. Law and P. Lewis (eds.), *The Public Face of Wilkie Collins: The Collected Letters*, 4 vols. (London: Pickering & Chatto 2005), vol. II, p. 169. Hereafter cited as BGLL.
3. [M. Oliphant], 'Sensation Novels', *Blackwood's Edinburgh Magazine* 41 (May 1862), p. 569.
4. *The Saturday Review* (13 March 1875), p. 357.
5. W. Collins to Cassell, Petter and Galpin, 2 February 1871. BGLL, vol. II, p. 235.
6. W. Collins to W. F. Tindell, 29 January 1875, in W. Baker and W. M. Clarke (eds.), *The Letters of Wilkie Collins*, 2 vols. (London: Macmillan, 1999), vol. II, p. 388. Hereafter cited as B&C.
7. *The Graphic* (13 March 1875), p. 251.
8. C. Dickens to W. H. Wills, 26 July 1868, in M. House, G. Storey and K. Tillotson (eds.), *The Letters of Charles Dickens* (Pilgrim Edition), 12 vols. (Oxford: Clarendon Press, 1965–2002), vol. XII, p. 159. Hereafter cited as Pilgrim.
9. C. Dickens to Collins, 7 January 1860. Pilgrim, vol. IX, p. 195.
10. A. Trollope, *Autobiography*, 2 vols. (London: Blackwood, 1883), vol. I, p. 379.
11. W. Collins to Charles Ward, 11 January 1860. BGLL, vol. I, p. 189.
12. W. Collins to George Bentley, 29 June 1872. BGLL, vol. II, p. 352.
13. W. Collins to T. D. Galpin, 17 August 1869. BGLL, vol. II, p. 147.
14. W. Collins to James Payn, 9 April 1870. BGLL, vol. II, p. 176.
15. See W. Collins, *The Woman in White*, ed. J. Sutherland (Oxford World's Classics, 2008), Appendix A, p. 647. Novel hereafter cited as WW.
16. *All the Year Round* (26 November 1859), p. 95. Hereafter cited as *AYR*.
17. *AYR* (3 September 1861), p. 437.
18. W. Collins to Harriet Collins, 26 November 1867. BGLL, vol. II, p. 92.
19. W. Collins to Harriet Collins, 26 July 1860. B&C, vol. I, p. 184.
20. J. Sutherland, 'Two Emergencies in the Writing of *The Woman in White*', *Yearbook of English Studies* 7 (1977), pp. 148–56 (p. 149).
21. W. Collins to Harriet Collins, 17 August 1865. BGLL, vol. II, p. 19.
22. See Appendix A, WW, pp. 647–8.
23. Ibid., p. 647.
24. Ibid.
25. Ibid., p. 682; Sutherland 'Two Emergencies', p. 150.
26. Appendix A, WW, p. 647.
27. W. Baker, 'The Manuscript of Wilkie Collins's *No Name*', *Studies in Bibliography* 43 (1990), pp. 197–208 (pp. 206, 205).
28. Ibid., p. 199.

29 See C. Delafield, 'Novel/Magazine Interfaces: The "Long" Serialisation of Wilkie Collins's *Armadale*', *Australasian Journal of Victorian Studies* 23.1 (2019), pp. 1–13 (pp. 5–7).
30 *AYR* (5 October 1867), p. 360.
31 G. Law, 'The Professional Writer and the Literary Marketplace', in J. Bourne Taylor (ed.), *The Cambridge Companion to Wilkie Collins* (Cambridge University Press, 2007), pp. 97–111 (p. 101).
32 W. Collins, 'Preface to a New Edition', *The Moonstone*, ed. F. O'Gorman (Oxford World's Classics, 2019), p. lv.
33 [H. L. Mansel], 'Sensation Novels', *Quarterly Review* 113 (April 1863), pp. 481–514 (p. 483).
34 *AYR* (21 January 1860), pp. 291–2.
35 WW, p. 308; *AYR* (31 March 1860), p. 537.
36 Dickens to W. H. Wills, 30 June 1867. Pilgrim, vol. xi, p. 385.
37 *The Times* (30 October 1860), p. 6.
38 *AYR* (31 March 1860), p. 525; WW, p. 293.
39 *Cornhill Magazine* 13 (1866), p. 597.
40 Ibid., p. 610; W. Collins, *Armadale*, ed. Catherine Peters (Oxford World's Classics 2008), p. 616.

CHAPTER 18

Wilkie Collins and Sensation Fiction

Richard Nemesvari

The 3 February 1872 *Vanity Fair* caricature of Wilkie Collins poses him as a forceful and energised storyteller. Leaning forward in his chair, hands on his knees, enormous beard bristling, he focuses intently beyond the frame of the lithograph, the opacity of his spectacles increasing rather than lessening the intensity of his gaze and engagement with his audience (see frontispiece to this volume). Adriano Cecioni, one of the illustrators for the magazine's 'Men of the Day' series, has chosen his subject's posture well, for by the 1870s the epithet had been applied to Collins so often that *Vanity Fair*'s readers would have had no difficulty recognising either its semiotics or its implications, most obviously asserted by Justin MacCarthy's comments almost a decade earlier:

> [i]n our own literature Mr. Wilkie Collins is undoubtedly an admirable storyteller. He is not to be compared for a moment with Mr. Meredith in intellect, and fancy, and true perception of human feeling; but he is a good story-teller, and his books are read everywhere, while Mr. Meredith's novels only extort the half-reluctant admiration of some rare groups of intellectual readers.[1]

Through this contrast with George Meredith, Collins's success as an author is both acknowledged and dismissed, a critical strategy repeated in the biographical sketch accompanying Cecioni's depiction. In it, 'Jehu Junior' (the pen name of Thomas Gibson Bowles, founder and editor of the magazine) observes that 'Mr. Wilkie Collins ... recognised the rudeness of the contrivances hitherto in vogue, and by a far more artistic and conscientious treatment than had yet been attempted, he essayed to revive once more the interest in horrors. He is entitled to be called the novelist who invented Sensation.' This final phrase serves as the caption accompanying the image, which Bowles uses to draw towards his final, ambivalent conclusion:

> He has struck the note of that vast Superstition which lies in all of us as a recognition of the mystery of the world with a happy hand, and piling

> incident upon incident in the most lavish profusion, keeps his reader in a perpetual state of 'jumps' till he chooses to release them. Many of his characters are revolting, some are impossible, but many, like Fosco, are ingenious and startling; and some, like Fairlie, are exquisite.[2]

The assertion that Collins's novels consist only of plots 'piling incident upon incident' with the purpose of jolting his readers, and that his characters are 'revolting' and 'ingenious', 'impossible' and 'exquisite' in equal measure, provides an impressive two-sentence encapsulation of reviewers' responses directed at the author over his long career.

Perhaps equally interesting, however, is that nowhere in the piece appears the phrase 'sensation novel' or 'sensation fiction'. What, after all, does it mean to assert that a specific British novelist 'invented' sensation? As current scholarship notes, such an attribution is problematic on more than one level. Nicholas Daly notes that 'when the term "sensation" first came into widespread use in the early 1860s to describe cultural goods, it was more often identified with the theatre than with fiction',[3] while Graham Law expands this idea geographically by arguing that '[t]he evidence in fact points unmistakably towards the United States as the source of the attributive use of "sensation", with the earliest instances found from the late 1850s in notices of stage melodramas'.[4] At the time, however, *Vanity Fair* could be confident that its attribution would stand.

There can be little doubt, of course, that Bowles has in mind *The Woman in White* (1860), *No Name* (1863), *Armadale* (1866) and *The Moonstone* (1868),[5] Collins's novels of the 1860s that were perceived as foundational texts in the sensation 'craze', but it remains telling that he gives the author credit not for generating a new literary genre, but rather for the response that that genre provokes. In this instance the nineteenth-century magazine seems to concur with modern genre theory, which also problematises the idea that any writer can unilaterally generate a literary category through formalist innovation. It is especially difficult to systematise sensation fiction, since its putative examples vary widely in narrative approach, tone, theme and even plot elements, although this last was used most often to try and unify a disparate set of texts. The sensation novel is an especially apt illustration of Mikhail Bakhtin's position that 'individual examples of the novel are historically active, not a generic canon as such',[6] while Hans Robert Jauss argues that 'it is ... unimaginable that a literary work set itself into an information vacuum .... To this extent, every work belongs to a genre – whereby I mean neither more nor less than that for each work a preconstituted horizon of expectation must be ready at hand.'[7]

The 'horizon of expectation' necessary to classify sensation fiction, and the controversy which arose around it from the late 1850s throughout the 1860s, was produced by a complex mixture of cultural forces, critical reactions, audience demand and authorial responses to these macro-social influences. No single author, however significant, could by themself encompass such interwoven materialist forces.

Further, at the beginning of this process it was far from obvious that Collins was to assume the role of a progenitor even within the parameters being established. Reviews of his early novels had no compunction about attempting to assign him to pre-existing fictional forms, with H. F. Chorley in his unsigned *Athenaeum* review of *Antonina* (1850) feeling the need to 'warn Mr. Collins against the vices of the French school, – against the needless accumulation of revolting details',[8] while an unsigned review of *Basil* (1852) in *Bentley's Miscellany* places that novel in 'the Godwin school of fiction', because 'the *intense* everywhere predominates' (Page: 46). The anonymous reviewer for the *Westminster Review* in 1853 is likewise displeased, since *Basil* seems to 'revel in scenes of fury and passion', which the critic states places it in 'a very objectionable school [that] ... like others of the same kind, has not been without its admirers, [so] we shall state our reasons for condemning it' (Page: 52). These efforts to situate Collins in a somewhat nebulous 'school' of novel writing provide clear forerunners of the attacks that would be aimed at sensation fiction, but at this point they have not coalesced into the specific target necessary to provide a unified chorus of disapproval. Nonetheless, the critical *desire* to generate such a coherent focus for attack is obvious and indicates the increasing unease which prose fiction (and its modes of delivery) were arousing at this collective moment in Britain. Lyn Pykett provides the crucial rhetorical question when she wonders '[w]as the sensation novel actually a distinct genre or subgenre, or was it rather a label applied to a range of novels by certain kinds of reviewer to express and amplify a particular kind of cultural anxiety?'[9] while elaborating on the implied answer by observing that '[f]or many mid-nineteenth-century commentators (especially those writing in the middle-class quarterly reviews) the sensation phenomenon was a morbid symptom of modernity, the product of a commodified literary marketplace'.[10] In addition, we might ask why Collins was eventually so powerfully identified with both the 'label' and the 'cultural anxiety' being generated during this developing 'moment of modernity'.

Certainly, Collins's timing and productivity are important, since his arrival as a novelist at this particularly fraught juncture,[11] reinforced by his family background in the arts, and the sheer subsequent quantity of his writing, gave him a profile that was impossible to ignore. In other words, the cultural work of Wilkie Collins was obvious – but the cultural value of 'Wilkie Collins' as flashpoint for social/literary commentary and genre categorisation needed to be developed over time, and two interrelated elements contributed to that effect. The first was Collins's close and widely recognised relationship with Charles Dickens. Leaving aside questions of mentorship and professional advancement, Dickens eventually provided critics (both contemporary and subsequent) with a foil through which to create taxonomies of value and hierarchy that situated Collins as a minor figure connected to a lesser form of writing.[12] As well, Collins's equally prominent involvement with Victorian theatre (likewise connected to Dickens) established a link with melodrama that was cemented through dramatisations of his novels, both by himself and by unscrupulous theatre managers willing to pirate and capitalise on the success of his plots. The questionable status of this type of entertainment, connected as it was with an ostensibly unrefined mass audience, meant that Collins could act as a bridge between two forms of narrative that were reprobated, and for the same reasons – their supposed unsophisticated reliance on plot over character, and on crude visceral responses over 'proper' emotional engagement. Connected to this, Collins's desire to significantly expand the audience for his writing, to engage with an untapped audience existing beyond the usual outlets for 'serious' fiction, was seen by him as an opportunity to expand his market, but was perceived by others as a debasement of artistic endeavour that needed to be discouraged, if not actually prevented. Reviewers' attempts to construct the sensation novel as mere commodity, as a debased expression of commercialised modernity, was connected to the spectacular triumphs of melodramatic theatre, and allowed mass popularity to be constructed as a betrayal of the purposes of art. Collins's ability to sell widely became a negative indicator of why the newly formulated genre could be rejected, along with the author who came to represent its now-quantified artistic failures.

A real possibility at the time was that Dickens, rather than Collins, could have been construed as the founder of the Victorian sensation novel, as Anne-Marie Beller notes:

> For some critics in the early years of the debates of the 1860s [Dickens] was the leader of the 'sensation school'. One of the earliest uses of the term appeared in a *Sixpenny Journal* review essay, which included *A Tale of Two Cities* (1859) and *Great Expectations* (1860–61) as examples of 'sensation novels', while Margaret Oliphant also included Dickens in her 1862 survey of the trend, comparing *Great Expectations* unfavourably with *The Woman*

in White. However, as the critical campaign hardened, Dickens became conspicuously absent from the attacks levelled at sensation fiction.[13]

This conspicuous absence was based on two aspects of Dickens's success. First, he was simply too popular, and had been so for too long, to serve as a negative example of current novelistic failures. If he was the author who established this 'school', and its threatening excesses, then where had the critics and reviewers, with their worries and warnings, been for the last twenty years? As well, the longer Dickens's career lasted the more obvious it became that a key element of his fame rested on his fictional characters. Although in the Margaret Oliphant review mentioned by Beller the critic disapprovingly questions Dickens's tendency towards 'fantastic eccentricities, and ... high-strained oddity', she also confesses that in the past 'we all awaited with impatience and received with delight the new oddities with which the great novelist filled his pages', – even if that strategy supposedly fails in *Great Expectations*.[14] By 1862 Dickens could not meet the increasingly codified requirements of the domestic novel and psychological realism, but as 'the great novelist' his characters are simply too vividly embedded in Victorian culture to be dismissed. Collins, however, has not achieved that security.

The way in which the two authors are distinguished is rhetorically clever. Over and over in 1860s reviews Collins is associated with the word 'genius', but in such a way as to carefully qualify what is meant by the term. Here is Chorley again, this time writing in the 3 January 1863 *Athenaeum* on sensation fiction and *No Name*:

> At any rate we doubt if any English writer will carry this description of novel writing to a higher pitch of excellence than Mr. Collins. And yet, with all his many merits, we cannot help feeling that he does not belong to the same category as that to which in our own day Thackeray and Dickens and George Eliot have effected their entrance. However, we have no right to look a gift horse in the mouth. *No Name* does not profess to be anything more than an exciting story; and we have only made these remarks because we cannot help think that, with its author's unmistakable genius, he might rise to something higher than even a first-rate sensation novel. (Page: 135)

Along similar lines, an unsigned piece in the 16 June 1866 *Saturday Review* observes that

> Mr. Wilkie Collins has given us, in his latest novel, one more instance of his strange capacity for weaving extraordinary plots. *Armadale*, from beginning to end, is a lurid labyrinth of improbabilities .... To the accomplishment of this object he devotes great ingenuity, a curious genius for arranging and contriving mysteries, and a good deal of what may be called galvanic power. (Page: 151)

This passage is significant, because it introduces another repeated word in the period's response to Collins: ingenuity. The association of Collins with 'genius' is increasingly restricted to complex plots, so that the related but diminished idea that such a skill is merely 'ingenious' (a word applied by Bowles subsequently even to Collins's characters) can lead the same reviewer to declare '[t]he praise which *Armadale* merits for its ingenuity it cannot be said to deserve as a study of character' (Page: 152). A sign of Collins's cultural usefulness in this extended process of canon creation is that 'ingenuity' becomes a definingly dismissive word applied to sensation fiction in general. By reducing Collins's narratives to a series of transiently amusing riddles it becomes possible for an anonymous review in the *Nation* to say of *The Moonstone* that there

> is nothing new in Mr. Collins's stories, if the reader has ever read a book of puzzles, and they serve none of the recognized purposes of the novel. They reflect neither nature nor human life; the actors whom they introduce are nothing but more or less ingenious pieces of mechanism, and they are all alike – like each other and like nothing else. (Page: 174)

The novel's characters are explicitly identified as subsidiary to the mechanisms of the plot, and their resulting inability to meet the 'recognized purposes of the novel' means the entire endeavour collapses. The separation of Dickens from Collins through a carefully contrived separation of their use of character, which allows the older author to be placed in the company of George Eliot and William Makepeace Thackeray, while his younger colleague is placed in a thoroughly secondary position, serves to assign sensation fiction the same status. And the emphasis on plot which plays such a crucial role in this calculation is then available to be reinforced through linkages to melodrama, another form seen as substandard.

The lasting effectiveness of these constructions is demonstrated in T. S. Eliot's 1927 *Times Literary Supplement* essay, 'Wilkie Collins and Dickens'. In it he asserts that 'Dickens excelled in character, the creation of characters of greater intensity than human beings. Collins was not usually strong in the creation of character; but he was a master of plot and situation, of those elements of drama which are most essential to melodrama', and then later that 'Collins, in addition to his particular merits, was a Dickens without genius.'[15] The echoes here of Victorian reviewers, with their faint-praise acknowledgements and ranking system, might even suggest that Eliot read some of them before penning his own evaluation. What remain unstated are the wider cultural forces that, by the early twentieth century, had made assumptions about melodrama's inferiority automatic. As is well known,

Collins met Dickens 'for the first time ... when Wilkie dined with him and was present at a reading of the play *Not so Bad as We Seem*', an amateur production in which Dickens was to star and Collins to play his valet.[16] Not only did this foreshadow their eventual literary standing, but it also once again demonstrated that an association they shared could be used to distinguish between them, since 'it is the imaginative fecundity of Dickens that becomes a cultural yardstick with which to measure, and ultimately belittle, Collins's [melodramatic] art'.[17]

The dramatic impulse that led to sensation scenes in melodrama was easily mapped onto equivalent plots and scenes in sensation fiction. Plays such as Dion Boucicault's *The Colleen Bawn* (1860) and *After Dark* (1868), with their enactment of last-minute daring rescues in life-or-death situations, supported by the most current theatrical effects, not only achieved enormous box office receipts but had audiences returning to repeatedly experience the thrills they provided. Critics argued that those thrills were the *only* reason theatre-goers attended such entertainments, since it was obvious, at least to them, that neither the narratives nor the characters were sufficient to explain such popularity. The quick and phenomenally successful transfer of sensation novels such as Ellen Wood's *East Lynne* (1861) and Mary Elizabeth Braddon's *Lady Audley's Secret* (1862) to the stage, which often entailed a reduction in the number of characters and an increased emphasis on conflict, ensured that the perceived weakness of both forms became combined. As well, the ability of melodrama and sensation fiction to break down audience class boundaries posed a serious challenge to status-quo constructions of social hierarchy. Janice M. Allan argues that 'sensation fiction was perceived as a threat, not simply because it was associated with a variety of "lower" forms, such as melodrama ... but because it was able to disguise such dubious origins and masquerade as more worthy reading material for the middle classes'.[18] Although Collins's successful self-dramatisations of *The Woman in White* (1871), *Man and Wife* (1873), *The New Magdalen* (1873) and *Miss Gwilt* (1875 – the staged version of *Armadale*) occurred in the decade following the height of the sensation fiction debate, this simply confirmed the genre associations that created linkages back and forth between two kinds of sensationalism by then firmly established as subordinate in both artistic and status terms. Which returns us to *Vanity Fair* in 1872. Discussing Walter Benjamin's distinction between oral and print culture, Anastasia Nikolopoulou makes the following observation: '[t]he relationship between melodrama and storytelling goes beyond sharing generic and formal affinities ... The significance of melodrama's kinship to storytelling needs to be sought in their emotional economy. In reviving the performativity of ... narrative, the melodrama also redirects the emotional responses produced in the reader.'[19] Collins's ability to produce powerful storytelling effects, both on the page and in the theatre, ensured a prominent cultural profile even as it allowed him to be labelled in such a way as to undercut the value of his achievements.

The reaction to sensation fiction was never limited to a single author, with Braddon, Wood, Charles Reade, Sheridan Le Fanu and Marie Louise de la Ramée (Ouida), to name only a few of the most prominent writers, also placed in this category and subjected to the dismissals it attracted. But the ideological impetus to create that classification, caused by changing modes of publication, mass entertainment as spectacle, political unrest, gender role uncertainty and imperial tensions, meant that a focal point needed to be generated to concentrate and address the anxieties provoked. Collins, through his prominent working relationship with Dickens, along with his direct, unapologetic connection to Victorian theatre and the melodramatic mode, not to mention his combative prefaces, provided reviewers with an obvious writer around whom to organise their responses. Collins could not individually invent the sensation novel, but he had significant utility as a reification of sensationalism. Contrary to his detractors' attempts at limiting his accomplishments, recognising his very real genius at creating intense reader immersion in fully realised expressions of nascent modernity, through both narrative *and* character, helps expose the tendentious nature of the realism/sensation fiction dichotomy they manufactured. Since we are now in a position to acknowledge that 'attempts to demarcate strict boundaries between "high" and "popular" – "legitimate" and "illegitimate" – forms of fiction were inextricably bound up with the material position of the professional critic at mid-century', we can likewise resist efforts to restrict Collins only to the world of sensation fiction, and accept his role as an unqualifiedly important Victorian novelist.[20]

Notes

[1] J. McCarthy, 'Novels with a Purpose', *Westminster Review* 26 (July 1864), pp. 38–9.
[2] T. Gibson Bowles, 'Men of the Day. No. 39. Mr. Wilkie Collins', *Vanity Fair* 170 (3 February 1872), n.p.
[3] N. Daly, *Sensation and Modernity in the 1860s* (Cambridge University Press, 2009), p. 55.
[4] G. Law, 'Sensation Fiction and the Publishing Industry', in A. Mangham (ed.), *The Cambridge Companion to Sensation Fiction* (Cambridge University Press, 2013), pp. 168–81 (p. 169).
[5] Bowles believes that Collins's 'best work is perhaps "Armadale"'.

6. M. Bakhtin, *The Dialogic Imagination: Four Essays*, ed. M. Holquist, trans. C. Emerson and M. Holquist (Austin: University of Texas Press, 1981), p. 3.
7. H. R. Jauss, *Toward an Aesthetic of Reception*, trans. T. Bahti (Minneapolis: University of Minnesota Press, 1980), p. 79.
8. N. Page (ed.), *Wilkie Collins: The Critical Heritage* (London: Routledge, 1974), p. 41. Further references to this work will appear in the text in parenthesis as Page.
9. L. Pykett, 'Collins and the Sensation Novel', in J. Bourne Taylor (ed.), *The Cambridge Companion to Wilkie Collins* (Cambridge University Press, 2006), pp. 50–64 (p. 50).
10. Ibid., p. 51.
11. See D. Brown, 'Realism and Sensation Fiction', in P. K. Gilbert (ed.), *A Companion to Sensation Fiction* (Oxford: Wiley-Blackwell, 2011), pp. 94–106.
12. See, for example, the unsigned review in *Harper's New Monthly Magazine* of October 1868, which declares that Collins 'writes always good sound English ... but he has none of the delicacies or mannerisms of style which characterize the works of Dickens and Thackeray' (Page, p. 178), and A. Lang in the *Contemporary Review* of January 1890, where the critic states that Collins 'cannot equal ... the excellence of Dickens, of Thackeray, of George Eliot, of Charles Reade, or even of Anthony Trollope. The *genre* of novel to which Mr. Collins devoted himself was lower than theirs' (Page, p. 271).
13. A.-M. Beller, 'Sensation Fiction in the 1850s', in Mangham (ed.), *The Cambridge Companion to Sensation Fiction*, pp. 7–20 (p. 9).
14. M. Oliphant, 'Sensation Novels', in J. Shattock, E. Jay, J. Wilkes and V. Sanders (eds.), *The Selected Works of Margaret Oliphant, Part 1: Literary Criticism and History* (New York: Routledge, 2016), pp. 257, 258.
15. T. S. Eliot, 'Wilkie Collins and Dickens', in R. Dickey, J. Formichelli and R. Schuchard (eds.), *The Complete Prose of T. S. Eliot: The Critical Edition*: Vol. III: *Literature, Politics, Belief, 1927–1929* (Baltimore, MD: Johns Hopkins University Press, 2015), pp. 164–74 (pp. 165, 167).
16. C. Peters, *The King of Inventors* (Princeton University Press, 1991), p. 96.
17. A. Radford, *Victorian Sensation Fiction: A Reader's Guide to Essential Criticism* (Basingstoke: Palgrave Macmillan, 2009), p. 24.
18. J. M. Allan, 'The Contemporary Response to Sensation Fiction', in Mangham (ed.), *The Cambridge Companion to Sensation Fiction*, pp. 84–98 (p. 92).
19. A. Nikolopoulou, 'Historical Disruptions: The Walter Scott Melodramas', in M. Hays and A. Nikolopoulou (eds.), *Melodrama: The Cultural Emergence of a Genre* (New York: St Martin's Press, 1996), pp. 121–43 (p. 135).
20. J. M. Allan, 'Introduction: "Other Sensations"', *Critical Survey* 23.1 (2011), p. 3.

CHAPTER 19

Wilkie Collins and Scott

Lizhen Chen

When Sir Walter Scott died at Abbotsford on 21 September 1832, Wilkie Collins was only eight years old. There is no proof of his direct personal association with the Scottish novelist. It is widely known, nevertheless, that Collins was a great admirer of Scott. He was one of Collins's favourite novelists, along with James Fenimore Cooper and Honoré de Balzac. Collins termed these three great novelists 'the three Kings of fiction'.[1] This is emphasised by the many references in his letters: 'a hundred and fiftieth reading of the glorious Walter Scott' (B&C II: 453); 'reading "A Legend of Montrose" again for the 100th time' (B&C II: 482); or 'reading "Guy Mannering" again for the 50th time at least' (B&C II: 540). As a towering figure in the field of nineteenth-century British literature, Scott became a role model for young writers. His centrality to the English novel in the first decades of the nineteenth century was certified by the amazing number of sales. William St Clair argues that 'During the romantic period, the "Author of Waverley" sold more novels than all the other novelists of the time put together.'[2] The strong influence of Scott could also be seen in his impact on contemporary writers and the younger generation of novelists. When Collins started his literary career in the 1840s, the historical novel was still highly influential in the United Kingdom, though incomparable to the vogue that reached its peak in the 1820s. Many young writers imitated Scott's style and followed the trail he blazed.

Collins's deep attachment to Scott can probably be traced back to his parents. As is known, Collins was taught at home by his mother Harriet, who was a governess before marriage, until he was eleven years old. His mother's favourite novelist was Walter Scott.[3] It is reasonable to draw the conclusion that the literary taste of his mother had quite a strong influence on him. While receiving his early education at home, the young Collins

> immersed himself in his mother's collection of Ann Radcliffe's Gothic romances and the poetry of Shakespeare, Pope, Scott, Shelley, and Byron,

as well as the usual fictional fare of a middle-class boy of the nineteenth century: tales of Robin Hood, *Don Quixote*, *The Vicar of Wakefield*, *The Arabian Nights Entertainment*, and the novels of Frederick Marryat and Sir Walter Scott.[4]

Collins showed good potential for storytelling, which paved the way for him to become a good writer in the future.

He had a more tangible connection with Scott through his father, William Collins, a famous landscape painter, and his godfather David Wilkie, a highly distinguished Scottish painter from whom Wilkie Collins got his middle name. David Wilkie was a close friend of Scott's, and is mentioned many times in Scott's letters, journals and diary. David Wilkie painted portraits for Scott and his family and contributed illustrations for the Magnum Opus edition of the 'Waverley Novels'. William Collins was acquainted with Scott, William Wordsworth, Robert Southey and many other famous men of letters of his time. In August 1822, William Collins and David Wilkie went to Scotland on a tour recording the historical moments of King George IV's official visit to Edinburgh and painting Scottish landscapes. They also visited Scott at his home at Abbotsford. William Collins wrote a letter asking his fiancée Harriet Geddes to come to Edinburgh where they could solve their matrimonial problem and be married. In consideration of the insecure financial status of William Collins, his parents did not give consent to the marriage. A new Marriage Act, which required the oaths and formal consent of parents for marriages in England, but not Scotland, had been passed on 22 July 1822. The marriage took place in the English Episcopal Church in Edinburgh in September 1822. After the marriage, the couple lived at 11 New Cavendish Street, London, where Wilkie Collins was born on 8 January 1824.

At the age of seventeen, Collins left school, was apprenticed to the tea merchant Mr E. Antrobus, and went into the tea trade profession in 1841. In the summer of 1842, Collins paid a visit to Edinburgh and the Shetland Islands of Scotland with his father, who accepted a commission from the Edinburgh publisher Robert Cadell to illustrate the Waverley edition of Scott's novel *The Pirate*, the scenes of which were also set in the Orkney and Shetland Islands.[5] They went on an expedition to Sumburgh Head to relive the dramatic experience of Captain Cleveland's shipwreck in Scott's historical novel. In his *Memoirs of the Life of William Collins, Esq., R.A.* (1848), a book that was finished as a fulfilment of his father's wish,[6] Collins recorded his father's sketching of the scene from Scott's novel in vivid detail:

the immense precipice of Sumburgh Head, hanging over as if it would fall into the sea, with the waves writhing about its jagged base, and hundreds on hundreds of sea-birds whirling above its mighty summit, was, he declared, one of the sublimest natural objects he had ever beheld. He made a careful sketch of it from the beach; from which he produced a striking and original illustration of the scene in 'The Pirate', where Cleveland is saved from the wreck of his vessel by Mordaunt Mertoun.[7]

Altogether, Collins witnessed his father sketch five views for *The Pirate*, which were engraved for the Abbotsford edition of the novel, and during this trip they 'paid a pilgrimage' to Abbotsford.[8] Perhaps Collins took inspiration from his journey to Scotland and visit to Scott's home, as he developed a stronger interest in literature and started to read and write intensely. Collins depicted Scotland in his novels *Man and Wife* (1870) and *The Law and the Lady* (1875), and addressed the issues of political and cultural conflicts between England and Scotland. Anne Longmuir maintains that 'like Scott, Collins subscribes to the commonly held perception of Scotland as a country divided between the metropolitan and sophisticated Lowlands and the rugged and barbaric Highlands'.[9] As an English novelist, Collins focused mainly on life and events that happened in England.

The widely acknowledged debut of Collins was his short story 'The Last Stage Coachman', which appeared in *The Illuminated Magazine* in August 1843, and throughout his career Collins lavished praise on Scott.[10] Like many readers in the first decades of the nineteenth century, he regarded Scott as the leading novelist of his day. In a letter to William Winter of 14 January 1883, he wrote: 'An armchair and a cigar – and a hundred and fiftieth reading of the glorious Walter Scott (King, Emperor, President, and God Almighty of Novelists) – there is the regimen that is doing me good!'[11] As an ardent admirer, Collins had a large collection of Walter Scott's books. Graham Law and Andrew Maunder note that 'At his death his library contained nearly a hundred well-thumbed volumes by the writer, including the poetical works and miscellaneous prose, in addition to the Waverley Novels themselves.'[12] William Baker observes that in Collins's library there were four multi-volume editions of Walter Scott.[13]

It seems that among all of Scott's novels, *The Antiquary* was Collins's favourite. In a letter to J. A. Stewart of 9 January 1888, he held that 'After more than thirty years' study of the Art, I consider Walter Scott to be the greatest of all novelists, and "The Antiquary" is, as I think, the most perfect of all novels' (B&C 11: 552). It was not the only occasion in which Collins expressed his opinion in this way. He held, in a letter written on 29 December 1883, that Scott deserved well the baronetcy conferred on him and that he 'ought to have been created a Prince if he had only written "The Antiquary" and "Ivanhoe"' (B&C 11: 464). When Collins became a writer, he often made references to Scott and his work in his own novels.

For example, he introduced the 'Deaf Mute' character Madonna (Mary Grice) in *Hide and Seek* (1854). As he stated clearly in a note to his book, he did this in order to exhibit the effects and afflictions produced by the loss of sensory faculties, and mentioned the famous Fenella in Scott's *Peveril of the Peak* as an example of the same type of character.[14] In chapter 10 of *The Law and the Lady*, a novel serialised in *The Graphic* from 1874 to 1875, Collins mentions the books of Scott alongside Voltaire and Shakespeare. In chapter 2 of Book VII of *The Fallen Leaves* (1879), when the hero Amelius Goldenheart goes into his library and reads *Rob Roy*, Collins's narrator states: 'Wisely inspired, he turned to the truer history next, which men call fiction. The writings of the one supreme genius, who soars above all other dramatists – the writings of Walter Scott – had their place of honour in his library.'[15] *Heart and Science*, Collins's book about science and vivisection in the Victorian age, was serialised in *The Manchester Weekly Times* from July 1882 to January 1883 and in *Belgravia* from August 1882 to June 1883. When it was published in volume form in 1883, Collins wrote a preface explaining how he came to think of writing this book. He quoted opinions from three people: Shakespeare, Scott and Michael Faraday. In a letter to Hall Caine of 15 March 1888, Collins talked about the importance of contrast in literature. He argued that *Hamlet* and *The Bride of Lammermoor* were 'two of the greatest of tragic stories', asking Hall Caine to notice 'how Shakespeare and Scott take every opportunity of presenting contrasts, and brightening the picture at the right place' (B&C 11: 554). Collins also made brief references to Scott and his 'Waverley Novels' in his essay 'The Unknown Public' (1858); in Book II, chapter 3 of his novel *Armadale* (1866); in his story 'The Poetry Did it: An Event in the Life of Major Evergreen' (1885); in his novella *The Guilty River* (1886); and in many other places. These allusions to Scott are traces of the high tribute Wilkie Collins paid to this great novelist and the tradition that he started.

At the same time, as a biographer, he had a high opinion of J. G. Lockhart's biography, *Memoirs of the Life of Sir Walter Scott* (1837–8). He published his short story 'Your Money or Your Life' in the *Belgravia* 1881 Christmas number, which 'draws upon an episode in the fifth volume of J. G. Lockhart's *The Life of Sir Walter Scott* for the foundation of this story'.[16] Collins published the essay 'Books Necessary for a Liberal Education' in *Pall Mall Gazette* on 11 February 1886. He recommended, in a frank way, to inexperienced readers some of the books that would educate them and make them better Christians. In his mind, the most valuable result of a liberal education was to produce good citizens. He took Scott and Dickens to be two of his most trustworthy writers and chose Lockhart's *Life of Sir Walter Scott* as a masterpiece of biographical work for general reading.

While an apprentice with the London tea merchants Antrobus & Co., Collins started to write the novel *Ioláni; or, Tahíti as it Was: A Romance* in the autumn of 1844. It was rejected by Longman and Chapman & Hall in 1845 and was never published in his lifetime. The manuscript was rediscovered in 1991 and published by Princeton University Press in 1999. This novel is a mixture of sensational plot, Gothic romance, 'exotic' atmosphere and historical imagination. The book's editor, Ira Nadel, makes clear Collins's indebtedness to Scott: 'For Collins, Scott represented the historical in fiction and the successful union of fact with imagination. In using Scottish history to fashion his stories, Scott showed Collins how to employ actual events in an imaginative construct.'[17] Law and Maunder hold that 'Collins's passion for Scott is reflected already in the choice of subject of his first two novels, both historical romances, which at the same time make a claim to documentary accuracy.'[18] He published his first novel *Antonina; or, The Fall of Rome* in 1850, which was, at a first glance at its title, a historical romance in the style of Scott and tinged with the colour of the works of Edward Gibbon and Edward Bulwer-Lytton. *Antonina* was quite a success and paved a solid way for Collins's literary career. It received many favourable comments:

> *The Observer*, for instance, described it as 'a remarkable book', and the *Morning Post* hailed it as 'sufficient to place [its author] in the very first rank of English novelists'. In addition to these, *Harper's* (July 1850) lauded its 'splendour of imagination', and the *Athenaeum* (No. 2) and the *Eclectic Review* (April 1850) both compared Collins to Shakespeare.[19]

As a major writer in the Victorian age, Wilkie Collins was highly energetic and inventive. Even though he worshipped Scott, he would not stick to his old-fashioned style. In his second novel *Basil* (1852), he switched his orientation and wrote the story with a contemporary setting. Collins achieved great fame in the 1860s with a series of novels including *The Woman in White* (1860), *No Name* (1863), *Armadale* (1866) and *The Moonstone* (1868). When Collins published *The Moonstone*, he was renowned as a master of the 'sensation novel'. The subtitle of *The Moonstone* is 'A Romance', which can be considered as his effort to revive this literary genre. In nineteenth-century English literature, the success of 'romance', which emphasised the qualities of fictionality and things that are different from real existence and daily life, is attributed to Gothic romance, and to Walter Scott and his historical romances. Daniel Brown holds that 'Scott and Austen both shift the focus on literature away from the shocking and inexplicable events of the Gothic and towards the sober explorations of individual psychology which distinguish realism.'[20] A dominant mode of the English novel in the Victorian age was domestic realism, which was reinforced by the works of William Makepeace Thackeray, Anthony Trollope, George Eliot, Elizabeth Gaskell and many other novelists. It was defined by believable descriptions of the daily lives of common people. Collins went against the grain. His name was often associated with the genre of sensation fiction which was formally inaugurated by *The Woman in White*. In this sense, Collins inherited the literary legacy of Walter Scott. He fostered and enhanced Scott's merit of wrapping the imaginary and romantic in a realistic and concrete historical setting. With his genius and inventiveness, Collins infused elements of suspense, violence and mystery into his work to create his modern urban romances.

Notes

[1] W. Baker and W. M. Clarke (eds.), *The Letters of Wilkie Collins*, 2 vols. (London: Macmillan, 1999), vol. II, p. 476. Hereafter cited parenthetically in the text as B&C.

[2] W. St Clair, *The Reading Nation in the Romantic Period* (Cambridge University Press, 2004), p. 221.

[3] I. B. Nadel, 'Introduction' to W. Collins, *Ioláni; or, Tahíti as It Was: A Romance*, ed. I. B. Nadel (Princeton University Press, 1999), p. xvi.

[4] L. Pykett, *Authors in Context: Wilkie Collins* (Oxford University Press, 2005), p. 4.

[5] A. Lycett, *Wilkie Collins: A Life of Sensation* (London: Hutchinson, 2013), p. 53.

[6] Pykett, *Authors in Context*, pp. 8–9.

[7] W. Collins, *Memoirs of the Life of William Collins, Esq., R.A.: With Selections from His Journals and Correspondence*, 2 vols. (London: Longman, Brown, Green, and Longmans, 1848), vol. II, pp. 217–18.

[8] Lycett, *Wilkie Collins*, p. 53.

[9] A. Longmuir, 'The Scotch Verdict and Irregular Marriages: How Scottish Law Disrupts the Normative in *The Law and the Lady* and *Man and Wife*', in

A. Mangham (ed.), *Wilkie Collins: Interdisciplinary Essays* (Newcastle: Cambridge Scholars Publishing, 2007), pp. 166–77 (p. 167).
[10] In 2008, Daniel Hack discovered a reprint of a previously undiscovered short story, 'Volpurno', which was published in New York on 8 July 1843 in *The Albion, or British, Colonial, and Foreign Weekly* and at least two other periodicals.
[11] W. Collins to William Winter, 14 January 1883. B&C, vol. II, p. 543.
[12] G. Law and A. Maunder, *Wilkie Collins: A Literary Life* (Basingstoke: Palgrave Macmillan, 2008), p. 12.
[13] W. Baker, *Wilkie Collins's Library: A Reconstruction* (Westport, CT, and London: Greenwood, 2002), p. 37.
[14] W. Collins, *Hide and Seek* (London: Sampson Low, 1861), p. 355.
[15] W. Collins, *The Fallen Leaves*, 2 vols. (Leipzig: Bernhard Tauchnitz, 1879), vol. II, p. 100.
[16] W. Baker, *A Wilkie Collins Chronology* (Basingstoke: Palgrave Macmillan, 2007), p. 187.
[17] Nadel, 'Introduction' to Collins, *Ioláni*, p. xxxiv.
[18] Law and Maunder, *Wilkie Collins*, p. 12.
[19] N. Page (ed.), *Wilkie Collins: The Critical Heritage* (London and New York: Routledge, 1974), p. 6.
[20] D. Brown, 'Realism and Sensation Fiction', in P. K. Gilbert (ed.), *A Companion to Sensation Fiction* (Oxford: Wiley-Blackwell, 2011), pp. 94–106 (p. 95).

CHAPTER 20

Wilkie Collins and Dickens

Emily Bell

Although Wilkie Collins was twelve years younger than Charles Dickens, first meeting the more established writer on 12 March 1851 at the age of twenty-seven (Dickens was thirty-nine), Collins was never numbered among Dickens's 'young men'. This group of younger writers who gathered around Dickens, first at his journal *Household Words* (1850–9) and then *All the Year Round* (1859–70), and including among their number George Augustus Sala, Edmund Yates, Blanchard Jerrold, James Payn and John Hollingshead, were viewed largely as imitating the style of their 'Chief'. Collins's collaboration with one of the most monumental literary figures of the age was of a very different nature.

Academic approaches to literary collaboration have shifted over time. Lillian Nayder's *Unequal Partners: Charles Dickens, Wilkie Collins, and Victorian Authorship* (2001) highlighted the gap in scholarship about collaborative literary work in the Victorian period, coming as it did after the solidification of a romantic idea of the man of letters as hero and lone genius, and taking place amidst a changing legal framework for understanding copyright and intellectual property. Nayder's volume brings the focus back to collaboration as creative partnership, exploring not only the specific collaborative writing of the two authors but also the imaginative influence each had on the other's individual works. More recently, Martin Hewitt's work on generations (2019) has shown how formative experiences such as major political events and cultural shifts created a sense of community and shared interests among Victorians of the same generation. Collins and Dickens were arguably of different generations, and thus the dynamics of this relationship had a significant impact on the development of each writer, pushing each to experiment in ways their other collaborators and literary peers did not, beyond the boundaries of a mentor-disciple relationship and also beyond a shared generational background.

These changing attitudes to collaboration and influence are also evident in the authors' afterlives: for example, Dan Simmons's biofictional novel

Drood (2009), about Dickens, Collins and mesmeric influence after the Staplehurst railway accident of 1865, explores the psychological and subtle nature of influence, suggesting a more deliberate manipulation of Collins by Dickens. Nayder's work is similarly critical of the older writer, situating the two writers in an ongoing conflict of political difference, competing priorities (i.e., Dickens's focus on his journals as under his conductorship, and Collins's desire to build a name for himself) and problematic family ties – both Collins's unconventional relationships, and Dickens's growing exasperation with Collins's younger brother, who married Dickens's daughter Katey in 1860 and suffered from ill health for the entirety of their married life.

Our understanding of Collins's place among Dickens's circle is further influenced by the deliberate shaping of Dickens's posthumous reputation enacted by friends, family and biographers after the author's death in June 1870: the first major biography of the author (1872–4), written by his friend John Forster, minimises the role of Collins in Dickens's life, focusing as it does on Dickens's letters to Forster (incidentally, born the same year as Dickens and thus part of the same generation). Although Collins did not publish a biography of Dickens, what we know of his marked copy of Forster's *Life of Charles Dickens*, sold at auction and lost to private hands, shows that he would have most likely been more critical than Forster: where Forster had written that Dickens was 'the most popular novelist of the century', Collins added 'after Walter Scott'.[1] He disagreed with Forster's judgment in several places, including his description of Dickens's personal characteristics. This scrap of critical and biographical judgment is one of the only pieces of evidence remaining to modern scholars: Dickens's burning of his correspondence also contributes to the rather one-sided view of their friendship which can be found in scholarship on the two writers. In 1860, Dickens made a bonfire of his correspondence, and this practice of destroying letters was carried out periodically over the following years.

The friendship between the two writers spanned nearly twenty years: Collins and Dickens were introduced by the artist Augustus Egg in 1851, who was assisting Dickens with putting together an amateur theatrical troupe to perform Edward Bulwer-Lytton's *Not so Bad as We Seem*, which was to be played at Devonshire House before the Queen. The friendship which formed between the two men continued until Dickens's death in 1870, although with increasing distance during the 1860s. Collins's first contribution to *Household Words*, 'The Traveller's Story of a Terribly Strange Bed', appeared in April 1852. A follow-up story,

'Mad Monkton', was rejected by Dickens in February 1853, while 'Gabriel's Marriage' appeared in April 1853. Other works of Collins's which appeared in *Household Words* include 'Sister Rose', and its backdrop of the French Revolution may have inspired Dickens in the preparation of *A Tale of Two Cities* (1859).

Friendship with Dickens gave Collins access to other major writers of the day, including George Eliot, William Makepeace Thackeray and Elizabeth Gaskell, among others. The older writer's encouragement continued throughout their acquaintance, with Collins becoming a regular contributor to *Household Words* from 1852. Collins's contributions to *Household Words* increased from spring 1856, and he was appointed a staff writer later that year. Dickens wrote to his subeditor W. H. Wills when proposing the appointment: 'He is very suggestive, and exceeding quick to take my notions. Being industrious and reliable besides, I don't think we should be at an additional expense of £20 in the year by the transaction.'[2] Collins accepted the position, but was perhaps not as suggestible as Dickens hoped, ensuring it was understood that any new, long story would appear under his name. In that year, the Christmas number was, for the first time, co-written by Collins and Dickens. Collins would resign his staff position at *All the Year Round* in January 1861, after five years, and the two writers would not collaborate again until 'No Thoroughfare' in 1867, although Collins contributed a chapter to the short story, 'Tom Tiddler's Ground', which formed the 1861 Christmas number. While Collins was no longer a staff writer, he took over the editorship of *All the Year Round* temporarily in 1867 while Dickens was in the United States.

In addition to their working relationship, Collins holidayed with Dickens on several occasions. Their various excursions formed the basis for articles and stories; this is particularly evident in 'The Lazy Tour of Two Idle Apprentices', published in *Household Words* in 1857, which presents a fictionalised account of a walking tour of Cumberland taken by the two writers. The closeness of one's relationship to Dickens, at least in the words of his friends and family after his death, was indicated by engagement with the author's family, invitations to his home and inclusion in holidays. Thus it is significant that Collins acted in theatricals at Dickens's home, Tavistock House, including the 1855 Twelfth Night theatricals, and his holidays with Dickens included a long stay at Folkestone in the same year, where planning for the Christmas number, *The Holly Tree Inn*, took place; Collins contributed 'The Ostler' (1855). Collins's excursions with Dickens included an extended holiday to

Switzerland and Italy in 1853, as well as visits to Paris and night walking in London in search of material for the journals. In 1856, Collins spent six weeks in Paris living next door to Dickens and his family.

As many of Dickens's young men noted after his death, their 'Chief' was a firm and rather overbearing editor, making radical changes to their copy to ensure a consistent editorial tone, and largely publishing their writing anonymously while signing his own contributions in journals 'conducted' by Dickens. Collins was, in many ways, an exception to this: the success of his early serialised works meant that eventually Collins's own name appeared attached to his work, and not just 'By the author of . . .'. *The Dead Secret* and *The Moonstone*, for example, appeared under Collins's name, at the writer's insistence, after the successful but anonymous run of *The Woman in White* in *All the Year Round* in 1859. However, Dickens's heavy-handed editing occasionally makes it difficult to disentangle the work of the two writers, most notably in the case of 'No Thoroughfare', 'A House to Let' and 'The Lazy Tour of Two Idle Apprentices', for which there is no surviving manuscript. The discovery of an annotated set of *All the Year Round* in 2015 brought to light new articles written by Collins but published anonymously, as well as revealing that Collins had mistakenly been credited with several other pieces which appeared in the journal's pages. In a letter to the publisher Frederic Chapman, who was hoping to ascertain which parts of 'No Thoroughfare' Collins had written so that he could cut them out, Collins claimed: 'I inserted passages in his chapters, and he inserted passages in mine. I can only tell you that we as nearly as possible *halved* the work. We put the story together in the Swiss chalet at Gad's Hill, and we finished the Fourth Act side by side at two desks in his bedroom at Gad's Hill.'[3] This invocation of the private, domestic space – Dickens's country home at Gad's Hill, Kent, and the Swiss chalet in its grounds in which he wrote during the summer – resists the easy delineation of the work of the two men, highlighting the blurring of the personal and professional, and the importance of the time the writers spent together, at home and abroad, in their literary collaboration.

Dickens's decision to keep contributions to his journals largely anonymous, though very much in keeping with common practice in newspapers and periodicals at the time, caused some friction between the two men. Collins's aim to create a reputation for himself was at odds with this policy, and Nayder argues that these tensions were heightened by political differences, suggesting the conflict is most evident in 'The Perils of Certain English Prisoners' (1857). Dickens was also more conservative than his young friend, and some frustration with Collins's choice of themes, as well as his unconventional lifestyle, coloured their personal and professional interactions. Dickens was clearly both attracted and repelled by Collins's more radical politics and relationships: the two men explored the underbelly of London and Paris together, Dickens writing, when in need of a break from *Hard Times* (1854):

> The interval I propose to pass in a career of amiable dissipation and unbounded license in the metropolis. If you will come and breakfast with me about midnight – anywhere – any day – and go to bed no more until we fly to these pastoral retreats – I shall be delighted to have so vicious an associate.[4]

Dickens's advice to, and encouragement of, his 'vicious associate' were vital. He was the first to recognise the originality of *Basil* (1852), Collins's first novel of contemporary life, which drew hostile reviews for its outspoken depiction of sexual obsession. Collins dedicated his third novel, *Hide and Seek* (1854), to Dickens 'as a token of admiration and affection'; this is the most obviously Dickensian of his novels, drawing on Collins's own childhood experiences. Dickens's later criticisms of Collins's writing centred on narration and style: for example, he was critical of the use of multiple narrators in *The Moonstone* (1868). Dickens's unfinished novel, *The Mystery of Edwin Drood* (1870), has been seen as a response to Collins's themes of imperialism and an attempt by Dickens to write a sensational novel, in the vein of Collins's work. The two writers' work on *The Frozen Deep* (1857), and in particular its staging, influenced Dickens's *A Tale of Two Cities* (1859). The theatrical collaborations between the two men had a clear impact on their individual works: in particular, the connections between melodrama as a theatrical mode and sensation fiction as a genre.

The first connection between the writers centred on the stage rather than the page, and Collins wrote his first play, *The Lighthouse*, in 1855, performing it at Tavistock House, before having it professionally staged at the Olympic Theatre in 1857. This was followed by *The Frozen Deep*, which was also staged by Dickens's amateur company before having a professional run in the Free Trade Hall in Manchester. Dickens, playing the lead, met and began his relationship with the actor Ellen Ternan, who had been brought in with her mother and sister to replace Dickens's sister-in-law and daughters' roles. After the failure of *The Red Vial* (1858), Collins returned his focus to journalism. At around this time, the relationship between the two men grew more distant; this coincided with Dickens's separation from his wife, Catherine, in favour of Ternan, while Collins was establishing a household with Caroline Graves. The marriage of Collins's brother Charles to Dickens's daughter Katey, a match of which Dickens disapproved, increased this sense of separation. The last existing correspondence between the two men took place in January 1870, when Dickens wrote a legal formal letter acknowledging Collins's copyright in the articles written for his journals. An accompanying note on Collins's health, reflecting the rather awkward and detached nature of their relationship by this time, ends 'I don't come to see you, because I don't want to bother you. Perhaps you may be glad to see me bye and bye. Who knows!'[5] Dickens died only five months later.

The influence the two writers had on each other is complex and multifaceted: a shared love of the theatre led to many fruitful collaborations, and manifested thematically in the novels of both. Collins's more sensational style influenced Dickens's later experiments, most notably *A Tale of Two Cities* and *The Mystery of Edwin Drood*, while *Hide and Seek* is, in turn, the most Dickensian of Collins's novels. There are shared thematic interests, from disenfranchisement to illegitimacy, empire and crime. Dickens's rather heavy editorial hand can be felt in Collins's pieces for *Household Words* and *All the Year Round*, and yet Collins was never the servile imitator of Dickens that other contributors to the journals were (or were seen to be). The nature of the relationship transcends the 'Chief' and his 'young men' dynamic that many other writers had with Dickens, with Collins a more confident, independent literary force. However, there is still research to be done on the extent and nature of their collaboration, including the division of several collaborative texts. This collaborative model has, perhaps, the most in common with theatrical writing, and the mutual enthusiasm for the theatre shared by Collins and Dickens was potentially also responsible for the more fluid, adaptive nature of their nearly twenty years of collaboration.

Notes

[1] 'Wilkie Collins About Charles Dickens (From a Marked Copy of Forster's "Dickens")', *Pall Mall Gazette* (20 January 1890), p. 3.
[2] C. Dickens to W. H. Wills, 16 September 1856, in M. House, G. Storey and K. Tillotson (eds.), *The Letters of Charles Dickens* (Pilgrim Edition), 12 vols. (Oxford: Clarendon Press, 1965–2002), vol. VIII, p. 188. Hereafter cited as Pilgrim.
[3] Quoted in F. G. Kitton, *The Minor Writings of Charles Dickens* (London: Elliott Stock, 1900), p. 173.
[4] C. Dickens to W. Collins, 12 July 1854. Pilgrim, vol. VII, p. 366.
[5] C. Dickens to W. Collins, 27 January 1870. Pilgrim, vol. XII, p. 471.

CHAPTER 21

Wilkie Collins, Mary Braddon and Other Women Writers

Jeanette Roberts Shumaker

In an 1887 interview, the popular sensation novelist Mary Elizabeth Braddon said that 'Wilkie Collins is my literary father', according to Susan Calovini in 'A "Secret" Novel of Her Own'.[1] Yet Braddon's works were long forgotten, unlike Collins's. In their 2014 introduction to *Rediscovering Victorian Women Sensation Writers*, Anne-Marie Beller and Tara MacDonald write that Braddon 'arguably constitutes one of the most successfully recovered authors of modern times'.[2] Wilkie Collins's masterpiece *The Woman in White* (1860) pioneered the sensation novel's depiction of doubles, crime and criminals, madness, secrets, amateur detectives, gender issues, captivity and impersonation that Braddon reworked in her bestselling *Lady Audley's Secret* (1862). Collins's influence on Braddon and other female sensation novelists of the 1860s has been extensively explored by leading scholars such as Jenny Bourne Taylor. In her *In the Secret Theatre of Home* (1988), Bourne Taylor contends that both novelists critique the Victorian Angel in the House: 'Collins and Braddon are each in different ways challenging the blonde child-wife stereotype.'[3]

Unlike Collins's impact on Braddon, Braddon's apparent influence on Collins's sensation novels written after *Lady Audley's Secret* has not been exhaustively examined. Collins's *Armadale* (1866) shows the influence of *Lady Audley's Secret* through its portrayal of a murderess who is a more complex and sympathetic figure than Braddon's. Another way in which *Armadale* shows an affinity with *Lady Audley's Secret* is through its focus upon male friendship. In *The Woman in White*, there is a friendly alliance between the two villains, Count Fosco and Sir Percival Glyde, with the older Fosco acting as a father figure who manipulates the younger man. In *Lady Audley's Secret*, however, a close friendship between two young men is a catalyst for the plot, motivating an amateur detective, Robert Audley, to pursue the woman who he believes murdered his best friend, George Talboys. In *Armadale*, an even closer friendship between two young men dominates the lengthy novel, queering it further than *Lady Audley's Secret*.

The homosocial friendship in *Armadale* challenges Victorian prejudice more than the one in *Lady Audley's Secret* does, since one of the friends in *Armadale*, Ozias Midwinter, has a Black mother and grew up poor, experiencing homelessness, beatings and manual labour. By contrast, in Braddon's novel, Robert and George are both white and affluent. By making Midwinter the protagonist of *Armadale*, Collins challenges racism and class snobbery to an extent rarely seen in nineteenth-century British fiction.

A further reason that *Armadale* is a more thought-provoking novel than *Lady Audley's Secret* is that *Armadale* includes a diary written by a murderess, along with letters to her accomplices, which help readers understand her motives, whereas Braddon's murderess remains somewhat opaque. Both negative and positive traits make Collins's killer, Lydia Gwilt, a more appealing, well-developed figure than Braddon's would-be killer, Lady Audley. Beaten across the face by her habitually abusive first husband, Lydia poisoned him. By contrast, Lady Audley tried to kill the husband who was devoted to her in order to protect her bigamous second marriage to a wealthy aristocrat. Though Lady Audley occasionally takes laudanum to escape her fear that her crimes might be discovered, Lydia seems to be addicted to it: she comments in her diary, '"Drops," you are a darling!'[4] Lydia's guilt, loneliness and despair cause her addiction and suicide attempts. After Lydia's second husband, a rogue from Cuba, abandoned her, she tried to kill herself for the first time. As well as using drugs, Lydia copes with depression by playing the piano at a level of proficiency that allows her to give music lessons and perform in lowly professional venues. Lydia's skill as a pianist along with her eloquence as a letter writer suggest that her mental powers exceed Lady Audley's. In addition, Lydia is a sympathetic character because she falls in love with Midwinter, even though he is neither wealthy nor white. She remarks, 'Why not live out all the days that are left to me, happy and harmless in a love like this!' (A: 616). By contrast, Lady Audley pities the aristocratic husband she deceives, but does not love him. Lydia ends up poisoning herself after accidentally nearly killing Midwinter, when she had intended to kill his rich namesake, Allan Armadale. Lydia's suicide seems to be a twisted gesture of atonement for her crimes, perhaps moving readers to forgive her when she writes to Midwinter: 'It is not hard for me to die, now I know you will live' (A: 806). Unlike Lydia, Lady Audley gives no sign that she repents of her crimes.

Greed drives both Lady Audley and Lydia to try to kill their husbands (or pretend husbands) to enable them to benefit from counterfeit marriages to wealthy men. Lacking mothers, both women were raised by erratically paid women who beat and at times starved them. As a result, they grew up overvaluing wealth, and learned to see their beauty and charm as the traits that would enable them to avoid poverty by marrying up. Collins and Braddon suggest that murder can be the result of such a commodification of women.

Avoiding such mercenary connections, Robert falls in love with George's sister Clara, in a kind of substitution of sister for brother that queers the novel, while recalling Shakespeare's *Twelfth Night*. In *Armadale*, by contrast, Midwinter and Armadale are rivals for Lydia's affection. Lydia tries to resist her attraction to Midwinter due to his intelligence, sensitivity and the marks of suffering from his impoverished childhood that remind her of her own. Collins satirises the marriage market seen in many Victorian novels when Lydia pretends that she prefers the dull but kindly Armadale because his wealth makes him a highly eligible suitor.

Collins's *No Name* is another novel that may have been influenced by *Lady Audley's Secret*. The publication of *No Name* in serial form began after the serialisation of *Lady Audley's Secret* had started: Braddon's novel appeared as a serial in 1861–2, while *No Name* was serialised in 1862–3. As with *Armadale*, *No Name* builds on features seen in Braddon's novel to create a more subversive text than *Lady Audley's Secret*, for Braddon's female impostor-villain becomes the resourceful, if law-breaking, heroine in Collins's novel. The deceitful Magdalen Vanstone in *No Name* is more psychologically complex than Lady Audley, too. Further, Collins uses his heroine's story to attack the lack of inheritance rights for illegitimate children, as well as excoriating the stigma against them that upholds such practices. Less obviously, Collins attacks the privileging of the inheritance rights of men over women, as well as exposing the ugliness of primogeniture.

Like *Lady Audley's Secret*, *No Name* reveals the cruelty of the marriage market, as Magdalen plots to marry the man who was left the wealth she would have inherited, had she been born legitimate. Magdalen reflects, 'Thousands of women marry for money . . . Why shouldn't I?'[5] But unlike Lady Audley, Magdalen suffers profoundly due to selling herself into marriage, even though she thinks that regaining her and her sister's inheritance is the goal she must attain through any sacrifice. However, the prospect of her hollow marriage 'petrified all feeling in her' (NN: 481). Wed to a man she hates, Magdalen sinks into depression, bitterness and self-contempt. As she writes to her former governess, Miss Garth, Magdalen is 'Nobody's Child, Somebody's Wife' (NN: 590). Magdalen has wrecked her sense of self by adopting a role she detests. This is ironic, since Magdalen felt a sense of agency when developing her plan to entrap her bridegroom, but lost her feeling of power as soon as she started enacting her plot. Magdalen's self-estrangement due to becoming a purchased wife contrasts with Lady Audley's joy in wealth obtained through bigamy, suggesting Magdalen has a moral sense that Lady Audley lacks.

After her first husband's death, Magdalen impersonates a parlourmaid in the home of his relative, an admiral who has inherited her husband's fortune. Magdalen's assumption of a working-class role in her second use of a disguise to regain her inheritance shows her obsessiveness. As a maid, Magdalen experiences the low-status, financially insecure position that many illegitimate children of the era were forced to cope with. Whereas Lady Audley started her life in relative poverty, Magdalen embraces it in adulthood as a desperate expedient in her failed plot to regain the wealth she once knew. To ensure his readers' forgiveness of his penitent impostor at the end of *No Name*, Collins has Magdalen become seriously ill, before turning her into a submissive Angel in the House when she marries again, this time for love. Collins's Magdalen moves beyond the unidimensional impostor figure pioneered by Braddon's Lady Audley, who is unable or unwilling to reform; by contrast, Magdalen grows from her many mistakes.

Ellen Wood was another major sensation novelist who may have influenced Collins. Lady Isabel in Wood's bestselling *East Lynne* (1861) provided the figure of the female household employee who is an impostor; such a figure stars in *No Name* and *Armadale*. In '"She Had Her Role to Play": The Performance of Servanthood in *East Lynne* and Other Sensation Novels' (2011), Elizabeth Steere explains that '[t]he invisibility expected of servants within a household offers further anonymity for criminal or illicit acts'.[6] Servants would have been considered potential 'fallen women', much like actresses.[7] Like Wood's adulterous Isabel, Collins's 'fallen' Lydia in *Armadale* uses her acting skills while serving as a governess to conceal her real identity from her employers. Similarly, Magdalen Vanstone assumes a false identity as a maid in *No Name* so she can search for a legal document that belongs to her employer.

The focus upon jealousy in *East Lynne* recalls a similar focus in Collins's *The Law and the Lady* (1875). In *East Lynne*, jealousy of an imagined rival for her husband's love leads Lady Isabel to leave him for another man, in order to revenge herself upon her husband. Ironically, Isabel's supposed rival, Barbara Hare, had felt intense jealousy of Isabel since she had long loved Isabel's husband, Archibald Carlyle, without him reciprocating her feelings. After Isabel returns home years later to serve her ex-husband as their children's governess while wearing a remarkably effective disguise, she feels keen jealousy of Barbara again; this time, her jealousy makes sense, since Barbara has married Carlyle. Later, when Isabel is dying, she finally reveals her identity to Carlyle. Admitting her jealousy of Barbara, Isabel hopes that after both she and Carlyle have died, he might love her again in heaven. She tells him, 'Keep a little corner in your heart for your poor lost Isabel.'[8] Though sounding penitent and pious, Isabel manages to sound a bit adulterous, too.

The enduring painfulness of Isabel's thwarted longing for her husband's affection, as well as her jealousy, may be a forerunner of Sara's motivation for suicide in *The Law and the Lady*. Sara's deathbed letter to her husband, Eustace Macallan, describes her intense jealousy of Mrs Helena Beauly, whom Eustace loves instead of Sara. Reading Eustace's diary has led Sara to realise that her husband will never love her, so Sara poisons herself. She writes to Eustace, 'I have already sacrificed everything but my life to my love for you. Now I know that my love is not returned, the last sacrifice left is easy. My death will set you free to marry Mrs. Beauly.'[9] Sara manages to cast herself as a domestic saint even as she violates Christian precepts by killing herself to escape her pain and perhaps to punish her husband; fortunately, for his peace of mind, Eustace never reads Sara's letter.

As in *East Lynne*, in *The Law and the Lady* a climactic moment of jealousy and frustrated love before a besotted woman's death gains power because of the many examples of jealousy among the other characters. In *East Lynne*, Carlyle's older sister is intensely jealous of Isabel because she threatens not only to usurp Carlyle's sister's role as housekeeper, but also her role as the primary attachment in Carlyle's life. In *The Law and the Lady*, Valeria, who marries Eustace long after Sara dies, is jealous of Helena, just as Sara was. Likewise, Eustace's mentally unstable friend Miserrimus Dexter, who loved Sara and is attracted to Valeria, displays extreme jealousy of Eustace. Dexter's servant Ariel provides the most extreme case of jealousy in the novel, since, without reason, she fears Valeria will replace her as Dexter's attendant because of his inappropriate interest in Eustace's new wife. Both *East Lynne* and *The Law and the Lady* suggest that jealousy can be fatal at times, whether it be well founded or not. Destructive jealousy in these two novels may symbolise the envy of prosperous acquaintances that afflicted Victorians, as a result of the growth in middle-class jobs that came with increasing industrialisation and empire-building.

Collins's best novels are of a higher quality than those by Braddon and Wood. Winifred Hughes, in *The Maniac in the Cellar: Sensation Novels of the 1860s* (1980), asserts that 'where Braddon and Wood casually invoke "the hand of Destiny" as a matter of narrative convenience, Collins explicitly poses the philosophical questions of fate in opposition to accident, and of character in opposition to both'.[10] Through such philosophical implications, Collins proves his ability to write serious novels, a talent that Braddon and Wood lack. However, some critics think Braddon's best novels are as deeply probing as Collins's. Speaking generally about Collins's and Braddon's novels, Beller contends that the protagonists experience 'a sudden point of discovery that overturns everything they thought they knew about themselves and their world ... [that moment] epitomizes ... emerging ontological uncertainty in the wake of scientific advances and challenges to traditional religious absolutes'.[11] In *Lady Audley's Secret*, Robert and George, not the stunted Lady Audley, are the characters who experience epiphanies that might be seen as symbolic of those of Victorians who struggled to cope with sudden cultural changes.

The influence of Collins on later women novelists has been investigated, though not as fully as his influence on Braddon and her peers. Collins, like women authors of sensation novels, 'focus[es] on the female point of view', Hughes argues.[12] In her 2012 article, 'Why Novels Are Redundant', Emily Steinlight sees Collins and several women sensation novelists as similarly critical of marriage: 'The novels of Wilkie Collins, Mary Elizabeth Braddon, Ouida, Ellen Wood, and Rhoda Broughton shifted emphasis from the perils of the marriage market to the sanctuary of the household – revealing marriage itself to be equally crowded and unstable.'[13] Both *The Woman in White* and *Lady Audley's Secret* use chains as an important motif 'for the binding power of the conventional marriage plot', writes Elizabeth Meadows in 2014, in 'Entropy and the Marriage Plot'.[14]

As well as benefiting from Braddon and Wood, Collins was influenced by much earlier women writers such as Ann Radcliffe. According to Tamara Heller in *Dead Secrets: Wilkie Collins and the Female Gothic* (1992), 'For Collins, then, as for Radcliffe and Shelley, the Gothic was the site of ideological conflict, a vehicle through which at once to criticize domesticity and to pose its values as a barrier against rebellion and social change.'[15] Collins saw Mary Wollstonecraft's *Maria; or, The Wrongs of Woman* (1792) as a model for his own Gothic novels of 'social protest'; Wollstonecraft's daughter Mary Shelley's *Frankenstein* (1818) was his model for the 'discourse of class ... that intersects with its discourse of gender'.[16]

In 1867, Margaret Oliphant argued that Jane Eyre was the model for heroines of sensation novels, notes Lyn Pykett in *The Nineteenth-Century Sensation Novel* (2011).[17] Heller points out that Collins may be making the same point about women's writing in his *The Dead Secret* (1857) as Brontë was in *Jane Eyre*: for *The Dead Secret* may be read, as Sandra M. Gilbert and Susan Gubar famously read *Jane Eyre*, as containing 'a covert subtext ... [which is] paradigmatic of nineteenth-century women's writing'.[18]

Collins, along with female sensation novelists, influenced major Victorian women writers such as George Eliot. Steinlight regards *Daniel Deronda* (1876) as a sensation novel and Pykett agrees.[19] Pykett names other descendants of Collins's and Braddon's sensation novels such as *Felix Holt* (1866) and *Middlemarch* (1871–2).[20] In *Felix Holt*, according to Hughes, 'Eliot's handling of the material of illicit sex, which she shares with the sensation novelists, shows more than a trace of their influence.'[21] Pykett posits that the New Woman novel was another descendant of the sensation novel: 'The critical debate on the New Woman novel picked up some of the main threads of the sensation debate, focusing on transgressive, independent heroines, and representations of the female body and women's feelings.'[22] Further, Beth Palmer explains in 'Are the Victorians Still with Us?' (2009) that Collins may have also influenced neo-Victorian thriller writers like Sarah Waters and Michel Faber;[23] in addition, Pykett sees links between Collins and A. S. Byatt and Margaret Drabble.[24] Collins's championing of marginalised women along with his insight into their psychology in such novels as *Armadale* make his work almost as relevant to contemporary neo-Victorian women writers as it once was to female sensation novelists.

Notes

[1] S. Calovini, 'A "Secret" Novel of Her Own: Mary Elizabeth Braddon's Rewriting of Dickens and Collins', *Tennessee Philological Bulletin* 38 (2001), pp. 19–29 (p. 20).

[2] A-M. Beller and T. MacDonald (eds.), *Rediscovering Victorian Women Sensation Writers: Beyond Braddon* (London: Routledge, 2014), p. 3.

[3] J. Bourne Taylor, *In the Secret Theatre of Home: Wilkie Collins, Sensation Narrative, and Nineteenth-Century Psychology* (1988; Brighton: Victorian Secrets, 2013), p. 18.

[4] W. Collins, *Armadale*, ed. C. Peters (Oxford World's Classics, 1999), p. 514. Hereafter cited parenthetically in the text as A.

[5] W. Collins, *No Name*, ed. V. Blain (Oxford World's Classics, 1999), p. 489. Hereafter cited parenthetically in the text as NN.

6. E. Steere, '"She Had Her Role to Play": The Performance of Servanthood in *East Lynne* and Other Sensation Novels', *Victorian Network* 3.2 (2011), pp. 52–77 (p. 53).
7. Ibid., p. 55.
8. E. Wood, *East Lynne*, ed. E. Jay (Oxford University Press, 2008), p. 616.
9. W. Collins, *The Law and the Lady*, ed. J. Bourne Taylor (Oxford World's Classics, 1992), p. 391.
10. W. Hughes, *The Maniac in the Cellar: Sensation Novels of the 1860s* (Princeton University Press, 1980), p. 137.
11. A-M. Beller, 'Detecting the Self in the Sensation Fiction of Wilkie Collins and Mary Elizabeth Braddon', *Clues: A Journal of Detection* 26.1 (2007), pp. 49–61 (p. 49).
12. Hughes, *The Maniac in the Cellar*, p. 30.
13. E. Steinlight, 'Why Novels Are Redundant: Sensation Fiction and the Overpopulation of Literature', *English Literary History* 79.2 (2012), pp. 501–35 (p. 505).
14. E. Meadows, 'Entropy and the Marriage Plot in *The Woman in White* and *Lady Audley's Secret*', *Dickens Studies Annual* 45 (2014), pp. 311–31 (p. 318).
15. T. Heller, *Dead Secrets: Wilkie Collins and the Female Gothic* (New Haven, CT: Yale University Press, 1992), p. 37.
16. Ibid., p. 17.
17. L. Pykett, *The Nineteenth-Century Sensation Novel*, 2nd ed. (Tavistock, Devon: Northcote/Liverpool University Press, 2011), p. 104.
18. Heller, *Dead Secrets*, p. 3.
19. Steinlight, 'Why Novels Are Redundant', p. 512; Pykett, *The Nineteenth-Century Sensation Novel*, p. 120.
20. Pykett, *The Nineteenth-Century Sensation Novel*, p. 120.
21. Hughes, *The Maniac in the Cellar*, p. 171.
22. Pykett, *The Nineteenth-Century Sensation Novel*, p. 126.
23. B. Palmer, 'Are the Victorians Still with Us? Victorian Sensation Fiction and Its Legacies in the Twenty-First Century', *Victorian Studies* 52.1 (2009), pp. 86–94 (p. 87).
24. Pykett, *The Nineteenth-Century Sensation Novel*, pp. 127–8.

PART IV

Contexts: Cultural and Social

CHAPTER 22

Money

Paul Lewis

Money is the common thread that runs through the novels of Wilkie Collins. Having it. Needing it. Seeking it. Inheriting it. Losing it. It is a theme too in his letters. The pleas of a young Wilkie from Paris to his mother when he was running out of cash. The joy of being paid £5,000 for *Armadale*. The fear he would go overdrawn. He earned around £62,000 during his life but he spent all of it and more, leaving his two lovers and their children with rather less than he had inherited from his parents.

Collins's financial life has been largely ignored by his biographers and in scholarly research. This brief study looks at the personal finances of Wilkie Collins. Where he got his money. What he spent it on. How he managed it. It draws on the 3,000 known letters and analyses his bank account at Coutts.

Earning It

Wilkie Collins opened his own bank account on 23 August 1860 at the age of thirty-six. He was at the beginning of his great success. *The Woman in White* had powered sales of Charles Dickens's periodical *All the Year Round*.[1] The final serial part had just been published and the three-volume novel a week earlier on Wednesday, 15 August 1860.[2] A week later he wrote to his mother Harriet Collins, 'the first impression was sold on the day of publication ... 350 copies of the second edition sold in five days!'[3]

That day Collins went to the publisher Sampson Low to collect his first payment – £500 in cash. He kept £200 and opened his account at Coutts the next day with the £300 balance. From then until his death most of his financial affairs are laid out in the annual copies of his bank account in the Coutts archives.[4]

Careful analysis of those accounts shows that from 23 August 1860 to his death on 23 September 1889 Collins's income is recorded as £67,200. But a total of £10,000 of that came from inheritance. About £3,000 was inherited directly after his mother's death and ultimately spent, and around £7,000 came from dividends on investments left by his father or bought with money he inherited from his mother and later sold. That leaves £57,200 which came from his own work.

His accounts do not tell the whole story. He was earning money as a writer for at least seventeen years before he opened his own bank account. He had eight books published between 1848 and 1857. He also wrote a total of eighty-seven known pieces in monthly and weekly publications including *Bentley's Miscellany*,[5] *The Leader*[6] and of course Dickens's *Household Words*.[7] This essay ignores those amounts save to say that the author estimates the total earned outside his Coutts account was of the order of £4,500. Adding that to the £57,200 from his accounts we can reckon Collins earned close to £62,000 in his lifetime from his writing. In current terms that is approximately £6.2 million, or in terms of earned income around £40 million. See the section 'Money Values' below for the methodology.

Collins recognised the value of his work and sold it as many times as he could. His novels came out as a serial, in three volumes, in one volume, as a cheaper edition and often as a play as well. He sold the rights in America usually at the same time as a work was published in London, and sold for later publication in other countries in English or translated.

His earnings from the initial publication of a book peaked with his third great novel *Armadale* (1866). Despite his great success with *The Woman in White* both in Dickens's *All the Year Round* and in three volumes by Sampson Low, accompanied by a commitment to write his next novel for the same publishers, he sold the book after that to George Smith of Smith, Elder to serialise in his monthly *The Cornhill Magazine* and then publish in volume form. He wrote to his mother, 'Smith & Elder have bought me away from All The Year Round [they] offer me (in writing) for a work of fiction a little longer than The Woman In White … the sum of – Five Thousand Pounds ! ! ! ! ! ! Ha! ha! Ha'.[8]

Collins was not just joyful about large payments. Throughout his life he battled with foreign pirates who stole his work to publish in their own country in English or in translation without paying him.[9] He had an acrimonious correspondence with the Dutch publishers Belinfante Brothers over the proposed theft – as he saw it – of *Man and Wife* to be published in translation in their periodical *Stuivers Magazijn*. But eventually, after the letters were made public, the publisher gave in: 'The enclosed is a triumph! A bill for a hundred guilders (£8.6.8!!!) extracted from the Dutch Publishers !!!!! for "Man & Wife". I never was so excited in my life.'[10] Over the next ten years Belinfante made five payments totalling £44.13.

The diversity of Collins's earnings as his professional life developed can be seen from just one year: the Coutts banking year 24 June 1871 to 23 June 1872. In that year Collins's total income from all his work was £3,417.07. His biggest earner was the story *Poor Miss Finch*. He sold it six times for a total of £2,130.81 or 62 per cent of his writing income that year. Table 22.1 shows how he protected his copyrights to sell his work in different formats and countries. The much shorter *Miss or Mrs?* was sold four times. His successful dramatisation of *The Woman in White* opened at the Olympic Theatre on 9 October 1871 and ran for twenty weeks. He earned 10 per cent of the box office receipts when they topped £400 in a week and 5 per cent for weeks below that.[11] He was also paid by the publisher Smith, Elder for new editions of six old titles, stretching back to his first published novel, *Antonina* (1850).

Collins received a total of £226.64 in dividends, mainly from the investments left by his father which, after his mother's death in 1868, came equally to him and his brother Charles. He had also invested some money in American bonds.

In that year his total income from all sources was £3,688.71. It is a microcosm of Collins's working life coming from publishing his work in London, in North America and in Europe, both in English and translated. It comes from books and periodicals, from new work and from reprints as well as a major West End play. In addition – and always overlooked – there are dividends which ultimately arose from his inheritance.

Spending It

Collins had a substantial income but he spent almost all of it. From 23 August 1860 to his death on 23 September 1889, his total actual expenditure was £66,638, just £558 less than his total income when the £10,005 from inheritance and investments is added to his recorded earned income of £57,191. In other words, he spent almost every penny he earned and inherited.

Since 1856 – aged thirty-two – he had lived with his companion Caroline Graves, a widow he met in the mid-1850s, and her daughter Harriet Elizabeth whom Collins adopted in all but name. Between the autumn of 1860, when she was nine, and 1868, he paid a total of £426.84 for her education.[12]

Sending her to boarding school was convenient for Collins, as he wanted to take Caroline to Paris after he finished *The Woman in White*.

Table 22.1 *Wilkie Collins – Income, 24 June 1871–23 June 1872*

INCOME FROM WRITING

Poor Miss Finch			*The Woman in White* drama		
Cassell's (serial)	£600.00		At 10% of box office	£302.86	
Bentley (3-vols. initial payment)	£750.00		At 5% of box office	£183.63	
Harper (New York publication)	£600.00			£486.49	14%
Hunter Rose (Canadian serial)	£102.50		**Smith, Elder new editions**		
Tauchnitz (Continental)	£70.00		4,000 copies *Woman in White*	£40.00	
Belinfante (Dutch publication)	£8.33		*Antonina*	£16.67	
	£2,130.83	62%	2,000 *Hide and Seek* & 2,000 *Dead Secret*	£33.33	
Miss or Mrs?			*Basil* and *Armadale*	£73.33	
Graphic Christmas number	£400.00			£163.33	5%
Tauchnitz (Continental)	£50.00		**Various**		
Hunter Rose (Canadian)	£35.00		Kleinan (translations)	£40.00	
German translation	£10.00		per Letter (unidentified)	£41.67	
	£495.00	14%	Smith, Elder (balance for *Man and Wife*)	£59.75	
				£141.42	4%
Total income from writing			**£3,417.07**		

INCOME FROM OTHER SOURCES

Dividends			**Miscellaneous**		
From father £5,807 15s	£169.88		Naylor Benzon (unknown)	£25.00	
From father £700 re Gray	£20.48		Frank Beard (loan repaid)	£20.00	
From $6,000 US 6 pcts	£36.28			£45.00	
	£226.64	6%			
Total income other sources			**£271.64**		
TOTAL INCOME			**£3,688.71**		

They travelled first class and stayed two weeks at the Hotel Meurice in the rue de Rivoli. Among the luxuries of Paris they ate at Les Trois Frères Provençaux, one of Dickens's favourite restaurants.[13]

Table 22.2 *Wilkie Collins – Trip to Europe*

13 April–23 June 1863	
Cash	
Travelling expenses	£100.00
via Charles Ward	£20.00
at Lafitte in Paris	£50.00
	£170.00
Hotels and servants	
Wintgens (Aix-la-Chapelle)	£100.00
M. Klumpp (Hôtel de l'Ours, Wildbad)	£150.00
R. Sorranend (Paris?)	£26.13
Mr Nidecker (travelling servant)	£16.65
	£292.78
TOTAL FOR 72-DAY TRIP	**£462.78**

Foreign travel took a lot of Collins's budget. He went on an extended trip with Caroline to France and Germany from 13 April to 23 June 1863. It was partly a health cure – he and Caroline had been unwell – and they went to the sulphurous spa in Aix-la-Chapelle and then on to spend three weeks taking the waters in Wildbad in Germany's Black Forest before returning via Paris. It was not a cheap trip, costing him £462.78 at a time when his annual income was £2,051 (Table 22.2).[14] But hiring Nidecker was a good investment. Collins wrote to Harriet: 'The courier does admirably – an attentive competent servant, who saves me worlds of trouble.'[15]

The bonus from the trip was that the hotel in Wildbad provided him with the first chapter of his next novel, which was already badly delayed by his rheumatic gout: 'IT was the opening of the season of eighteen hundred and thirty-two, at the Baths of WILDBAD'.[16]

Collins suffered from this gout most of his adult life. It affected many parts of his body including his eyes, sometimes sending him blind. It cost him significantly in medical bills, medicines and laudanum. On his return he paid his doctor, Frank Beard, £100.

His next stop was to Henry Poole, his Savile Row tailor. That was just one of eleven fittings between 1861 and 1867, costing him £147.73. After that Collins seems to have transferred his custom to John Steckleback, a German tailor whom he patronised until 1880, spending £269.41. His many extant photographs show that he liked to dress in fashionable day-suits and cravats.[17]

In the early 1860s Collins paid £110 a year to rent the top floors of 12 Harley Street. Wilkie and Caroline had two servants aged sixteen and twenty-six to look after them and Caroline was recorded in the 1861 census as 'Author's wife'. She drew £40 out of his account in 1864/65, and withdrawals marked 'House' totalling £190 may well have gone to her as well to pay for food and servants. Collins himself drew out £370 in cash, partly to pay for two trips to Boulogne and Paris. But it was his trip to Great Yarmouth in 1864 that was to change all their lives. He went there to research the Broads for scenes in the book he was writing which was to become *Armadale*. He took out £75 from his bank on 29 July 1864, travelled to Norfolk and stayed at the Victoria Hotel in Great Yarmouth at a cost of £51.89. While he was there he met Martha Rudd, then a nineteen-year-old barmaid, and within a couple of years he had set her up in rooms in London in 33 Bolsover Street. There she was known as Martha Dawson, and, if anyone asked, her husband who visited her frequently was William Dawson, barrister. At that address the first two of their three children were born, Marian on 4 July 1869 and Harriet Constance on 14 May 1871.

Caroline left him briefly but was certainly back in time for the April 1871 Census, though listed as a housekeeper and not his wife. At the time he was paying Martha between £20 and £30 a month for her expenses. Collins's relationship with the two women continued for the rest of his life.

In August 1867 he had moved with Caroline and her daughter to 90 Gloucester Place where he stayed for more than twenty years. Detailed analysis of his spending in 1871/72 (Table 22.3) shows the house took more than a fifth of his money in that period. He belonged to three clubs – two in London and the Royal Victoria Yacht Club on the Isle of Wight. Apart from his own doctor, Frank Beard, he made one payment of £20 to Adolphe Didier, a 'medical galvanist' for electric baths.[18] His chemist's bills – probably largely for laudanum – totalled £33.62. The payments to three distant relatives were all obligations under various wills. Charles Whiting printed the dramatic version of *The Woman in White* used in the production at the Olympic Theatre. The payment to George Vining may be related to that play, in which he took the lead. The payment to Charles Fechter may have been related to other payments made to him in 1869–70.[19] Altogether Collins spent £254 more than his income (see Table 22.1), mainly because of his investments in US Bonds which he sold later in 1872 when he needed money.

His main hotel expense was two weeks at the Queen's Hotel near Crystal Palace – to 'breathe a mouthful of this fine air', he wrote to his lawyer William Tindell: 'I am drunk with it after London. N.B. The champagne is good and dry.'[20]

Table 22.3 *Wilkie Collins – Spending, 1871–1872*

House etc.	Entries	Amount	per cent
Bills, wages, sundries, coal, gas, water	33	£658.68	16.7
Rent	4	£176.25	4.5
Rates	2	£31.25	0.8
Benham (furniture)	1	£7.11	0.2
		£873.29	22.1
Personal			
Wine (Justerini, Dremel, Morel)	4	£161.66	4.1
Cash	12	£130.00	3.3
Clubs (Three incl. Athenaeum)	9	£69.95	1.8
Doctors (Frank Beard, M. Didier)	4	£69.20	1.8
Hotels (Crystal Palace and Ramsgate)	3	£60.53	1.5
Tailors (Stecklebeck, Geoghegan)	4	£53.54	1.4
Cigars (Fribourg)	1	£49.30	1.3
Chemist (Corbyn)	5	£33.62	0.9
Charity (various)	5	£23.15	0.6
Stationery (Bacon)	1	£6.65	0.2
Jeweller (Tessier)	1	£6.30	0.2
Books (Sotheran)	1	£5.93	0.2
		£669.82	17.0
Family			
Martha	12	£295.00	7.5
Aunt Gray, Aunt Dyke, Cousin Jones	10	£55.12	1.4
Caroline	1	£5.00	0.1
		£355.12	9.0
Actor friends			
Charles Fechter	1	£100.00	2.5
George Vining	4	£27.94	0.7
		£127.94	3.2
Publishers			
Chatto & Windus	1	£116.00	2.9
Charles Whiting (printing of *The Woman in White: A Drama*)	1	£60.06	1.5
		£176.06	4.5
Unidentified traders			
Mainly single bills	10	£198.93	5.0
Finances			
Investment (US bonds, Artisan homes)	3	£1,317.88	33.4
Mr Shean (lawyer)	2	£162.90	4.1
Tax (Income and assessed)	1	£53.75	1.4
Life Insurance	1	£4.25	0.1
Stamps on documents	5	£2.78	0.1
		£1,541.55	39.1
TOTAL SPENDING	**142**	**£3,942.71**	**100.0**

Dry champagne was a great love of Collins, it was the one drink that did not seem to upset his gout and he believed 'there is no tonic for the exhausted nervous system, so effectual and so harmless'.[21] Around twenty wine merchants appear in his accounts. Justerini & Co. was a favourite for nearly twenty years from 1860 to 1878, whose bills over that time totalled £662.48. Later he patronised Beecheno, Yaxley & Co. from 1883 to his death in 1889. The nineteen letters to that firm which survive give an insight into his tastes:

> I have got through my little supply of your Champagne – with good results, due no doubt to the genuine dryness of the wine, which also possesses the great merit of delicacy. Thus encouraged, I shall be obliged if you will send me Six dozen half bottles of the same 'Vin Brut' – and the sooner they arrive (in the present state of the weather) the more welcome they will be.[22]

Three months later he ordered the same again – and again for his home with Martha Rudd, together with 'a three-dozen case' of sherry for both. That order cost him £20.55 and in total he paid the firm £90.81. He also bought ice from the Wenham Lake Ice Co. Over seven years from 1862 to 1868 he spent £54.50, perhaps to keep his champagne cool.

Alongside the bills from Justerini often came one from the tobacconist Fribourg. Collins loved a good cigar, and over fifteen years he spent £510.42 there. As early as 1845 Collins tells his mother from Paris that he 'smoked cigars, imbibed coffee'[23] and his letters are sprinkled with invitations to friends: 'we should be more snug over a cigar, in a couple of arm-chairs here'[24] or 'Can you kindly look in on Wednesday afternoon next? and keep me company with a cigar?'[25]

Collins described his smoking habits to the journalist J. Maynard Saunders in 1886:

> When I take up my pen, after breakfast, I take up my cigar with it. When I return to my pen, after lunch, I return to my cigar. When I do my best, in the evening, to digest my dinner (N.B. I am sixty two years old) my cigar helps me. I have only to add that I feel the most unfeigned pity for those unfortunate persons who do not smoke.[26]

With two households and four children to support, holidays and trips abroad, luxury tastes and travel around the UK, it is not surprising that Collins spent just about all his income. And inevitably sometimes he feared that his expenditures might exceed it.

Managing It

From his earliest days Wilkie Collins frequently ran out of money. In August 1844, the twenty-year-old was planning a trip to Paris and wrote to his mother from the office at the Strand where he worked, which was conveniently next door to Coutts bank where her account was held: 'I am very much obliged for the permission to bleed the Estate. I shall take my money in £5 notes. They change them in Paris at an advantage to the English.'[27]

His annual trips to Paris in his twenties were all characterised by pleas for a little more money. But when he was earning enough to be independent, he was meticulous with his mother about taking only his own money out of her account. In Paris again in 1856, he writes to her:

> I find by reckoning up my accounts, that you have advanced me £10 – send a cheque for [erased word] £20 more to Ward to be paid into Lafitte's here for me. You will then have advanced me £30, and you will have £40 to reimburse you at Coutts's at the beginning of April ... No need [to] turn up your eyes – You won't advance more than I can already pay back.[28]

When he ran his own account at Coutts, Collins had periodic fears that he would not have enough to cover his spending. During the thirty banking years for which he had his own account his expenditure exceeded his income in sixteen of them – including 1871/72 (Tables 22.1 and 22.3). It took judicious juggling to ensure he never went overdrawn, with the help of his good friend Charles Ward who was his banker at Coutts. On one occasion Collins wrote to Ward: 'I am very glad you warned me – I will draw no cheques before the 19th.'[29]

Concerned in June 1871 that he might be about to spend all his money, he asked Ward to sell the remainder of an investment in American bonds which he had bought two years earlier. He received £403.88 on 16 June, leaving him happily in funds.

Collins first invested money in 1864 in government bonds called 'Consols' yielding 3 per cent a year. But by 1867 he had sold them. Over the next seven years he bought and sold more American bonds and overall his investments made him a profit of £445.23. Much of the money he invested was from part of the £3,000 he inherited from his mother after her death in 1868. He sold the last of them in 1878, and his inheritance from Harriet was simply absorbed into his own income.

Wilkie Collins died on 23 September 1889. After the sale of his books and manuscripts his estate was valued at £11,414.80, rather less than the total of £11,815 his own father had left for his family forty-two years earlier, and which Collins ultimately inherited. He had spent all he had earned and inherited in his life bar £862.63 in his bank account, some of which arrived *post mortem*.

His estate was shared equally between his two lovers Caroline Graves and Martha Rudd. His will specified and named both them and their children.

Money Values

Until 1971 the UK's currency was pounds, shillings and pence, with twenty shillings to the pound and twelve pence to the shilling. All amounts in this essay are converted to decimals.³⁰

Translating value from the nineteenth century to today is notoriously tricky. The website measuringworth.com explains the difficulties and does the conversion. Prices from Collins's time to 2020 have risen about 100-fold. So, £138.45 in the nineteenth century is the equivalent of £13,845 today. However, this conversion only takes account of price rises. Wages have risen far more, and converting wages then to wages now would need a factor of around 650, so earning £100 then is equivalent to earning £65,000 now. Neither conversion by prices or by wages is completely satisfactory.

Notes

1. See R. L. Patten, *Charles Dickens and His Publishers* (Oxford University Press: 1978), p. 464.
2. A. Gasson, '*The Woman in White* – A Chronological Study', Wilkie Collins Society (September 2010), pp. 3–5.
3. W. Collins to Harriet Collins, 22 August 1860, [0369]; BGLL, vol. 1, p. 209. The most up-to-date edition of Collins's letters is W. Baker, A. Gasson, G. Law and P. Lewis (eds.), *The Collected Letters of Wilkie Collins*, Past Masters (Charlottesville, VA: InteLex, 2019). Each letter there begins with a unique four-digit number in square brackets. Those references have been used here, together with the reference to B&C (W. Baker and W. M. Clarke [eds.], *The Letters of Wilkie Collins*, 2 vols. [London: Macmillan, 1999]) or BGLL (W. Baker, A. Gasson, G. Law and P. Lewis [eds.], *The Public Face of Wilkie Collins: The Collected Letters*, 4 vols. [London: Pickering & Chatto, 2005]).
4. Coutts accounts for Wilkie Collins from 1860 to 1890, for his father William John Thomas Collins, R. A., and for his executors' account from 1845 to 1869, were kindly made available to me by the Coutts archives. Any reference to money into or out of Collins's account refers to these accounts unless referenced otherwise.
5. Bentley Receipts, British Library, Add. Ms. 46652, ff. 163–5.
6. See G. Law (ed.), '"The New Dragon of Wantley: A Social Revolution", A Lost Tale by Wilkie Collins, with Further Discussion of His Contributions to *The Leader*', Wilkie Collins Society (November 2007).
7. See Anne Lohrli (compiler), 'List of Contributors', in *Household Words: A Weekly Journal, 1850–1859 Conducted by Charles Dickens* (University of Toronto Press, 1973).

8. W. Collins to Harriet Collins, 31 July 1861, [0429]; B&C, vol. I, pp. 197–8.
9. See W. Collins, 'Considerations on the Copyright Question. Addressed to an American Friend', *International Review* (June 1880), pp. 609–18.
10. W. Collins to Charles Ward, 14 April 1871, [1087]; BGLL, vol. II, pp. 251–2.
11. P. Lewis, 'The Woman in White at the Olympic Theatre', Wilkie Collins Society Newsletter Supplement (August 2009).
12. P. Lewis, 'Educating Elizabeth Harriet Graves', Wilkie Collins Society (May 2010).
13. See C. Dickens to W. Collins, 4 October 1860, in M. House, G. Storey and K. Tillotson (eds.), *The Letters of Charles Dickens* (Pilgrim Edition), 12 vols. (Oxford: Clarendon Press, 1965–2002), vol. IX, p. 331.
14. The average of his income for 1862/63 and 1863/64.
15. W. Collins to Harriet Collins, 21 April 1863, [0534]; B&C, vol. I, pp. 219–20.
16. W. Collins, *Armadale*, ed. C. Peters (Oxford World's Classics, 1989), p. [1].
17. For several examples, see 'Wilkie and photographs', www.wilkiecollins.com menu item 3.
18. W. Collins to Charles Kent, 28 June 1871, [1100]; BGLL, vol. II, p. 259.
19. W. Collins to Charles Ward, 9 June 1870, [0989]; BGLL, vol. II, pp. 192–3.
20. W. Collins to William Tindell, 15 August 1871, [1119]; BGLL, vol. II, pp. 270–1.
21. W. Collins to Arthur Reade, 19 April 1883, [2141]; BGLL, vol. III, p. 400.
22. W. Collins to Beecheno, Yaxley & Co., 17 September 1885, [2468]; BGLL, vol. IV, p. 118.
23. W. Collins to Harriet Collins, 9, 10 September 1845, [0025]; B&C, vol. I, pp. 26–7 (dated [9 September 1845]).
24. W. Collins to Edward Benham, 5 January 1867, [0719]; BGLL, vol. II, p. 58 (as to Charles Benham), amended in Past Masters.
25. W. Collins to Frank Archer, 5 December 1887, [2786]; BGLL, vol. IV, p. 284, amended in Past Masters.
26. W. Collins to J. Maynard Saunders, 7 September 1886, [2609]; BGLL, vol. IV, p. 190, amended in Past Masters.
27. W. Collins to Harriet Collins, 8 August 1844, [0020]; BGLL, vol. I, pp. 10–11.
28. W. Collins to Harriet Collins, 16 March 1856, [0233]; B&C, vol. I, pp. 151–2.
29. W. Collins to Charles Ward, March 1860–late December 1864, [0611]; BGLL, vol. I, p. 333.
30. See www.paullewis.co.uk, 'Victorian coinage', for more information about this system.

CHAPTER 23

Gender

Tamara S. Wagner

The most memorable characters of Wilkie Collins's novels include the resolute Marian Halcombe and the enervated drawing-master Walter Hartright in *The Woman in White* (1860), Collins's breakthrough and still best-known sensation novel. Strong women and highly sensitive men reappear in his fiction, embodying a sustained concern with gendered attributes and emotions in Victorian culture. Yet, Collins does not promote a simple inversion of the normative gender identities of the time. In *The Woman in White*, Marian operates as her half-sister's double, accentuating Laura Fairlie's 'womanly charms', 'the graces and gentleness of her character', by force of contrast.[1] With a 'dark down on her upper lip [that] was almost a moustache', 'a large, firm, masculine mouth and jaw', Marian's expression may be 'bright, frank, and intelligent', but 'altogether wanting in those feminine attractions of gentleness and pliability, without which the beauty of the handsomest woman alive is beauty incomplete' (WW: 32). Similarly, Hartright returns from explorations overseas with renewed energies that seem also to have imbued him with more traditional masculine qualities, since his 'will had learnt to be strong, [his] heart to be resolute, [his] mind to rely on itself', enabling him to face his 'future ... as a man should' (WW: 415). Hartright's marriage to Laura appears to reaffirm heteronormativity. In a triangulation of different degrees of nervousness, the cultural idealisation of feminised weakness has meanwhile been exorcised through the death of Laura's other half-sister, whose physical likeness to Laura underpins the main mystery. Seemingly 'twin-sisters of chance resemblance', complete with a 'nervous uncertainty about the lips', their exchangeability complicates the representation of both nervousness and femininity in the text (WW: 96). In addition, Laura never fully recovers from her identification with and indeed as the mad woman in white – an identification that yokes together a pliability that is traditionally coded feminine with a weak-mindedness close to imbecility – whereas the family arrangement with which the novel concludes needs

Marian's strengthening presence. While redeploying traditional associations with feminine and masculine qualities, the text dramatises their impasses by tracing a spectrum of nervousness, and ultimately questions expected narrative resolutions as the ending identifies 'Marian [as] the good angel of our lives' (WW: 643).

Throughout his writing, Collins experiments with the representation of non-normative family constellations, resolute women and highly strung anti-heroes with their heart in the right place, often with speaking names (Hartright in *The Woman in White*, Goldenheart in *The Fallen Leaves* [1879] and Ovid Vere in *Heart and Science* [1883]). Although several narratives indisputably sensationalise transgressive behaviour or appearance, including Miserrimus Dexter in *The Law and the Lady* (1875), and present powerful women as dangerous (Mrs Fontaine in *Jezebel's Daughter* [1880]), these figures form part of a more encompassing fabric of transnormative rejections of gendered behaviour patterns. Despite his sadism and selfishness, Dexter's tragic end evokes sympathy. The same novel features a successful female detective figure, who solves the mystery enveloping her husband. A marginalised character, the latter remains, in his mother's words, 'one of the weakest of living mortals', and yet he deserves to be rescued by his wife.[2] Collins challenges the limits of Victorian gender ideology in depicting characters and relationships that would have been considered subversive. His self-consciously alternative representations of gendered attributes and household arrangements range from satires of newly fashionable ideals of 'muscular Christianity' in *Man and Wife* (1870) to the many nurturing men in his adoption novels, narratives otherwise as different as his proto-sensation foundling tale, *Hide and Seek* (1854), the family melodrama surrounding child custody in *The Evil Genius* (1886), and the dramatisation of debates on nature versus nurture through a religious minister's adoption of a murderess's infant in *The Legacy of Cain* (1888). Driving his sensational exposure of Victorian mores, Collins's critical engagement with gender, in fact, can usefully be divided into three categories: (1) a critique of gendered domestic ideologies, which operates through both a domestic Gothic and a celebration of alternative family constellations; (2) his indictment of marriage and custody laws; and (3) his subversion of gendered character traits, in particular of prevailing portrayals of masculinity.

Domestic ideologies formed a definitional aspect of Victorian culture. Prioritising home, family and privacy, these ideologies were based on the concept of 'separate spheres', the public and the private. At a time when work from home became increasingly common among the middle classes, men were regarded as the main breadwinners, while women were expected to run the household. This concept scripted home as a place of rest – for the professional middle-class man, who came home from work elsewhere. In John Ruskin's often-cited words, home promised a 'place of Peace' and a 'shelter' from 'the anxieties of the outer life', a space separated from labour other than the housework that, according to this gendered ideology, was deemed to be invisible. Ruskin's lecture 'Of Queens' Gardens' (1865) influentially summed up a binary system of gender values that came to structure middle-class culture:

> Now their separate characters are briefly these. The man's power is active, progressive, defensive. He is eminently the doer, the creator, the discoverer, the defender. His intellect is for speculation and invention; his energy for adventure, for war, and for conquest ... But the woman's power is for rule, not for battle, – and her intellect is not for invention or creation, but for sweet ordering, arrangement, and decision.[3]

Cultural historians emphasise that this concept of separate spheres constituted a prescriptive ideal rather than an actuality. Claudia Nelson points out that '[as] constructed by Ruskin and countless other cultural commentators, home and family were potent forces, amounting, at least in the abstract, to a secular religion. But the ways in which Victorian society practiced this "religion" varied enormously.'[4] Regardless of its various interpretations or its implementation, the myth of separate spheres nonetheless formed a pervasive, inescapable presence in nineteenth-century print culture. Household manuals and domestic magazines contributed to a thriving market of advice material. While offering practical instructions on how to manage a household, these publications reinforced gendered expectations, admonishing women readers to attend to their domestic duties for the betterment of mankind. In January 1845, the inaugural issue of *The British Mothers' Magazine* asserted that in 'discharg[ing] their duties aright', mothers could guarantee 'future eminence and joy', but in the case of maternal failure, their children would 'as surely become the pests of society and the plagues of the earth'.[5] In *The Mothers of England: Their Influence and Responsibility* (1843), the best-selling writer of conduct books Sarah Stickney Ellis evoked this significance as a truism, claiming that '[f]ew subjects are more hackneyed, or more common to all writers, than that of maternal influence'.[6] The much-stressed moral superiority of women and their redemptive quality formed a key component of Victorian gender ideology, further prising apart and neatly classifying feminine and masculine attributes.

Although Victorian literature influentially contributed to the aestheticisation and circulation of these binaries, it also critiqued, satirised and variously undermined expectations of the so-called separate spheres. Popular writers drew not just the practicality, but also the desirability of such dichotomies into question. In *Great Expectations* (1861), Charles Dickens describes Wemmick's self-division into his office life and his private identity – fortified behind a miniature drawbridge in his suburban 'Castle' – as a comical idiosyncrasy that nonetheless articulates a growing trend: 'the office is one thing, and private life is another. When I go into the office, I leave the Castle behind me, and when I come into the Castle, I leave the office behind me.'[7] For Dickens, this split precludes social responsibility. In informing middle-class self-definition, in fact, the separate spheres ideology was premised on a set of exclusions. Cementing middle-class ascendancy by asserting a putative moral superiority, several of these exclusions were class-based. Bourgeois domesticity became demarcated against aristocratic moral licence on the one hand and the perceived failures of the working classes to implement the recommended domestic ideals on the other. Vilified aristocrats widely populate nineteenth-century fiction (including the false Sir Percival Glyde and the foreign Count Fosco in *The Woman in White*), yet while some authors indisputably patronised 'the poor' in an endeavour to propagate middle-class concepts, fiction also pleaded the cause of the excluded and condemned social injustice. Sentimentalised abandoned babies routinely expressed a call for social change in Victorian fiction, whereas the portrayal of fallen women could be more controversial. In the 1867 Christmas story and play *No Thoroughfare*, co-written by Collins and Dickens, the mystery surrounding two foundlings helps to channel a sympathetic representation of a mother who seeks to reclaim her illegitimate child to bequeath to him the fortune she has made as a businesswoman. In *The New Magdalen* (1873), Collins went further in depicting an erstwhile prostitute who is also an impostor, but who is scripted as more deserving than the socially respectable woman she replaces. *The Fallen Leaves* (1879) concludes with Goldenheart's marriage to a former child prostitute. A projected sequel was to detail their married life, but Collins decided that the reading public was not ready yet, regretting that 'certain important social topics ... are held to be forbidden to the English novelist ... by a narrow-minded minority of readers, and by the critics who flatter their prejudices'.[8] Although Collins wrote more hopefully of 'that wholesome audience of the nation at large [that] has done liberal justice' to his earlier novels, he instead raised, in *Jezebel's Daughter*, the novel he decided to write meanwhile, 'the interesting moral problem' whether 'maternal love' counterbalances 'an otherwise cruel, false, and degraded nature'.⁹

In these representations of prostitutes, illegitimate children and the mothers yearning for them, Collins eschewed a central component of Victorian gender ideologies. Another key binary, in fact, involved the split into the fallen woman and the domestic angel, often termed 'the Angel in the House', after the title of Coventry Patmore's poem (1854). Although the eponymous angel of Patmore's piece is love itself, in particular married love, similar phrases appear throughout nineteenth-century writing to describe idealised female characters, such as Agnes Wickfield in Dickens's *David Copperfield* (1850): 'the better angel of the lives of all who come within her calm, good, self-denying influence'.¹⁰ When Collins describes Marian Halcombe, associated throughout the text with masculine qualities, as 'the good angel of our lives' at the end of *The Woman in White*, he therefore already seeks to alter the parameters of this definition (WW: 643). *The Dead Secret* (1857) and *The Fallen Leaves* describe women forced to suppress their love for their illegitimate children, whereas *No Name* (1863) sympathetically presents an illegitimate female impostor, anticipating the more radical treatment of the theme in *The New Magdalen*, the text that most explicitly upends the binary. In *The New Magdalen*, in her work as a nurse the former prostitute is introduced as her patients' 'guardian angel', whereas 'fierce' and 'savage' are adjectives associated with the putatively respectable woman whose identity she has stolen.¹¹

Whereas the unmasking of seeming respectability and hypocrisy forms part of the sensation genre's domestic Gothic, Collins simultaneously challenges normative gender alignments in his representation of blended families, including informal adoption, and alternative domestic arrangements. Collins himself established two households: Caroline Graves was known as his housekeeper, whereas he lived with Martha Rudd and their three children under an assumed name, Mr and Mrs Dawson. Collins's reputed first meeting with Caroline Graves in the early 1850s may be partly apocryphal, but it has long been believed to have inspired *The Woman in White* and possibly also *The Fallen Leaves*, which he dedicated to Caroline.¹² In his fiction, Collins criticises the social opprobrium surrounding non-normative arrangements and indicts the limited marriage, divorce and custody laws. *Man and Wife* lays bare the easily exploited legal inconsistences of divergent marriage laws across Victorian Britain, while also arguing the case for a Married Woman's Property Act. Collins's divorce and child-custody novel, *The Evil Genius*, anticipated

Henry James's *What Maisie Knew* (1897) by over ten years. The Custody of Infants Act of 1839 permitted mothers to petition in court for the custody of children under seven and for access to older children; after 1873, Chancery could decide as it saw fit; by the 1880s, it had become customary to grant custody of young children to their mothers. Whereas in *Heart and Science*, Mr Gallilee overcomes his irresoluteness and saves his children from an emotionally cold amateur scientist after his divorce from her, *The Evil Genius* dramatises the divorced father's painful separation from his daughter. Both novels foreground the father's emotional investment in young children. Similarly, Collins depicts the precariousness of adoptive relationships prior to the Adoption of Children Act (1926). In *Hide and Seek*, Valentine Blyth hides the clue to his adopted daughter's identity because he fears that she might be claimed by relatives, whereas *The Legacy of Cain* redeploys the form of the adoption novel to explore contested theories of heredity. Instead of using adoption as a pat ending, these narratives demonstrate the challenges of families that are not legally recognised as such. Geraldine Jewsbury's *The History of an Adopted Child* (1853) was the first novel to address this issue as a main theme, and Dinah Craik's *King Arthur: Not a Love Story* (1886) explicitly tackled the absence of adequate laws regulating adoption. Scholars often also consider Emily Brontë's *Wuthering Heights* (1847), Dickens's *Bleak House* (1853) and *Great Expectations*, and George Eliot's *Daniel Deronda* (1876) as examples of 'the Victorian adoption novel'.[13] Recently, queer studies approaches to elective families, as well as new interest in historical fatherhood, have drawn attention to 'literary celebrations of the caring male' in the context of non-biological adoption.[14]

Increasingly, Collins specifically targeted the ideals of muscular Christianity, with its focus on the body at the expense of intellectual and ethical education. This school of thought stressed athletics and character-building through team sports in the public school system, as influentially outlined in Thomas Hughes's *Tom Brown's School Days* (1857). While Collins already satirises the muscular Christian in Godfrey Ablewhite in *The Moonstone* (1868), in *Man and Wife* he exposes the 'cant of the day' that takes 'physically-wholesome men for granted, as being morally-wholesome men into the bargain'.[15] Embodying the 'model young Briton of the present time', with 'features ... as perfectly regular and as perfectly unintelligent as human features can be', Geoffrey Delamayn is a sly murderer and dies in a competitive race (M&W: 68, 76). Introduced as a 'strong personal contrast', the novel's wavering anti-hero, Arnold Brinkworth, is 'slow and awkward', while his tears 'honoured the man who shed them' (M&W: 274). Although Charles Kingsley as well as Hughes promoted muscular Christianity in their novels, Victorian fiction registers various attempts to reconceptualise the ideal, which could range from the physically strong scientist Roger Hamley in Elizabeth Gaskell's *Wives and Daughters* (1866) to nurturing male characters, often copiously shedding tears, in Charlotte Yonge's fiction, most notably in *The Pillars of the House* (1873). Androgynous or queer bodies in Collins's novels often act as doubles further to redefine gender identity. Collins repeats this strategy, starting with the nervous, physically delicate anti-hero of *Basil* (1852), who disfigures his beautiful rival, continuing with the projection of Eustace Macallan's feminine qualities onto Miserrimus Dexter's androgyny in *The Law and the Lady*, and through to the violent showdown between the anti-hero and his disabled, mixed-race doppelganger in the late novella *The Guilty River* (1886). With eyes 'so entirely beautiful that they had no right to be in a man's face', 'the pale delicacy of his complexion, [and] his finely shaped sensitive lips', juxtaposed with an 'expression of power about his head, and the signs of masculine resolution presented by his mouth and chin', the latter embodies both dangerous virility and effeminacy.[16] Their simultaneity externalises the anti-hero's sense of unease with his own gender identity.

Although Collins repeatedly challenged gender norms, his renegotiation of shifting ideals frequently worked through such projections onto doubles. Collins's strong women generally fall into two categories: dangerous and supportive. Whereas his representation of female murderers, from Lydia Gwilt in *Armadale* (1866) to Mrs Fontaine in *Jezebel's Daughter*, reflects his interest in new scientific studies of the criminal mind, impostors as embodiments of transgressiveness are sympathetically presented (*No Name*, *The New Magdalen*), and if Marian Halcombe already forms an important power in solving the mystery in *The Woman in White*, in *The Law and the Lady* Collins created one of the markedly few female detectives in nineteenth-century fiction. His persistent rejection of prescriptive gender attributes, while often self-conscious, testifies to the multiplicity of experiences and discourses surrounding gender in Victorian Britain.

Notes

[1] W. Collins, *The Woman in White*, ed. J. Sutherland (Oxford: Oxford World's Classics, 2008), p. 216. Hereafter cited in the text as WW.
[2] W. Collins, *The Law and the Lady*, ed. D. Skilton (London: Penguin, 1998), p. 183.

3 J. Ruskin, *Sesame and Lilies* (London: Cassell, 1909), pp. 73–4.
4 C. Nelson, *Family Ties in Victorian England* (Westport, CT: Praeger, 2007), p. 7.
5 Anon., *The British Mothers' Magazine* (1 January 1845), p. 2.
6 S. Stickney Ellis, *The Mothers of England: Their Influence and Responsibility* (London: Fisher, Son & Co., 1843), p. 56.
7 C. Dickens, *Great Expectations*, ed. M. Cardwell (Oxford World's Classics, 2008), p. 191.
8 W. Collins, *Jezebel's Daughter*, ed. J. D. Hall (Oxford World's Classics, 2016), p. 3.
9 Ibid., p. 4.
10 C. Dickens, *David Copperfield*, ed. N. Burgis and A. Sanders (Oxford World's Classics, 2008), p. 262.
11 W. Collins, *The New Magdalen: A Novel* (Stroud: Sutton, 1993), pp. 25, 96.
12 W. M. Clarke, *The Secret Life of Wilkie Collins* (1988; Chicago: Ivan R. Dee, 1991), pp. 90–1. Clarke terms it a 'story [that] plainly improved in the retelling'.
13 Nelson, *Family Ties*, pp. 161–6.
14 H. Furneaux, *Queer Dickens: Erotics, Families, Masculinities* (Oxford University Press, 2009), p. 57. Recent work builds on John Tosh's seminal discussion of men's complex positioning in the Victorian home, as they newly felt that they needed to stake 'a claim to be at the centre of family life at a time when motherhood was being placed on a pedestal'. See Tosh, *A Man's Place: Masculinity and the Middle-Class Home in Victorian England* (New Haven, CT: Yale University Press, 1999), p. 82.
15 W. Collins, *Man and Wife*, ed. N. Page (Oxford World's Classics, 1995), pp. 68–69. Hereafter cited in the text as M&W.
16 W. Collins, *The Guilty River*, in *Miss or Mrs?, The Haunted Hotel, The Guilty River*, ed. N. Page and T. Sasaki (Oxford World's Classics, 1999), p. 277.

CHAPTER 24

Science and Medicine

Laurence Talairach

Wilkie Collins's novels were informed by contemporary scientific, medical and psychological discourses, from debates revolving around insanity to those dealing with heredity and transmission. Whether suffering from melancholy, nervousness, monomania, delusional behaviour, insanity or epilepsy, many of his characters are marked by symptoms of degeneration. Some also suffer from heart complaints or blindness; others undergo surgery or take drugs. Evolving as they do in a nerve-racking modern world, they consult medical practitioners, from physicians and quacks to surgeons and anatomists. The contagious 'nervousness' of the characters in *The Woman in White* (1860), just like the 'detective fever' which strikes characters in *The Moonstone* (1868), map out the rise of nervous disorders in Victorian Britain, as this chapter will argue, following the evolution of Collins's novels and their use of science and medicine. More and more foregrounding the threat of determinism, Collins's novels condemned contemporary science and medical experimentation, especially as science and medicine increasingly defined morality and conscience in purely materialistic terms, suggesting therefore that crime resulted from brain mechanisms which were morbid but could, perhaps, be manipulated to ensure moral reform.

It was in the midst of heated debates around the nature of criminality that Collins's sensational characters took shape. Though William Baker's reconstruction of Collins's library shows that Collins owned very few medical books, citations and allusions to medical figures and textbooks appear in his novels, from John Elliotson and William Carpenter in *The Moonstone* to David Ferrier in *Heart and Science* (1883).[1] The idea that humans' criminal propensities were located in their brains and that disorders of the mind were not 'due to the presence of an evil spirit in the sufferer, or to the enslavement of the soul by sin'[2] was validated by the work of the English psychiatrist Henry Maudsley (1835–1918), which particularly emphasised the links between the criminal and the insane in Victorian England.[3]

In Collins's early works, such as *Basil* (1852) and 'Mad Monkton' (1855), monomania is used as a sensational plot device to revamp the theme of ancestral legacy. In *Basil*, the son of an ancient family is lured by a linen-draper's daughter and blinded by his passion. The eponymous hero's obsession with Margaret Sherwin eventually leads him to the brink of madness, whilst the son of his father's employee (who was hanged for forging Basil's father's name), Robert Mannion, is monomaniacally obsessed with taking revenge on Basil. In 'Mad Monkton', Alfred Monkton, who looks for the unburied corpse of his uncle, is believed to be insane. The narrative relates the story of the Monktons of Wincot Abbey, plagued with hereditary insanity. However, the mental disease, which furnishes a rational explanation for Monkton's delusions, is linked with the crimes of the past which Monkton discovers by reading ancient manuscripts in the library of the abbey: the ancestors' immoral behaviour is physiologically encoded and transmitted through hereditary insanity, as a physiological punishment inherited by their descendants.

Monomania informs as well *The Woman in White*. Constructed as 'a curse narrative in reverse',[4] since we only know at the end of the novel that the sins of the father have been visited on the children, *The Woman in White* foregrounds the character of Anne Catherick, the illegitimate daughter of Laura Fairlie's father. Monomaniacally obsessed with the colour white – and with baronets – the young woman has been wrongly incarcerated in a lunatic asylum by Sir Percival Glyde so that she may not reveal the secret she claims to possess. The serialisation of *The Woman in White* corresponded with the publication and widespread discussion of the Parliamentary Select Committee Inquiry into the Care and Treatment of Lunatics and Their Property of 1858–9 (whose members included John Forster and Richard Monckton Milnes, two of Collins's acquaintances).[5] With his friend Dickens, who supported the asylum reform movement, Collins met many of the significant figures connected with psychological medicine, such as Bryan Procter (1787–1874), who was a Lunacy Commissioner between 1832 and 1861 and was the dedicatee of *The Woman in White*.[6]

Tellingly, Anne Catherick quickly contaminates the other characters with forms of anxiety: Hartright develops a 'nervous spasm' about his lips and eyes,[7] Sir Percival Glyde shows 'an unsettled, excitable manner' (WW: 404) after his marriage to Laura Fairlie, and the latter's sister, Marian Halcombe, becomes suspicious.[8] In addition, when the characters reach the most Gothic locale of the novel – Blackwater Park – the narrative strengthens the connection between Gothic *topoi* and pathology: the curse on the lake is believed to be due to potential miasmatic infection: its waters, 'black and poisonous' (WW: 207), with rats slipping in and out, recall the cholera epidemic in London between 1849 and 1850, and the medical authorities' focus on stagnant water as a source of infection (WW: 680, n. 234). The most Gothic villain, Count Fosco, is also regarded as potentially contagious, with his 'faint livid yellow hue' (WW: 240) making him look like 'a walking-West-Indian epidemic' likely to 'dye the very carpet he walked on with scarlet fever' (WW: 358). In addition, *The Woman in White* foregrounds Hartright's attempts to help Laura recover memory after her incarceration in the lunatic asylum – a theme to which Collins will return, as in *Heart and Science*, which shows the doctor Ovid Vere prescribing chemicals to help the heroine recollect the fragmented pieces of her brain and remember 'trifles' from her life before the shock. In both cases, contemporary psychology informs the description of the characters' physiological reaction to stimulation: their minds appear as disorderly scattered fragments, their brains made up of layers. If former layers sometimes seem to have been effaced by the passing of time – or by sustained anxiety and emotional shocks – they nevertheless remain buried in the depths of the mind, like haunting thoughts likely to visit the upper layers of consciousness when excited.

The echoes between *The Woman in White* and *Heart and Science*, published more than two decades later, typify Collins's reworking of many of the themes and motifs. In *The Moonstone*, likewise, memory plays a central part in the plot, becoming pivotal in constructions of the self, both novels alluding to current research in mental physiology and hinting at the work of champions of associationism, such as Alexander Bain, or to the theories of William Carpenter. However, while Carpenter saw memory as continuous and simply lying in the dark recesses of the mind,[9] Laura Fairlie's wandering memory in *The Woman in White* appears chaotic and discontinuous. Such discontinuity bears a striking resemblance to the motif of the palimpsest, which became a leading metaphor for the brain and mental processes in the second half of the nineteenth century and which Collins increasingly employed in his novels throughout his literary career, as in *The Haunted Hotel: A Mystery of Modern Venice* (1879).

The private lunatic asylum on which the plot of *The Woman in White* revolves appears again in *Armadale* (1866), a novel which similarly plays upon doubles and where one of the 'villains' is Dr Downward (later called Le Doux), an abortionist who becomes the owner of a sanatorium for nervous invalids. Embodying the figure of the enterprising doctor, the unqualified Dr Le Doux also dabbles in chemistry, providing the poison meant to kill Allan Armadale. Showing how the development of medicine, whether lay or professional, went hand in hand with the rise of free-market economy, *Armadale* foregrounds as well the significance of science and modern inventions. The novel is set in 1851, when the 'marvels' of science and industry displayed at the Great Exhibition were often discussed in lay journals such as *The Cornhill Magazine* in which *Armadale* was serialised between November 1864 and June 1866.[10] The issue of transmission and electromagnetism, which informs the novel, was the focus of an earlier essay on 'Electricity and the Electric Telegraph', which, as John Sutherland suggests, Collins had most probably read.[11] Throughout the novel, science enables Collins to conflate the natural and the supernatural: telegraphy was very much linked to animal magnetism, since it resulted from the applications of electromagnetism.[12] Hence the novel's play upon electromagnetic forces, such as those fatally attracting the dark-haired Ozias Midwinter to the fair-haired Allan Armadale, and the allusion to the invisible links between individuals permitting the transmission of thoughts. Thus, whilst the characters actually use the telegraph or telegraphic style to communicate, the narrative relies upon the allegation that the body possesses latent electricity, which explains magnetic phenomena as the transmission of 'some invisible aura, or electric, or electro-magnetic current ... from the operator to the brain and nerves of the patient'.[13]

In *The Moonstone*, the character of Rosanna Spearman, who suffers from fainting fits and eventually commits suicide, highlights once again Collins's interest in heredity and his use of tropes of infection: the deformed character, who has one shoulder bigger than the other, is physically branded by her ancestors' crimes and, as already mentioned, appears to contaminate the detectives with a mysterious 'detective fever'. Moreover, the quest for the Moonstone is punctuated by allusions to mesmerism, clairvoyance and magnetic discourse. Collins's sympathy for mesmerism, or 'animal magnetism', had been evinced in his letters to *The Leader*, 'Magnetic Evenings at Home' (1852), which recorded six accounts of mesmerism and clairvoyance Collins had witnessed.[14] In these experiments, the magnetic influence exercised by the mesmerist is seen as 'a curative agent', particularly designed for nervous diseases.[15] In *The Moonstone*, Franklin Blake, whose nervous system is out of order, is administered an opiate by Dr Candy for his distrust of medical science. Blake's opium-induced trance, which leads him to steal the diamond, stands halfway between the field of medicine and that of mesmerism: Collins uses the experiment to stress his belief in animal magnetism as a curative agent, as he intimates further on in the novel by citing the work of

John Elliotson and comparing it with William Carpenter's researches in mental physiology.[16] The narrative is also framed by the Indians' clairvoyant experiment in the opening and by Ezra Jennings's mesmeric experiment at the end: 'it looked like a piece of trickery, akin to the trickery of mesmerism, clairvoyance, and the like'.[17]

The training of the will to harness the automatic self and combat humans' potential reversion into brutes, much encouraged by Victorian mental physiologists, informs *Poor Miss Finch* (1872), which features an epileptic patient and plays upon evolutionary motifs, such as human transformation and interconnectedness between the characters, notably between the twins Oscar and Nugent Dubourg. Just like *The Legacy of Cain* (1888), which questions the inheritance of morbid propensities and biological determinism, in *Poor Miss Finch* epilepsy becomes an index of immorality. Nevertheless, the character is not doomed by his weak will and lack of volitional control but ironically by his medical treatment, since the use of silver nitrate turns him into a 'Blue Man' – a monstrous figure who terrifies the heroine. In addition, the novel borrows from the electric and magnetic language of nineteenth-century mesmerism and spiritualism to connect the lovers, climaxing with the novel's closure as Nugent, the real villain of the narrative, who is also in love with Lucilla Finch, embarks upon an Arctic expedition: recalling contemporary polar expeditions, such as the quest for the North-West passage, the end of the novel evokes Collins's fascination with John Franklin's lost expedition (as illustrated by his stage play, *The Frozen Deep* [1857], which he revised for book publication in 1874, or his later short story, 'The Devil's Spectacles' [1879], also set in the Arctic). Moreover, like Oscar, who is unconscious during his fits, Lucilla, who is blind, is as though entranced; deprived of the sense of sight, she trusts voices and the magnetic impressions she receives through skin contact. With her enhanced senses, the heroine heralds Collins's later female characters who experience cataleptic fits, such as Carmina's hystero-catalepsy in *Heart and Science*. Both female characters become the patients (or victims) of surgeons/anatomists: Herr Grosse, a German eye surgeon, aims to cure Lucilla of her cataract in *Poor Miss Finch*, whilst in *Heart and Science*, Dr Benjulia is a vivisectionist who intends to experiment on Carmina's weak will. In the latter case, the novel's concern with vivisection may be paralleled with anxieties related to women falling prey to medical malpractice and experimentation – already visible in the form of experimental gynaecological surgery.[18] Indeed, the novel aligns women and animals, an association which anti-vivisection campaigns often stressed. Just like the London physician famous for handling female cases 'in all their varieties' in *The Haunted Hotel*,[19] Dr Benjulia treats especially sensitive female subjects, from the half-witted Zoe to Carmina, whose hysterical disorder shows forth when she falls into a cataleptic state. Other surgical acts appear in *The New Magdalen* (1873), where Grace Roseberry is injured by a shell wound on the head and undergoes a surgical operation, and in *The Black Robe* (1881), where a silver plate is placed on the right parietal bone of Emma Winterfield's skull after her fall in the circus, whilst the surgeon George Germaine figures in *The Two Destinies* (1876).

The influence of the past upon the present and the future, which heavily marks Collins's plots, from *The Moonstone* to *Man and Wife* (1870) and *The Law and the Lady* (1875), in which the female characters are all haunted by the ghosts of the past and doomed to experience their mothers' and other female characters' fate, evinces Collins's fascination with evolutionary constructions of human physiology. All three novels feature detectives digging up texts and gathering the fragments of former texts to restore an original narrative in a way like neurologists. However, if Ezra Jennings in *The Moonstone* successfully reconstructs Dr Candy's fragmented discourse and is pivotal to the exploration of Franklin Blake's unconscious, in *The Haunted Hotel* the unconscious confession of the villainess (through a play she writes to redeem her conscience) refuses to restore the original text, leaving only traces for the reader to imagine the solution to the mystery of Lord Montbarry's murder. Similarly, in *The Law and the Lady*, the key to the mystery is concealed in a Gothic intertext which reveals the part played by the legless villain, Miserrimus Dexter: devising a Gothic story to make the heroine suspect that her husband's first wife, Sara Macallan, was poisoned, Dexter unconsciously intersperses past memories which betray his knowledge of the woman's suicide. Once again, solving an enigma is intermingled with reading a character's degenerate physiology and pathological mind: the secret is buried in the self, stored among other memories which the investigation rekindles.

Though suppressed memory marks Collins's early novels, such as in *The Dead Secret* (1857) in which Sarah Leeson is gnawed by guilt, in *The New Magdalen* Mercy Merrick's hysterical symptoms function as manifestations of her buried – and immoral – past; whilst the connection between memory and conscience reaches a climax in Collins's later novels, as in *The Haunted Hotel*, since the Catholic murderess's repressed crime threatens to entail 'double consciousness'. But Collins's exploration of memory in *The Haunted Hotel* goes a step further in his later novel, *The Legacy of Cain*, in which the transmission of criminality from the guilty mother (executed for the murder of her husband) to the innocent daughter is figured as a 'hereditary taint',[20] and the repressed shameful material is, as a result, framed by evolutionary fears. Eunice Gracedieu's 'slowness of mind and laziness of body' (LC: 44) align her with children whose moral sense, as criminal anthropologists following Cesare Lombroso believed, was wanting. Uninhibited, excitable and impressionable, the adopted girl is contrasted with Reverend Abel Gracedieu's own daughter, Helena, who recalls Grace Roseberry in *The New Magdalen*, whose self-control is yet shown to be a pathological symptom linked to her head injury. When Eunice realises that Helena has captured her lover's attentions, her beastly nature emerges, turning her into 'a wild animal' (LC: 131), hence testifying to her regression and proving the transmission of her mother's inheritance. As in *The Haunted Hotel*, memory and conscience work in tandem: the surging up of past memories triggers Eunice's 'animal instincts'. But as Eunice writes about her uncurbed passions, she trains her will and gains self-control, showing the extent to which virtue depends, in fact, upon physiological mechanisms. Like Hans Grimm (*alias* Jack Straw), the patient from Bethlehem Hospital who has been taught to weave in *Jezebel's Daughter* (1880), the writing activity in *The Legacy of Cain* prevents the character from drifting into madness – and crime. By way of contrast, in *Man and Wife*, the 'barbarous darkness in [Geoffrey Delamayn's] mind' corresponds to the latent instincts which have not been disciplined by any education of the will.[21] The muscular athlete reacts like other 'savage[s]' (M&W: 177), illustrating contemporary views on criminal physiology. Even in the field of psychology, as Alexander Bain's work underlined, the 'physiognomy of strength' could conceal malevolence.[22]

In addition to medical practitioners, scientists pursuing the quest for Faustian knowledge are found in several novels. Colonel Herncastle in *The Moonstone* and Baron Rivar in *The Haunted Hotel* are both looking for the secrets of the philosopher's stone. Experimental chemistry is alluded to in *The Woman in White*, since Count Fosco has discovered a means of petrifying the body after death, and used in *Jezebel's Daughter*, where Dr Fontaine and Paracelsus, a Hungarian experimental chemist, work on two 'resuscitated poisons'[23] which can be employed either to kill or cure, depending on the dose administered (like arsenic, used both as a cosmetic or tonic and as a deadly poison in *The Law and the Lady*). *Heart and Science* denounces too the abuses of modern science through the character of Mrs Gallilee, the Gothic heroine's heartless aunt who dabbles in science. Collins resorted time and again to such scientific female figures as, for instance, Mrs Lecount in *No Name* (1863) whose 'taste for science' and love of snakes intimate her insensitive nature.[24] In *Heart and Science*, physics and biology are Mrs Gallilee's favourite subjects and her thirst for knowledge is not only a sign of her transgression of Victorian gender spheres but also a symptom of her depraved character. Her success in 'dissecting the nervous system of a bee'[25] and her passion for dissecting flowers, turn her into a female counterpart of vivisectionist Dr Benjulia, the 'dissector of living creatures' (HS: 176).

In the latter novel Collins makes clear from the beginning that David Ferrier's experimental studies of cerebral localisation inform his narrative, and even quotes a sentence from Ferrier's *The Localisation of Cerebral Disease* (1878). The physiologist was Professor of Forensic Medicine at King's College Hospital and Medical School, London. Between 1873 and 1874, he carried out vivisections on live animals and executed post-mortem experiments on the patients of the Wakefield Lunatic Asylum, to which the laboratory he used was attached.[26] The vivisection controversy raged in many periodicals in the late 1870s and early 1880s. Though Collins was not officially a member of one of the many anti-vivisection societies, he actively communicated with Frances Power Cobbe, who founded the Society for the Protection of Animals from Vivisection (later known as the Victoria Street Society).[27] The propagandist purposes of *Heart and Science* were evident at the time of its publication: deemed a novel 'with a purpose', *Heart and Science* was written, as Collins argues in his preface, to help 'the cause of the harmless and affectionate beings of God's creation' (HS: 2). Other scientific figures wend their way through the novel, from Michael Faraday and Hermann von Helmholtz, one of Johannes Peter Müller's pupils, both associated with electricity and its applications in physiology, to Joseph John Thomson, whose work paved the way for the discovery of the electron at the end of the nineteenth century.

Thus, whilst the rise of sensation fiction was seen as a 'collective cultural nervous disorder', a 'morbid addiction' and 'suggested in a single figure the most primitive and atavistic of human responses', as Jenny Bourne Taylor has argued,[28] Collins's novels found their sources of inspiration in the latest medical and scientific discourses. Revisiting villainy by equating moral and mental dysfunction so as to provide up-to-date *frissons*, his narratives proposed much more complex villains than eighteenth-century Gothic novels. They also revamped ghosts, using states of double consciousness or even suspended animation, as in *Jezebel's Daughter* (a novel which hinted at the activism against premature burial), whilst scientists and medical practitioners plot murders and keep secrets, like the London surgeon in *'I Say No'* (1884), who conceals from his goddaughter the reasons for her father's death – and even play tricks, like Dr Candy in *The Moonstone*.

Notes

[1] W. Baker, *Wilkie Collins's Library: A Reconstruction* (Westport, CT: Greenwood Press, 2002).
[2] H. Maudsley, *Body and Mind: An Inquiry into their Connection and Mutual Influence, Specially in Reference to Mental Disorders* (New York: D. Appleton & Co., 1871), p. 12.
[3] See N. Davie, *Tracing the Criminal: The Rise of Scientific Criminology in Britain, 1860–1918* (Oxford: Bardwell Press, 2005).
[4] R. Mighall, *A Geography of Victorian Gothic Fiction: Mapping History's Nightmares* (Oxford University Press, 1999), p. 121.
[5] J. Bourne Taylor, *In the Secret Theatre of Home: Wilkie Collins, Sensation Narrative, and Nineteenth-Century Psychology* (London: Routledge, 1988), p. 30.
[6] H. Small, *Love's Madness: Medicine, the Novel, and Female Insanity, 1800–1865* (Oxford: Clarendon Press, 1996), p. 185.
[7] W. Collins, *The Woman in White*, ed. J. Sutherland (Oxford World's Classics, 1996), p. 158. All further references to this edition are given parenthetically in the text as WW.
[8] D. A. Miller, '*Cages aux Folles*: Sensation and Gender in Wilkie Collins's *The Woman in White*', *Representations* 14 (Spring 1986), pp. 107–36.
[9] See J. Bourne Taylor, 'Obscure Recesses: Locating the Victorian Unconscious', in J. B. Bullen (ed.), *Writing and Victorianism* (London and New York: Longman, 1997), pp. 137–79.
[10] See for instance [Anon.], 'At the Great Exhibition', *The Cornhill Magazine* 5 (January–June 1862), pp. 665–81.
[11] [Anon.], 'Electricity and the Electric Telegraph', *The Cornhill Magazine* 2 (July–December 1860), pp. 61–73. See W. Collins, *Armadale*, ed. J. Sutherland (Harmondsworth: Penguin, 1995), p. 697.
[12] Charles Wheatstone, the inventor of the telegraph, was also involved in electric tests carried out on magnetic subjects; see A. Winter, *Mesmerized: Powers of Mind in Victorian Britain* (University of Chicago Press, 1998), p. 54.
[13] [Anon.], 'Medico-Botanical Society: Animal Magnetism', *Lancet* 9 (June 1838), pp. 367–71, cited in Winter, *Mesmerized*, p. 57.
[14] W. Collins, 'Magnetic Evenings at Home', *The Leader* 3.95 (17 January 1852), pp. 63–4; 3.99 (14 February 1852), pp. 160–1; 3.100 (21 February 1852), pp. 183–4; 3.101 (28 February 1852), pp. 207–8; 3.102 (6 March 1852), pp. 231–3; 3.103 (13 March 1853), pp. 256–7; reprinted in W. Collins, *Magnetic Evenings at Home*, ed. P. Lewis, Wilkie Collins Society (November 2001).

15 Collins, 'Magnetic Evenings at Home' (17 January 1853), pp. 63–4; Wilkie Collins Society reprint, p. 5.
16 John Elliotson was a young professor at University College London, founder and first president of the Phrenological Society, who explored the extent to which life and mind were mechanical, turning supernatural seemings into natural phenomena. He advocated artificial somnambulism to cure nervous disorders. However, he also claimed that the method of induced trance entailed divining 'psychic powers', such as in clairvoyance.
17 W. Collins, *The Moonstone*, ed. D. Blair (London: Penguin, 1986), p. 452.
18 See C. Lansbury, 'Gynaecology, Pornography, and the Antivivisection Movement', *Victorian Studies* 28.3 (Spring 1985), pp. 413–37; and G. Depledge, '*Heart and Science* and Vivisection's Threat to Women', in A. Mangham (ed.), *Wilkie Collins: Interdisciplinary Essays* (Newcastle: Cambridge Scholars Publishing, 2007), pp. 149–63. Lansbury argues that the Austrian vivisectionist Emanuel Klein inspired Collins's Dr Benjulia and H. G. Wells's Dr Moreau.
19 W. Collins, *The Haunted Hotel: A Story of Modern Venice* [1879] (Stroud: Alan Sutton Publishing, 1994), p. 1.
20 W. Collins, *The Legacy of Cain* [1888] (Stroud: Alan Sutton Publishing, 1993), p. 153. All further references to this edition are given parenthetically in the text as LC.
21 W. Collins, *Man and Wife*, ed. N. Page (Oxford World's Classics, 1995), p. 213. All further references to this edition are given parenthetically in the text as M&W.
22 A. Bain, *The Emotions and the Will* [1875], 3rd ed. (New York: Cosimo, 2006), p. 199.
23 W. Collins, *Jezebel's Daughter* [1880] (Stroud: Alan Sutton Publishing, 1995), p. 118.
24 W. Collins, *No Name*, ed. V. Blain (Oxford World's Classics, 1986), p. 323.
25 W. Collins, *Heart and Science* [1883] (Stroud: Alan Sutton Publishing, 1994), p. 35. All further references to this edition are given parenthetically in the text as HS.
26 V. Pedlar, 'Experimentation or Exploitation? The Investigations of David Ferrier, Dr Benjulia and Dr Seward', *Interdisciplinary Science Reviews* 28.3 (September 2003), pp. 169–74 (p. 169).
27 W. Collins, *Heart and Science*, ed. S. Farmer (Peterborough, ON: Broadview Press, 1997), p. 22.
28 Taylor, *In the Secret Theatre of Home*, p. 4.

CHAPTER 25

Language

Melissa Raines

William Makepeace Thackeray claimed that Wilkie Collins's *The Woman in White* (1860) was one of a few novels that caused him to look back on periods of illness 'with a great deal of pleasure and gratitude'; he went on to say, 'Think of a whole day in bed, and a good novel for a companion. No cares: no remorse about idleness: no visitors: and the Woman in White ... to tell me stories from dawn till night!'[1]

This source for the oft-repeated anecdote that Thackeray sat up all night to finish the novel is indicative of a wider trend in Collins criticism: a consensus on the power of a good story. Collins was an extremely popular author who received measures of praise and derision from critics and fellow novelists in his lifetime, but most agreed that whatever his faults, he had an ability to construct plots that inspired intense readerly interest. What is also implied – and sometimes explicitly stated – is that Collins's talents as a master plotter came at the expense of characterisation and style. Indeed, an anonymous review in *Harper's New Monthly Magazine* described Collins as 'the one great "story-wright"' while simultaneously noting that '[i]t would be hard to find in all [Collins's] characteristic works a page which from mere form of expression any one could declare to be his rather than that of any other person who understands grammar and has at command a good store of words'.[2]

While not all critics are this dismissive, Collins's use of his 'good store of words' has received relatively little attention; those who do discuss his style often focus on the broader movements of his narratives or on the novelist's need to write in language that could transmit the story as quickly and lucidly as possible, suggesting that pace itself is ideal in experiencing his work. However, the inventive plots and experimental narratives that are associated with Collins's fiction often demand more than mere transmission.[3] One need only think of the collected documents that make up the narrative of *The Woman in White*. Walter Hartright, compiler of the documents and hero of the story, makes the choice to appeal to those most 'closely connected ... with the incidents to be recorded' in each case, switching between narrators as appropriate; his goal is 'to present the truth always in its most direct and most intelligible aspect'.[4] Yet just as this courtroom-emulating narrative approach raises questions of perspective and the impossibility of the very objectivity it seeks, so Collins's seemingly transparent language destabilises the notion of straightforward representation by, as Janice Allan expresses it, 'consistently acknowledg[ing] the instability of language' itself.[5] This conflict is most noticeable when considering Collins's realist approach to sensationalism, as well as his centring of texts and the act of writing within his stories.

'The Light of Reality'

The mid-Victorian literary critic's devaluing of plot is by extension a devaluing of sensation fiction – of which Wilkie Collins is seen as a founding father – in favour of realism. Many critics felt that sensation fiction's only purpose was a dangerous stimulation of the reader's nerves and a potentially corrupting discussion of subjects such as crime and adultery. Even before the publication of the genre-defining *The Woman in White*, Collins felt the need to defend his inclusion of such topics in the letter of dedication that prefaced *Basil* (1852), his second published novel, by saying that they were a realistic part of human existence. Collins would insist on the importance of engaging with life's darker aspects throughout his career, refusing to be limited by 'the Clap-trap morality of the present day'.[6] Indeed, if the critics of the time often saw Collins's work and sensation novels more broadly as morally questionable, it is interesting that in the introductory letters and prefatory remarks to so many of his texts, Collins presents a kind of ethical imperative in terms of the underlying reality of the sensational, whether through his inclusion of 'the light of Reality' in *Basil*, 'a resolute adherence, throughout, to the truth as it is in Nature' in *No Name* (1863), or writing 'fiction ... founded on facts' in *Man and Wife* (1870).[7] Collins would also make direct reference to consultations with lawyers, doctors and others with relevant professional expertise in arguing for the validity of particular incidents within his novels, so that even in his sensational texts, there is a consistent commitment to his idea that 'the business of fiction is to exhibit human life' (B: 6). Richard Nemesvari has argued that the ideologically charged generative process of 'defin[ing] realism and sensationalism in relationship to each other' – and indeed, in opposition to each other – in the mid-nineteenth century, not only strengthened the conceptions of genre boundaries for each of the evolving novel forms, but also 'reified "the realistic"'.[8] What makes Collins's novels so provocative then is that, as Walter Kendrick puts it, his work 'is founded in the realistic faith which it violates' primarily because it insists on being 'read as if it were realistic'.[9]

Collins's best-known novels, *The Woman in White* and *The Moonstone* (1868), provide the most fundamental formal challenges to the realist approach through their inherent questioning of the authority of the omniscient narrator, but even Collins's own omniscient narrators help to undermine realism's mimetic purpose. Sundeep Bisla contends that the opening of Collins's sixth published novel, *No Name*, is one of many of the author's 'elaborately prepared traps for the reader'; with its specificity of time and place and descriptions of the early morning hours of a happy family home, complete with ticking clock and snoring dog, the intensely mundane scene is 'artfully constructed' as an 'imitation of the realist novel'.[10] What is of interest at the microscopic level is what completes the paragraph describing that 'mysterious morning stillness':

> Who were the sleepers hidden in the upper regions? Let the house reveal its own secrets; and, one by one, as they descend the stairs from their beds, let the sleepers disclose themselves. (NN: 7)

The paragraphs that follow revert to the prosaic detail of the dog crying to be let out and the servants responding, in a definitive retreat back to domesticity, but these simple lines with their focus on what is *not* known (think of the use of 'mysterious', 'hidden', 'secrets', 'disclose') are a kind of uncanny disruption of what feels innately safe and secure. The softly repetitive narratorial command to '[l]et the house' and 'let the sleepers' reveal their stories through display and action respectively, cautions against the anticipation that was ironically prompted by that opening question, for who *is* sleeping upstairs after all? The question seems to crystallise a subconscious moment in the reading process in language – that interrogative impulse that pushes us to the next sentence, the next paragraph and, in this particular case, to the mysterious letter that will disturb the seeming peace of the family home once we are acquainted with its inhabitants. Even when the initial disruption caused by the letter has passed and the story seems to have moved on without revealing its contents, it remains the source of further narrative questions:

> Had the house revolution run its course already? Was the secret, thus far hidden impenetrably, hidden for ever?
>
> Nothing in this world is hidden forever. (NN: 34)

The paragraph break suggests a wavering hopefulness that the definitive pronouncement extinguishes. If the reader were at all inclined to forget, the recurring questions do not allow it, constantly highlighting the sinister persistence of the unknown, and thus the narrator revises the question not to 'if' or even 'what', but to 'how': 'How was the secret now hidden in the household ... doomed to disclose itself?' (NN: 34). It is almost as if the ticking clock from the opening scene is counting down to the moment of crisis.

Patrick Brantlinger argues that '[t]he forthright declarative statements of realistic fiction', when written within a sensation novel, are 'punctuated by question marks'.[11] In *No Name*, and in Collins's fiction more broadly, this is quite literally the case, as his novels are riddled with these questions that prefigure the ones his readers might ask if they paused long enough over a sentence to do so, paradoxically creating a fleeting, suspenseful delay even as they propel us forward. In the case of *No Name*, Collins admits a particular fascination with the suspected future: he explains that after the revelation of the secret of Norah and Magdalen Vanstone's illegitimacy, 'all the main events of the story are purposely foreshadowed, before they take place – my present design being to rouse the reader's interest in following the train of circumstances by which these foreseen events are brought about' (NN: 6). The reveal does not stop the anticipatory questions, although it does shift their focus as the two sisters react to the news that they are legally 'Nobody's Children', and the 'icy resignation' (NN:143) of Magdalen in particular suggests a darker side to her character:

> Was the promise of the future shining with prophetic light through the surface-shadow of Norah's reserve; and darkening with prophetic gloom, under the surface-glitter of Magdalen's bright spirits? If the life of the elder sister was destined henceforth to be the ripening ground of the underdeveloped Good that was in her – was the life of the younger doomed to be the battle-field of moral conflict with the roused forces of Evil in herself? (NN: 147)

The reflective pause created by these questions is more extended than that of the opening, in line with the seriousness of the issues raised. In a sense, it is a literal extension of that initial query: 'Who were the sleepers?' becomes 'What has been sleeping within these young women?' The parallel phrasing, shifting between the 'surface-shadow' of Norah's 'underdeveloped Good' and the 'surface-glitter' of Magdalen's 'roused forces of Evil', gives the passage a cadenced inevitability that the interrogatives themselves belie, just as it reminds us of Collins's well-known preoccupation with doubles and duality. In this case, the duality is not just between but within the two sisters; the shifts in character are precipitated by the sensational event of their revealed illegitimacy. As such the questions posed carry the reflexive subtext of the reader's own 'inbred forces of Good and Evil', poised 'at the mercy of the liberating opportunity' (NN: 146).

Not all critics were convinced of the effectiveness of Collins's technique. Indeed, many seem to feel that there was a heavy-handedness to some of his stylistic choices: Charles Dickens told his friend, 'you know that I always contest your disposition to give an audience credit for nothing, which necessarily involves the forcing of points on their attention'.[12] Kendrick posits that this consistent forcing of 'the reader's attention on the chains that constitute a novel's plot' within sensation fiction detracted from the reality – and by extension, seriousness – of the literary undertaking.[13] While this may have been the case to the mid-Victorian critic, I would argue that the frequent questions, readjustments and reflexive moments within Collins's narratives are meant to work along with the reading process rather than against it. And in revealing the minute movements of 'the train of circumstances' that make a sensational plot, Collins reminds us of the harsh reality that even the most peaceful domestic setting can, at any moment, be disrupted by catastrophe – in other words, of the inherent reality of the sensational.

'I Am Making My Own Flesh Creep With What I Am Writing'

If genre is a contested site within Wilkie Collins's works that has a direct impact on his language, so too is the act of writing and the centrality of texts within his texts. Collins's description of his writing of the dream sequence in *Armadale* 'making [his] own flesh creep'[14] is not unlike descriptions of the reading of sensation fiction; it also alludes to the visceral, and often emotional, aspect of writing itself. The significance, of course, is that writing is expected of so many of Collins's characters and sometimes with serious consequences. Marian Halcombe, narrator of a substantial portion of *The Woman in White* via her diary entries, practically 'writes herself into illness' in attempting to document her sister's tragedy, as Karen Beth Strovas argues.[15] Marian's impassioned relationship with her writing process is what makes the widely accepted reading of Count Fosco's entry in her diary as a textual rape such a convincing one.

Lydia Gwilt, the primary first-person narrator in the largely omnisciently narrated *Armadale* (1866), has a fraught relationship with her diary as well: she writes what she knows that she shouldn't – namely, details that could reveal her criminal past to others and, even more importantly, reveal her potential criminal future to herself. Her realisation that she can capitalise on the secret identity of Ozias Midwinter, who legally shares the name Allan Armadale with his unknowing and wealthy best friend, comes to her as she writes, and she begins to plot to marry Midwinter under his legal name, murder Armadale, and claim his widow's inheritance. The difficulties in executing the plan arise from her unexpected love for Midwinter, and she struggles to recount the details of the 'miserable made-up story' that she told him as a necessary part of her deception (A: 594). She should include a detailed record of the lies that she told in order to be able to 'refer to it consistently on after-occasions', but she cannot put into writing what she actually said:

> There was nothing new in what I told him: it was the common-place rubbish of circulating libraries. A dead father; a lost fortune; vagabond brothers, whom I dread ever seeing again; a bed-ridden mother dependent on my exertions – No! I can't write it down! I hate myself, I despise myself, when I remember that *he* believed it because I said it – that *he* was distressed by it, because it was my story! (A: 594–5)

The fragments of Lydia's 'miserable made-up story' could constitute the beginnings of a Wilkie Collins novel on their own, but the syntaxless list lacks the intensity of what follows: the guilt that arises due to Midwinter's naive belief and loving sympathy. Lydia's refusal to make narrative sense of the details of her lies within the diary is significant, because her diary is so often her space for exploration of the worst sides of herself – the confessed 'secret friend of her wretchedest and wickedest hours' (A: 659). The absence of a full 'made-up story' foreshadows her commitment, on the eve of her wedding to Midwinter, 'never to open [the diary] again' (A: 624), just as the fevered vacillations between self-interest and self-loathing throughout her entries anticipate her return to her 'second self' (A: 659) through writing and, eventually, her tragic end. Unlike *The Woman in White* and *The Moonstone*, with their carefully delineated narrative strategies, there is never any reasoning given for the reliance upon Lydia's diary for substantial sections of *Armadale*; no other character has the same level of narrative privilege and exposure, and even with the sections of her diary, a great deal of Lydia's past experience is revealed through other characters. At the age of twelve and under the direction and approval of the adults in her life, Lydia Gwilt wrote a 'miserable made-up story' that poisoned her future both figuratively and literally. By giving the reader access to Lydia's diary at key moments in the novel, the impact of that early abuse is made manifest, as Collins provides an even darker exploration of 'the struggle of a human creature, under those opposing influences of Good and Evil' (NN: 5).

What emerges throughout Collins's work is the vital significance of texts themselves in terms of the contribution of their varied voices and their direct impact on the intricate stories within the novels. The connections with texts within stories can be intensely personal, such as Lydia's with her diary or Magdalen's decision to copy portions of her father's will and his final letter and keep them close to her heart; but there is also the importance of legal letters and documents, whether in an official sense or, of course, as collections of evidence. Darcy Irvin notes that *The Woman in White*, and I would argue Collins's novels more broadly, are not only 'deeply interested in the presentation and reproduction of the documents that make up the story', but also 'consumed with suspicion of images, texts, and image-texts'.[16] These documents – from the written testimonies of *The Woman in White* and *The Moonstone* to the letters, wills, registries and marriage licences that function in a more official capacity – are seen as a source of truth, but there are many times throughout the novels when texts – whether personal or official – are imprecise if not 'wholly inaccurate'.[17] The most glaring example, of course, is what Kendrick describes as the 'striking moment when language is negated by the sight of a living face' – when Walter Hartright meets the woman he loved and believed he had lost, Laura, Lady Glyde, standing by her grave.[18] The undoing of textual authority here only reinforces what has been suggested throughout: that textual renderings, even when chiselled in stone, are never absolute, and that truth is only ever an illusion.

Notes

[1] W. M. Thackeray, from 'De Finibus', *The Cornhill Magazine* 6.285 (August 1862), in N. Page (ed.), *Wilkie Collins: The Critical Heritage* (London: Taylor & Francis, 2005), p. 117. Hereafter cited as Page.

[2] Page, p. 177.

[3] B. A. Booth, 'Wilkie Collins and the Art of Fiction', *Nineteenth-Century Fiction* 6.2 (September 1951), pp. 131–43 (p. 132); Page, p. xi.

[4] W. Collins, *The Woman in White*, ed. J. Sutherland (Oxford World's Classics, 2008), p. 2.

[5] J. M. Allan, '"A Lock without a Key": Language and Detection in Collins's *The Law and the Lady*', *Clues: A Journal of Detection* 25.1 (Fall 2006), pp. 45–57 (p. 46).

6. W. Collins, *Armadale*, ed. C. Peters (Oxford World's Classics, 2008), n.p. (hereafter cited parenthetically in the text as A).
7. W. Collins, *Basil: A Story of Modern Life*, ed. D. Goldman (Oxford World's Classics, 2008), p. 5 (hereafter cited parenthetically in the text as B); W. Collins, *No Name*, ed. V. Blain (Oxford World's Classics, 2008), p. 5 (hereafter cited parenthetically in the text as NN); *Man and Wife*, ed. N. Page (Oxford World's Classics, 2008), p. 5.
8. R. Nemesvari, '"Judged by a Purely Literary Standard": Sensation Fiction, Horizons of Expectation, and the Generic Construction of Victorian Realism', in K. Harrison and R. Fantina (eds.), *Victorian Sensations: Essays on a Scandalous Genre* (Columbus: Ohio State University Press, 2006), pp. 15–28 (pp. 19, 17).
9. W. M. Kendrick, 'The Sensationalism of *The Woman in White*', *Nineteenth-Century Fiction* 32.1 (June 1977), pp. 18–35 (p. 21).
10. S. Bisla, 'Overdoing Things with Words in 1862: Pretense and Plain Truth in Wilkie Collins's *No Name*', *Victorian Literature and Culture* 38.1 (2010), pp. 1–19 (pp. 1, 2).
11. P. Brantlinger, 'What Is "Sensational" about the "Sensation Novel"?', in L. Pykett (ed.), *Wilkie Collins: Contemporary Critical Essays* (Basingstoke: Macmillan, 1998), pp. 30–57 (p. 30).
12. Page, p. 81.
13. Kendrick, 'Sensationalism', p. 72.
14. W. Collins to Mrs Harriet Collins, 9 September 1864, in W. Baker and W. M. Clarke (eds.), *The Letters of Wilkie Collins*, 2 vols. (Basingstoke: Macmillan Press, 1999), vol. 1, p. 250.
15. K. B. Strovas, '"Oh my God! Am I Going to Be Ill?": Narratives of Sleep and the Sickbed in Wilkie Collins's *The Woman in White*', *CEA Critic* 75.1 (March 2013), pp. 22–35 (p. 30).
16. D. Irvin, 'Image-Texts in *The Woman in White*', *Rocky Mountain Review* 63.2 (Fall 2009), pp. 225–32 (pp. 228, 230).
17. Ibid., p. 230.
18. Kendrick, 'Sensationalism', p. 32.

CHAPTER 26

Collins and the Artists
Leonee Ormond

As the son of a painter, Wilkie Collins was born into the artistic community. His father, William Collins, was a Royal Academician with a gift for landscapes and for scenes painted near the coast. His parents gave their son his father's name, William, followed by that of a particular friend of his father's, the Scottish artist David Wilkie, who was the child's godfather. At the christening, David Wilkie looked carefully at the baby's eyes, and decided that 'He sees.'[1] William and Harriet Collins's younger son, Charles Allston Collins, born in 1828, became an artist, so that, as a writer of fiction, Collins was working in a different field from his close relatives. Not surprisingly, however, he would introduce artists into his novels and stories.

The family lived in various locations while their son was young, including Ramsgate and Hampstead Square, before moving into Porchester Terrace, near Hyde Park, in 1830. When Collins was twelve, they set out to travel to Italy. This was a journey which his father had long wanted to make, but, after a short time in Paris, they were delayed in Nice due to a cholera epidemic in Italy. Six weeks later they moved on to Rome, where they arrived in January 1837 and took an apartment near the Villa Borghese. Collins would tell friends that he had his first love affair there, aged fourteen. From Rome the family went to Naples, where Collins's father was taken ill. After his recovery, they returned to Rome and, in August 1838, they were back in London and living on Avenue Road near Regent's Park. Collins was then sent to an Academy school in Islington, where he remained for two-and-a-half years and which he much disliked. He was already contemplating becoming an author while his father hoped that he would be a clergyman.

Collins began to write his first novel, *Ioláni; or, Tahíti as it Was; A Romance*, in 1844, on his return from a visit to Paris. While he was there he had gone to the Louvre, but was not greatly impressed. Only two history paintings caught his imagination. On another visit to Paris and the Louvre, the following year, he

> showed a strange mix of enthusiasm and disdain, extravagantly comparing a history painting exhibited at Versailles, Horace Vernet's *The Capture of Abd-el-Kader's Camp at Taguim*, to Michaelangelo's [sic] *Last Judgement*, while concluding that two shows of up-and coming landscape and history painters were dire – 'the worst Suffolk street landscape is superior to the best picture' in the former, while the standards in the latter were 'ineffably below those of the Royal Academy students'.[2]

In the summer of 1845, an exhibition of projected frescoes for the new House of Lords was held, and again, Collins was not impressed:

> Oh those frescoes! Upon my honor I can fancy the spirit of Raffael wandering round the Hall at night and weeping for shame and sorrow as he looks at them. Maclise is the only man there is any hope of. He seems to understand his material at least.[3]

Collins knew the Irish artist Daniel Maclise through his friends Ned and Henrietta Ward, who were Maclise's neighbours. Maclise was indeed, in 1847 and 1849, to paint two frescoes for the House of Lords, *The Spirit of Chivalry* and *The Spirit of Justice*. He had been very close to Dickens, but, as Nancy Weston explains in her biography of the artist: 'After Maclise, Dickens picked Wilkie Collins, a dozen years younger than he, to be his companion on the sort of youthful and free-spirited outings that he had enjoyed previously with Maclise.'[4]

Other artists whom Collins knew well were from the Pre-Raphaelite Brotherhood, founded in 1848. One friend was John Everett Millais, whom Collins met from time to time at his club, the Athenaeum. A sinister Collins story, published on 23 December 1851, is 'Mr Wray's Cash-Box: A Christmas Sketch', for which the young Millais drew his first published illustration. In the story, Wray, who has made a cast of the bust of Shakespeare in Stratford-upon-Avon, is worried that this will be regarded as a criminal act and conceals it in his cash-box. Millais's drawing shows Martin Blunt from the side, with Wray's grand-daughter, Annie, fixing his neckerchief. The *Athenaeum* published a negative review of the story and the illustration on 10 January 1852.

In the same year, Collins published 'A Passage in the Life of Mr Perugino Potts (Extracted, by Permission, from the Italian Journal of Mr P.P.)' in *Bentley's Miscellany*. The publication was anonymous, perhaps because the writer felt that, as an artist's son and a journalist, he should not be identified as the writer of such a satire on the art world. The third paragraph tells us that, like the author, the speaker comes from a family with a connection to the arts:

> I was destined to be an artist from my cradle; my father was a great connoisseur, and a great collector of pictures; he christened me 'Perugino', after the name of his favourite master, left me five hundred a year, and told me with his last breath to be Potts, RA, or perish in the attempt. I determined to obey him; but, though I have hitherto signally failed in becoming an RA, I have not the slightest intention even of so much as *beginning* to perish, in compliance with the alternative suggested to me by my late lamented parent. Let the Royal Academy perish first! I mean to exist for the express purpose of testifying against that miserably managed institution as long as I possibly can.[5]

Pietro Perugino was an Italian artist of the fifteenth and sixteenth centuries, and by choosing the more down to earth name 'Potts' for the other half of his character's surname, Collins provides his story with an amusing title.

The narrator tells us that he has been trying without success to join the Royal Academy. In the first year he sent in a painting of *The Smothering of the Princes in the Tower* and in the second he was equally unlucky with *The Wise and Foolish Virgins*:

> ten angular women, in impossible attitudes, with a landscape background, painted from the anti-perspective point of view – turned out! The third year I changed to the sentimental and pathetic; it was Sterne's *Maria*, this time, with her goat; Maria was crying, the goat was crying, Sterne himself (in the background) was crying.[6]

Collins continues with this satirical account of the Royal Academy's practices, telling his readers that, in the fifth year, the artist 'gave up figures' and sent in a classical landscape with 'three ruined columns, five pine-trees, a lake, a temple, distant mountains, and a gorgeous sunset'.[7] This painting, for which he was charging 50 guineas, and which also showed dancing nymphs in Roman togas, was turned down. In his small seventh-year painting, he chose an everyday subject and showed 'a pot of porter, a pipe, and a plate of bread and cheese', but this 'one little ewe-lamb of a picture, was – turned out!'[8] Now, in the eighth year, the artist tells us that he is in Rome: 'I, Perugino Potts! vowed to grapple with Raphael and Michaelangelo on their own ground! Grand idea!'[9] Collins published the story four years after the founding of the Pre-Raphaelite Brotherhood, and his character's determination to grapple with Raphael and Michelangelo clearly reflects this, together with the writer's support for his brother, Charles.

In the biography of his father, John Guille Millais explains that, although he does not have much to say about Collins in connection with the arts, he knows that both Wilkie and Charles Collins were 'for many years amongst Millais' most intimate friends, and no one more admired his [Collins's] brilliant talent as a novelist'.[10] J. G. Millais then describes how, on one of their walks, in the late 1850s, the friends saw an attractive woman, dressed in white, running through Regent's Park. Wilkie Collins ran after her, and on the next day he told them that she had been kept prisoner by a man in a nearby villa. There have been suggestions that this was the inspiration for the opening of Collins's novel, *The Woman in White*, published in 1860. However, Collins himself said that he took the plot of the novel 'from Maurice Méjan's *Recueil des causes célèbres, et des arrêts qui les ont décidées*, a collection of French legal cases published at the start of the century'.[11]

Around 1850, J. E. Millais painted a portrait of Collins, which is now in the National Portrait Gallery, London. It shows the writer with his fingers touching and in smart dress, with a bow tie and raised collar. It would seem that he is contemplating some of his writing, and he has an obviously thoughtful expression. Alison Smith has suggested that William Holman Hunt may have been inspired by Collins's novel *Basil* of 1852, with its story of a rich young man's marriage to a tradesman's daughter, when, in 1852–3, he was painting one of his best-known pictures, *The Awakening Conscience* (Tate Britain, London). The painting shows a woman who has leapt from the lap of a man, presumably her lover, who has been playing the piano. Smith argues that a passage in chapter 10 of the novel, in which Collins describes 'the drawing room of the girl's father's house, could almost be taken as a description in prose of the interior in Hunt's painting':

> Everything was oppressively new ... the paper on the walls, with its gaudy pattern of birds, trellis-work and flowers ... the showy window curtain of white and sky blue, and the still showier carpet of red and yellow ... the round rosewood table was in a painfully high state of polish ... Never was a richly furnished room more thoroughly comfortless than this – the eye ached at looking round it.[12]

Judith Bronkhurst, in her *Catalogue Raisonné* of Hunt's paintings, suggests that the cat 'tormenting' a bird painted under the man's chair is symbolic of the relationship between the man and woman in *The Awakening Conscience*. And, like Smith, she speculates that 'The latter may have been inspired by a scene in Wilkie Collins's novel *Basil*', quoting from Hunt's own statement about the imagery of the screen behind the woman in the painting: 'The corn and vine are left unguarded by the slumbering cupid watchers and the fruit is left to be preyed upon by thievish birds'.[13]

In a letter written to Millais in 1863, Collins told him that he had been:

> miserably ill with rheumatic gout ever since that pleasant dinner at your house and I am only now getting strong enough to leave England in a few days and try the German baths ... I hear great things of a picture of yours [*The Eve of St Agnes*], but there is no chance of my getting to see it. If I am alive, I hope to be back in June and see it at the Academy. All the little strength I have got is now wanted for preparations for the start.[14]

Collins goes on to lament the death of another painter friend, Augustus Egg: 'Poor dear Egg! No such heavy distress as that has tried me for many and many a year past. And I know you must have felt it too.'[15]

Not surprisingly, Collins sometimes includes accounts of the lives of artists and descriptions of paintings in his narratives. In his 'The Traveller's Story of a Terribly Strange Bed', published in *Household Words* in 1852, the narrator is staying in a gambling house in Paris. After he has bolted the door he falls asleep, but when he wakes in the morning he sees a 'dark old picture' of a man 'in a high Spanish hat, crowned with a plume of towering feathers'. The subject is

> A swarthy sinister ruffian, looking upward, shading his eyes with his hand, and looking intently upward – it might be at some tall gallows at which he was going to be hanged. At any rate, he had the appearance of thoroughly deserving it.[16]

The narrator counts the feathers in the hat:

> they stood out in relief – three white, two green. I observed the crown of his hat, which was of a conical shape, according to the fashion supposed to have been favoured by Guido Fawkes. I wondered what he was looking up at. It couldn't be at the stars; such a desperado was neither astrologer nor astronomer. It must be at the high gallows, and he was going to be hanged presently.[17]

Studying the painting makes the man uneasy at being in 'a strange house of the most suspicious character', and he finds that there is a 'murderous canopy' in the ceiling over the bed.[18] He realises that he has been drugged, but survives and escapes.

With his father and his brother as artists, Collins had personal experience of the importance of becoming an Academician in an artist's career.

On 7 November 1853, he and his younger brother Charles were out of London, as were John Millais and his brother William. This was also the day on which the election for associate members of the Academy was to take place. On their return to London, they heard that Millais, who was twenty-four, had been elected. Just over a year later, on 29 January 1855, Collins's mother, Harriet Collins, gave a dinner party with her sons, Wilkie and Charles. J. G. Millais reports:

> Millais and Charles Dickens met (I think) for the first time. After dinner they talked till a late hour on pictures, and particularly on the subject of 'The Rescue,' on which Millais was then engaged. Dickens, it will be remembered, objected strongly to Millais' treatment of 'Christ in the House of His Parents,' and had made no attempt to disguise his feeling in speaking of the picture in *Good Words*.[19]

As Millais's biographer G. H. Fleming notes: 'Thanks largely to amiable, tactful Harriet Collins, everything proceeded smoothly. Millais mentioned his new picture, whereupon Dickens offered to send him a copy of an article on the London fire brigade' from *Household Words*, the journal in which Dickens had attacked the Pre-Raphaelites.[20] It came with a note in which Dickens expressed his current admiration for Millais's more recent work. Collins must have been proud to have achieved this important meeting.

It is not surprising that Wilkie Collins should choose to write about artists and art works in his fiction, and his novels and stories give us an insight into a world which he knew well. He is also a talented storyteller, so that, as readers, we are not only drawn into a world which he understood, but also gripped by the stories themselves.

Notes

[1] A. Lycett, *Wilkie Collins: A Life of Sensation* (London: Windmill Books, 2014), p. 22.
[2] Ibid., p. 63.
[3] W. Baker and W. M. Clarke (eds.), *The Letters of Wilkie Collins*, 2 vols. (Basingstoke: Macmillan, 1999), vol. 1, p. 21.
[4] N. Weston, *Daniel Maclise: Irish Artist in Victorian London* (Dublin: Four Courts Press, 2001), p. 118.
[5] W. Collins, *The Dream-Woman and Other Stories*, ed. P. Miles (London: Phoenix, 1998), p. 19.
[6] Ibid., p. 20.
[7] Ibid.
[8] Ibid.
[9] Ibid.

10. J. G. Millais, *The Life and Letters of Sir John Everett Millais*, 2 vols. (New York: F. A. Stokes, 1899), vol. 1, p. 278.
11. Lycett, *Wilkie Collins*, p. 198.
12. A. Smith, 'The Awakening Conscience', in T. Barringer, J. Rosenfeld and A. Smith, *Pre-Raphaelites: Victorian Avant-Garde* (London: Tate Publishing, 2012), p. 134.
13. J. Bronkhurst, *William Holman Hunt: A Catalogue Raisonné: Paintings* (London: Paul Mellon Centre, 2006), p. 166.
14. J. G. Millais, *The Life and Letters*, vol. 1, pp. 281–2.
15. Ibid., vol. 1, p. 282.
16. Collins, *The Dream-Woman*, pp. 10–11.
17. Ibid., p. 11.
18. Ibid., p. 13.
19. J. G. Millais, *The Life and Letters*, vol. 1, 248–9.
20. G. H. Fleming, *John Everett Millais: A Biography* (London: Constable, 1998), p. 144.

CHAPTER 27

Music

Allan W. Atlas

Writing to his wife from Florence on 21 November 1853, Charles Dickens commented about his friend and travelling-companion, Wilkie Collins:

> On music too, he is very learned, and sometimes almost drives me into a frenzy humming and whistling whole overtures – with not one movement correctly remembered from the beginning to the end. I was obliged to ask him, the day before yesterday, to leave off whistling the overture to William Tell. 'For by Heaven,' said I, 'there's something the matter with your ear – it must be the cotton which plays the Devil with the commonest tune.'[1]

Yet whether Collins had a tin ear or not, he deeply appreciated music and had an educated amateur's knowledge of both the classical canon and various vernacular traditions. A contemporary description catches him listening to music: 'I was astonished at the capacity for enjoyment that ... Collins seemed to have ... He seemed to absorb the music ... He told me afterwards that it ... made him feel ten years younger.'[2] Here we will concentrate exclusively on Collins's attitude toward classical music, specifically on his strong and unwavering likes and dislikes, which he spelled out clearly in both his letters and, more importantly, in his works.

We begin with what Collins did not like: German music of the 'modern school', which he associated first and foremost with Robert Schumann. As he wrote to Elizabeth Benzon, on 20 February 1869: 'I hope you were not the worse for this concert. As for me, Herr Schumann's music, Madame Schumann's playing, and the atmosphere of St. James's Hall, are three afflictions as I never desire to feel again.'[3] (Note that Collins had ample opportunity to hear Clara Schumann during the weeks just prior to the letter; beginning on 30 January, she performed in London on at least five occasions.)[4]

It was, however, in four works from the 1870s to 1880s that Collins made his views known to his readers. In *Miss or Mrs?* (1873) the renowned pianist 'Bootmann' is playing at the home of Lady Winwood, who says to one of the guests:

> the great Bootmann is playing the Nightmare Sonata in the next room ... You have only to shut your eyes, and you fancy you hear four modern German composers playing, instead of one, and not a ghost of a melody among all the four.[5]

The narrator adds:

> The great Bootmann had arrived at that part of the Nightmare Sonata in which musical sound ... principally [in] the left hand ... describe[s] beyond all possibility of mistake, the rising of the moon in a country churchyard, and a dance of Vampires round a maiden's grave. (MM: 50)

Needless to say, 'Bootmann' = Schumann (an equation that Collins likely derived from the curmudgeonly critic at *The Athenaeum*, Henry Chorley, who had dubbed Clara Schumann the 'shoewoman');[6] and though gender goes unmentioned, the real-life reference is surely to Clara, who was a mainstay on the London recital stage from the mid-1850s on. As for the 'Nightmare': it resists identification, if, in fact, there is even a real sonata to identify. (One candidate: Beethoven's Piano Sonata No. 17 in D minor, op. 31, no. 2, the 'Tempest', which Collins could have heard Clara Schumann perform in February 1867.)[7]

In *The Fallen Leaves* (1879), Collins calls modern German music 'pretentious instrumental noises ... impudently offered ... as a substitute for melody ... musical quackery',[8] while two years later, in *The Black Robe* (1881), he confesses, through Lord Loring, 'I don't understand modern German music'.[9] Finally, there are the stinging indictments in *Heart and Science* (1883), where he takes aim not only at German instrumental music, but also at German opera and the degree to which German music in general has taken over the musical life of London. As the music-master Mr Le Frank puts it: 'My composition has been carefully based on fashionable principles ... the modern German school. As little tune as possible',[10] while earlier in the novel, the seventeen-year-old Carmina Graywell had expressed things from the concert-goer's point of view:

> Is there no Italian music in London? ... Reading the advertised programmes, Carmina found them in one remarkable respect, all alike. They would have led an ignorant stranger to wonder whether any ... Italian ... French ... and English composers had ever existed. The music offered to the English public was music of exclusively German (and for the most part modern German) origin. (HS: 54–5)

When Carmina tries again to find some musical entertainment:

> The so-called Italian opera was open that night ... Fortune was still against them. A German opera appeared on the bill. Carmina turned to the music-seller in despair. 'Is there no music, sir, but German music to be heard in London?' (HS: 57–8)

Indeed, Carmina might well have been faced with Wagner, Wagner and more Wagner, for it was in 1882, just as *Heart and Science* was being issued in serial fashion, that London heard its first performances of *Tristan und Isolde*, *Die Meistersinger* and *Der Ring*.

And at the root of all this modern German music, thought Collins, lay Beethoven. As Collins confessed to Nina Lehmann (and her sisters) in a letter dated 12 June 1860, 'the "Great Kreutzer Sonata" [op. 47, for piano and violin] has upset me about classical music ... The whole violin part of "The Great K.S." appeared to me to be the musical expression of a varying and violent stomach-ache with intervals of hiccups.'[11]

In *No Name* (1863), Mr Vanstone describes what I believe is Symphony No. 7 in A major, op. 92, as 'Nothing but Crash-Bang, varied now and then by Bang-Crash',[12] while *Armadale* (1866) finds Beethoven guilty by association with the villainous Lydia Gwilt who dotes on him.[13]

What, then, did Collins like? In one word: *melody*, especially when it was unencumbered by thick, complicated accompaniments and counterpoint. And this he found in three repertories. First, there was Italian opera: Bellini in both *The Law and the Lady* (1875)[14] and *Armadale* (A: 493); Donizetti in *The Woman in White* (1860), where *Lucrezia Borgia* is 'delicious music';[15] and Rossini, whose *Moses in Egypt* is a 'sublime oratorio' and the Overture to *Guillaume Tell* a 'symphony under another name' (WW: 336).

Another source was the piano music of Chopin, Mendelssohn (both in NN: 69) and Schubert (*Poor Miss Finch* [1872]),[16] as well as a piece that Collins cites as the '"Last Waltz" of Weber' (*The Dead Secret* [1857]),[17] which can be identified more precisely as 'Webers letzter Gedanke', no. 5 in Karl Gottlieb Reissiger's *Danses brillantes pour le piano*, op. 26 (c.1824), which was generally known in England as 'Weber's Last Waltz'.[18] That Collins offers no criticism here is no doubt a sign of tacit approval. And that he could discern the difference between Robert Schumann's full-fledged, literary-influenced romanticism and the classicism that still pervades the music of Mendelssohn and Schubert speaks well for his sense of musical style (but see below).

Finally, there is Mozart: 'the king of all music-composers that ever lived', as Joseph Buschmann calls him in *The Dead Secret* (185), and one of the 'gods in this world' (along with Shakespeare and Raphael) according to Valentine Blyth in *Hide and Seek* (1854).[19] For Madame Pratolungo, Mozart's piano sonatas are 'divine serenity and completeness ... raised above all other music that was ever written (PMF: 163), while in *Man and Wife* (1870) Julius Delamayn says of the 'Adagio' of the 'Fifteenth' sonata for violin and piano: 'If ever there was divine music written by mortal man, there it is!'[20]

On two occasions, Collins assigns a quasi-dramatic role to Mozart's music. In *The Woman in White*, Laura Fairlie plays 'new music of the ... tuneless, florid kind' for the depraved Sir Percival Glyde, whom she has been forced to marry; on the other hand, she plays 'lovely old melodies of Mozart' for her true love, Walter Hartright, and does not play them again after his departure (WW: 187). As much as anything else, then, music tells us where Laura's heart lies. Finally, in *The Dead Secret*, it is a music box that once belonged to Mozart himself that becomes a character of sorts; though it chimes tunes from *Don Giovanni* – Zerlina's 'Batti, batti' (DS: 144–6) and the Act I minuet (DS: 166) – it falls silent at the recollection or experience of moments of heartbreak (DS: 220–1, 349). Thus, Mozart's music represents life itself, both in the present and in the nostalgic past.

In all, and with the partial exception of his harsh criticism of Beethoven, Collins's views on music – adulation of Mozart, acceptance of Mendelssohn, Chopin, Schubert and the Italian *bel canto* composers, and an inability to come to terms with the 'modernism' of Schumann and Wagner – place him squarely within the mid-century, conservative mainstream of Victorian taste as exemplified by such critics as the previously mentioned Henry Chorley, along with J. W. Davison, chief critic at *The Times*. Like them, Collins had trouble 'hearing' past the past.

Four Miscellaneous Observations

Collins's Music Library

Among the music-related items in Collins's library were two biographies of Mozart: that by Edward Holmes, *The Life of Mozart* (1845) – at the time the most authoritative English-language treatment of the composer – and Otto Jahn's monumental *The Life of Mozart* (in the 1882 translation by Pauline Townsend). Also on the shelves: Ignaz Moscheles's English version of Anton Felix Schindler's *The Life of Beethoven* (1840) and the revised edition (1881) of Berlioz's *Mémoires* (in the original French).[21]

A Mozart Misattribution

In chapter 13 of *The Frozen Deep* (the 1874 novella version), Mrs Crayford plays the piano for Clara Burnham: 'Mozart's "Air in A, with Variations"... the lovely melodies... of that unpretending and unrivalled work'.[22] Though I initially assumed that this was the first movement of the well-known Piano Sonata in A, K. 331 (this despite Mrs Crayford's arriving at variation 9 – the Mozart sonata has only six – 'literary licence', I thought), Nicky Losseff has argued persuasively that the piece in question was the widely circulated *Air in A with Variations* (ten of them) by the now largely forgotten Emanuel Aloys Förster, and that Collins's favourable judgment of the work may well have been influenced by his mistakenly thinking that it was by Mozart (was his stylistic sense not quite as well honed as I implied above?).[23]

Amateur versus Professional

Collins seems to have been in full accord with the Victorian suspicion of professional musicians. In *Heart and Science*, the pianist/music teacher, Mr Le Frank, turns out to be the villain of the story; likewise, Miss Hoighty, the would-be opera singer in *The Law and the Lady*, is vulgar, speaks ungrammatically and is motivated mainly by the prospect of making money (LL: 91). On the other hand, Collins praises Julius Delamayn: though he 'practised the *foreign vice* of perfecting himself in the art of playing on an instrument [violin]', he remained an amateur (M&W: 160; my emphasis), while in the same work, Anne Silvester chillingly says about her own daughter: 'Don't bring her up like me!... Don't let her act! Don't let her sing! Don't let her go on the stage' (M&W: 42). No wonder that Collins's favourite pianist was his dear friend and *amateur* musician Nina Lehmann.[24]

Gendered Instruments

Finally, the Victorians had strong convictions about which instruments were appropriate for women and which for men. Until the third quarter of the century, well-bred 'ladies' (and the governesses who looked after them) did not play string instruments (and heaven forbid puffing up their cheeks on the winds); rather they sang or they played piano, harp (by mid-century in steep decline), guitar or the extremely popular (especially with the upper crust) English concertina.[25] Indeed, the Royal Academy of Music did not accept its first female violin student until January 1872. Likewise, English 'gentlemen' did not play the piano; their instrument was the violin. And with all of this, Collins toed the line. Among his pianists: Laura Fairlie, Lucy Crayford, Madame Pratolungo and many others, all of whom were women; as for the violin: we count Julius Delamayn and Basil's older brother Ralph in *Basil* (1852).[26]

Only upon bridging the period's rigid social conventions did Collins step over the equally hard-drawn distinctions with respect to instruments. Thus in *The Fallen Leaves*, Amelius Goldenheart plays the piano; but 'Mel' (as he chooses to be called), despite looking forward to a handsome inheritance, had been raised by the Primitive Christian Socialists in Illinois (FL: 20), had turned his back on hard-and-fast class differences and had rescued Sally, a teenage prostitute, from the streets (they eventually wed); and Sally: she played the violin (FL: 156–7).

In sum, although Collins never burrowed deeply into the music he cites (he lacked the training with which to do so), he used music consistently, not only to express his own likes and dislikes, but to round out his characters and to imbue his work with, as Richard Altick calls it, 'the presence of the present'. Indeed, Altick goes so far as to place Collins alongside George Eliot as one of the two Victorian novelists 'whose serious musical interests exceeded the norm for the time'.[27]

Notes

[1] G. Storey, K. Tillotson and A. Easson (eds.), *The Letters of Charles Dickens* (Pilgrim Edition), Vol. VII: *1853–1855* (Oxford: Clarendon Press, 1993), pp. 203–5.

[2] P. Lewis (ed.), 'Mary Cunliffe's Recollection of Wilkie Collins', Wilkie Collins Society (2020), p. 3; C. Peters, *The King of Inventors: A Life of Wilkie Collins* (Princeton University Press, 1991), p. 324.

[3] W. Baker and W. M. Clarke (eds.), *The Letters of Wilkie Collins*, 2 vols. (London: Macmillan, 1999), vol. II, p. 319. Hereafter cited as B&C.

[4] N. B. Reich, *Clara Schumann: The Artist and the Woman*, rev. ed. (Ithaca, NY: Cornell University Press, 2001).

[5] W. Collins, *Miss or Mrs?* (Stroud: Alan Sutton, 1993), p. 49. Further references to this work will appear parenthetically in the text as MM.

[6] R. T. Bledsoe, *Henry Fothergill Chorley: Victorian Journalist* (Aldershot: Ashgate, 1998), p. 269.

[7] A. W. Atlas, 'Wilkie Collins on Music and Musicians', *Journal of the Royal Musical Association* 124.2 (1999), pp. 255–70 (p. 260).

[8] W. Collins, *The Fallen Leaves* (Stroud: Alan Sutton Publishing, 1994), p. 59. Further references to this work will appear parenthetically in the text as FL.

9. W. Collins, *The Black Robe* (Stroud: Alan Sutton Publishing, 1994), p. 61.
10. W. Collins, *Heart and Science*, ed. S. Farmer (Peterborough, ON: Broadview Press, 1996), p. 267. Further references to this work will appear parenthetically in the text as HS.
11. B&C, vol. 1, p. 194 (there dated 1861).
12. W. Collins, *No Name*, ed. V. Blain (Oxford World's Classics, 1986), p. 3. Further references to this work will appear parenthetically in the text as NN.
13. W. Collins, *Armadale*, ed. J. Sutherland (Harmondsworth: Penguin, 1995), p. 142. Further references to this work will appear parenthetically in the text as A.
14. W. Collins, *The Law and the Lady*, ed. J. Bourne Taylor (Oxford World's Classics, 1992), p. 73. Further references to this work will appear parenthetically in the text as LL.
15. W. Collins, *The Woman in White*, ed. J. Symons (Harmondsworth: Penguin, 1974), p. 588. Further references to this work will appear parenthetically in the text in as WW.
16. W. Collins, *Poor Miss Finch*, ed. C. Peters (Oxford World's Classics, 1995), p. 26. Further references to this work will appear parenthetically in the text as PMF.
17. W. Collins, *The Dead Secret* (New York: Dover, 1979), p. 249. Further references to this work will appear parenthetically in the text as DS.
18. Atlas, 'Wilkie Collins on Music and Musicians', p. 264, n. 28; R. Newsome, *Brass Roots: A Hundred Years of Brass Bands and their Music, 1836–1936* (Aldershot: Ashgate, 1998), p. 149.
19. W. Collins, *Hide and Seek*, ed. N. Donaldson (New York: Dover, 1981), p. 20.
20. W. Collins, *Man and Wife*, ed. N. Page (Oxford World's Classics, 1995), p. 435. Further references to this work will appear parenthetically in the text as M&W.
21. W. Baker, *Wilkie Collins's Library: A Reconstruction* (Westport, CT: Greenwood Press, 2002), p. 62.
22. W. Collins, *The Frozen Deep* (London: Hesperus Press, 2004), p. 65.
23. Atlas, 'Wilkie Collins on Music and Musicians', p. 265; N. Losseff, 'Absent Melody and "The Woman in White"', *Music and Letters* 81.4 (November 2000), pp. 532–50 (pp. 538–9).
24. J. Lehmann, *Ancestors and Friends* (London: Eyre & Spottiswoode, 1962), p. 161; Peters, *The King of Inventors*, p. 124.
25. P. Gillett, *Musical Women in England, 1870–1914: 'Encroaching on All Man's Privileges'* (New York: St Martin's Press, 2000); W. A. Atlas, 'Ladies in the Wheatstone Ledgers: The Gendered Concertina in Victorian England, 1835–1870', *Royal Musical Association Research Chronicle* 39.1 (2006), pp. 1–234.
26. W. Collins, *Basil: A Story of Modern Life*, ed. D. Goldman (Oxford World's Classics, 1990), pp. 17, 276.
27. R. D. Altick, *The Presence of the Present: Topics of the Day in the Victorian Novel* (Columbus: Ohio State University Press, 1991), p. 468.

CHAPTER 28

Politics

Patricia Cove

Disguised as a parlour-maid while searching for information about the 'Secret Trust' related to her lost fortune, Magdalen Vanstone listens in on Admiral Bartram's dinner conversation at St Crux: 'Politics, home and foreign, took their turn with the small household history of St. Crux: the leaders of the revolution which expelled Louis Philippe from the throne of France, marched side by side, in the dinner-table review, with old Mazey and the dogs'.[1] Exasperated and anticipating future talk of the Secret Trust, Magdalen hopes, 'They could hardly talk again tomorrow, they could hardly talk again the next day, of the French Revolution and the dogs' (NN: 645). This scene from *No Name* (1863) illustrates several key points about politics in the writing of Wilkie Collins. Politics is ingrained in everyday, mundane life in Collins's work, featuring among the trappings of Victorian realism that frame Collins's sensational plots and lending a pervasive political atmosphere to his writing. However, despite Collins's tendency to include social commentary and critique in his work, especially in his so-called novels with a purpose, politics is not central and political references do not coalesce around any particular political ideology or agenda. In this scene, Magdalen's plot takes precedence over the exciting political developments in Europe, and indeed Great Britain, in April 1848, when this scene is set. Magdalen's dismissiveness of 'the French Revolution and the dogs' as equally unimportant items of conversation transfers to the reader invested in her scheming. In addition, this scene pinpoints *No Name* in political time; though the novel is not explicitly about 1848 or the revolutions of that year, awareness of political currency underlies this novel and much of Collins's work. While politics tends to highlight characterisation and setting in Collins's novels, rather than presenting a coherent political perspective, political context is nevertheless ubiquitous in his work.

Many of Collins's thesis novels cite specific political targets: the United Kingdom's diverse and problematic marriage laws in *Man and Wife* (1870) or the vivisection debate and the 1876 Cruelty to Animals Act in *Heart and Science* (1883), for example. These issues, along with well-known exposures of Victorian social ills, such as the treatment of women and mental illness in *The Woman in White* (1860), demonstrate the importance of social and political critique for Collins. Nonetheless, several of his novels show a pattern of casually and comically minimising politics alongside Collins's thrilling plots. In *The Moonstone* (1868), when describing Colonel Herncastle's compelling history for Franklin Blake, for example, Gabriel Betteredge ironically begs, 'Try if you can't forget politics, horses, prices in the City, and grievances at the club'.[2] Similarly, Collins depicts the lunch conversation at Windygates in *Man and Wife* with the aside: '(topics Politics and Sport – and then, when a change was wanted, Sport and Politics)'.[3] In *Hide and Seek* (1854), Valentine Blyth, one of Collins's most pleasant characters, is resoundingly apolitical, having 'never read a leading article or a parliamentary debate in his life'.[4] References to Parliament mix Collins's trademark exposure of Victorian hypocrisy with light offhandedness. Paternal parliamentarians include the fathers of Basil, Franklin Blake, Catherine Linley and Anne Silvester, whose despicable father, John Vanborough, views his 'estimable wife' as an 'obstacle' to his success (M&W: 21). Lord Holchester and his son Julius are also Members of Parliament, providing a contrast between the ambitious, strategic father and the compassionate, politically timid son. Disturbingly, Sir Percival Glyde, having 'fought successfully two contested elections and ... come out of the ordeal unscathed', uses Parliament as a respectable cover to conceal his true character and crimes.[5] By contrast, Pesca's excited hope, 'One of these days, I go into your noble Parliament. It is the dream of my whole life to be Honourable Pesca, M. P.!' (WW: 61), is benign and comic.

Parliamentary and constitutional reform are sometimes addressed obliquely in Collins's work, as in the allegory of the owls in the summer house at Windygates; the owls' adherence to their constitutional privileges and resistance to reform – in the shape of home renovations – is dated to 1868 (M&W: 54–5). Parliamentary and constitutional high seriousness, particularly speechifying, are also targets for comic deflation. The steward at Porthgenna Tower 'address[es] Uncle Joseph as if he was the Speaker of the House of Commons';[6] Betteredge compares his customary annual birthday speech for Rachel with the Queen's speech opening Parliament (M: 115); and Finch intones 'Parliamentary speeches by Burke or Sheridan' to an exasperated audience, including Madame Pratolungo, who develops 'implacable hostility (on every question of the time) to the policy of Mr Burke'.[7] Collins reserves a serious place for specific bills, debates and targets of reform, like the marriage laws in which *Man and Wife*'s Vanborough finds a legal loophole to dissolve his Irish marriage, using 'the Legislature of Great Britain ... [as] the humble servant of his treachery, and the respectable accomplice of his crime' (M&W: 40), and gaining a seat in Parliament as reward. *Man and Wife* further identifies the Commission on marriage laws and its report (M&W: 231–2) and explicitly indicts English marriage laws, particularly related to women's property, in Hester Dethridge's embedded narrative (M&W: 581–607).

As this interest in women's rights and abuses of domestic power indicates, Collins is heavily invested in exposing authoritarianism and combatting reactionary politics. Collins critiques patriarchal authoritarians like Zack Thorpe's father, whose parlour is likened to 'a cell in Newgate, or a private torturing chamber in the Inquisition' (H&S: 12), as well as retrograde political views like Miserrimus Dexter's claim that women themselves, and not 'the defective institutions of the age they live in', are to blame for inequality.[8] Often, however, offhand political references simply typify a quirky character, like the unflappable governess Miss Sturch of *The Dead Secret*, who, 'If she had lived in a royalist family, during the civil wars in England, ... would have rung for the cook, to order dinner, on the morning of the execution of Charles the First' (DS: 42). Frequent allusions to Napoleon in Collins's work illuminate character and layer suggestively with Collins's themes, like abuses of power in the private sphere in *The Woman in White*, for example. When acting out, six-year-old Zack comically mirrors the authoritarian and insurrectionary political legacies of the French Revolution; he stands 'holding his hands behind him in unconscious imitation of the favourite action of Napoleon the Great', while 'from his bright blue eyes Rebellion looked out frankly mischievous' (H&S: 20). Dexter, with more sinister effect, reveals a personality divided between emulating the autocratic Emperor, when he cries 'I am Napoleon, at the sunrise of Austerlitz!' (LL: 206), and being compelled by the chaos of the Terror, evident in his possession of a leather shirt described as 'Skin of a French Marquis, tanned in the Revolution of Ninety Three. Who says the nobility are not good for something? They make good leather' (LL: 247–8). Such apparent contradictions suggest a continuum between the anarchy of the Revolution and the repressive Empire that succeeded it.

Collins elaborates on Napoleon's attraction in an interview late in his life with Edmund Yates: 'You tell me that the first Napoleon was, in the opinion of his contemporaries, a mean scoundrel and a shameless liar', yet 'men in our own day [are] blinded, as you think, by the Napoleonic legend. It is good to tell the truth about Napoleon, of course; but you cannot break the idol, for his deeds strike the imagination. He was a dramatic man'.[9] 'The Great Napoleon' (WW: 241) is, of course, most visible in the 'strik[ing]' and 'dramatic'[10] figure of Count Fosco, who is also a spy for the Austrian Empire, a byword for continental illiberalism in Victorian Britain. Fosco's need to travel 'abruptly' to Vienna, instead of Rome (WW: 226), indicates his association with Austrian authoritarianism, which is confirmed in Madame Fosco's biography, vindicating his supposed 'Martyr[dom]' serving the established powers and the hereditary privilege they protect (WW: 615). Marian unpleasantly associates the pet mice crawling over Fosco's body with 'hideous ideas of men dying in prison, with the crawling creatures of the dungeon preying on them undisturbed' (WW: 254), an image that resonates with British perceptions of authoritarian continental rule and prison narratives like those by Silvio Pellico and Felice Orsini, whose harrowing experiences as political prisoners raised Italian nationalism's profile for British readers. Pellico, writer and editor of the liberal *Il Conciliatore*, was confined in the Austrian prison Spielberg for a decade and wrote about his experience in his widely translated memoir, *Le Mie Prigioni* (1832). Orsini published two memoirs, *The Austrian Dungeons in Italy* (1856) and *Memoirs and Adventures of Felice Orsini* (1857), and lectured across England and Scotland in 1856–7 after escaping from the Austrian prison San Giorgio. Orsini attempted to assassinate Napoleon III in 1858, spurring France's 1859 military intervention in Austrian-ruled Lombardy alongside Piedmont, which led to Italian unification in 1861. Orsini planned his attack while living in Britain as a refugee, and the affair led to a diplomatic crisis between Britain and France, the Palmerston government's 1858 fall over its response to that crisis, and the creation of the Liberal Party.

Italian by birth, resembling Napoleon and serving Austria, Fosco is a spy stationed in Britain 'charged with a delicate political mission from abroad' (WW: 591) and leading a team of agents, including the Rubelles, assigned to the Great Exhibition. His scandalous extracurricular activity as Sir Percival Glyde's domestic 'spy', 'informer' (WW: 315) and criminal accomplice reminds readers of the spy scandals of previous decades. Topical instances of state spying include the use of spies in the 1794 Treason Trials of several well-known British radicals; the high-profile scandals around spies and provocateurs like John Castle and William Oliver in 1810; and the 1844 Post Office scandal, when Thomas Slingsby Duncombe revealed in Parliament that Italian refugee

Giuseppe Mazzini's letters had been secretly opened by the British government and shared with continental regimes. These revelations of covert state letter-opening associate Fosco's abuses of power as a state-sanctioned and domestic spy with the practices of the British government. Like the Chartist W. J. Linton, whose detective work helped uncover the spying on Mazzini, Walter Hartright earns his living as an engraver while he investigates the conspiracy against Laura. Scenes of domestic spying recur in later novels by Collins, including *Heart and Science* and *The Evil Genius* (1886), though without the state backing that complicates Fosco's intrigue at Blackwater Park.

The counterparts to spies and agents of tyrannical governments, like Fosco, appear in the European revolutionaries and refugees present across Collins's work, mirroring the public awareness of European refugees from Italy, Poland, Hungary and elsewhere who arrived in Britain after each wave of revolution and repression in Europe, such as the 1820–1 uprisings in Italy or the 1848 revolutions. Pesca, who 'had left Italy for political reasons' (WW: 52), is the most famous example of an Italian political radical turned exile among Collins's characters, but he finds a precursor in an Italian 'political refugee, dependent for the bread he ate, on the money he received for teaching languages' in *Basil*.[11] *Heart and Science*'s Roman refugee, Egisto Baccani, like his fictional predecessors, 'got into some political scrape, and took refuge, like the rest of them, in England; and got his living, like the rest of them, by teaching languages'.[12]

Unlike Pesca, whose arrival in England predates the 1848 European revolutions, Baccani's timeline places him in Rome in the late 1860s when Carmina is born. Baccani's 'political scrape' (HS: 219), then, could relate to efforts to overthrow Papal rule in Rome or to promote the Papal States' union with Italy; however, this explanation does not account for his remaining in England after Rome joined Italy in 1870. Finally, the Cuban Manuel, Lydia Gwilt's ex-lover, fraudulently presents himself to Allan Armadale 'as "a political refugee"' in Naples before attempting to rob and murder his dupe.[13] The incredibility of this cover story in the early 1850s, when *Armadale* (1866) is set, is one among many indicators of Armadale's gullibility: Naples, part of the notoriously repressive Bourbon-ruled Kingdom of the Two Sicilies until captured by Giuseppe Garibaldi's army of volunteers in 1860, is an unlikely safe harbour for exiles and, instead, was the origin of many of the displaced people who fled to Britain in the decades before Italian unification.[14]

Though not a refugee herself, Madame Pratolungo in *Poor Miss Finch* (1872) is a formerly active participant in the liberal international with a revolutionary history reminiscent of the Brazilian Anita Garibaldi, whose guerrilla fighting with her husband in 1830s and 1840s South America and in defence of the Roman Republic was legendary;[15] or the British Jessie White Mario, who built a career championing Italian unification and who translated Orsini's *Austrian Dungeons*. White and her future husband, Italian republican Alberto Mario, were held in Genoa's Sant'Andrea prison for their involvement in Mazzini's planned uprisings across Piedmont in 1857, and she later volunteered as a nurse during Garibaldi's expedition to southern Italy. Madame Pratolungo is an amalgam of nineteenth-century political radicalisms, as she participates in and propagandises for nationalist independence movements, republicanism and socialism, and she has links to South America, Italy – through her husband's Italianate name – and France.

As the novel is set in the late 1850s, Madame Pratolungo's revolutionary career is aligned with the 1848 revolutions. She spent her honeymoon on 'the sacred duty of destroying tyrants' in South America (PMF: 1), reminding readers of White Mario's engagement in prison and the Garibaldis' early careers, while her history includes a period of English exile, 'when my glorious Pratolungo and I, succumbing to Fate and tyrants, fled to England for safety; martyrs to that ungrateful Republic (long live the Republic!) for which I laid down my money and my husband his life' (PMF: 236). According to this timeline, Madame Pratolungo's history may have included participation in the 1848 revolutionary Roman Republic and the defence of Rome against counter-revolutionary French intervention, or residence in her home country of France during the French Second Republic, followed by the rise of Louis-Napoleon as French President and, later, Emperor Napoleon III. Like White Mario, Madame Pratolungo gains battlefield nursing experience (PMF: 81) and, like an exaggerated version of Garibaldi, who was exiled from liberalised Piedmont for defending the Roman Republic, Pratolungo was 'fifteen times exiled' when he met his future wife (PMF: 2). When Madame Pratolungo's final words, 'Long live the Republic! Farewell' (PMF: 427) are uttered in 1871, twelve years after the novel's events, the Paris Commune, unjustly a target of anti-revolutionary paranoia among members of the British middle classes, would have been the most immediate republican context. Collins does not indulge histrionic anti-republican or anti-communist fears through Madame Pratolungo, who is primarily a non-threatening, domestic figure (unlike Charles Dickens's bloodthirsty Madame Defarge in *A Tale of Two Cities*), perhaps because, even by 1859, her revolutionary moment is already safely in the past.

The 1859 context of *Poor Miss Finch*'s setting also resonates with Italian revolutionary history; Madame Pratolungo travels with her father to Rome, 'that hotbed of the enemies of mankind', in the first weeks of 1859 (PMF: 116), underlining the shift from pre-unification Papal Rome to the new Italian Rome of the 1870s, when the novel appeared. The Second War of Italian Independence occurred shortly thereafter, in April–July 1859, when allied Piedmont and France pushed the Austrian Empire from Lombardy, a political context Collins highlights when Oscar Dubourg travels to Turin (PMF: 378) and nurses the wounded in the aftermath of 'the famous campaign of France and Italy against Austria' (PMF: 379–80). Oddly, Madame Pratolungo, perhaps distracted by domestic events, does not seem heavily invested in the Italian war, and the plot ends before Garibaldi's 1860 southern campaign, of which Pratolungo's career is heavily reminiscent. Eustace Macallan of *The Law and the Lady* is Oscar's successor, volunteering with the Red Cross in Spain, where he is injured (LL: 196, 306): the 1859 Battle of Solferino, whose wounded Oscar nurses (PMF: 385–7), moved civilian eyewitness Henri Dunant to create the Red Cross.

Madame Pratolungo and Pesca are both comic, non-threatening characters, despite Pratolungo's overt investment in revolutionary violence and Pesca's embroilment with the pseudo-carbonarist Brotherhood. By contrast, the 1880s Irish revolutionaries of *Blind Love* (1890) are presented unsympathetically, perhaps because Ireland's 1879–82 Land War was more immediate – temporally, geographically and in terms of internal British politics – when Collins wrote his final, unfinished novel. *Blind Love*'s prologue features contemporary political acts, including 'conspiracy and assassination', evictions and boycotts.[16] Irish 'political excitement' is described as 'infection' (BL: 84), while the secret society Lord Harry joins, the Invincibles, is 'nothing better than a society of assassins' (BL: 75), a 'network of political conspiracy' led by 'Irish-American desperadoes' (BL: 91). One might question how this Irish 'murderous brotherhood' (BL: 97) differs from *The Woman in White*'s equally murderous Brotherhood, which is the instrument of retribution against Fosco, just as Lord Harry eventually allows himself to be pursued and killed by the Invincibles, whom he has betrayed, providing resolution in both novels. Fosco's combination of the roles of political agent and domestic spy matches this fate and partially legitimises the Brotherhood's actions, as does the organisation's affiliation with the sympathetic refugee Pesca, who defends his youthful decision to join the ranks of a political society whose goal is 'the destruction of tyranny, and the assertion of the rights of the people'

(WW: 569). Despite his Anglophilia, Pesca highlights the pressing need for revolution as a response to tyranny in Italy, arguing that the English 'have conquered your freedom so long ago, that you have conveniently forgotten what blood you shed, and what extremities you proceeded to in the conquering' (WW: 569). Pesca's affiliation and Hartright's awareness of reports of political murders (WW: 574–5) set the stage for what appears to be a justified political assassination in Fosco's case. In *Blind Love*, however, the Invincibles seem to be merely used to frame Lord Harry's adventures and the romance plot involving him, Iris Henley and Hugh Mountjoy; therefore, the extremely negative depiction of Irish revolutionaries, as compared with Pesca or Madame Pratolungo, stands out as politically motivated and anti-Irish. Interestingly, an early version of *Blind Love* (titled *Iris*) featured early nineteenth-century French settings and Italian exiles, which aligns the draft's emphasis on continental European political contexts with Collins's interests in much of his other work.[17]

Given the prevalence of continental exiles and revolutionaries in Collins's work, it is unsurprising that European revolution features as the backdrop to many of his novels, particularly those, including *The Woman in White*, *No Name* and *The Moonstone*, that are set in the radical 1840s. As noted above, the 1848 French Revolution is a topic of discussion at St Crux in April of that year (NN: 644–5). Continental revolution appears similarly comically in *The Moonstone*, when, to divert his daughter Penelope from the topic of the mysterious diamond in June 1848, Gabriel Betteredge claims 'that Mr Franklin and I had both talked of foreign politics, till we could talk no longer, and had then mutually fallen asleep in the heat of the sun' (M: 100). Like the newly married Glydes, who travel to Rome in 1849–50, several *Moonstone* characters travel across revolutionary Europe in 1848–49. Franklin Blake arrives from Europe in May 1848, then leaves England again, destination unknown, the same summer (M: 250). Miss Clack begins her 'foreign exile' in Brittany in 1848, following a financial crisis connected to the 1848 French Revolution (M: 319), and remains there when she composes her narrative in 1850 (M: 256), while Godfrey Ablewhite travels to Brussels in June 1849 (M: 430–1).

The 1840s was also the heyday of British radicalism, the pinnacle of influence for the Chartist movement. Though an exchange 'about the spread of democracy in England' at Rachel Verinder's birthday dinner (M: 126) suggests Chartism's political importance in 1840s Britain, alongside Collins's insistent references to 1840s European revolutions, British radicalism is minimised. For example, Magdalen Vanstone's encounter with the sleepwalking Admiral Bartram and her discovery of the Secret Trust letter in *No Name*, occurs in the early overnight hours of 7 April 1848 (NN: 663–74), just days before the planned mass Chartist rally set for Kennington Common on 10 April 1848. George Bartram criss-crosses the Channel between London and Paris at the same time, seemingly unaware of the Kennington Common rally: his letter to his uncle indicating that he will follow Norah to republican Paris to propose to her is dated 3 April 1848 from London (NN: 681), while his letter to Miss Garth explaining Norah's refusal and his planned return to England is dated 13 April 1848 from Paris (NN: 681–2). Though effective state policing ensured the rally's failure and led to the dwindling of Chartism's power in the protest's aftermath, as the date approached in April 1848, what Dickens described as 'la revolution anglaise' seemed imminent.[18] Chartism's absence from the otherwise politically conscious *No Name* is therefore conspicuous.

Of course, readers understand that Collins does not agree with the Windygates butler's admiration for the villain Geoffrey Delamayn, expressed through the political sentiment, 'Ah! Foreign nations may have their revolutions! foreign aristocracies may tumble down! The British aristocracy lives in the hearts of the people, and lives forever!' (M&W: 243). By contrast, Collins's sympathy with working people is articulated through Lucy Yolland's vengeful anger towards Blake following Rosanna Spearman's death, tellingly dated from 1848: 'Ha, Mr Betteredge, the day is not far off when the poor will rise against the rich. I pray Heaven they may begin with *him*. I pray Heaven they may begin with *him*' (M: 248; original emphasis). Still, Lucy's is merely a lone voice exposing the untenable inequality of mid-Victorian society and lacking the sustained and collective strength of 1840s Chartism, invisible in Collins's work. The dominance of exciting plot, strongly delineated characters and highly realised setting in Collins's writing seems conducive to the inclusion of cross-continental travel, non-English despots, revolutionaries and refugees with quirky personalities and distant revolutionary backdrops. Despite Collins's sympathy for working people and specific critiques of social wrongs, however, a concerted programme for domestic reform or political radicalism is overlooked, even out of place, in fictional worlds in which disappearing diamonds, disguised identities and nocturnal searches of ancestral mansions take precedence.

Notes

1. W. Collins, *No Name*, ed. V. Blain (Oxford World's Classics, 2008), p. 644. All future references will be cited in the text as NN.
2. W. Collins, *The Moonstone*, ed. S. Farmer (Peterborough, ON: Broadview Press, 1999), pp. 83–4. All future references will be cited in the text as M.
3. W. Collins, *Man and Wife*, ed. N. Page (Oxford World's Classics, 1995), p. 257. All future references will be cited in the text as M&W.
4. W. Collins, *Hide and Seek*, ed. C. Peters (Oxford World's Classics, 1999), p. 44. All future references will be cited in the text as H&S.
5. W. Collins, *The Woman in White*, ed. M. K. Bachman and D. R. Cox (Peterborough, ON: Broadview Press, 2006), p. 120. All future references will be cited in the text as WW.
6. Ibid.
7. W. Collins, *The Dead Secret*, ed. I. B. Nadel (Oxford World's Classics, 2008), p. 199. All future references will be cited in the text as DS.
8. W. Collins, *Poor Miss Finch: A Domestic Story*, ed. C. Peters (Oxford World's Classics, 2008), p. 132. All future references will be cited in the text PMF.
9. W. Collins, *The Law and the Lady*, ed. J. Bourne Taylor (Oxford World's Classics, 1999), p. 246. All future references will be cited in the text as LL.
10. E. Yates, 'Mr. Wilkie Collins in Gloucester-Place', *Celebrities at Home*, 3rd series, No. 72, *The World* (1879), p. 156.
11. W. Collins, *Basil: A Story of Modern Life*, ed. D. Goldman (Oxford World's Classics, 2008), p. 11.
12. W. Collins, *Heart and Science: A Story of the Present Time*, ed. S. Farmer (Peterborough, ON: Broadview Press, 1996), p. 219. All future references will be cited in the text as HS.
13. W. Collins, *Armadale*, ed. C. Peters (Oxford World's Classics, 1989), p. 560.
14. See W. E. Gladstone, *Two Letters to the Earl of Aberdeen, on the State Prosecutions of the Neapolitan Government*, 3rd ed. (London: John Murray, 1851), www.gale.com/primary-sources/nineteenth-century-collections-online
15. See, for example, Elizabeth Barrett Browning's *Casa Guidi Windows* (1851), which describes Anita Garibaldi's death after the fall of the Roman Republic in 1849; in M. Stone and B. Taylor (eds.), *The Works of Elizabeth Barrett Browning*, Vol. II: *Poems* (London and New York: Routledge, 2010), ll. 2.678–94.
16. W. Collins, *Blind Love*, ed. M. K. Bachman and D. R. Cox (Peterborough, ON: Broadview Press, 2004), p. 63. All future references will be cited in the text as BL.
17. See ibid., Appendix E for an excerpt from *Iris*.
18. C. Dickens to Count D'Orsay, 31 March 1848, in G. Storey and K. J. Fielding (eds.), *The Letters of Charles Dickens* (Pilgrim Edition), Vol. V: *1847–1849* (Oxford: Clarendon Press, 1980), p. 268.

CHAPTER 29

Law

Anne-Marie Beller

> socially, morally, legally – dead.
>
> *The Woman in White*

The nineteenth century witnessed widespread legal reform and an unprecedented expansion of bureaucracy, so it is unsurprising that novelists of the period engaged so extensively and transformatively with the law in their fictions. The creation of a unified police force, the rise of forensic science in the detection of crime, extensive public interest in criminal trials and the nature of evidence, and the rise of the legal professional all contributed to a new literary emphasis on the role of the law. Wilkie Collins was foremost among the writers who negotiated the contemporary legal world. Collins trained as a lawyer, studying at Lincoln's Inn beginning in May 1846, but never practised after being called to the Bar in November 1851. This legal training nevertheless inflected his fiction, not only at the level of narrative and plot, but more fundamentally in its ideological, philosophical and polemical aspects. As Catherine Peters claims in her 1991 biography of Collins, 'the intricacies and inconsistencies of the law interested him' and 'he could have made a good lawyer'.[1]

In a practical sense, his legal background must have been invaluable in the habits of attention to detail and an ordered mind required for structuring his complicated plots. These plots often had their origins in historical or contemporaneous legal cases and criminal trials. Collins acknowledged that *The Woman in White* was inspired by his reading of a collection of French trials, and William Baker has demonstrated that he possessed various law books in his personal library.[2] In addition, Collins also drew parallels between literature and legal discourse through his experiments with narrative form. The multiple narrators of *The Woman in White* (1860) and *The Moonstone* (1868) are key aspects of his narratorial innovations, which are imitative of legal trials and testimony. Walter Hartright begins his narration in *The Woman in White* like a barrister assembling his evidence: 'As the Judge might once have heard it, so the Reader shall hear it now.'³

The shortcomings of the law are a central theme in most of Collins's major novels, providing the entire impetus for the plot in *The Woman in White*, *No Name* (1863), *The Law and the Lady* (1875) and *Man and Wife* (1870) in particular. Collins was still engaging with contemporary legal questions up until his final novel, *Blind Love* (1890), in which he examines Fenian politics through the dual lens of the Irish Question and the Woman Question. In Collins's fiction, the law is always inextricably entangled with the moral and the social. There is rarely a sense of 'pure' justice, no legal question untainted by moral implications. As Philip O'Neill argues, what Collins shows in a novel such as *No Name* is that 'Life must be organised around the dictates of the law rather than the dictates of the heart and the emotions. The law determines how we should lead our lives and a challenge to the law is an attack on society itself.'⁴ The law, then, for Collins, is always a complex and tangled entity, which cannot be separated from individual social and psychological identity.

From the outset of *The Woman in White*, Collins makes clear his critical stance in regard to the law, which he implies is not only imperfect, but also potentially corrupt. 'If the machinery of the Law could be depended on', Hartright suggests, 'the events which fill these pages might have claimed their share of the public attention in a Court of Justice. But the Law is still, in certain inevitable cases, the pre-engaged servant of the long purse' (WW: 1). A decade later, Collins took similar swipes at the ways in which the law could be complicit with immoral actions. In the prologue to *Man and Wife* (1870), John Vanborough manages to dispose of his unwanted wife, Anne, when his unprincipled lawyer, Mr Delamayn, informs him of a convenient legal loophole relating to the Irish marriage laws. Collins revisits the trope of the law being in service to wealth and iniquity, declaring 'the Legislature of Great Britain' to be 'the humble servant of [Vanborough's] treachery, and the respectable accomplice of his crime'.⁵ In stipulating an action endorsed by law as a 'crime', Collins disrupts the stable categories of licit and illicit, thereby calling into question accepted notions of 'justice'.

Collins's fiction, generally, is fascinated by abstruseness, contradiction and liminality, so it is unsurprising that ambiguous points of law and convoluted legal discourse furnish the impetus for many of his plots. For Collins, those points of law where the moral and the judicial are in conflict provide the ideal scenario because they produce extreme psychological states and social situations generative of dramatic interest. Abigail

Boucher has persuasively demonstrated that 'Collins's works reveal a deeper, steadier, and less easily resolved interaction with the law at a philosophical level. Many of his texts affirm that the law requires regular revision to keep pace with social norms and morals.'[6] As a leading proponent of the sensation novel, which dominated literary discourse and popular sales through the 1860s, Collins was working within a genre characterised by explicit engagement with the legal debates of the day. If crime and transgression were the hallmarks of sensation fiction, then these tropes were reflective of contemporary social change, including debates around the marriage laws and increased newspaper reportage of high-profile divorce and bigamy cases. Collins's novels in particular demonstrate the centrality of the law in determining women's identity and their position within society.

In *The Woman in White* the issue of female identity is complex. The theft of Laura Fairlie's identity by Count Fosco and Sir Percival Glyde is comprehensive, touching every part of her existence: as Hartright defines Laura's situation, she is 'socially, morally, legally – dead' (WW: 329). The 'death' of Laura resultant on her marriage may be seen as symbolic of a woman's fate under the Victorian marriage laws, where her entire legal entity was 'covered' by that of her husband and thereby erased. Collins posits that modern identity itself has become a matter to be evidentially proven and, in doing so, exposes the various ways in which the law colludes against women who are victimised by unscrupulous men. As Matthew Finley claims, Collins 'puts the law on trial by engaging the interplay between legal questions of witness credibility and testimonial evidence and their impact on social factors such as class and gender'.[7] *The Woman in White* reveals the fragmentary and vulnerable nature of identity, and also the different ways in which men and women may be constructed through legal processes. Thus, where Sir Percival is ultimately denied his rightful identity through an *absence* of marriage (i.e., his illegitimacy), Laura is stripped of her identity as a *result* of marriage, when, in legal and social terms, she ceases to exist.

In his subsequent novel, Collins returned to the issue of illegitimacy. *No Name* attacks 'The law of England, as it affects illegitimate offspring' as 'a disgrace to the nation'.[8] This 'disgrace' is dramatised through the plight of Norah and Magdalen Vanstone, whose affluent and secure existence is abruptly terminated on the death of their parents. It emerges that the Vanstones had only been married for a short time prior to their untimely demise, and that the daughters are therefore illegitimate. Even though a will had been drawn up to provide for them, the subsequent marriage invalidates this document, and the sisters are dispossessed of their inheritance in favour of a distant male cousin.

For Collins, who never married the mother of his own children, Martha Rudd, the laws governing the fate of illegitimate offspring was a deeply personal interest. His novel is outspoken in its disgust at what Collins sees as the false morality governing such laws, and for some contemporary critics, his indignation was a step too far. One reviewer complained that, in *No Name*, Collins attempted 'to gild one of the greatest offences a man can commit against the laws of morality' and 'excit[ed] sympathy for that which should be visited with stern reprobation'.[9] The Vanstone's family solicitor, Mr Pendril, becomes Collins's mouthpiece in excoriating the laws which disinherit Magdalen and Norah: 'It violates every principle of Christian mercy ... It is not the law of Scotland, not the law of France, not the law ... of any other civilized community in Europe' (NN: 59). Whereas Scottish law is the target of criticism in *The Law and the Lady* and *Man and Wife*, here, Collins emphasises that, in this matter, it is English law that is less civilised and merciful than that of other nations.

In their legal position as *filius nullius* ('nobody's child'), the Vanstone sisters embody a familiar state in Collins's fiction: one where identity itself is rendered unstable either through legal uncertainties or legal injustice. In *The Law and the Lady*, for example, the heroine's uncertain status as either a married or single woman is figured through confusion over her legal name. Eustace Macallan has married Valeria Brinton under an assumed name (Woodville), and it is unclear which of these three names Valeria is entitled to use. It is pointed out to Valeria that she is 'neither maid, nor wife, nor widow. You are worse than nothing, madam', which underlines her liminal state in the eyes of the law and society.[10] The impact of the law on social identity is seen again in *Man and Wife*, where Anne Silvester's uncertain marital status subjects her to a similar loss of identity. As Anne Longmuir argues: 'Unless she can legitimate her marriage to Geoffrey Delamayn, Anne Silvester faces losing her social identity, as Lady Lundie's refusal to refer to Anne's sex or name indicates.'[11]

Unlike Anne, Magdalen and Laura, Valeria Macallan's dilemma does not stem from institutionalised gender inequalities *per se*, but her attempt to remedy that problem reveals those very injustices. Her resolve to uncover the truth of her husband's past by stepping into the male sphere of the law elicits resistance and hostility from several characters, including Valeria's uncle, who reacts with disgust to his niece's proposal to read the transcript of Eustace's murder trial: 'Nice reading for a young woman! You will be wanting a batch of nasty French novels next' (LL: 121). Valeria's trespass into a traditionally male domain is connected to sexual aberrance, and her uncle's objections to what he terms 'lawyers in petticoats' (LL: 121) connotes an unease surrounding the whole issue of women and knowledge.

Of all Collins's literary engagements with the law, it is arguably in *Man and Wife* that he mounts his most sustained and polemical critique. In the preface, Collins announces his intention to tackle 'the present scandalous condition of the Marriage Laws of the United Kingdom'.[12] This was eminently topical, as the Royal Commission set up to enquire into the state of the marriage laws had issued its report in 1868, the year in which the action of the novel is set. Collins makes direct reference to this Commission in his preface and in the novel itself, and he even includes an appendix, directing his reader to specific parts of the report as evidence that his 'fiction is founded on facts'.[13]

Collins's villain, Geoffrey Delamayn, has seduced Anne Silvester and reneged on his promise to marry her. Unbeknownst to both Geoffrey and Anne, the former's father was instrumental in the ruin of Anne's mother, through his legal advice to John Vanborough, as discussed above. In a familiar Collinsian theme of history repeating itself through subsequent generations, Geoffrey manages to cast aside Anne by pretending to believe that she is already married to Arnold Brinkworth. Arnold is engaged to marry Anne's best friend, Blanche, but fears he has accidentally married Anne under the Scottish laws governing irregular marriages. The main thrust of the plot involves the untangling of these legal threads to ascertain the precise marital status of the central characters. To this end, Collins's novel features a whole array of lawyers, from the compassionate Sir Patrick Lundie to the ruthless Delamayn. The latter's momentary sympathy for Anne Vanborough (the woman he has helped to ruin) is immediately dismissed by his reflection that 'It *is* the law': 'he owned it was hard on her ... But the law justified it' (M&W: 28, 38). Sir Patrick is ranged with Collins's benign legal professionals, such as Pendril (*No Name*), Pedgift (*Armadale*) and Bruff (*The Moonstone*), whereas Delamayn's self-interest aligns him with the criminal lawyers of his mentor Charles Dickens's fiction, such as Tulkinghorn and Jaggers.

Between these two extremes of critical interpretation of the law and inhuman inflexibility, there is a whole class of undistinguished legal drones, of whom Collins is candidly dismissive. Lady Lundie's solicitor in *Man and Wife* is described as 'one of that large class of purely mechanical and perfectly mediocre persons connected with the practice of the law who will probably, in a more advanced state of science, be superseded by machinery' (M&W: 502). Whether ruthless in their own interests or merely ineffectual, the lawyers who are critiqued in Collins's novels lack humaneness. Their dogmatic adherence to laws which Collins lambasts as cruel and unjust sets them apart from those who are willing to work creatively with, or even outside of, those laws where necessary for the attainment of justice.

In *Man and Wife*, it is not only the laws relating to irregular marriages that are subject to Collins's critique as 'an outrage on common decency and common-sense' (M&W: 230). The legal rights of the husband over his wife's body, as inscribed in the law of coverture, are also castigated by Collins. Once Geoffrey Delamayn has been proven by the disputation of lawyers to be Anne's legal husband, another injustice of the law is immediately exposed. Geoffrey's power over the woman he now hates, and wishes to be rid of by any means, is absolute, and upheld by the laws of the land: '"The law tells her to go with her husband," he said. "The law forbids you to part Man and Wife"' (M&W: 526). Forced to cohabit with a man who is plotting her murder, Anne is afraid equally for her safety and her virtue: 'There were outrages which her husband was privileged to commit, under the sanction of marriage, at the bare thought of which her blood ran cold'; 'Law and Society armed her husband with his conjugal rights' (M&W: 550).

Margaret Oliphant, in a broadly complimentary review, felt bound to protest that Anne's predicament at this climactic moment in the novel was implausible:

> though she ... and everybody else believes, her very life to be in danger – there is not one about her, though she is surrounded by lawyers, who has sufficient presence of mind to assure her that the law does not require her to give herself over to be killed, even to her husband.[14]

Oliphant's objection is reasonable, but it is not necessarily sound. Anne's friends lack definite evidence that Geoffrey intends to do her harm and, more importantly, legal precedents had highlighted the reluctance of the law to protect the rights of married women. The Cochrane Decision of 1840, in which a judge upheld Alexander Cochrane's right to confine his wife, Cecilia Maria, until she resumed her wifely duties, had disturbingly shown how women were vulnerable to abusive male control under Victorian marriage laws.

Collins was obviously writing thirty years after this case, but the judge's ruling had been precedent-setting and campaigners for women's rights frequently cited the Cochrane Decision as a key example of the need for legal change. Writing in *The Westminster Review* in 1856, Caroline Frances Cornwallis reminded her readers of the details of the case and concluded that 'the common law views the relation of husband and wife as that of master and bondwoman. A *hired* servant could not be so treated.'[15] Given that it was not until 1891 that a High Court ruling denied a husband the right to imprison his wife in pursuit of his conjugal rights, and another century before British law finally passed legislation overturning the marital exemption to the law of rape in 1991, Collins's powerful representation of Anne's predicament is not far-fetched: 'The law sanctioned the sacrifice of her as unanswerably as it had sanctioned the sacrifice of her mother before her' (M&W: 526).

Having attacked the Irish and Scottish marriage laws, Collins then proceeds, through the character of the servant, Hester Dethridge, to confront the English married woman's property laws. Married to a wastrel, who appropriates her earnings and modest inherited property to fund his tastes for strong liquor, Hester is compelled to seek assistance from the law. A sympathetic policeman explains to her that, under English law, she is not entitled to own property and that everything she possesses legally belongs to her husband. Collins encourages his readers to question this state of affairs through Hester's pathetic plight and unanswerable logic:

> I've been told by wiser heads than mine that we all pay our taxes to keep the Queen and the Parliament going; and that the Queen and the Parliament make laws to protect us in return. I have paid my taxes. Why, if you please, is there no law to protect me in return? (M&W: 586–7)

Deprived of any protection from her increasingly abusive husband, Hester finally resorts to murdering him as the only escape she perceives as possible from her legally endorsed subjection.

Collins arguably includes the personal history of Hester Dethridge to demonstrate that women from all social classes are subject to these legal inequities. However, it is noteworthy that Anne's story is able to resolve happily because she has affluent and influential friends. Hester, on the other hand, descends into total insanity and is incarcerated for the rest of her life. Perhaps the most powerful aspect of Collins's critique of unjust laws in *Man and Wife* is his disquieting depiction of the psychological harm done to women, the consequences of which he renders physically on their bodies. Hester's elective mutism and her increasing insanity are the collateral damage of her abusive marriage. Similarly, Anne's emotional ordeal at the hands of Delamayn is depicted visibly through a steady physical deterioration and loss of vitality and beauty. Her pregnancy and traumatic delivery of a stillborn baby are barely confronted by the novel, encoded as too traumatic to articulate fully. In Anne's refusal to speak of her trauma to any of the other characters, she is linked to the mute Hester, and their shared silence is indicative of the psychological harm inflicted on women with the permission of the law.

Despite attacks on specific laws, particularly those affecting women and illegitimate children, Collins's broader treatment of jurisprudence is arguably conservative. Though he seeks to rectify isolated abuses, he never really interrogates the *institution* of the law at a fundamental level. As Boucher points out, both Laura Fairlie and Magdalen Vanstone are finally restored to their rightful positions *through* the machinery of the law: 'Although Collins expresses disappointment in the law, he does not call for any revocation of the legal system; in fact, he reifies society's reliance upon statutes, technicalities, and legal systems even as he subverts that reliance.'[16]

Yet Collins was a key voice in the debates about women's rights and legal reform in the second half of the nineteenth century, and his novels constituted an important part of the national conversation. Shortly after the publication of *Man and Wife* in 1870, the Irish marriage laws were reformed and the first Married Women's Property Act was passed. In his preface to the second edition, Collins noted the shortcomings of the latter act, but conceded that it was 'better than no law at all'.[17] Norman Page argues that 'Collins was as a propagandist less a trail-blazer than a popularizer ... he used his creative powers to bring home to the minds and hearts of his readers questions that were already in the public domain.'[18] Collins's championing of such causes within some of the most widely read novels of the day undoubtedly lent momentum to the popular mandate for change.

Notes

[1] C. Peters, *The King of Inventors: A Life of Wilkie Collins* (Princeton University Press, 1991), p. 69.
[2] See W. Baker, *Wilkie Collins's Library: A Reconstruction* (Westport, CT: Greenwood Press, 2002).
[3] W. Collins, *The Woman in White*, ed. J. Sutherland (Oxford World's Classics, 2008), p. 1. Hereafter cited parenthetically in the text as WW.
[4] P. O'Neill, *Wilkie Collins: Women, Property, and Propriety* (Totowa, NJ: Barnes & Noble, 1988), p. 162.
[5] W. Collins, *Man and Wife*, ed. N. Page (Oxford World's Classics, 2008), p. 40. Hereafter cited parenthetically in the text as M&W.

6. A. K. Boucher, 'The Nature of the Law: Struggles between Statute and Universal Morality in Wilkie Collins's *The Woman in White* and *No Name*', *The Wilkie Collins Journal* 14 (2017), n.p.
7. M. Finley, 'Hearsay Evidence: Legal Discourse, Circumstantiality, and *The Woman in White*', *Global Tides* 10 (2016), Article 1, https://digitalcommons.pepperdine.edu/globaltides/vol10/iss1/1, p. 1.
8. Wilkie Collins, *No Name*, ed. V. Blain (Oxford World's Classics, 2008), p. 59. Hereafter cited parenthetically in the text as NN.
9. [Unsigned review], *London Quarterly Review* (October 1866), in N. Page (ed.), *Wilkie Collins: The Critical Heritage* (London and New York: Routledge, 1974), p. 141.
10. W. Collins, *The Law and the Lady*, ed. J. Bourne Taylor (Oxford World's Classics, 1992), p. 40. Hereafter cited parenthetically in the text as LL.
11. A. Longmuir, 'The Scotch Verdict and Irregular Marriages: How Scottish Law Disrupts the Normative in *The Law and the Lady* and *Man and Wife*', in A. Mangham (ed.), *Wilkie Collins: Interdisciplinary Essays* (Newcastle: Cambridge Scholar's Publishing, 2008), pp. 166–77 (p. 171).
12. W. Collins, Preface to *Man and Wife*, ed. N. Page (Oxford World's Classics, 2008), p. 5.
13. Ibid.
14. [M. Oliphant], 'New Books', *Blackwood's Edinburgh Magazine* 108 (November 1870), p. 630.
15. C. F. Cornwallis, 'The Property of Married Women', *Westminster Review* 66 (1856), pp. 181–97 (p. 187, n.).
16. Boucher, 'The Nature of the Law', n.p.
17. Quoted in N. Page, 'Introduction' to Collins, *Man and Wife*, p. xiv.
18. Page, 'Introduction' to Collins, *Man and Wife*, p. xiii.

CHAPTER 30

Geography and Places

Susan R. Hanes

A comprehensive discussion of the works of Wilkie Collins would not be complete without considering the travels that influenced his writings. Although he was born in London and lived most of his life in the central district of Marylebone, he recognised at an early age the importance of travel to broaden his experience and develop his eye for description.

Collins's father, landscape painter William Collins, R.A., instilled in his young sons the importance of observation. In 1829, the family travelled to Boulogne when the boys were aged five and one. They spent four months in Wales in 1834 while William searched for new subjects for his paintings. Finally, the elder Collins was able to free himself from obligations at home where he was providing for his mother and brother and his wife's family in addition to his own. In 1836, he took his family on a two-year tour of France and Italy. The timing was propitious for young Wilkie, who at twelve was at a receptive age to absorb the culture and scenery of the continent and gain proficiency in Italian and French. It was a trip that he later maintained was critical to his development as a novelist.

Collins's earliest writings reveal a fascination with the uncharted worlds of travel. His first novel, *Ioláni*, was set in Tahiti and displayed 'a youthful imagination [run] riot among the noble savages', as he recalled in an interview for *Appleton's Journal* in 1870.[1] Though it was written in 1844, it was not published until 1991 when the manuscript emerged from private ownership.

The first book inspired by his own observations was *Antonina; or, The Fall of Rome*, published in 1850. In addition to borrowing from Edward Gibbon's *Decline and Fall of the Roman Empire* (1776–88), he used his impressions of Rome in 1837 to describe the Rome of 408 CE:

> Beyond the walls immense suburbs stretched forth in the days of old. Gorgeous villas, luxurious groves, temples, theatres, baths – interspersed by colonies of dwellings belonging to the lower orders of the people – surrounded

the mighty city. Of these innumerable abodes hardly a trace remains. The modern traveller, as he looks forth over the site of the famous suburbs, beholds, here and there, a ruined aqueduct, or a crumbling tomb, tottering on the surface of a pestilential marsh.[2]

Collins drew on the suburbs of London to imbue his narratives with significance. In *Basil*, published in 1852, he contrasts the sophisticated city with a suburban landscape of new and unfinished homes, thus revealing the class division between his characters. The description of the home of the linen-draper gives the reader a vivid contrast with that of the aristocratic title character:

Everything was oppressively new. The brilliantly-varnished door cracked with a report like a pistol when it was opened; the paper on the walls, with its gaudy pattern of birds, trellis-work, and flowers in gold, red, and green on a white ground, looked hardly dry yet.[3]

He featured the London suburb of Hampstead in several of his novels. Not only had he been brought up there, but he later became familiar with the area during long walks and visits with friends. Hampstead was the location that advanced the theme of identity central to *The Woman in White* (1860) when Walter Hartright's meandering walk home brings him to his dramatic encounter with Anne Catherick:

I determined to stroll home in the purer air by the most roundabout way I could take; to follow the white winding paths across the lonely heath; and to approach London through its most open suburb by striking into the Finchley Road, and so getting back, in the cool of the new morning, by the western side of the Regent's Park.[4]

In 1870, Collins stayed with Frederick and Nina Lehmann at their Hampstead home while he was writing *Man and Wife*. The opening scene of the novel takes place at a villa in Hampstead. There are also allusions to Hampstead in *Armadale* (1866), *The Moonstone* (1868) and *Blind Love* (1890).

At the age of twenty, Collins toured Europe with an older friend, Charles Ward. Liberated from the constraints of parental oversight, he enjoyed seeing the sights, attending the theatre and indulging in French cuisine. Less than a year later, he returned to Paris, this time unaccompanied, which he discovered he preferred. Being alone allowed him to follow his own tastes and inclinations, including visits to the seamier districts of the city. Of particular fascination to him was the central morgue, a popular Paris attraction where bodies were displayed for public viewing. In the final scene of *The Woman in White*, Count Fosco, stabbed to death and then dragged out of the Seine, ends up in the Paris Morgue. Collins undoubtedly drew upon his memory of the visits he had made there:

> Slowly, inch by inch, I pressed in with the crowd, moving nearer and nearer to the great glass screen that parts the dead from the living at the Morgue – nearer and nearer, till I was close behind the front row of spectators, and could look in. There he lay, unowned, unknown, exposed to the flippant curiosity of a French mob! (WW: 643)

Another advantage of time spent in France was his growing command of French. Collins was captivated by the books of Honoré de Balzac. He considered Balzac, Walter Scott and James Fenimore Cooper the greatest of all storytellers. He was inspired by Balzac's meticulous attention to detail and careful observation that created an authentic sense of place in his narratives, and noted how Balzac's descriptions revealed his characters as real people. In 'Portrait of an Author, Painted by his Publisher', which first appeared in Charles Dickens's *All the Year Round* in 1859 and later in *My Miscellanies*, he writes of Balzac:

> The framework in which his idea is set is always wrought with a loving minuteness which leaves nothing out. Everything which in this writer's mind can even remotely illustrate the characters that he depicts, must be elaborately conveyed to the minds of his readers before the characters themselves start into action.[5]

Wandering the streets of Paris with Dickens on a later trip, he came across an old set of Maurice Méjan's *Recueil des causes célèbres* at one of the *bouquinistes* (used and antiquarian booksellers on the banks of the Seine). This collection of eighteenth-century legal cases, 'a sort of French *Newgate Calendar*', as Collins referred to it, would provide him with some of his best plots, including that of *The Woman in White*. The actor Wybert Reeve later recalled Collins's delight when he told him about finding this 'prize':

> In speaking of his own works, [Collins] said nearly all his plots were founded on facts, on some incidents he had heard of or read, or on his desire to expose or correct in the shape of a novel some abuse. ... When speaking of the charge brought against him, that in some of his books, as in *The Woman in White*, he was too sensational and exceeded the bounds of all probability, he said, 'It has angered me, and shows how much some of the critics know about it ... I know of very few instances in which fiction exceeds the probability of reality.[6]

In *My Miscellanies*, his 1863 collection of essays and stories, Collins included several pieces based on French cases that he undoubtedly found in Méjan, including an account of the 1657 murder of the Marquis Monaldeschi and 'The Poisoned Meal', a story of a woman falsely accused of murder. Late in his career, Collins alluded to the Méjan cases in *The Guilty River* (1886), describing the use that the Lodger plans to make of the French Trials that he receives on approval from a bookseller: 'I more than approve – I admire; and I more than admire – I imitate. These criminal stories are told with a dramatic power, which has impelled me to try if I can rival the clever French narrative.'[7]

In 1850, instead of returning to the continent, Collins arranged a hiking tour of Cornwall with the artist Henry Brandling. *Rambles Beyond Railways* was published in 1851. It was an illustrated travelogue filled with descriptions of the sites they had visited and a documentation of local customs and stories. Their hike to the Devil's Throat in Kynance Cove inspired his description of Mannion's death in *Basil*, which was published the following year:

> The wet sea-weed slipped through his fingers. He struggled frantically to throw himself towards the side of the declivity; slipping further and further down it at every effort. A tremendous jet of spray hissed out upon him at the same moment. I heard a scream so shrill, so horribly unlike a human cry, that it seemed to silence the very thundering of the water. (B: 325)

The legend of a lost vessel in *Rambles* appears again in his story of 'Mad Monkton' (1855; 1859). Also, in *The Dead Secret* (1857), the scenes of Porthgenna resemble Lanhydrock House, nestled in the shadow of a dense forest near Bodmin in central Cornwall:

> There, below them, was the dark, lonesome, spacious structure of Porthgenna, with the sunlight already stealing round towards the windows of the west front. There was the path winding away to it gracefully over the moor... The mansion had been originally built in the form of a square and had been strongly fortified.[8]

In the 1850s, Collins returned to Europe on several occasions. He visited Dickens in Boulogne in 1853. In his 1881 novel, *The Black Robe*, Collins sets the opening chapters in Boulogne, to which Lewis Romayne travels to see his dying aunt. He mentions the 'smell of the harbour' and 'the oysters ... at the restaurant on the pier', which Collins undoubtedly enjoyed himself.[9] In October of that year, the artist Augustus Egg joined Collins and Dickens for a trip through Switzerland and Italy. Collins, commenting as Marian in *The Woman in White*, wrote that Italy was 'the most interesting country in the world' (WW: 207), and enjoyed experiences that found their way into several of his subsequent works. In *Armadale*, Lydia Gwilt and Ozias Midwinter live in Naples, '(for economy's sake) far away from the expensive English quarter, in a suburb of the city, on the Portici side'.[10] *The Haunted Hotel* (1879), set in Venice, is the home of Lord Montbarry and Countess Narona who lived in a mouldering palace that became a fashionable hotel. The building is located on the water, with 'its fine Palladian front looking on the canal'.[11] He depicts the Venetian atmosphere later in the novel:

> The canal beneath the window looked like a black gulf; the opposite houses were barely visible as a row of shadows, dimly relieved against the starless and moonless sky. At long intervals, the warning cry of a belated gondolier was just audible, as he turned the corner of a distant canal, and called to invisible boats which might be approaching him in the darkness. Now and then, the nearer dip of an oar in the water told of the viewless passage of other gondolas bringing guests back to the hotel. (HH: 198)

The mid-1850s found Collins travelling extensively in the British Isles. He sailed to the Scilly Islands with Edward Pigott in September 1855 – a trip so successful that sailing became his favourite outdoor occupation. He cheerfully described their misadventures in 'The Cruise of the *Tomtit*' for that year's Christmas number of Dickens's *Household Words*.

A walking tour of Cumberland with Dickens in the late summer of 1857 resulted in their collaboration, *The Lazy Tour of Two Idle Apprentices*, published in *Household Words* in October that year. In that book, Collins recounted how he suffered a badly sprained ankle when the two men became disoriented in the fog on Carrock Fell. Cumberland also featured in several of his other books. It was the site of Limmeridge House in *The Woman in White*; Noel and Magdalen Vanstone honeymoon there in *No Name* (1863); and, in *The Evil Genius* (1886), Catherine takes her daughter Kitty to Cumberland with Mrs Presty.

From his youth, Collins frequented the Thanet district of Kent to escape the oppressive heat of London and take in the fresh sea air. He joined the local yacht club with his old friend Edward Pigott, and often rented rooms at Ramsgate both with Caroline Graves and with his family, Martha Rudd and their children. He also stayed in nearby Broadstairs, using it as a base for sailing trips to Dunkirk and as a retreat for his writing. The North Foreland Lighthouse was even said to have inspired him with the title of *The Woman in White*.[12] He frequently holidayed there with

Dickens. His love affair with the area was diminished by the death of Dickens in 1870, after which he determined that Broadstairs held too many memories for him. However, Ramsgate remained a refuge and inspiration throughout his life. So familiar was he with the area that he used it to create an atmosphere of pleasure and contentment in several works. In *Poor Miss Finch* (1872), 'The bracing air of Ramsgate was all that was wanting to complete the success of the operation.'[13] He continues:

> To-day, we went out together for a walk on the cliffs. What a delight it was to move through the fresh briny air and see the lovely sights on every side of me! ... All sorts of diversions were going on. Monkeys, organs, girls on stilts, a conjurer, and a troop of negro minstrels, were all at work to amuse the visitors. I thought the varied color and bustling enjoyment of the crowd, with the bright blue sea beyond, and the glorious sunshine overhead, quite delightful – I declare I felt as if two eyes were not half enough to see with! (PMF: 338–9)

In *The Fallen Leaves* (1879), he describes the scene:

> The blue lustre of the sky was without a cloud; the sunny sea leapt under the fresh westerly breeze. From the beach, the cries of children at play, the shouts of donkey-boys driving their poor beasts, the distant notes of brass instruments playing a waltz, and the mellow music of the small waves breaking on the sand, rose joyously together on the fragrant air.[14]

Valeria and Eustace Macallan enjoy their honeymoon at Ramsgate in *The Law and the Lady* (1875):

> The scene on that fine autumn morning was nothing less than enchanting. The brisk breeze, the brilliant sky, the flashing blue sea, the sun-bright cliffs and the tawny sands at their feet, the gliding procession of ships on the great marine highway of the English Channel – it was all so exhilarating.[15]

Collins's other seaside locations are a contrast with his glorious settings in Kent. After visiting Aldeburgh in Suffolk, he created the memorable scene in which Magdalen looks out at the passing ships from her window and wrestles with her fate in *No Name*:

> She seated herself close at the side of the window, with her back towards the quarter from which the vessels were drifting down on her – with the poison placed on the window-sill, and the watch in her lap. For one half hour to come, she determined to wait there, and count the vessels as they went by. If, at that time, an even number passed her – the sign given, should be a sign to live. If the uneven number prevailed – the end should be Death.[16]

Collins travelled to Whitby, a seaside town in Yorkshire, with Caroline in 1861, staying at the Royal Hotel. Driven away by a brass band that played beneath their window every afternoon, they headed 'high up on the Yorkshire coast and close by the sea', the setting for *The Moonstone*.[17] Mulgrave Castle may have been the inspiration for Frizinghall, the Verinder estate in the novel. Collins learned of the castle when he discovered that Maharajah Duleep Singh, owner of the Koh-i-Noor diamond – the Moonstone of the title – had rented the castle near Whitby. His description of the Shivering Sands was based on his observations along the Yorkshire coast. The hamlet of Cobb's Hole that features in the book is probably Hob Holes, located between Sandsend and Runswick Bay:

> The raging sea, and the rollers tumbling in on the sand-bank, and the driven rain sweeping over the waters like a flying garment, and the yellow wilderness of the beach with one solitary black figure standing on it – the figure of Sergeant Cuff. (M: 196)

Collins's travels were critical in enabling him to craft a sense of place in his novels. His romanticised landscapes enhanced the aura of mystery that was essential to his storytelling. His attention to detail aided a rich imagination to create atmosphere and define the personalities of his characters. In *The Woman in White*, Marian's description of Blackwater Park becomes an important metaphor for its owner, Sir Percival Glyde:

> As I walked down to the lake, I saw that the ground on the farther side was damp and marshy, overgrown with rank grass and dismal willows. The water ... looked black and poisonous opposite to me, and the rank overhanging thickets and tangled trees. (WW: 227–8)

On a subsequent trip to Whitby in 1864, he travelled to Great Yarmouth in Norfolk where he first met nineteen-year-old Martha Rudd, who was to become his common-law wife. Nearby Horsey Mere, or as Collins calls it, Hurle Mere, offered the perfect backdrop for the dramatic appearance of Lydia Gwilt in *Armadale*. His description of the 'broad lonely pool' (A: 321) enhances the enigmatic air that shrouds the character of Lydia Gwilt when Allan Armadale and Midwinter first encounter her:

> The sun was sinking in the cloudless westward heaven. The waters of the Mere lay beneath, tinged red by the dying light. The open country stretched away, darkening drearily already on the right hand and the left. And on the near margin of the pool, where all had been solitude before, there now stood, fronting the sunset, the figure of a woman. (A: 320)

A trip to the Isle of Man with Caroline and her daughter in 1863 gave Collins further descriptive material for *Armadale*. In a letter to his mother, he revealed that, although he found the trip uncomfortable, the wild scenery suited his purpose in creating a crucial scene in the novel. He wrote that it was 'wild and frightful, just what I wanted – everything made for my occult literary purposes':[18]

> Little by little the cliffs rose in height, and the rocks, massed wild and jagged, showed rifted black chasms yawning deep in their seaward sides. Off the bold promontory called Spanish Head, Midwinter looked ominously at his watch. But Allan pleaded hard for half an hour more, and for a glance at the famous channel of the Sound, which they were now fast nearing ... and of which he had heard some startling stories from the workmen employed on his yacht. The new change which Midwinter's compliance with this request rendered it necessary to make in the course of the boat brought her close to the wind; and revealed, on one side, the grand view of the southernmost shores of the Isle of Man, and on the other, the black precipices of the islet called the Calf, separated from the mainland by the dark and dangerous channel of the Sound. (A: 144–5)

Following Dickens's advice to seek therapy for his gout in the healing waters of European spa towns, Collins travelled to Aix-la-Chapelle and Wildbad with Caroline in 1863. The places he described in a letter to his mother became almost word for word the first chapter of *Armadale*. The scene is the town in which Mr Neal is asked to transcribe the deathbed confession of Allan Armadale:

> The evening shadows were beginning to gather over the quiet little German town, and the diligence was expected every minute. ... The light of a May evening was still bright on the tops of the great wooded hills watching high over the town on the right hand and the left; and the cool breeze that comes before sunset came keenly fragrant here with the balsamic odor of the first of the Black Forest. (A: 708)

By the end of the 1860s, Collins was a celebrated novelist. The popularity of his books had grown precipitously on both sides of the Atlantic. He frequently wrote to Harper & Brothers, his American publishers, questioning details of the publication of his novels, and was also in contact with his Canadian publishers, Hunter, Rose, arranging for the release of his novel *Man and Wife* in Canada in order to thwart the recurring piracy of his American publications. He soon recognised that a visit to his New World publishers would be a prudent business move, and determined to follow the example of Dickens and William Makepeace Thackeray by undertaking a reading tour of America with the expectation that he might achieve the same financial reward that they had realised. He further hoped to promote his books, meet with important men of influence and, as always, collect material for his writing.

On 13 September 1873, Collins set sail from Liverpool aboard the Cunard Line's *Algeria*, one of a trio of modern ships built in the 1860s. The ship steamed into New York harbour on Thursday, 25 September, and Collins was met by his old friend the actor Charles Fechter. After hearty greetings, the two went to the cosy Westminster Hotel at Irving Place in which they were to stay. Delegations from the exclusive Arcadian and Lotos Clubs were stationed at the hotel to greet the novelist and welcome him to the city. After extricating himself from his well-wishers, Collins was shown to his rooms, the same suite, with a private door and staircase, that Dickens had occupied on his own reading tour six years earlier.

During the six months that he spent in North America, Collins gave twenty-five readings in twenty-two locations. He used New York and Boston as bases from which he travelled to his readings. He made short trips from these cities to nearby places, including Philadelphia, and completed four major circuits, heading northwest to upstate New York, north to Canada, west to Chicago and south to Washington, DC. His first circuit took him to Albany, Troy, Utica and Syracuse. His second was to Baltimore and Washington. The third was to Montreal, Toronto, Niagara and Buffalo. The final circuit took him west to Cleveland, Sandusky, Toledo, Detroit and Chicago.

His readings were not the greatest achievement of Collins's tour. Although he seemed to be pleased with his reception and wrote enthusiastically to his friends about his appearances, his descriptions often contradicted the newspaper reviews. He made nowhere near the money that Dickens or Thackeray brought home. However, fascination with Wilkie Collins, the man, was pervasive. His performances drew crowds that came principally to see the distinguished writer. He was swarmed by admirers and met some of the most influential men in the United States. He was extravagantly entertained and gloriously fêted. He earned the admiration and respect of nearly everyone he met, basking in the knowledge that the American people lionised him as the greatest living novelist.

Collins enjoyed a genuine affinity with his American hosts and they with him, enabling him to gain a solid understanding of the American character. His experiences in North America enriched his writing for the remainder of his life.

Collins's visit to the Oneida Community in Wallingford, Connecticut, was an inspiration for Tadmor, a utopian colony of 'Primitive Christian Socialists' where Amelius Goldenheart grew up in *The Fallen Leaves*. He employed Wallingford again in *The Legacy of Cain* (1888), in which the villain Helena Gracedieu becomes the leader of an American religious cult. The theme of social equality that appears in *The Guilty River* was born of his observations as he travelled in the United States during the period of Reconstruction.

While in America, he even managed to complete a book, *The Dead Alive* (1874), a wrongful-conviction thriller based on a true story recounted in a pamphlet presented to him in Troy, New York. Also, in *The Two Destinies* (1876) and *Blind Love*, he employed North America as a faraway place where he could send certain characters to keep them from encountering each other.

His understanding of the American temperament is demonstrated in a scene in the *Haunted Hotel*, published four years after he returned to London:

> Henry's attention was attracted by an angry voice protesting, in a strong New England accent, against one of the greatest hardships that can be inflicted on a citizen of the United States – the hardship of sending him to bed without gas in his room. The Americans are not only the most hospitable people to be found on the face of the earth – they are (under certain conditions) the most patient and good-tempered people as well. But they are human; and the limit of American endurance is found in the obsolete institution of a bedroom candle. The American traveller, in the present case, declined to believe that his bedroom was in a complete finished state without a gas-burner. (HH: 168–9)

From the time that Collins's father first exposed his sons to the experience of travel, he kindled in young Wilkie an appetite for adventure and an aptitude for observation. Throughout his life, Collins revelled in the opportunity to witness and document scenes and customs that enriched him as a writer. His broad experience of places and people enabled him to leave a legacy of works that has continued to captivate legions of readers to this day.

Notes

[1] [Unsigned], 'Wilkie Collins', *Appelton's Journal* 4.75 (3 September 1870), p. 279.

[2] W. Collins, *Antonina; or, The Fall of Rome* (New York: Harper & Brothers, 1904), p. 49.

3 W. Collins, *Basil: A Story of Modern Life*, ed. D. Goldman (Oxford World's Classics, 1992), p. 61. Future references will be cited in the text as B.
4 W. Collins, *The Woman in White*, ed. M. Sweet (London: Penguin Classics, 1985), p. 46. Future references will be cited in the text as WW.
5 W. Collins, 'Portrait of an Author, Painted by His Publisher', in *My Miscellanies* (New York: Harper & Brothers, 1874), p. 155.
6 W. Reeve, 'Recollections of Wilkie Collins', *Chambers's Journal* 9 (June 1906), pp. 458–61 (p. 459).
7 W. Collins, *The Guilty River*, in *Miss or Mrs?, The Haunted Hotel, The Guilty River*, ed. N. Page and T. Sasaki (Oxford World's Classics, 1999), p. 270. Future references will be cited in the text as GR.
8 W. Collins, *The Dead Secret*, ed. I. B. Nadel (Oxford World's Classics, 1997), p. 167.
9 W. Collins, *The Black Robe* (Stroud: Alan Sutton Publishing, 1994), pp. 2, 4.
10 W. Collins, *Armadale*, ed. C. Peters (Oxford World's Classics, 1989), p. 663. Future references will be cited in the text as A.
11 W. Collins, *The Haunted Hotel*, in *Miss or Mrs?, The Haunted Hotel, The Guilty River*, ed. Page and Sasaki, p. 158. Future references will be cited in the text as HH.
12 A. Gasson, *Wilkie Collins: An Illustrated Guide*, consultant ed. C. Peters (Oxford University Press, 1998), p. 117.
13 W. Collins, *Poor Miss Finch*, ed. C. Peters (Oxford World's Classics, 1995), p. 307. Future references will be cited in the text as PMF.
14 W. Collins, *The Fallen Leaves* (Coln St Aldwyn: Echo Library, 2005), pp. 11–12.
15 W. Collins, *The Law and the Lady*, ed. J. Bourne Taylor (Oxford World's Classics, 1992), p. 26.
16 W. Collins, *No Name*, ed. M. Ford (London: Penguin Classics, 1994), p. 408.
17 W. Collins, *The Moonstone*, ed. S. Kemp (Harmondsworth: Penguin, 1977), p. 55. Future references will be cited in the text as M.
18 W. M. Clarke, *The Secret Life of Wilkie Collins* (1988; Chicago: Ivan R. Dee, 1991), p. 108.

CHAPTER 31

Victorian Environments
Mark Frost

As an individual and as a writer, Wilkie Collins was intensely social – a highly sociable man whose works vividly depict human society. Given this, it might seem unreasonable to expect his novels to provide the sustained engagement with the non-human evident in the works of many of his contemporaries. Even so, it is surprising that environments, at first glance, appear to play a relatively minor role in his fictional worlds, that they seem so strongly overshadowed by the social, and that so many of his nature descriptions are conventional. It is surprising because of his background in a family of landscape artists, and because of the intense preoccupation with nature characterising the nineteenth century. While Collins's fictions often provide limited representations of nature, they do, however, reward closer investigation. Placing them alongside his non-fiction travel narrative, *Rambles Beyond Railways* (1851), moreover, complicates the impression they may give of a writer uninterested in environment.

This essay firstly sketches the contexts against which Collins's approach to nature can be most effectively evaluated: the state of the environment and its intersections with the socio-economic transformations of British society during his lifetime; the key scientific and cultural engagements with nature during the period; and the biographical factors that shaped him. It then turns to key tropes in his fictional representations of environment, and particularly his construction of Gothic landscapes. I will also argue that the characteristically Victorian environment which Collins most astutely described was that curiously pastoral phenomenon, the suburb. The final section will turn to *Rambles Beyond Railways* in order to explain why the impression often given by Collins's fiction of an underwhelming engagement with Victorian environments may be misleading, and that a more nuanced understanding is required.

Contexts

Victorian environments were by no means easy to ignore. The effects of rapid industrialisation and urbanisation were a daily sensory experience for city dwellers like Collins, through unwelcome proximity to polluted air, water and earth – all bound up with the fourth primal element, fire, via the Victorian God of coal, the burning of which (at work and at home) did much to establish our Anthropocene age. The sight of animal body-parts floating in rivers of industrial and human effluent was a quotidian reminder of the impacts of human activity on the natural world. While multiplying urban populations turned sections of Britain's cities into impromptu sewers and brought unprecedented levels of epidemic disease, the countryside also changed rapidly, drawing British agriculture more inexorably into the complex networks of laissez-faire capitalism; and witnessing the development of 'improvements' in plant and animal breeding, agricultural chemistry, mechanisation, drainage and land management (in a countryside largely enclosed by the time of Collins's birth in 1824). Collins lived through the 'hungry forties' (which included the Irish Famine and widespread social discontent and suffering in rural Britain), a period of mid-century agricultural prosperity and the Great Agricultural Depression (1873–96). Nineteenth-century rural environments saw significant changes, including the loss of many woodland, bog, meadow and marshland environments to agriculture. While the countryside had always featured industrial activity, the rapid expansion of quarries, mines, ironworks, brickworks and mills often made it difficult to distinguish between urban and rural. The dominant social role of the aristocracy and gentry owed as much to their industrial and colonial investments as it did to their supposedly timeless roots in British soil.

The Victorian period witnessed an intensification of scientific engagements with nature that had gathered pace since the sixteenth century. The golden age of British geology, it also saw the advent of biogeography, Darwinism and ecological science, and a massive expansion of interest in zoology and botany. The scientists Alexander von Humboldt, Richard Owen, John Gould and Charles Darwin achieved celebrity status, while a growing middle-class readership eagerly sought accounts of scientific travels to 'exotic' lands and indulged in crazes for ferns, orchids and aquaria.

Unsurprisingly, the arts reflected these various developments, and helped ensure that the concept of 'nature' became increasingly sanctified as environments were placed under intensified pressures. The impact of the Picturesque and Romantic schools in forming more sympathetic modes of engagement with the non-human world cannot be overstated. While the wider tendency to view nature as an exploitable commodity intensified, it was accompanied by a Romantic veneration of landscapes (and particularly wilder environments previously viewed with suspicion or dread) as sites of transcendent experience in which narrow human experiences could be reflected upon and transformed. The idea that nature had value in and of itself, and that particular environments were worthy of protection, was not a Romantic invention (the roots of conservationism and environmentalism are much deeper), but the overwhelming appeal of the Romantic view of nature to their successors was immense. The often-individualised responses of the Romantic poets were conjoined in the Victorian age to an intense desire to engage with the social life of the countryside: for George Eliot, John Ruskin, Richard Jefferies, Thomas Hardy and others, it was insufficient and unseemly to seek picturesque pleasures in tumbledown cottages, and better by far to investigate the lives of those who lived within their walls. Politically informed engagements with nineteenth-century environments were evident in a range of social writers – from William Cobbett and Friedrich Engels to Elizabeth Gaskell and Charles Kingsley – while Victorian commentators and journalists set out to quantify, analyse and understand rural life.

Collins's father William was a celebrated Royal Academician of the John Constable/J. M. W. Turner era, whose works combined landscapes and figures, while his brother, Charles Allston Collins was associated with the Pre-Raphaelite Brotherhood. This reminds us of Wilkie's close proximity to significant traditions of British landscape art that were strongly linked (via Ruskin) to the idea of 'going to nature' to paint real, rather than idealised, landscapes. Collins, however, appears to have been relatively unenthusiastic about these movements, and of the intense activity, upheaval and excitement in ecological, social, political and cultural aspects of environment outlined so far, there are limited traces in his fiction. That this is so clearly requires some explanation.

Fictional Landscapes

That Collins might be antithetical to Romantic attitudes to nature and humanity is suggested by Walter Hartright's reflections in chapter 8 of *The Woman in White* (1860), where he asserts that 'admiration of those beauties of the inanimate world, which modern poetry so largely and so eloquently describes, is not, even in the best of us, one of the original instincts of our nature': neither children nor 'uninstructed' adults possess this feeling, while 'those whose lives are most exclusively passed amid the ever-changing wonders of sea and land are also those who are most universally insensible to every aspect of Nature not directly associated with the human interest of their calling'.[1] Speaking of trees, and voicing a Romantic belief in environment as a test of human morality, Ruskin opined that:

> this race of plants, deserving boundless affection and admiration from us, becomes, in proportion to their obtaining it, a nearly perfect test of our being in right temper of mind and way of life; so that no one can be far wrong in either who loves the trees enough, and every one is assuredly wrong in both who does not love them, if his life has brought them in his way.[2]

When Ruskin claims that 'if human life be cast among trees at all, the love borne to them is a sure test of its purity',[3] he argues that landscape feeling is innate in unspoiled individuals: to love nature is, for Ruskin, natural, but for Hartright it is cultural. 'Our capacity of appreciating the beauties of the earth we live on', he asserts, 'is one of the civilised accomplishments which we all learn' (WW: 53). While for Ruskin, innate love of nature may be nurtured or suppressed by human society, Hartright detects a 'want of inborn sympathy between the creature and the creation around it' and a social desire to turn instead to 'the smallest human interest that the pure heart can feel' (WW: 53, 54).

Does Collins share Hartright's allegiance to human culture in preference to nature, as well as his belief that landscape feeling is a sophisticated product of civilisation? This initially seems to be borne out by his novelistic representations of environment, in which landscapes are routinely subordinate to human experience. Collins often uses environments as conventional backdrops or as reflections of mood or plot, most frequently rendering natural backdrops in Gothicised ways. In *The Woman in White*, this is evident in the spectral environment of Hampstead Heath where Hartright first encounters the titular female figure; and in the 'wild, weird, and gloomy' (WW: 233) Hampshire heaths, lake and plantations of Sir Percival's estate where the criminal plot builds.

Perhaps the most famous of Collins's Gothic landscapes is the 'lonesome and horrid retreat' of the Shivering Sands in *The Moonstone* (1868).[4] Situated at 'the loneliest and ugliest little bay' on the Yorkshire coast, it is 'most horrible' not purely because of its topography but by association with the gloomy, suicidal character of Rosanna Spearman (M: 23, 22).

Similarly Gothic landscapes abound elsewhere; in *Armadale* (1866) there are the ghastly, sublime seascapes of the Isle of Man, replete with 'low, black, lurking rocks, and the broken waters of the channel, pouring white and angry into the vast calm of the westward ocean'; and the 'wilderness of winding water and lonesome marsh' of the Norfolk Broads.[5] In the same category are the Cornish landscapes of *Basil* (1852) and *The Dead Secret* (1857), or the Scottish moorlands of *Man and Wife* (1870), their dramatic excess mere reflections of the plots for which they form largely cursory backdrops: only in *Basil* are landscapes described in detail.

There are glimpses of other environments amidst Collins's headlong pursuit of human action: the American 'wildernesses' beloved of Matthew Grice and Zack Thorpe in *Hide and Seek* (1854); Somerset, Suffolk and Dumfriesshire in *No Name* (1863); and the South Downs of *Poor Miss Finch* (1872), approvingly described by Madame Pratolungo, a revolutionary figure thus connected to Romantic sentiments. Collins rarely shows much attention to these places, however, and there is nothing in his fiction to match the sustained engagement with rural environments and societies in the works of Eliot, Jefferies or Hardy. In general, his landscape descriptions are as underwhelming as those of his friend, mentor and rival, Charles Dickens.[6] Only when Collins turns his urban gaze upon that quintessentially Victorian environment, the suburb, is he capable of displaying his acuity.

The phenomenon of Victorian suburbs is well documented as a distinctive feature of rapid population growth and urbanisation. As Sarah Bilston points out, villages on the edges of towns were absorbed by growing cities, 'while open land in between and around built-up areas was sold and built into terraces, quadrupling the population of the metropolis in a century'.[7] Bilston suggests that the allure of suburbs lay in 'the development of a new space, or more properly a space that expressly called into question the binary of country and city that had structured life and ways of thinking about the human experience of modernity for centuries'.[8] For Bilston, the Victorians regarded suburbs as a new form of urban life, but they were also marked by rural tropes. In this we can identify a collapse of the solidly dependable structural roots of pastoral in binary oppositions of rural and urban, in which the former is always superior. Read in this way, Victorian suburbs are a distinctive but disturbing reflection of the power of urban capitalism to reshape every environment and to create novel cultural constructions of 'nature'.

Given Collins's decided preference for London living it is perhaps surprising that he views its suburbs as baneful and sordid, but this is evident throughout his work. That Mrs Gallilee, the villainess of *Heart and Science* (1883) resides in suburbia is only one indication of a decided antipathy. In *The Law and the Lady* (1875), the heroine, Valeria Macallan, visits the forbidding Miserrimus Dexter in 'the great northern suburb of London', 'a dingy black labyrinth of streets' interspersed with 'dismal patches of waste ground which seemed to be neither town nor country'.[9] Breaking pastoral oppositions, this threateningly in-between landscape features 'forlorn outlying groups of houses with dim little scattered shops among them, looking like lost country villages wandering on their way to London' (LL: 201). Amidst 'the half-completed foundations of new houses' and 'gaunt scaffolding poles' lies a 'second desert', in which 'the ghastly white figures of vagrant ducks gleamed at intervals in the mystic light' (LL: 202). Neither city nor country, and uncanny in their half-resemblance to both, these scenes are again Gothic, their unease and disquiet created by the disruptions and dislocations of suburbia.

Hide and Seek opens in suburbia, where the houses of the suggestively named Baregrove Square sit amidst vegetation that 'seemed to be absolutely rotting away in yellow mist and softly-steady rain', a landscape rendered yet more indistinct and 'dirtily mournful' by 'the smoke from the chimney-pots [that] was lost mysteriously in deepening superincumbent fog'.[10] The narrator later looks back to that opening scene, dating it to 1837 when Baregrove Square 'was the farthest square from the city, and the nearest to the country, of any then existing in the north-western suburb of London', before moving readers forward fourteen years to a time when Baregrove 'had lost its distinctive character altogether' because 'other squares had filched from it those last remnants of healthy rustic flavour from which its good name had been derived' (H&S: 27). Remorselessly cataloguing the processes by which 'other streets, crescents, rows, and villa-residences had forced themselves pitilessly between the old suburb and the country', Collins suggests London's rampant outward urge 'had suspended for ever the once neighbourly relations between the pavement of Baregrove Square and the pathways of the pleasant fields' (H&S: 27). This note of pastoral elegy becomes urgent as the narrator unfavourably compares the conquests of Alexander and Napoleon to 'the modern Guerrilla regiments of the hod, the trowel, and the brick-kiln' as they 'march through the kingdom of nature, triumphantly bricklaying beauty' and leaving behind 'the mournful modern sight of the last tree standing, on the last few feet growing, amid the greenly-festering stucco of a finished Paradise Row, or the naked scaffolding-poles of a half-completed Prospect Place' (H&S: 26, 27). Anticipating George Orwell's disgust with

London's suburbs in *Coming Up for Air* (1939), Collins's alarm at the rise of suburbia is powerfully expressed, far outdoing his rural representations precisely because it articulates a far greater commitment to the natural scenes that are simultaneously represented and despoiled: amongst scenes of devastation, something important is, at last, at stake. That Collins is capable here of a sustained, meaningful engagement with nature suggests a need to re-evaluate his broader attitudes, and to question whether he really does share Hartright's apparent dismissal of landscape feeling. To develop this idea further, we must turn to his non-fiction.

Cornish Landscapes

Rambles Beyond Railways (1851) was written when Collins's only publications were an early short story, an 1848 memoir of his father, and a little-noticed novel, *Antonina; or, The Fall of Rome* (1850). His career in fiction had barely begun, and it would be almost a decade before *The Woman in White* made him a literary celebrity. *Rambles* is a skilfully engaging entry into the publishing marketplace of a novice writer keen to establish his place. With a canny eye for opportunities, he declares Cornwall undervalued in comparison to the all-too-familiar landscapes of Scotland, Wales, the Lakes and Devon, comparing it to Kamchatka 'as an unexplored region offered to the curiosity of the tourist'.[11] His chatty travel guide also expresses that other structural binary of traditional pastoral (the preference for the past over the present) in celebrating the old-fashioned pleasures of pedestrian travel in a bygone county:

> You, who in these days of vehement bustle, business, and competition, can still find time to travel for pleasure alone – you, who have yet to become emancipated from the thraldom of railways, coaches, and saddle-horses – patronize, I exhort you, that first and oldest-established of all conveyances, your own legs![12]

While *Rambles* devotes many pages to social encounters during Collins's travels with H. C. Brandling (the book's illustrator), it also offers winning coverage of Cornwall's history, customs and economic activities. Amongst all of this are many sustained landscape descriptions that suggest a keener eye for rural environments than evidenced in his later novels. Indeed, he declares a strong feeling for landscape while describing contemplative moments at the ancient St Cleer's Well near Liskeard:

> Recollections began to rise vividly on my mind of other ruins that I had seen in other countries, with friends, some scattered, some gone now – of

pleasant pilgrimages, in boyish days, along the storied shores of Baiæ, or through the desolate streets of the Dead City under Vesuvius – of happy sketching excursions to the aqueducts on the plains of Rome, or to the temples and villas of Tivoli; during which, I had first learned to appreciate the beauties of Nature.[13]

While this does not conflict with Hartright's assertion that appreciation of natural beauty is learned, it also implies Romantic feeling. Sustained, vivid landscape descriptions in *Rambles* suggest that the travel narrative rather than the novel offered Collins opportunities to express his pleasure in landscape and his keen eye for the comings-together of human and natural histories. There are impressive, often moving descriptions of landscape, including Looe Harbour, the Lizard and Kynance Cove (the latter far finer than their counterparts in *Basil*), but it is perhaps Bodmin Moor that provides his most memorable engagements: looking down from the moors above St Cleer, 'the whole plain appeared like the site of an ancient city of palaces, overthrown and crumbled into atoms by an earthquake', a silent, almost empty landscape in which 'the majestic loneliness and stillness of the scene were almost oppressive both to eye and ear'.[14] Characteristically, the urban wanderer is particularly attuned to industrial landscapes, including a copper mine:

> All about us monstrous wheels were turning slowly; machinery was clanking and groaning in the hoarsest discords; invisible waters were pouring onward with a rushing sound; high above our heads, on skeleton platforms, iron chains clattered fast and fiercely over iron pulleys, and huge steam pumps puffed and gasped, and slowly raised and depressed their heavy black beams of wood.[15]

Unlike the empty landscapes described earlier, this environment is created by humans and characterised by human suffering: Collins gazes down upon 'men, women, and children [who] were breaking and washing ore in a perfect marsh of copper-coloured mud and copper-coloured water'.[16]

Rambles provides Collins with the means to articulate his essentially urban engagement with environment, and, like Dickens, this urban gaze is valuable precisely because it largely avoids the tendency of traditional pastoral to idealise rural life and to occlude rural labour. Instead, he sees the Victorian countryside for what it was: an integral part of a wider economic nexus in which environmental violence was both the impetus and the means for human sovereignty over the non-human other. The sensitivity with which Collins engages with London's suburbs and Cornwall's complex cultural landscapes belies the impression given by his novels of a writer so immersed in the social that he has little trace of landscape feeling or environmental understanding: indeed, it is his understanding that environments are simultaneously natural and cultural that makes his work insightful. While we should look elsewhere for the profoundest insights into Victorian environments, there is still a great deal to value in Collins's unique approach to cultural landscapes.

Notes

1. W. Collins, *The Woman in White*, ed. J. Sutherland (Oxford World's Classics, 1999), p. 53. Hereafter cited parenthetically in the text as WW.
2. E. T. Cook and A. Wedderburn (eds.), *The Library Edition of the Complete Works of John Ruskin*, 39 vols. (London: George Allen & Unwin, 1903–12), vol. VII, p. 16.
3. Ibid., vol. VII, p. 17.
4. W. Collins, *The Moonstone*, ed. F. O'Gorman (Oxford World's Classics, 1999), p. 23. Hereafter cited parenthetically in the text as M.
5. W. Collins, *Armadale*, ed. C. Peters (Oxford World's Classics, 1990), pp. 247, 119.
6. On this, see M. Frost, 'Journeys *through* Nature: Dickens, Anti-Pastoralism and the Country', *Réprésentations* 6, special issue, 'Dickens and the Environment' (Summer 2016), pp. 53–71.
7. S. Bilston, *The Promise of the Suburbs: A Victorian History in Literature and Culture* (New Haven, CT: Yale University Press, 2019), p. 4.
8. Ibid., p. 5.
9. W. Collins, *The Law and the Lady*, ed. J. Bourne Taylor (Oxford World's Classics, 2008), p. 201. Hereafter cited parenthetically in the text as LL.
10. W. Collins, *Hide and Seek*, ed. C. Peters (Oxford World's Classics, 1999), p. 9. Hereafter cited parenthetically in the text as H&S.
11. W. Collins, *Rambles Beyond Railways; or, Notes in Cornwall Taken A-Foot* (London: Richard Bentley, 1851), p. 7.
12. Ibid., p. 25.
13. Ibid., p. 57.
14. Ibid., p. 61.
15. Ibid., p. 60.
16. Ibid.

CHAPTER 32

Race and Empire
Melisa Klimaszewski

One cannot separate race and empire as entities discrete from other aspects of the Victorian times in which Wilkie Collins existed. As with any historical epoch, various identities or status markers – social class/rank, gender, religion, sexuality, physical size and ability, perceived racial identity – affected one's experience of the nineteenth-century world. These identities and concepts, however, were not left unquestioned. Victorian readers, writers and thinkers actively interrogated definitions of personhood; legislators and politicians debated reform laws in mostly unsuccessful attempts to minimise social inequality, reduce poverty and broaden the franchise; and fiction writers imagined plots that challenged the legitimacy of patriarchy. The concept of race was also in flux, with philosophers, essayists and scientists disagreeing over theories of racial composition and the primacy of whiteness, a slippery concept. Simultaneously, the British state actively perpetrated colonial violence, and those activities intensified debates about racialised British identity.

Black and Brown people have a long history in Britain, but popular misperceptions about that fact are slow to change. Peter Fryer's path-breaking work opens with a reference point in the third century of the Common Era: 'There were Africans in Britain before the English came here.'[1] Gretchen Holbrook Gerzina notes that seventeenth- and eighteenth-century Londoners would have seen Black city dwellers routinely, as it would have been impossible to exist in a sphere that did not include 'Africans and their descendants working and living alongside the English'.[2] Places like Liverpool and Bristol, which had provided ports for the trading of human slaves, were home to sizable multiracial populations. It was not unusual to see young Black children serving as pages in rural manor houses, and their presence is represented frequently in aristocratic portraiture. Queen Victoria herself welcomed a Black 'daughter', Sally Bonetta Forbes, into the royal household after a naval captain presented the young girl as a 'gift' from a West African king.[3] The Queen also insisted, rather controversially, on forming a close relationship with attendant Abdul Karim, an Indian man she called 'Munshi', who had been sent with a delegation to deliver a ceremonial gift and was asked by the monarch to become her Urdu teacher and companion of sorts. These actions occurred simultaneously with great colonial violence and existed alongside racist ideologies, exemplifying the complex negotiations of race that permeate individual and institutional relationships. The nineteenth century did not herald the sudden arrival of people of colour or the invention of the concept of race in Britain. Rather, long-standing and fluctuating discourses of difference, complexion and power continued to morph and change, and the influence of scientific language increased.

Wilkie Collins's works routinely ponder questions of racial identity, and his family history included important engagement with debates about the morality of slavery. Wilkie's grandfather, William Collins, was a successful painter and freelance journalist who composed an abolitionist piece, 'The Slave Trade: A Poem Written in 1788', which inspired George Morland's Royal Academy painting on the same theme. Wilkie Collins's life spanned the period of Britain's greatest reach as an imperial power. Britain outlawed trading in slaves in 1807, but when Collins was born, the practice of human enslavement continued in British colonial territories and was not formally ended until 1833, after which brutal working conditions and entrenched oppression (officially in the form of 'apprenticeships') persisted whilst the British government compensated slave owners for the value of their human property. In the 1850s and 1860s, the decades of Collins's career in which he published his most notable works, British colonial territories were vast and included Australia, Canada, the Cape Colony and Natal (regions of present-day South Africa), Guyana on the northeast coast of South America, Jamaica and other islands in the Caribbean (labelled the West Indies, from a clearly British viewpoint), India, Ireland, Malta, New Zealand and Sierra Leone. Some of the most frequently cited statistics about British imperial dominance note that, by the end of the nineteenth century, British colonies 'comprised more than a quarter of all the territory on the face of the earth' and 'one in four people was a subject of Queen Victoria'.[4]

Imperial identity suffused all aspects of nineteenth-century British life. Embedded in the fibres used for textile production, in the raw materials used to power the Industrial Revolution, in tea leaves and sugar crystals, was the exploited human labour and plundered resources of territories in the Caribbean and India. Early in the century, abolitionists launched boycotts of sugar in recognition of the connections between English tea tables and the abuse of enslaved Africans on Caribbean plantations. The clerkships of middle-class Londoners in counting houses and offices of all sorts linked vast networks of international trade to family incomes and everyday domestic life. Most of the world's actual money passed through private banks in England or the Bank of England, whose dominance increased throughout the century as Britain's imperial might grew. Tea, a commodity cultivated in China and India, became a crucial ideological component in idealised Englishness: 'According to nineteenth-century tea histories and advertisements, tea helped to define English identity, character, and class values. Tea united the English people, temporarily erasing the boundaries between groups to unify the nation into a coherent whole.'[5] Such aspirational coherence inextricably links domestic English identity to colonial interests and the labour of racialised others. Drinking tea, going to work, spotting a print advertisement for coffee, or walking down the road and spotting a textile mill in the distance, all contributed to a sense of national identity predicated on British imperial dominance.

Still, war and fears of invasion were a constant feature of nineteenth-century British politics and governance. Following the conclusion of the Napoleonic Wars with France in 1815, Britain's military challenges included a badly managed war against Russia in the Crimea (1854–6), ongoing resistance to British rule in Ireland and armed insurrections in India and the Caribbean. Britain also fought wars with China over the opium trade (1839–42 and 1856–60), which led to British control of Hong Kong in 1841. The Opium Wars offer a glimpse of the interconnected, violent relationships that enabled English domestic consumption: 'The largest cash crop produced in British India and one that the Indian peasantry was forced to grow, opium was smuggled into China in exchange for tea imported to Britain.'[6] It was this lucrative arrangement, which filled pots on tea tables at all levels of British society and put opium into the nervous systems of fussy babies and chronic pain sufferers like Wilkie Collins, that Britain fought to protect.

In addition to the sacrifice of lives and ever-present compromises of human dignity, the ideological maintenance of racial and national identities required active, sometimes extravagant, effort. The Great Exhibition of 1851 was one such display. The project of Prince Albert, vast displays were meant to showcase the industrial and technological advancements of the entire world, with England, of course, at the apex. Although the event was called the Great Exhibition of the Works of Industry of All Nations, only 'thirty-four nations participated, grouped together in the East Wing, while Britain alone dominated the West'.[7] The exhibition event took place in

Hyde Park for nearly six months as millions of people walked through Joseph Paxton's Crystal Palace, a massive building of glass and iron. Some of the exhibits exoticised the residents of colonial lands, and the whole affair, attended by throngs of visitors, was satirised in the periodical press. The power and scope of the Great Exhibition's vision of global capitalism continued to grow and advance mercilessly in the decades to follow, with white-identified imperial powers reaping the vast majority of the financial benefits. Other popular exhibitions throughout the nineteenth century focused on human beings themselves as spectacles. In 1853, a group of Black Zulu South Africans was described in animalistic terms in newspaper coverage and exhibited by the merchant A. T. Caldecott and his son Charles at St George's Gallery at Hyde Park Corner before touring the country.[8] Such was the England of Wilkie Collins's adulthood.

Just six years after the Great Exhibition, one of Britain's most intense colonial crises took place in India. The Rebellion of 1857 (which Victorians called the Mutiny) shook Britons abroad and at home, and its consequences reshaped British rule in India. Prior to 1857, Britain governed lands in India via indirect rule and the government-backed strong arm of the East India Company. Indian soldiers, called sepoys, supported British interests and vastly outnumbered British troops. Multiple underlying causes and histories of mistreatment underpin the uprising of 1857; the event that set it off was news that new cartridges for the Enfield rifles of sepoys were greased with cow and pig fat. Given that the consumption of such fats contravenes Hindu and Muslim religious beliefs, outraged soldiers turned their guns on the British, who could not re-establish control for well over a year. A slaughter at Cawnpore in which British women and children were killed caused massive public outrage and calls for harsh reprisals, which were already happening as the British massacred entire villages. The crisis led ultimately to the British Crown instituting direct governmental rule and to Queen Victoria being named Empress of India in 1876. Wilkie Collins reacted to widespread racism and incidents of colonial violence with complexity in his writing. His personal papers and his published works contain viewpoints about race and racism that are sometimes contradictory. Even when seeming to compliment Black waiters in the United States, for instance, Collins used offensive terminology in his correspondence. Examples of racist language and stereotyping are present in his works, and they exist alongside strong challenges to racist behaviour and racialised identities.

In the midst of the 1857–8 conflict in India, Collins published 'Sermon for Sepoys' in the pages of *Household Words*, Charles Dickens's weekly periodical.⁹ Dickens's reactions to the uprising were harsh, but he does not seem to have hesitated to publish Collins's more tempered views in the journal, which identified itself as 'Conducted by Charles Dickens' and did not include by-lines for individual pieces. In 'Sermon for Sepoys', Collins calls the Indian rebels 'betrayers and assassins' yet also asserts that Muslim beliefs and stories have a long, respectable history and would be superior to Christian texts at achieving moral reform. This piece may have provided Collins with a way to temper the racism of *The Perils of Certain English Prisoners*, the Christmas number he co-wrote with Dickens to conclude 1857. Although some view the *Perils* chapters for which Collins is the primary author as more comic and less intensely racist than those for which Dickens is the primary author, the full text is collaborative, and all of its chapters direct denigrating, racist anger at Black bodies.

A decade later, *The Moonstone* (1868) continues to explore the moral consequences of imperial violence, the ways in which violence against colonial subjects affects those living in England, and racism. The novel begins with a long account of the history of unjust colonial plunder and concludes with a peaceful, if exoticised, awe-inspiring scene of the return of a diamond to its rightful Hindu shrine. The central plot features a multiracial hero whose endurance of racist attitudes augments his sympathy, a villain who dies in brown face paint and Indian men whose murder of an Englishman the novel seems to approve. Scholars continue to debate the extent to which the novel challenges or reinscribes troublesome imperialist mindsets, illustrating that matters of empire and race are inseparable from the generic developments in detective fiction that Collins contributed to the literary landscape.

The Moonstone is not unique in Collins's oeuvre in addressing questions about the relationships between complexion, definitions of race, individual morality and oppression. The first novel Collins wrote, *Ioláni* (1845), which he did not regard highly and never published in his lifetime, is set in Tahiti and features troubling stereotypes of Pacific Islanders. Yet the target of its most severe critique is the patriarchy that colonisers practise just as intensely as the people they designate 'uncivilised', and the novel 'subvert[s] the usual polarities of missionary writing'.¹⁰ Most of Collins's published works offer more nuanced depictions of both white-identified British characters and characters of colour. *Armadale* (1866) features a heroic character, Ozias Midwinter, whose mother is of African descent, and its sensational plot explores the multi-generational consequences of slavery in Barbados and Trinidad. The novel depicts Midwinter's archetypal 'gypsy' and Creole-identified traits, such as being emotionally passionate, positively, and those aspects of his character exist alongside a sometimes poignant homoeroticism between him and the novel's doubled protagonist, Allan Armadale. Collins's fiction, particularly in regard to Creole identity, converses with other texts of the era, such as Mary Seacole's *The Wonderful Adventures of Mrs. Seacole in Many Lands* (1857). Seacole's memoir indicts racism and invokes stereotypes of passionate Creole women in order to empower its Creole subject, Seacole herself.

Collins's works repeatedly address legacies of slavery and continued violence in the Caribbean, contributing to public discourse surrounding the American Civil War (1861–5) and the brutal actions of Governor Edward Eyre in Morant Bay, Jamaica in 1865. Uprisings against British rule in the Caribbean had a long history and 'took place on average once every five years'.[11] The 1865 rebellion in Jamaica sought reform to improve the living conditions and livelihoods of formerly enslaved Black labourers. In response, Governor Eyre instituted martial law, presided over the killing of over 400 Jamaicans and the whipping of hundreds more, and executed George William Gordon.[12] Gordon was a well-respected elected official whose mother had been enslaved, and he was a vocal critic of Eyre. Eyre's terrible governing skills and killing of Gordon ignited fierce public debate in England and outpourings of racist sentiments about free Black people in newspapers and journals. In contrast, other powerful figures and voices formed a committee that attempted (and failed) to indict Gordon and some of those under his command for murder. The only official punishment was Eyre's removal from the governorship. Continuing to write fiction that engaged with the colonial histories that led to such crises and debates, Collins wrote *Miss or Mrs?* for the 1871 Christmas issue of *The Graphic*. The piece tells the story of a multiracial protagonist, Natalie Graybrook, whose deceased Martiniquais mother was of African descent. Given Collins's constant investment in exposing the absurdities of patriarchy and the disempowered positions of women, it is not surprising that his writing would also address questions of racial mixture, particularly in light of the weaving together of those issues in popular, if often paranoid, consciousness. As Jennifer DeVere Brody states, 'the English preoccupation with the problem of purity' invariably links discourses of morality, race and gender, as 'the supposed instability, plasticity, and variableness of the feminine "woman" generates contradictory narratives of her value and power, as well as prescriptive tracts detailing strategies for her control'.[13] In *Miss or Mrs?*, Graybrook's Creole traits are not maligned, and she is morally superior to her white European father, Sir Joseph, who attempts to force her into a marriage for financial gain.

The 'whiteness' of English men in Collins's works was a negotiated identity that interacted dynamically with such mechanisms of sexual control and with shifting definitions of race. Collins's villains are not only men like Count Fosco, a swarthy 'foreign' man in *The Woman in White*, but also Sir Percival Glyde, the social epitome of aristocratic whiteness who derives financial gain and pleasure from imprisoning women. In *The Moonstone*, the racial 'purity' of both the villain and the sympathetic protagonist, Godfrey Ablewhite and Franklin Blake respectively, is unstable, complicating definitions of whiteness. *Poor Miss Finch* (1872), whilst delivering a blistering critique of the irrationality of racism, practically lampoons the whole notion of race through its depiction of a blind protagonist who claims to be terrified of dark-skinned people then falls in love with a man who has blue skin. Perhaps most directly, such definitions and identities are questioned deeply in a play Collins co-wrote with Charles Fechter, *Black and White* (1869). Set in Trinidad, the melodrama centres around Maurice de Leyrac, an aristocratic, white-identified Frenchman who discovers his Black heritage while courting a woman whose rival exploits Leyrac's newfound legal status as an unfree person. The play both indulges and challenges biological essentialism. The lovers' feelings about racial identity and enslavement morph as quickly and arbitrarily as the legal identity of Leyrac, who 'ultimately reworks the significance of "black blood" to empower himself'.[14] These works of fiction clearly contribute to debates about biological determinism, race and natural selection that were fuelled by texts like Robert Knox's *The Races of Men* (1850), Charles Darwin's *On the Origin of Species* (1859) and feuding works by Thomas Carlyle and John Stuart Mill.[15] Works that designated themselves as non-fictional discussions of science, economics or character did not exist in a vacuum sealed off from literary fiction or its arguments about the relationships among racial identity, gender inequality and institutional power.

To understand some elements of the world in which Wilkie Collins lived and the plots he imagined, one must accept that 'racism informed virtually all aspects of Romantic and Victorian culture'.[16] Collins's oeuvre addresses race and empire in complicated and sometimes contradictory ways, often signalling that understandings of racial identities, racist behaviour and imperial power were unstable. Collins's writings show that he participated regularly in ongoing print conversations about racial identity and the moral failings of the British empire, and the conclusions of those contributions resist hasty categorisation.

Notes

1. P. Fryer, *Staying Power: The History of Black People in Britain* (1984; London: Pluto Press, 2010), p. 1.
2. G. Holbrook Gerzina, *Black London: Life Before Emancipation* (New Brunswick, NJ: Rutgers University Press, 1995), p. 2.
3. J. Anim-Addo, 'Queen Victoria's Black "Daughter"', in G. Holbrook Gerzina (ed.), *Black Victorians, Black Victoriana* (New Brunswick, NJ: Rutgers University Press, 2003), pp. 11–19.
4. C.-A. Christ, 'Introduction', in C.-A. Christ (ed.), *The Norton Anthology of English Literature*, Vol. 2B: *The Victorian Age*, 7th ed. (New York: Norton, 2000), p. 1044.
5. J. E. Fromer, '"Deeply Indebted to the Tea-Plant": Representations of English National Identity in Victorian Histories of Tea', *Victorian Literature and Culture* 36.2 (2008), pp. 531–47 (pp. 531–2).
6. L. Nayder, 'Collins and Empire', in J. Bourne Taylor (ed.), *The Cambridge Companion to Wilkie Collins* (Cambridge University Press, 2006), pp. 139–52 (p. 147).
7. J. Marsh, 'Spectacle', in H. F. Tucker (ed.), *A Companion to Victorian Literature and Culture* (Oxford: Blackwell, 1999), pp. 276–88 (p. 283).
8. *The Illustrated London News* 22. 624 (28 May 1853), pp. 409–10.
9. [W. Collins], 'Sermon for Sepoys', *Household Words* 414 (27 February 1858), pp. 244–7.
10. Nayder, 'Collins and Empire', p. 142.
11. G. Moore, 'Empires and Colonies', in S. Ledger and H. Furneaux (eds.), *Charles Dickens in Context* (Cambridge University Press, 2011), pp. 284–90 (p. 289).
12. C. Bolt, *Victorian Attitudes to Race* (London: Routledge, 1971), p. 82; L. Callanan, *Deciphering Race: White Anxiety, Racial Conflict, and the Turn to Fiction in Mid-Victorian English Prose* (Columbus: Ohio State University Press, 2006), p. 98.
13. J. DeVere Brody, *Impossible Purities: Blackness, Femininity, and Victorian Culture* (Durham, NC: Duke University Press, 1998), pp. 4–5.
14. M. Klimaszewski, *Collaborative Dickens: Authorship and Victorian Christmas Periodicals* (Athens: Ohio University Press, 2019), p. 211.
15. [T. Carlyle], 'Occasional Discourse on the Negro Question', *Fraser's Magazine* 40 (December 1849), pp. 670–9; [J. S. Mill], 'The Negro Question', *Fraser's Magazine* 41 (January 1850), pp. 25–31.
16. P. Brantlinger, *Taming Cannibals: Race and the Victorians* (Ithaca, NY: Cornell University Press, 2011), p. 7.

CHAPTER 33

Class Status and Social Identity

Jenny Bourne Taylor

One of the most chilling moments of *The Woman in White* (1860) is Walter Hartright's account of Frederick Fairlie's refusal to recognise Laura on her return to Limmeridge House following her rescue from the asylum where she had been confined as 'Anne Catherick'. 'The daughter of Philip Fairlie and the wife of Percival Glyde might still exist for her sister, might still exist for me', writes Walter Hartright; 'but to all the world beside she was . . . . socially, morally, legally – dead.'[1] Traumatised, neither Laura nor her half-sister, Marian Halcombe, is able to reassert her position; but it is the loss of her place within class and family which compounds the complete collapse of Laura's former self.

The slipperiness of identity runs through Collins's fiction. He plays on the instability of boundaries: between legitimacy and illegitimacy, sanity and madness, gender and racial categories, inside and outside; but these distinctions are underpinned by those of class. Class status is often a primary marker of identity: Magdalen Vanstone in *No Name* (1863), for example, is identified in a handbill as having 'the manners and habits of a refined, cultivated lady'.[2] Yet later, Magdalen herself stresses the performativity and instability of class distinction: 'Shall I tell you what a lady is?' she asks her maid before they exchange places: 'A lady is a woman who wears a silk gown, and has a sense of her own importance' (NN: 613). Ambiguous status also generates profound unease. Anne Catherick has neither 'the manner of a lady . . . [nor] the manner of a woman in the humblest rank of life', compounding Walter's cognitive confusion when he first encounters her (WW: 21); Gabriel Betteredge notes of Rosanna Spearman in *The Moonstone* (1868) that 'there was just a dash of something that wasn't like a housemaid, and that *was* like a lady, about her'.[3] The perception of social class is a central concern in most mid-nineteenth-century fiction, but Collins's preoccupation with disguised, appropriated and exchanged identities and with marginal and liminal figures dramatises contemporary tensions around its meaning particularly sharply, and his reworking of

Gothic and melodramatic tropes in contemporary settings gave his work a subversive currency.

Modern urban consumer society came to maturity between 1850 and 1880. The radicalism of the 1830s and 1840s had not completely disappeared, but it had been largely replaced by a more quiescent population and a recognition that political legitimacy depended on the inclusion of wider parts of it, that the 1867 Reform Act in part addressed. The Great Exhibition of 1851, a celebration of British industry and imperial reach that is mentioned in *The Woman in White* and *Armadale* (1866); the development of the railway as a form of mass transport, and with it the suburbs; new technologies of mass commodity production, including the proliferation of diverse print media and of advertising; and population growth and a broad increase in living standards (alongside continuing extreme poverty) all contributed to a sense that older hierarchies were being eroded.

Yet Britain remained a highly stratified society. The landed gentry still commanded the greatest part of the nation's wealth, with estates passed down through primogeniture and the exchange of women in marriage. This closed group retained its economic dominance despite some wealthy industrialists and commercial magnates joining its ranks – indeed its cultural power grew. The Church and the Law remained closely linked to the gentry; but the middle class was dividing into new professions and shifting social and cultural hierarchies. The legal profession expanded; medicine became increasingly specialised; the growth of print media generated diverse groups of writers, journalists and artists. This broadening of the middle class meant that domestic servants made up over an eighth of the working population – the majority of them women – by 1880. Notions of social distinction were also changing as the concept of rank gave way to class as an economic and social category. The idea of society as an organic whole persisted but took on newly ambivalent meanings. The shift away from conservative conceptions of a static hierarchy brought with it a recognition of the advantages of upward mobility; but this very fluidity also generated a profound unease about the collapse of social distinctions and a horror of an encroaching mass culture, often articulated through biological metaphors of heredity and disease and amplified from mid-century through the language of degeneration. The critical response to the sensation novel as an 'indication of a widespread corruption', and of making 'the literature of the kitchen the favourite reading of the Drawing Room', highlighted these fears.[4]

Collins's fiction plays on these transformations. He twists the familiar theme of the challenge to hereditary power by emerging class formations and scrutinises the meanings of 'inheritance' itself. He highlights the fundamental fictiveness of class distinction while exposing the ultimate limits of individual agency and mobility: mistress and maid often swap places, but only briefly and for limited purposes. The early novels *Basil* (1852) and *The Dead Secret* (1857) both draw heavily on Gothic tropes in their very different explorations of the morbid residual power of the landed gentry. Subtitled 'A Story of Modern Life', *Basil* unpicks the idea of hereditary rank through the retrospective confession of the eponymous protagonist, as he is banished to the edge of society and threatened by an enemy to whom he is bound by the past, and by sexual rivalry. Presenting himself as a typical younger son of an ancient family with a father obsessed by caste, Basil is a strangely ineffective figure, at the mercy of Margaret Sherwin, the linen-draper's daughter he clandestinely marries, her father, and Sherwin's mysterious clerk, Robert Mannion. Estranged from his family by his cross-class transgression, Basil nonetheless shares his class's horror of modern mass culture. He first sees Margaret on an omnibus, where 'persons of all classes ... are so oddly collected together';[5] traces her to the modern Gothic 'suburb of new houses ... its newness and desolation .... revolted me' (B: 30–1); and is deeply disturbed by the Sherwins' 'oppressively new' (B: 53) drawing-room.

The opposition between Margaret and Basil's sister Clara articulates class difference as an opposition between fairness and darkness, and Margaret's racialised class identity becomes increasingly pathologised, culminating in her death from typhus. Mannion's ambiguous social position, in contrast, is manifested in his face – 'so inexpressive that it did not even look vacant' (B: 91) – and in the mismatch between his economic status and his cultural demeanour – 'he had all the quietness and self-possession of a gentleman' (B: 91) – which consolidates his power over Sherwin and his sexual hold on Margaret (B: 111). Bound together by their fathers' intertwined histories manifested in the next generation, Basil and Mannion nonetheless ultimately both lack agency. Mannion's letter to Basil describes how his father's execution for forgery, condoned by Basil's father, thwarts his own attempts at self-improvement until his position with Sherwin gives him a new commercial middle-class status that is thwarted by Basil in turn. And although Basil is finally reassimilated into his family, there is no way forward to a new social identity – he remains a redundant member of his caste.

The traces of a former affliction are 'deeply and strikingly visible' in the lady's maid Sarah Leeson in *The Dead Secret*.[6] Servants are given real complexity in Collins's fiction, and *The Dead Secret* turns *Basil* inside out by making the underside of the ancient family the bearer and protector of its secret – that Rosamond Treverton, the heiress to the semi-ruined Cornish estate Porthgenna Tower, is actually Sarah's illegitimate daughter. As Collins made clear in the 1861 preface to the novel, the interest lies in the effect of its repression on Sarah herself, as she perversely highlights what she tries to conceal. But equally 'dead' is the notion of hereditary status that Basil's father embodied. Rosamond's husband Leonard Frankland is from an ancient family enriched by trade whose father's ambition has been 'to sink the merchant in the landed grandee' (DS: 58) by acquiring the crumbling Porthgenna Tower, along with its mines and fisheries. His early assertion that Rosamond should not 'confuse those distinctions in rank on which the well-being of society depends' is countered by her modern organicism: there are not 'such very wide distinctions between us. We have all got the same number of arms and legs' (DS: 73), and when Rosamond's parentage is finally disclosed, its effect on her husband is negligible – her class status remains intact.

Collins's novels of the 1860s stress the tension between inherited structure and individual agency more sharply, as class position becomes more labile and identities more unknowable. In *The Woman in White*, the revelation that the aristocratic villain Sir Percival Glyde is actually illegitimate exposes both the fragility and performativity of rank as much as its roots in very real forms of economic and ideological power. Philip Fairlie passes his wealthy daughter to his friend in an act of homosocial class solidarity, while the figures serving the family from older established professions – the lawyers Gilmore and Kyrle and the housekeeper, the downwardly mobile clergyman's widow Mrs Michelson – are, initially at least, in awe of the aristocracy. Walter notes that 'the Law is still ... the pre-engaged servant of the long purse' (WW: 5), while deploying the techniques of the courtroom to present the story. He combines the roles of specific narrator and general editor of others' testimony to dramatise his transformation from artist dependent on aristocratic patronage to becoming the father of the family's next heir. But to complete this process, he must fashion a new class status himself. Hardened by colonial exploration, reborn as 'an obscure unnoticed man, without patron or friend to help me' (WW: 420–1), Walter's upward mobility is achieved by becoming a successful member of the growing class of artists and intellectuals created by an expanding media. The closing scene of the novel represents a new accommodation between the emerging creative industries and older landed interests that had been impossible in *Basil*.

Such an accommodation is also impossible in *No Name* as it follows Magdalen Vanstone's fight to reclaim her social identity. The disclosure of Magdalen and Norah's illegitimacy highlights their economic powerlessness, but it also sets inheritance based on entail against the agency of testamentary freedom. Andrew Vanstone's wealth is derived from industry and based on capital not land; the daughters' disinheritance results from his will being nullified by his marriage, not their illegitimacy *per se*. This move defamiliarises primogeniture: the money reverts back to his elder brother and thus to his son Noel, as against the sisters' 'natural rights ... sanctioned by the direct expression of the father's wishes' (NN: 221–2). It also means that Magdalen is trapped between agency and entropy, as she assumes traditional feminine roles in the fight to reclaim her place: 'young lady at home'; older governess; married woman, and finally parlour maid. Posed by the narrator as a melodramatic struggle between 'Good' and 'Evil', Magdalen's shift between mutability and a rigidity in which her face becomes 'as still and cold as marble' (NN: 327) represents that impasse for middle-class women in which the way 'forward' can only be the way 'back' into the family.

The figures surrounding Magdalen play on this tension between mutability and fixity, often inverting class hierarchies in the process. Frank Clare and Noel Vanstone both embody the 'feminised' decadence of hereditary entitlement: Frank in his inability to forge a modern class status through industry or commerce; Noel through his miserly reluctance to invest or spend his capital. Norah regains the family fortune by marrying back into it, essentially recapitulating Magdalen's active moves as passive agent, and Norah and Noel are both dominated by powerful upper servants – the old governess Miss Garth and the resourceful Mrs Lecount. Against them, but also side-stepping this opposition, the specious 'relation' (NN: 28) Captain Wragge embodies and parodies the energy and endless self-reinvention of modern commodity culture, as comedy competes with melodrama. With his accounts and mania for 'order and propriety' (NN: 190), his many 'Skins to Jump Into' (NN: 322), and his belief in the power of confidence to overcome all odds, Wragge moves from 'Moral' to 'Medical Agriculture' (NN: 709), through fraud to commodity promotion to develop a successful pharmacological career based entirely on advertising, complemented by his put-upon wife: consumer *par excellence*.

Armadale inverts *Basil*'s theme of paired fathers and sons: Armadale/Midwinter's obsession with his father's legacy of murder and his struggles with his own morbid sense of hereditary destiny overturn the oppositions of the earlier novel. In *Armadale*, social distinction has no stable form or meaning, and never reaches a settled resolution, as it plays across the multiple identities of 'Allan Armadale', an empty name that reaches across place and time, but can be traced back to a colonial property. The history of the English estate of Thorpe Ambrose is intimately tied to the Barbadian slave plantation through the 'first' Allan Armadale. His adopted ward Allan Wrentmore (Armadale/Midwinter's father) takes the Armadale name with its legacy of slavery, which is passed, along with his crime, to his son. Midwinter's mixed enslaved and slave-owning heritage and his childhood as both servant and vagabond give him a hybridity and adaptability, in contrast with his namesake. While Allan Armadale is unwilling to play the role of landed gentleman to which he is unexpectedly assigned when he inherits the English estate, he is blissfully unconscious of, and protected from, the economic history of his class position and its psychological legacy by Midwinter himself. Other established roles tied to the English estate are also destabilised: the old family solicitor Darch is replaced by the upwardly mobile Pedgifts; the broken-down steward Dashwood is exploited by his private-detective son, while Midwinter finally finds a new social identity as a journalist and intellectual, like Walter, independent of patronage. His transformation is triggered, ironically, by his marriage to Lydia Gwilt, and Magdalen Vanstone's self-reinvention as a propertyless woman is taken to its limits in Collins's most intriguing villainess. Given the strongest voice and most complex subjectivity in the novel through the use of her diary and letters, Lydia expresses and acts upon a fundamentally class-based resentment that Midwinter the former servant and vagabond sublimates into a homosocial bond; but like Magdalen, her power is limited to a range of feminine roles: maid, governess, music teacher, wife.

The Moonstone also explores a morbid colonial legacy in Colonel Herncastle's expropriation of the sacred Indian diamond in the previous generation, but is set in the England of 1848–9, the end of a decade of political upheaval and conservative reaction, that is given voice by the fisherwoman Limping Lucy, one of the only figures not economically dependent on the landed gentry. As many critics have noted, this is Collins's most cognitively ambiguous novel, and in its portrayal of a social structure based on inherited wealth undermined from without and within, yet finally re-established, it is also one of his most politically ambivalent. The central story is made up of testimonies collated retrospectively by Franklin Blake, now husband of the wealthy heiress Rachel Verinder, and a wealthy landowner himself; but it is the servants who both uphold and undermine the class structure on which the family relies. The steward Gabriel Betteredge, who frames the inner Story, represents a nostalgic, organic social order based on familial relationships. Rising from pageboy through fifty years of service, his daughter Penelope raised to be Rachel's maid, his memory forms the glue that holds the family together, embodying a conscious sense of belatedness – 'dear old friend of the happy days that were never to come again' (M: 292), as Blake puts it. Conversely, Rosanna Spearman, the reformed, deformed thief taken into the family as housemaid, represents a modern, fluid organicism that recalls Rosamond's in *The Dead Secret*, but from a more subversive place. Her letter to Franklin expresses a radical, egalitarian subjectivity in her refusal to accept the boundaries of either class in her sexual desire for Franklin and her insistence on the class basis of Rachel's attractiveness. But finally Rosanna, too, maintains and protects Franklin's secret, obliterating herself and the apparent evidence of his guilt in the Shivering Sands.

The middle-class professionals that surround the family are in a state of flux as traditional roles are displaced by socially ambiguous scientists who nonetheless straddle amateur and professional identities. Colonel Herncastle is a gentleman scientist who combines 'smoking opium and collecting old books' with 'trying strange things in chemistry' (M: 31), and whose will 'founded a professorship of Chemistry at a northern university' (M: 36). The family lawyer Bruff plays a key narrative role and protects Rachel's financial interests from Godfrey Ablewhite; but his initial scepticism of the 'scientific experiment' (M: 412) that establishes Franklin's innocence consigns him to the position of spectator. Sergeant Cuff's celebrated status springs from his position in the by now well-established Metropolitan Police and from the methods of forensic science; the fear and mistrust with which he is initially treated by all levels of the household springs from his ambiguous class status, yet it is from retirement, as a gentleman horticulturalist, that he finally detects Godfrey Ablewhite. Franklin's unconscious taking of the Diamond is the product of the family doctor Candy's defence of establishment medicine and his inadequate understanding of the more complex psychological effects of opium. In contrast, his assistant Ezra Jennings is a modern mental scientist, the author of a book on the brain and nervous system, but treated with fear and mistrust by all the local community. With his parti-coloured hair and racial and gender ambiguity, both doctor and opium addict, Jennings is a hybrid figure that brings together many of the novel's oppositions – but it is latent class status that draws him to Franklin: 'he had . . . the *unsought self-possession*, which is a sure sign of good breeding . . . everywhere in the civilised world' (M: 365–6).

In 1879 Collins republished in volume form *A Rogue's Life, from his Birth to His Marriage*, a satire of the early nineteenth-century class structure that had first been serialised in *Household Words* in 1856. Offering himself as 'an example of some of the workings of the social system of this illustrious country of ours on the individual nature',[7] the downwardly mobile Frank Softly's confession is a comic reworking of *Basil*, while anticipating the slipperiness of social identity, and the narrow boundary separating criminal and respectable society in the novels of the 1860s. Like Basil's, Frank's upper-class family is obsessed with rank, but its pedigree has started to crumble: Frank's 'remarkably well-connected aristocratic mother' (whose ancestors were 'Rogues of great capacity and distinction in the Feudal times') has a brother who 'committed an outrage on the family by making a fortune in the soap and candle trade', while his brother-in-law 'made a fortune in the West Indies' (RL: 7, 2, 14). Like Basil, Frank goes to a prestigious public school; but his talent is for portraiture rather than literature, and his unsuitability for the gentlemanly professions leads him into caricature, then picture forgery, and finally (albeit against his will), coining, for which, like Mannion's father, he faces the death penalty. But in contrast with his working-class accomplice, Frank is fêted as a glamorous criminal celebrity and transported, rising again in Australia, from servant of his wife to a self-made man.

In the same year, 1879, Collins also published perhaps his most radical scrutiny of English society, *The Fallen Leaves*, a novel which, too, explores 'the workings of the social system' on the individual, but in a very different register and from the standpoint of the late nineteenth century. Like much of Collins's later fiction, *The Fallen Leaves* combines and reworks earlier motifs for explicitly tendentious ends often in bizarre ways, critically analysing the economic and social structures underlying class distinctions, while (as in much of his later fiction) laying greater emphasis on the relative power of environment and heredity. Like *The New Magdalen* (1873), *The Fallen Leaves* develops its critique through the device of upper-class radicals on the one hand and reformed prostitutes on the other – both novels end with transgressive marriages, and both draw heavily on melodrama in their use of concealed origins. Julian Gray and Amelius Goldenheart are both Christian Socialists who offer stirring critiques of economic and social inequality – Amelius, brought up in an American utopian community, in the 'Fatal Lecture', which excoriates English commercial society as 'organised systems of imposture, masquerading under the guise of banks and companies . . . . Everything we eat, drink and wear is . . . . [an] adulterated commodity.'[8] It is the shaping environment of capitalism, he insists, that shapes a class structure in which all classes are corrupted.

Yet in both novels, as in much of his late fiction, Collins also resists and amplifies the contemporary emphasis on heredity and degeneration in exploring the nature of social identity itself. *The New Magdalen* inverts *The Woman in White*'s substitution theme: the reformed prostitute Mercy Merrick steals the identity of the upper-class Grace Roseberry to gain a legitimate place in society. Yet her ability to fit the new social role she has stolen is presented as innate: manifested in her statuesque appearance and amplified by the revelation of her origins. In contrast, Grace, who has the rightful claim, is physically and socially 'unfit': both her physiognomy and her transgression of the rules of polite conduct undercut her class origins. And while the 'rescued' working-class child in *The New Magdalen* is an animalistic 'pet creation of the laws of political economy',[9] Sally, the adolescent prostitute in *The Fallen Leaves*, is 'saved' by her simple-mindedness: 'the appearance of the girl was artlessly virginal and innocent; she looked as if she had passed through the contamination of the streets without being touched by it' (FL: 185–6). The lost child of Emma Farnaby, Sally resists too the hereditary taint of both her parents – above all, her father John Farnaby, whose corrupt career as a venture capitalist is presented as both the product of his own 'low' origins, and an example of the system that Amelius rejects, but is unable to reform. Like Frank Softly in *A Rogue's Life*, neither Julian nor Amelius can be reassimilated into society; but while the Rogue's transportation leads to a new beginning, the self-made exiles of Collins's later fiction are given no clear social identity: both novels end ambiguously, without narrative closure as their protagonists move on to an undecided future.

Notes

[1] W. Collins, *The Woman in White*, ed. J. Sutherland (Oxford World's Classics, 1999), p. 421. All future references will be cited in the text as WW.
[2] W. Collins, *No Name*, ed. V. Blain (Oxford World's Classics, 2008), p. 189. All future references will be cited in the text as NN.
[3] W. Collins, *The Moonstone*, ed. J. Sutherland (Oxford World's Classics, 1999), p. 22. All future references will be cited in the text as M.
[4] [H. Mansel], 'Sensation Novels', *Quarterly Review* 113 (April 1863), pp. 481–514 (p. 482); [W. F. Rae], 'Sensation Novelists: Miss Braddon', *North British Review* 4 (September–December 1865), pp. 180–204 (p. 204).
[5] W. Collins, *Basil: A Story of Modern Life*, ed. D. Goldman (Oxford World's Classics, 1990), p. 27. All future references will be cited in the text as B.

6. W. Collins, *The Dead Secret*, ed. I. B. Nadel (Oxford World's Classics, 1997), p. 11. All future references will be cited in the text as DS.
7. W. Collins, *A Rogue's Life, from his Birth to his Marriage* (London: Chatto & Windus, 1890), p. 1. All future references will be cited in the text as RL.
8. W. Collins, *The Fallen Leaves* (London: Chatto & Windus, 1880), p. 156. All future references will be cited in the text as FL.
9. W. Collins, *The New Magdalen* (London: Chatto & Windus, 1891), p. 3.

CHAPTER 34

Disability

Heather Tilley

Disability is intrinsic to Wilkie Collins's novelistic project, and a significant area for critical attention in both the breadth and depth of attention that he focused on the experience and meaning of disability. The disability studies critic Martha Stoddard Holmes states that 'Wilkie Collins was one of the two most prolific producers of disabled characters in Victorian literature, along with ... Dickens',[1] and many of his plotlines are intricately bound up with characters' disabilities.[2] Despite the fantastical and sensational nature of his plotlines, Collins takes care to research and contextualise his depictions of physical and sensory impairments. This includes situating Madonna Blyth's deafness within contemporary sign-language debates in his early novel *Hide and Seek* (1854) and exploring the gender and class effects of Rosanna Spearman's visual difference in *The Moonstone* (1868). Collins departs from many of his contemporaries in his treatment of disability, refusing to use it as a cultural shorthand or metaphor for deviance, ignorance or purity. Instead, he is attentive to its lived experience, presenting disabled characters with a range of attributes, desires and challenges. Collins's interest in impairment was not simply vicarious: he lived with ill health throughout his life (developing an opium addiction to treat gout in the 1860s), and as a writer he was particularly attuned to the contingencies of the human body. His biographer Robert P. Ashley wrote that 'he had the chronic invalid's fascination for mental and physical deformities'.[3]

In this essay, I will briefly trace Collins's innovation in what lays claims to being one of the most radical treatments of disability in Victorian fiction, *Poor Miss Finch* (1872), before examining the complex and challenging treatment of disability in his next novel *The Law and the Lady* (1875). My focus here will be on Miserrimus Dexter, an instrumental agent in the novel's action, who was born without legs and becomes mad. Miserrimus's representation is clearly framed by contemporary medical discourses that linked mobility impairment with transgressive masculinity and mental instability. However, I propose that he is disabled not by his physical difference but rather by the way others respond to that difference, which renders his intellectual and artistic brilliance strange and his sexual energies repulsive. It is this distinction – between the natural and the socially and culturally constructed effects of impairment – that make Collins such a valuable narrator of Victorian disability for twenty-first-century readers.

Disability As It 'Is'?

In the preface to his melodramatic novel *Poor Miss Finch*, which explores the romantic and psychological ups and downs of Lucilla Finch, blind since infancy from congenital cataracts, Collins highlights an important aspect of his novelistic practice. He reveals that in creating a blind character he has 'carefully gathered the information necessary to the execution of this purpose from competent authorities of all sorts. Whenever "Lucilla" acts or speaks in these pages, with reference to her blindness, she is doing or saying what persons afflicted as she is have done or said before her.'[4] Collins's ambition to accurately and realistically depict blindness is at odds with the rather more far-fetched aspects of the novel, which utilises a staple of the melodramatic stage drama: the mistaken identity of identical twins (Oscar and Nugent), one of whom turns blue following treatment for epilepsy.[5] Significantly, the central drama of the novel turns around another spectacle familiar to melodrama audiences: the restoration of Lucilla's sight following the surgical removal of her cataracts.[6] Lucilla is motivated to undergo surgery so that she can *see* Oscar, the twin she has fallen in love with: however, she is victim to an elaborate deception in which Oscar exchanges places with Nugent, as he fears she will be disgusted by his blue skin when she has vision.

The plot certainly stretches the bounds of credulity, and indeed contemporary reviewers dismissed it, with one asking 'what is the aim of this story? That the blind should marry the dark-blue?'[7] It is noteworthy, however, that Collins exercises more restraint when it comes to exploring the experiences of Lucilla as a blind person, and the catastrophic effects of her cataract surgery. Sightedness causes her profound depression, so much so that she neglects care for her eyes and willingly becomes blind again. Collins's methodology for creating Lucilla's character – using research to try to better understand a blind person's lived experience and so exhibit 'blindness as it really is' – produced a new fictional model of blindness, with an unsigned reviewer for the *Saturday Review* noting how he departs from other literary writers who have 'idealised' blindness 'gracefully'.[8]

As literary disability studies scholars have noted, 'disabled' and 'disability' were not common terms in the Victorian period: instead, writers used terms such as 'the afflicted' and 'deformity'. This changing terminology exemplifies how the meaning of disability is itself fluid, changeable and historically constituted.⁹ However, scholars have also recognised the mid-Victorian period as a key moment in the development of our contemporary understanding of disability, as industrialisation contributed towards a normalisation of the body which in turn constructed disability as an undesirable identity. Minds and bodies which did not fit 'the norm' became a problem that needed to be addressed: for example, either treated or cured via medical practices or segregated in specialist institutions. The influential disability studies scholar Lennard Davis argues that this 'social process of disabling' was shored up by – and indeed shaped – nineteenth-century cultural forms, including the novel.¹⁰ Collins was certainly attentive to the medical causes of impairment: his depictions draw upon contemporary medical literature and he employs medical and legal perspectives on illness and impairment – including professional testimony of doctors and lawyers – within his multi-narrative texts. Indeed, his portrayal of Lucilla's cataract surgeon, Herr Grosse, was so successful that he received requests from readers to forward his address, as they believed he was a real and practising doctor (PMF: xl). However, Grosse's authority in *Poor Miss Finch* is undermined by Lucilla's own self-knowledge and confidence in her blindness: it is Grosse's 'cure' that most distresses her.¹¹

Collins also destabilises the notion that disability is a fixed, natural identity by using the multi-narrative structure and perspectives of the sensation novel to show that disability is produced by and within social and cultural relations. This process is central to the complex and challenging presentation of disability in his next novel, *The Law and the Lady*.

Miserrimus Dexter: How to Be Both?

The Law and the Lady was serialised weekly in the *Graphic* between 1874 and 1875. The novel is narrated by Valeria Woodville/Macallan, a recently married young woman who discovers her husband Eustace is shielding her from a mysterious secret: he has been tried in Scotland for poisoning his (undisclosed) first wife Sara with arsenic. The 'law' side of the novel relates to the morally ambiguous position Eustace has been left in after the murder case against him is found 'Not Proven' by the jury: they believed he was guilty but felt there was insufficient evidence to prove it. 'The Scotch Verdict' of not proven was anomalous in English law, whereby a jury could only find a defendant guilty or not guilty. In the process of setting out to prove her husband's innocence (an act which upsets traditional gender categories) she encounters his friend Miserrimus Dexter – born without legs and suggested to be mentally unstable.

We first meet Miserrimus not in person, but rather mediated through the court report of Eustace's trial. As the final witness, his testimony forms a dramatic conclusion to the trial, both in terms of the evidence he presents, and also his unusual physical appearance and demeanour. The description of him at the trial emphasises the duality of his character:

> The loss of [his coverlet] exposed to the public curiosity the head, the arms, and the trunk of a living human being: absolutely deprived of the lower limbs. To make this deformity all the more striking and all the more terrible, the victim of it was – as to his face and his body – an unusually handsome and an unusually well-made man. His long silky hair, of a bright and beautiful chestnut color, fell over shoulders that were the perfection of strength and grace. His face was bright with vivacity and intelligence.[12]

Miserrimus is held up as an object of 'curiosity' throughout the novel. Valeria is transfixed by his appearance, and by the tension between what she perceives as his 'deformity' and his unusual beauty and grace. She desires to see Dexter's limblessness in terms of monstrosity, but his upper form and appearance disrupt this. Yet she cannot turn her eyes away: on several occasions she lingers over his physical appearance, describing in detail his hair, face, exotic clothes and of course his 'deformity'. He is both sub- and superhuman: a 'fantastic and frightful apparition, man and machinery blended in one – the new Centaur, half man, half chair' (LL: 193). There is certainly discomfort in reading the novel today: as Clare Walker Gore stresses, we are very much invited to 'gawk' at Miserrimus. Collins both shows and exploits the emergence of disability as a maligned social identity in the nineteenth century, by viscerally detailing how visibly different bodies elicit disgust, shock and fear in non-disabled characters.

The complex narrative structure of Collins's novel blurs transcription and speculation in our introduction to Miserrimus: what seems to be the professional report of the court witness is actually Valeria's reconstruction of events, written down after she has met him in person. This is important, because it shows that Valeria's moral distaste and unease shapes our access to him as a character: we largely look at him through her particular perspective (she reveals a partiality for physiognomic reading of character throughout, interpreting moral values from a superficial scrutiny of facial features). Indeed, the chapters featuring Miserrimus are titled 'First View' and 'Second View'. However, as Gore also notes, whilst Valeria attempts to make Miserrimus 'stareable' (to use Rosemarie Garland-Thomson's term) by asserting her non-disabled gaze over him, he repeatedly troubles the proper direction of scrutiny.[13] She is disturbed by the lack of shame he displays when she occasionally mocks his eccentricities, and also details how he turns the gaze back on her, by scrutinising her face, body and walk. There is indeed much more frisson between Miserrimus and Valeria than between Valeria and her 'weak' and underwhelming husband – despite her protestations of passion for the latter. Notably, Eustace has a limp and walks with a cane: but this is no 'drawback' for Valeria, who exuberantly expresses her attraction towards him (and she falls pregnant on their honeymoon) (LL: 15). The novel establishes a way of reading disabled men as potential erotic and romantic objects in Valeria's desire for Eustace, but cannot sustain this in relation to Miserrimus.

Valeria is at pains to draw attention to Miserrimus's 'effeminate appearance', which goes some way to mitigating the sexual threat of this beautiful, strong disabled man, and his behaviour is also distinctly feminised (and infantalised). He tells Valeria of his 'unutterable nervous suffering' and describes himself as 'a very tender-hearted man ... capable of hysterics' (LL: 195, 203). The novel clearly suggests that Miserrimus's physical impairment renders him particularly sensitive, and susceptible to mental derangement which ultimately leads to the collapse of his health and his early death. As David Skilton notes, this reflects Collins's careful engagement with contemporary psychological discourse, which increasingly pathologised motor disorders as symptomatic of diseased minds.[14] The famous psychiatrist Henry Maudsley stated in 1873 that 'it is obvious that disorder of the motor centres may have, as I believe it has, no little effect upon the phenomena of mental derangement'.[15] Miserrimus exhibits symptoms of a condition contemporarily pathologised as monomania – defined by Maudsley as when a patient 'exhibits insane delusions on one subject or in regard to certain trains of thought, and talks sensibly in other respects'.[16] Collins's representation also shines light on the way that men with motor impairments were becoming a particularly troublesome category, as damaged nervous systems were recognised as incompatible with the demands of busy professional lives. This had been a particular feature of the contentious medical and legal debates over 'Railway Spine' in the 1860s, which, as the historian Mark S. Micale notes, is one arena in which men were psychopathologised as hysterical in British medical literature.[17]

Miserrimus's character is complex and contradictory: he is described as a man 'of far more than average ability' (LL: 167–8) but also in animalistic terms, likened variously to a monkey, a frog and an imp. This oscillating viewpoint undermines the certainty with which Miserrimus is pathologised. On Valeria's first meeting with him – at his home, notably on the margins of London in the 'great northern suburb' (LL: 188) – she is accompanied by her mother-in-law Mrs Macallan. Mrs Macallan draws attention in advance to Miserrimus's 'madnesses', directing both Valeria and the reader to his oddities (LL: 189). Notably, however, this is based on his refusal to sell the ruins on the grounds of his property to speculators, as he resists what he describes as the 'mean, dishonest, and grovelling constructions of a mean, dishonest, and grovelling age' (LL: 189–90): he is judged mad for being effectively anti-capitalist. Miserrimus himself challenges perceptions that he is 'mad', insisting instead that he is a 'visionary' (LL: 195).

Miserrimus is disabled and marginalised on multiple levels: his limblessness renders him visibly different and subject to pitying or fearful responses; and his motor impairment is associated with a mental illness that is exacerbated by the freakish status conferred on him. Notably, however, Collins resists portraying Miserrimus's physical impairment as naturally disabling. Instead, he draws attention to his physical capacity – his upper-body strength, his ability to move unsupported, alongside interdependence with his chair, which allows him to glide, 'self-propelled', easily: he asserts forcefully when someone attempts to steer his chair unprompted: 'My chair is Me ... how dare you lay hands on Me?' (LL: 163, 138). There is certainly competition between the narratorial and authorial perspectives on Miserrimus, who, with his complex, fragmented mind, is aligned with the creative force of the writer. As a 'student of human character' he writes poetry, composes music and paints imaginative scenes, and also, of course, creates false alternative plotlines for Valeria to unravel. As critics have noted, if Miserrimus is a parody of Collins, then Valeria – in her single-minded determination to uncover 'whodunnit' – is a stereotyped sensation- and detective-fiction reader.[18]

Although Lucilla Finch is granted a happy ending – she is both returned to blindness *and* marries Oscar – allowing a queer disabled man a similarly happy ending was seemingly too radical for Collins (or his publishers and readership).[19] Miserrimus is expunged firstly to a mental institution, and then to the graveyard. This ending is certainly problematic and exemplifies the narrative pattern for disability identified by David Mitchell and Sharon Snyder in their influential model of 'narrative prosthesis'. This model identifies both 'the dependency of literary narratives upon disability' and 'the notion that all narratives operate out of a desire to compensate for a limitation or to reign in excess' in relation to disabled characters.[20] Indeed, the latter part of the novel stages an alternative trial for the trustworthiness of Miserrimus's character (he is also named as a suspect): overturning the 'Not Proven' verdict increasingly depends on his word. Miserrimus is also, through a slow reveal of evidence and the piecing-together of Sara Macallan's suicide note – which he destroyed – suggested to be the novel's 'villain' (LL: 359), a stock role for disabled characters. However, the novel's serialised form – read over time, in parts – delays a simple, reductive response to Miserrimus. Sara Macallan's disgust for him arose in part because, as the lawyer Mr Playmore puts it, he was in love with her and had the temerity to ask her, 'deformed as he was' to be his wife (LL: 261). Even his obvious wealth and gentleman status cannot make a limbless man marriageable in the context of growing anxiety about the hereditary nature of certain impairments. The lack of an omniscient narrative voice means that the novel problematically articulates – even if it ironises – the viewpoint that disabled people should be asexual. However, it also acknowledges the complexities of disabled identity and recognises that disabled minds and bodies are also desiring and desired subjects. In so doing, it challenges newly unfolding notions of what constitutes 'normal' personhood.

The visibility of disability within Collins's novels led to a critical recoil against his work in the latter part of the nineteenth century. In an essay written after Collins's death, the poet Algernon Charles Swinburne commented:

> The remarkable genius of [Collins] for invention and construction and composition of incidents and effects was limited by an incapacity and dependence on a condition which cannot but be regarded as seriously impairing his claims to consideration as an artist or student. He could not, as a rule, get forward at all without the help of some physical or moral infirmity in some one of the leading agents or patients of the story.[21]

Swinburne's essay suggests that Collins's tendency to create disabled lead characters came to be seen as a defect of his writing: in fact, he cannot be treated as a serious artist because of it. This critical view of Collins re-enacts the denigration and reduction of Miserrimus's character, demonstrating how these social attitudes translated into issues of aesthetic taste and canon-formation. Collins's work is an important example of the way that literary representations do not simply reflect but also co-produce social attitudes to disability.

Notes

1. M. S. Holmes, *Fictions of Affliction: Physical Disability in Victorian Culture* (Ann Arbor: University of Michigan Press, 2004), p. 74.
2. For the sake of brevity, I will simply list here selected novels which use disability either as a central plot device or feature disabled central protagonists: *Hide and Seek* (1854): Madonna Blyth (deafness), Leonard Frankland (blindness); *The Woman in White* (1859): Anne Catherick (mental illness); *No Name* (1863): Matilda Wragge (learning disability); *The Moonstone* (1868): Ezra Jennings (chronic ill health, opium addiction), Rosanna Spearman (visual difference); *Poor Miss Finch* (1872): Lucilla Finch (blindness); *The Law and the Lady* (1875): Miserrimus Dexter and Ariel (physical disability and learning disability).
3. R. P. Ashley, *Wilkie Collins* (London: Arthur Barker, 1952), p. 37.
4. W. Collins, *Poor Miss Finch*, ed. C. Peters (Oxford World's Classics, 2000), p. xxxix. Further references will be cited in the text as PMF.
5. One of the most famous examples is Dion Boucicault's 1852 adaptation of Alexandre Dumas's novella *The Corsican Brothers*.
6. European writers and audiences were fascinated by the dramatic possibilities of experimental cataract surgery following the surgeon William Cheselden's account of his success in 1728. Whilst there were only a small number of successful cataract removals by the mid-nineteenth century, it became a popular subject for melodrama, usually featuring a blind girl whose sight is restored with medical intervention, allowing her to see and thus pursue a romantic relationship with a love interest. See, for example, Thomas Morton's sentimental comic opera, *The Blind Girl; or, A Receipt for Beauty* (1808); and George Roberts's, *Blind Love* (c.1850). Henrik Hertz's 1845 Danish play *King Rene's Daughter* – quickly translated and performed across Europe – was one of the most popular dramatic representations of sight restoration and inspired Tchaikovsky's final opera, *Iolanta* (1892). See also Elisabeth Gitter, 'The Blind Daughter in Charles Dickens's *Cricket on the Hearth*', *SEL: Studies in English Literature, 1500–1900* 39.4 (1999), pp. 675–89.
7. [Unsigned review], *The Nation* (7 March 1872), p. xiv.
8. 'Poor Miss Finch', *Saturday Review* 33.2 (2 March 1872), pp. 282–3 (p. 282).
9. See C. W. Gore, *Plotting Disability in the Nineteenth-Century Novel* (Edinburgh University Press, 2020), pp. 1–2.
10. L. J. Davis, *Enforcing Normalcy: Disability, Deafness, and the Body* (London: Verso, 1995), p. 24.
11. For a fuller discussion, see H. Tilley, *Blindness and Writing: From Wordsworth to Gissing* (Cambridge University Press, 2017), pp. 191–207.
12. W. Collins, *The Law and the Lady*, ed. D. Skilton (1998; London: Penguin, 2003), p. 163. Further references will be cited in the text as LL.
13. Gore, *Plotting Disability*, pp. 94–5.
14. D. Skilton, 'Introduction' to Collins, *The Law and the Lady*, p. xx.

[15] H. Maudsley, *Body and Mind: An Inquiry into their Connection and Mutual Influence, Specially in Reference to Mental Disorders*, 2nd ed. (London: Macmillan, 1873), p. 31. See also D. Tuke, *Illustrations of the Influence of the Mind upon the Body in Health and Disease* (London: J. & A. Churchill, 1872).

[16] H. Maudsley, *Responsibility in Mental Disease* (London: Henry S. King, 1874), p. 73.

[17] M. S. Micale, 'Hysterical Male/Hysterical Female: Reflections on Comparative Gender Construction in Nineteenth-Century France and Britain', in M. Benjamin (ed.), *Science and Sensibility: Gender and Scientific Enquiry, 1780–1945* (Oxford: Blackwell, 1991), pp. 200–39 (p. 201).

[18] Gore, *Plotting Disability*, p. 101.

[19] Indeed, the editor of the *Graphic* was outraged by and attempted to censor the scene in which Miserrimus kisses and fondles Valeria. See M. S. Holmes, 'Queering the Marriage Plot: Wilkie Collins's *The Law and the Lady*', in M. Tromp (ed.), *Victorian Freaks: The Social Context of Freakery in Britain* (Columbus: Ohio State University Press, 2008), pp. 237–58 (p. 249).

[20] D. T. Mitchell and S. L. Snyder, *Narrative Prosthesis: Disability and the Dependencies of Discourse* (Ann Arbor: University of Michigan Press, 2001), pp. 47, 51.

[21] A. C. Swinburne, 'Wilkie Collins', *The Fortnightly Review* 46.275 (November 1889), p. 589.

CHAPTER 35

Ethics

Biwu Shang

In her introduction to *The Cambridge Companion to Wilkie Collins* (2006), Jenny Bourne Taylor summarises the distinctive features of Collins's work as 'his exploration of how social identities and relationships are enacted and maintained, his fascination with the unstable boundary between the normal and the deviant, his reworking of Gothic conventions to explore the power relations at work in the Victorian family'.[1] In Taylor's view, these features have made Collins 'a particularly fruitful subject for many of the key theoretical and critical concerns of the 1980s and 1990s', which continues today.[2] Among these concerns, ethics is particularly important. Arguably, all of Collins's works are concerned with an ethical issue about one's identity and choice. I agree with Zhenzhao Nie, who argues that 'literature is not just an art of language but rather an art of text'.[3] In this chapter, I shall mainly use the novel *The Woman in White* (1860) as an example.

Most critics see this work as a sensation novel. Elizabeth Langland argues that 'it is Collins's achievement in *The Woman in White* that he found meaningful and fruitful ways to build sensation on issues of class, gender, sexual identity, and race that could unsettle his Victorian readers in 1859 in ways that are still effective today'.[4] Among all the issues that Langland relates with sensation, I would like to add ethics to the list. To a large degree, *The Woman in White* is a story about ethical chaos and ethical order/disorder in the disguise of a sensation novel. The novel's first sentence reads: 'This is the story of what a Woman's patience can endure, and what a Man's resolution can achieve'.[5] In other words, the story is a test to measure the woman's patience and the man's resolution. At issue is the question of whose patience and whose resolution is to be tested. What is the motivation for the patience and resolution? To address these questions, this chapter examines the ethical identities and ethical choices of Walter Hartright and Laura Fairlie, both of whom succeed in passing the test of patience and resolution, or to be more exact, the test of morality.

Ethics 319

Ultimately, the novel is a test for readers to see through the ethical chaos and confusion.

In the view of A. B. Emrys, the chaotic state is mainly manifested in issues of conduct by individuals:

> Sir Percival Glyde's father has appeared to marry his mother, who, however, had a living husband. The greedy and shallow Glyde fakes the parish register to secure his own position, but the fact is known by the aggressive social climber Mrs. Catherick, who blackmails him into elevating her position. Her frail and mentally unstable daughter Anne knows that a secret exists but not what it is. Glyde locks her away, and it is her escape, wearing her characteristic white, that begins the novel's action. Later, when Glyde proves unable to access Laura's money and Anne dies, he and Fosco switch the two women, who look alike, locking up Lady Glyde and declaring her dead.[6]

To continue thinking along the line of Emrys's argument and observation, I would like to say that the nature of the confusion is largely attributed to characters' misplaced ethical identities. According to ethical literary criticism, 'Almost all ethical issues in literature are concerned with ethical identities.'[7] Percival Glyde's mother marries his father, but he is not his father's son; Anne Catherick knows about Percival's secret but she does not know what the secret is; Laura Fairlie is alive but declared dead; Anne is dead but thought to be alive. The challenge for the protagonist Hartright is to help Laura restore her identity, while for readers, the challenge is to see through all the confusion and make their own ethical judgments accordingly.

The first test for Hartight is his accidental encounter with Anne, who is the woman in white and possesses a similar appearance to Laura. It is on one summer night that Hartright meets a solitary woman 'dressed from head to foot in white garments' (WW: 20). Hartright is wondering 'what sort of a woman she was, and how she came to be out alone in the high-road, an hour after midnight' (WW: 21). Instead of feeling panicked and frightened, he extends his sympathetic feelings. Hartright remembers, 'The loneliness and helplessness of the woman touched me. The natural impulse to assist her and to spare her, got the better of the judgment, the caution, the worldly tact, which an older, wiser, and colder man might have summoned to help him in this strange emergency' (WW: 22). Hartright's rich psychological activities reveal his ethical consciousness which enables him to make the right ethical choice of helping her arrive in London and making sure that she will safely go in the right direction. Readers, on the one hand, applaud Hartright's ethical action of doing the woman no harm and helping her out of difficulty, while, on the other hand, they wonder about the identity of the woman. It is assumed that readers also share Hartright's uncertainty of the woman's fate, which is intensified when he learns that she is a patient running from an asylum. It is not until then that he questions himself: 'What had I done? Assisted the victim of the most horrible of all false imprisonments to escape; or cast loose on the wide world of London an unfortunate creature, whose actions it was my duty, and every man's duty, mercifully to control?' (WW: 28–9). By using words such as 'false imprisonment', 'unfortunate' and 'mercifully', Hartright further shows his sympathy for the woman in white and extends his deep concern for her fate.

Hartright's worry about Anne is mixed up with his emotional engagement with Laura, whose physical appearance is similar to Anne's. Though already engaged to Percival Glyde by her father's will, Laura falls in love with Hartright. Thus, she is now in an ethical dilemma. For the sake of fulfilling her promise, she should keep her engagement and marry Glyde. However, to be faithful to her love, she should break the engagement and marry Hartright instead. In her conversation with Marian Halcombe, Laura confesses that 'I am miserably helpless – I can't control myself. For my own sake and for all our sakes, I must have courage enough to end it' (WW: 164–5). In the novel, Marian's immediate response is 'Do you mean courage enough to claim your release?' (WW: 165). To Marian and the readers' surprise, Laura decides to tell Glyde the truth, hoping that he will release her. It is a tragedy that Laura makes a decision by making no decision, and puts her fate in the hands of the very villain whose purpose of marriage is to take her money and possessions. In the novel, Laura pleads with Glyde to release her:

> 'I have found nothing in your conduct to blame,' she answered, 'You have always treated me with the same delicacy and the same forbearance. You have deserved my trust, and what is of far more importance in my estimation, you have deserved my father's trust, out of which mine grew. You have given me no excuse, even if I had wanted to find one, for asking to be released from my pledge. What I have said so far has been spoken with the wish to acknowledge my whole obligation to you. My regard for that obligation, my regard for my father's memory, and my regard for my own promise, all forbid me to set the example, on my side, of withdrawing from our present position. The breaking of our engagement must be entirely your wish and your act, Sir Percival – not mine.' (WW: 170)

In these lines, Laura makes a wrong judgment of Glyde in at least two senses. Firstly, she thinks that Glyde is trustworthy, and he deserves both her father's trust and hers. However, as is revealed in the letters between his lawyer and Fairlie's lawyer, Glyde's purpose is to demand the money and seize the inheritance from the Fairlie family. Secondly, Laura hopes that Glyde will release her from the engagement, which means the loss of a large possession for Glyde and thus makes it impossible for him to give her up. With his vicious purpose of marrying Laura, Glyde makes full use of Laura's confession and hypocritically answers her by saying: 'I am not heartless enough to resign a woman who has just shown herself to be the noblest of her sex' (WW: 173). Though readers agree with Glyde's claim that Laura is 'the noblest of her sex', they despise him for not releasing her from their engagement.

Viewed from the perspective of ethical literary criticism, Laura's dilemma is largely attributed to the confusion of her ethical identity. She is engaged to Glyde by her father, who trusted him. Laura regards her engagement as her remembrance of her father. As a dutiful daughter, she is reluctant to break the engagement and go against his will. Laura's guardianship is given to her uncle Philip Fairlie, who is obsessed with etchings and has no intention of interfering with his niece's engagement and marriage. He just does not want to be bothered and thus agrees with the unfavourable terms written by Glyde's lawyer. Given the circumstances, Laura's dilemma is that if she chooses to follow her heart and pursue her love, she will have to break the engagement, which means the betrayal of her father's trust in Glyde, bringing trouble and anxiety to her uncle. If she chooses to be a dutiful daughter of her father and a dutiful niece of her uncle, she will have to sacrifice herself and suffer a loveless marriage. Laura is faced with a choice between two identities: to be herself or to be the daughter of her father and the niece of her uncle. In such difficult circumstances, Laura chooses to make a confession to Glyde in the hope of asking him to release her from the engagement. If Glyde were to do so, Laura would be happy to break the engagement and be with Hartright without betraying her father and causing trouble to her uncle. Regrettably, Laura makes a wrong judgment of Glyde, who refuses to withdraw from the engagement. As for Laura, the consequence is that she acquires her new identity as Glyde's wife, which brings him closer to seizing the money left by Laura's father. Viewed in this sense, it is ironic for Laura to say that she has found nothing in Glyde's conduct to blame.

In his efforts to gain Laura's property and bury the secret of his false status, Glyde loses his ethical consciousness. With Count Fosco's assistance, he attempts to take away Anne's life, and tries to deprive Laura of her identity by making a false claim that she is dead. The conspiracy is confessed by Fosco, who admits that 'The bond of friendship which united Percival and myself was strengthened, on this occasion, by a touching similarity in the pecuniary position on his side and on mine. We both wanted money. Immense necessity! Universal want!' (WW: 614). In his confession, Fosco does not think there is anything wrong about their desperate need for money. The only possible solution they can think of is to make both Anne Catherick and Laura 'dead', so as to bury Glyde's secret and take Laura's property. Their conspiracy is to make several witnesses mistakenly see Anne as Laura; for instance, both Count Fosco's cook and the doctor witness Lady Glyde's death, and there is a tombstone marked with the name of Lady Glyde.

All visible evidence considered, Laura is supposed to be dead and buried. However, she is still alive, the situation described by Hartright as follows:

> In the eye of reason and of law, in the estimation of relatives and friends, according to every received formality of civilised society, 'Laura, Lady Glyde,' lay buried with her mother in Limmeridge churchyard. Torn in her own lifetime from the list of the living, the daughter of Philip Fairlie and the wife of Percival Glyde might still exist for her sister, might still exist for me, but to all the world besides she was dead. Dead to her uncle, who had renounced her; dead to the servants of the house, who had failed to recognise her; dead to the persons in authority, who had transmitted her fortune to her husband and her aunt; dead to my mother and my sister, who believed me to be the dupe of an adventuress and the victim of a fraud; socially, morally, legally – dead.
>
> And yet alive! Alive in poverty and in hiding. Alive, with the poor drawing-master to fight her battle, and to win the way back for her to her place in the world of living beings.
>
> Did no suspicion, excited by my own knowledge of Anne Catherick's resemblance to her, cross my mind, when her face was first revealed to me? Not the shadow of a suspicion, from the moment when she lifted her veil by the side of the inscription which recorded her death. (WW: 421)

As the victims of Fosco and Glyde's conspiracy, both Laura and Anne have lost their recognisable identities: though alive, Laura is claimed to be dead; while Anne, though dead, is mistakenly believed to be alive and missing. Anne is Laura's near double, which is used by Fosco and Glyde to confuse their identities. It is Hartright who keeps a keen sense of this confusing state and is determined to help Laura restore her identity as a living woman. To readers' relief, Hartright succeeds in correcting the errors and laying bare the crimes committed by Fosco and Glyde. To a larger degree, Hartright's resolution and his effort to restore Laura's ethical identity is to reassert ethical order and sort out ethical chaos. It needs to be noticed that all the confusion, chaos, misconduct and crime in the novel are caused and committed by the self-justifying characters who reveal their guilt as much as they deny it. For instance, in Fosco's confession of his crime, there is no single line expressing his regret and guilt. Instead, he is rather proud and takes the opportunity to express his affection for Marian Halcombe and to ask for the reader's sympathy.

In Nie's view, the task of literature is 'to depict how ethical relationships and moral order undergo changes, examine their consequences, and ultimately provide experience and lessons emerging from human life for the progress of human civilization'.[8] By telling a story of ethical chaos through multiple character-narrators in the form of a sensation novel, Wilkie Collins asserts the irreplaceable importance of maintaining ethical order and the disastrous consequences of ethical chaos caused by misplaced ethical identities.

Notes

[1] J. Bourne Taylor, 'Introduction', in J. Bourne Taylor (ed.), *The Cambridge Companion to Wilkie Collins* (Cambridge University Press, 2006), p. 2.
[2] Ibid., p. 2.
[3] Z. Z. Nie, 'Towards an Ethical Literary Criticism', *Arcadia* 50.1 (2015), pp. 83–101 (p. 83).
[4] E. Langland, '*The Woman in White* and the New Sensation', in P. K. Gilbert (ed.), *A Companion to Sensation Fiction* (Malden, MA: Wiley-Blackwell, 2011), pp. 196–207 (p. 206).
[5] W. Collins, *The Woman in White*, ed. J. Sutherland (Oxford World's Classics, 1996), p. 5. Hereafter cited in the text as WW.
[6] A. B. Emrys, *Wilkie Collins, Vera Caspary and the Evolution of the Casebook Novel* (Jefferson, NC: McFarland, 2011), p. 38.
[7] Z. Z. Nie, *Introduction to Ethical Literary Criticism* (Beijing: Peking University Press, 2014), p. 263.
[8] Z. Z. Nie, 'Ethical Literary Criticism: A Basic Theory', *Forum for World Literature Studies* 13.2 (2021), pp. 189–207 (p. 190).

Further Reading

Collins: Life

Biographies

Ackroyd, Peter. *Wilkie Collins* (London: Chatto & Windus, 2012).
Baker, William. *A Wilkie Collins Chronology* (Basingstoke: Palgrave, 2007).
  Wilkie Collins's Library: A Reconstruction (Westport, CT: Greenwood Press, 2007).
Clarke, William C. *The Secret Life of Wilkie Collins* (Stroud: Alan Sutton Publishing, 1996).
Gasson, Andrew. *Wilkie Collins: An Illustrated Guide*, consultant ed. Catherine Peters (Oxford University Press, 1998).
Klimaszewski, Melisa. *Brief Lives: Wilkie Collins* (London: Hesperus Press, 2011).
Law, Graham, and Andrew Maunder. *Wilkie Collins: A Literary Life* (Basingstoke: Palgrave, 2008).
Lycett, Andrew. *Wilkie Collins: A Life of Sensation* (London: Hutchinson, 2013).
Peters, Catherine. *The King of Inventors: A Life of Wilkie Collins* (Princeton University Press, 1991).

Letters

Baker, William, and William M. Clarke (eds.). *The Letters of Wilkie Collins*, 2 vols. (London: Macmillan, 1999).
Baker, William, Andrew Gasson, Graham Law and Paul Lewis (eds.). *The Collected Letters of Wilkie Collins*, Past Masters (Charlottesville, VA: InteLex, 2019).
Baker, William, Andrew Gasson, Graham Law, and Paul Lewis (eds.). *The Public Face of Wilkie Collins: The Collected Letters*, 4 vols. (London: Pickering & Chatto, 2005).

Collins: Works

Editions

Armadale. Ed. John Sutherland (London: Penguin, 1995).
Armadale. Ed. Catherine Peters (Oxford World's Classics, 2008).
Basil: A Story of Modern Life. Ed. Dorothy Goldman (Oxford World's Classics, 1990).

Blind Love. Ed. Maria K. Bachman and Don Richard Cox (Peterborough: Broadview Press, 2004).
The Dream-Woman and Other Stories. Ed. P. Miles (London: Phoenix, 1998).
The Evil Genius: A Domestic Story. Ed. Graham Law (Peterborough, ON: Broadview Press, 1994).
The Fallen Leaves. (Stroud: Alan Sutton Publishing, 1994).
The Guilty River. In *Miss or Mrs?, The Haunted Hotel, The Guilty River*. Ed. Norman Page and Toru Sasaki (Oxford World's Classics, 1999).
Heart and Science: A Story of the Present Time. Ed. Steve Farmer (Peterborough, ON: Broadview Press, 1996).
Hide and Seek. Ed. Catherine Peters (Oxford World's Classics, 1999).
'I Say No'. (New York: Peter Fenelon Collier, 1900).
Ioláni; or, Tahíti as It Was: A Romance. Ed. I. B. Nadel (Princeton University Press, 1999).
Jezebel's Daughter. Ed. Jason David Hall (Oxford World's Classics, 2016).
The Law and the Lady. Ed. Jenny Bourne Taylor (Oxford World's Classics, 1992).
The Legacy of Cain. (New York: Peter Fenelon Collier, 1900).
Man and Wife. Ed. Norman Page (Oxford World's Classics, 2008).
Miss or Mrs? (Stroud: Alan Sutton Publishing, 1993).
The Moonstone. Ed. Francis O'Gorman (Oxford World's Classics, 2019).
The Moonstone. Ed. Steve Farmer (Peterborough, ON: Broadview Press, 1999).
The New Magdalen: A Novel. (Stroud: Alan Sutton Publishing, 1993).
No Name. Ed. Virginia Blain (Oxford World's Classics, 1990).
Poor Miss Finch. Ed. Catherine Peters (1995; Oxford World's Classics, 2008).
A Rogue's Life, from his Birth to his Marriage. (London: Chatto & Windus, 1890).
The Woman in White. Ed. John Sutherland (Oxford World's Classics, 2008).

Other Works

Wilkie Collins: The Complete Shorter Fiction. Ed. Julian Thompson (New York: Carroll & Graf, 1995).
Hack, Daniel. 'Volpurno – or The Student: A Forgotten Tale of Madness by Wilkie Collins', *Times Literary Supplement* (2 January 2009), pp. 14–15.

Drama

The Lighthouse: A Drama in Two Acts. Introduction: Caroline Radcliffe and Andrew Gasson; Foreword: P. D. James (London: Francis Boutle, 2013).
The Red Vial: A Drama in Three Acts. Ed. Caroline Radcliffe (London: Francis Boutle, 2017).

Contemporary Responses

Bachman, Maria K., and Don Richard Cox (eds.). *Reality's Dark Light: The Sensational Wilkie Collins* (Knoxville: University of Tennessee Press, 2003).

Page, Norman (ed.). *Wilkie Collins: The Critical Heritage* (London and New York: Routledge, 1974).
Pykett, Lyn (ed.). *New Casebooks: Wilkie Collins* (Basingstoke: Macmillan, 1998).
Smith, Nelson C., and R. C. Terry (eds.). *Wilkie Collins to the Forefront: Some Reassessments* (New York: AMS Press, 1995).

Collins: Online

Wikipedia. 'Wilkie Collins'. https//en.Wikipedia.org/wiki/Wilkie_Collins
wilkiecollins.com 'The Wilkie Collins Pages'.

Criticism

Adaptation

Cox, Jessica. 'Narratives of Sexual Trauma in Contemporary Adaptations of Wilkie Collins's *The Woman in White*', in Nadine Boehm-Schnitker and Susanne Gruss (eds.), *Neo-Victorian Literature and Culture: Immersions and Revisitations* (New York: Routledge, 2014), pp. 137–50.
Laird, Karen E. *The Art of Adapting Victorian Literature, 1848–1920: Dramatizing Jane Eyre, David Copperfield, and The Woman in White* (Farnham, Surrey: Ashgate, 2015).
Malik, Rachel. 'The Afterlife of Wilkie Collins', in Jenny Bourne Taylor (ed.), *The Cambridge Companion to Wilkie Collins* (Cambridge University Press, 2006), pp. 181–93.
Mydla, Jacek. 'Sergeant Cuff and Spectacles of Detective Intrusion in *The Moonstone* and Its Adaptations', in Lucyna Krawczyk-Żywko (ed.), *Victorian Detectives in Contemporary Culture: Beyond Sherlock Holmes* (Cham, Switzerland: Palgrave Pivot: Springer Nature, 2017), pp. 27–41.
Warden, Rob (ed.). *Wilkie Collins's The Dead Alive: The Novel, the Case, and Wrongful Convictions*. Foreword: Scott Turow (Evanston, IL: Northwestern University Press, 2005).

Art

Bronkhurst, J. *William Holman Hunt: A Catalogue Raisonné: Paintings* (London: Paul Mellon Centre, 2006).
Fleming, G. H. *John Everett Millais: A Biography* (London: Constable, 1998).
Smith, A. 'The Awakening Conscience', in T. Barringer J. Rosenfeld and A. Smith (eds.), *Pre-Raphaelites: Victorian Avant-Garde* (London: Tate Publishing, 2012).
Weston, N. *Daniel Maclise: Irish Artist in Victorian London* (Dublin: Four Courts Press, 2001).

Collins and America

Hanes, Susan R. *Wilkie Collins's American Tour, 1873–4* (London: Pickering & Chatto, 2008).

Colonialism and Race

Brantlinger, Patrick. *Taming Cannibals: Race and the Victorians* (Ithaca, NY: Cornell University Press, 2011).
Callanan, Laura. *Deciphering Race: White Anxiety, Racial Conflict, and the Turn to Fiction in Mid-Victorian English Prose* (Columbus: Ohio State University Press, 2006).
Fryer, Peter. *Staying Power: The History of Black People in Britain* (1984; London: Pluto Press, 2018).
Gasson, Andrew, and William Baker. 'Forgotten Terrain: Wilkie Collin's Jewish Explorations.' *Jewish Historical Studies* 48 (2016), pp. 177–99.
Gerzina, Gretchen Holbrook (ed.). *Black Victorians/Black Victoriana* (New Brunswick, NJ: Rutgers University Press, 2003).
McClintock, Anne. *Imperial Leather: Race, Gender, and Sexuality in the Colonial Contest* (London: Routledge, 1995).
Salesa, Damon Ieremia. *Racial Crossings: Race, Intermarriage, and the Victorian British Empire* (Oxford University Press, 2011).

Disability

Davis. L. J. *Enforcing Normalcy: Disability, Deafness, and the Body* (London: Verso, 1995).
Gore, C. W. *Plotting Disability in the Nineteenth-Century Novel* (Edinburgh University Press, 2020).
Holmes, M. S. *Fictions of Affliction: Physical Disability in Victorian Culture* (Ann Arbor: University of Michigan Press, 2004).
  'Queering the Marriage Plot: Wilkie Collins's *The Law and the Lady*', in Marlene Tromp (ed.), *Victorian Freaks: The Social Context of Freakery in Britain* (Columbus: Ohio State University Press, 2008), pp. 237–58.
Tilley, Heather. *Blindness and Writing: From Wordsworth to Gissing* (Cambridge University Press, 2017).

Ecology

Bilston, Sarah. *The Promise of the Suburbs: A Victorian History in Literature and Culture* (New Haven, CT: Yale University Press, 2019).

Ethics

Baker, William, and Shang Biwu. 'Fruitful Collaborations: Ethical Literary Criticism in Chinese Academe', *Times Literary Supplement*, 31 July 2015, pp. 14–15.
Nie, Z. Z. *Introduction to Ethical Literary Criticism* (Beijing: Peking University Press, 2014).

Journalism

Law, Graham. 'The Professionalization of Authorship', in John Kucich and Jenny Bourne Taylor (eds.), *The Oxford History of the Novel in English*, Vol. III: *The Nineteenth-Century Novel, 1820–1880* (Oxford University Press, 2012), pp. 37–55.

'Wilkie Collins and the Discovery of an "Unknown Public"', in Joanne Shattock (ed.), *Journalism and the Periodical Press in Nineteenth-Century Britain* (Cambridge University Press, 2017), pp. 328–40.

Language

Allan, Janice M. 'A Lock without a Key: Language and Detection in Collins's *The Law and the Lady*', *Clues: A Journal of Detection* 25.1 (Fall 2006), pp. 45–57.

Bowen, John. 'The Man in White: Wilkie Collins's Styles', in Daniel Tyler (ed.), *On Style in Victorian Fiction* (Cambridge University Press, 2022), pp. 172–90.

Law

Finley, Matthew. 'Hearsay Evidence: Legal Discourse, Circumstantiality, and *The Woman in White*', *Global Tides* 10, Article 1 (2016), pp. 1–10. https://digitalcommons.pepperdine.edu/globaltides/vol10/iss1/1

Longmuir, Anne. 'The Scotch Verdict and Irregular Marriages: How Scottish Law Disrupts the Normative in *The Law and the Lady* and *Man and Wife*', in Andrew Mangham (ed.), *Wilkie Collins: Interdisciplinary Essays* (Newcastle: Cambridge Scholars Publishing, 2008), pp. 166–77.

Music and Musicians

Atlas, Allan W. 'Wilkie Collins on Music and Musicians', *Journal of the Royal Musical Association* 124.2 (1999), pp. 255–70.

Bledsoe, Robert Terrell. *Henry Fothergill Chorley: Victorian Journalist* (Aldershot: Ashgate, 1998).

Gillett, Paula. *Musical Women in England, 1870–1914: 'Encroaching on All Man's Privileges'* (New York: St Martin's Press, 2000).

Losseff, Nicky. 'Absent Melody and "The Woman in White"', *Music and Letters* 81.4 (November 2000), pp. 532–50.

Vorachek, L. 'Female Performances: Melodramatic Music Conventions and *The Woman in White*', in Sophie Fuller and Nicky Losseff (eds.), *The Idea of Music in Victorian Fiction* (Burlington, VT: Ashgate, 2004), pp. 105–28.

Weliver, P. 'The Prima Donna, Opera Chorus and Amateur Violinist: Music as "Event" in Wilkie Collins's *Man and Wife*', *Forum for Modern Language Studies* 48.2 (2012), pp. 178–94.

Science and Medicine

Hewitt, Martin. 'Victoria's Victorians and the Mid-Victorians', *Journal of Victorian Culture* 24.4 (2019), pp. 431–9.

Hurley, Kelly. *The Gothic Body: Sexuality, Materialism, and Degeneration at the Fin de Siècle* (1996; Cambridge University Press, 2004).

Lansbury, Coral. 'Gynaecology, Pornography, and the Antivivisection Movement', *Victorian Studies* 28.3 (Spring 1985), pp. 413–37.

Mangham, Andrew. *Violent Women and Sensation Fiction: Crime, Medicine and Victorian Popular Culture* (Basingstoke: Palgrave, 2007).

Pedlar, Valerie. 'Experimentation or Exploitation? The Investigations of David Ferrier, Dr Benjulia and Dr Seward', *Interdisciplinary Science Reviews* 28.3 (September 2003), pp. 169–74.

Small, Helen. *Love's Madness: Medicine, the Novel, and Female Insanity, 1800–1865* (Oxford: Clarendon Press, 1996).

Talairach, Laurence. *Gothic Remains: Corpses, Terror and Anatomical Culture, 1764–1897* (Cardiff: University of Wales Press, 2019).

Talairach-Vielmas, Laurence. *Wilkie Collins, Medicine and the Gothic* (Cardiff: University of Wales Press, 2009).

Sensation Fiction

Allan, Janice M. 'The Contemporary Response to Sensation Fiction', in Andrew Mangham (ed.), *The Cambridge Companion to Sensation Fiction* (Cambridge University Press, 2013), pp. 85–98.

  'To See Is to Suspect: Investigating the Private in Sensation Fiction', in Alistair Rolls and Rachel Franks (eds.), *Private Investigator* (Bristol: Intellect Books, 2016), pp. 172–83.

Beller, Anne-Marie. 'Detecting the Self in the Sensation Fiction of Wilkie Collins and Mary Elizabeth Braddon', *Clues: A Journal of Detection* 26.1 (2007), pp. 49–61.

  '"The Fashions of the Current Season": Recent Critical Work on Victorian Sensation Fiction', *Victorian Literature and Culture* 45.2 (2017), pp. 461–73.

  'Sensation Fiction in the 1850s', in Andrew Mangham (ed.), *The Cambridge Companion to Sensation Fiction* (Cambridge University Press, 2013), pp. 7–20.

Beller, Anne-Marie, and T. MacDonald (eds.). *Rediscovering Victorian Women Sensation Writers: Beyond Braddon* (London: Routledge, 2014).

Calovini, Susan. 'A "Secret" Novel of Her Own: Mary Elizabeth Braddon's Rewriting of Dickens and Collins', *Tennessee Philological Bulletin* 38 (2001), pp. 19–29.

Costantini, Mariaconcetta. *Sensation and Professionalism in the Victorian Novel* (Bern: Peter Lang, 2015).

  'Sensational Artists in Italy: Mid-Victorian Variations of the Künstlerroman Plot', *Journal of Anglo-Italian Studies* 13–14 (2014), pp. 161–73.

Daly, Nicholas. *Sensation and Modernity in the 1860s* (Cambridge University Press, 2009).
Emrys, A. B. *Wilkie Collins, Vera Caspary and the Evolution of the Casebook Novel* (Jefferson, NC: McFarland & Company, Inc., 2011).
Heller, Tamar. *Dead Secrets: Wilkie Collins and the Female Gothic* (New Haven, CT: Yale University Press, 1992).
Hughes, Winifred. *The Maniac in the Cellar: Sensation Novels of the 1860s* (Princeton University Press, 1980).
Ifill, Helena. *Creating Character: Theories of Nature and Nurture in Victorian Sensation Fiction* (Manchester University Press, 2018).
Law, Graham. 'Sensation Fiction and the Publishing Industry', in Andrew Mangham (ed.), *The Cambridge Companion to Sensation Fiction* (Cambridge University Press, 2013), pp. 168–81.
Meadows, Elizabeth. 'Entropy and the Marriage Plot in *The Woman in White* and *Lady Audley's Secret*', *Dickens Studies Annual* 45 (2014), pp. 311–31.
Nemesvari, Richard. '"Judged by a Purely Literary Standard": Sensation Fiction, Horizons of Expectation, and the Generic Construction of Victorian Realism', in Kimberly Harrison and Richard Fantina (eds.), *Victorian Sensations: Essays on a Scandalous Genre* (Columbus: Ohio State University Press, 2006), pp. 15–28.
Odden, K. M. '25 August 1861: The Clayton Tunnel Rail Crash, the Medical Profession, and the Sensation Novel', *Victorian Review* 40.2 (2014), pp. 30–4.
Pykett, Lyn. 'Collins and the Sensation Novel', in Jenny Bourne Taylor (ed.), *The Cambridge Companion to Wilkie Collins* (Cambridge University Press, 2006), pp. 50–64.
  The Nineteenth-Century Sensation Novel, 2nd ed. (Tavistock, Devon: Northcote House/Liverpool University Press, 2011).
Steinlight, Emily. 'Why Novels Are Redundant: Sensation Fiction and the Overpopulation of Literature', *English Literary History* 79.2 (Summer 2012), pp. 503–35.
Talairach-Vielmas, Laurence. 'Sensation Fiction: A Peep Behind the Veil', in Andrew Smith and W. Hughes (eds.), *The Victorian Gothic* (Edinburgh University Press, 2012), pp. 29–42.
  'Sensation Fiction and the Gothic', in Andrew Mangham (ed.), *The Cambridge Companion to Sensation Fiction* (Cambridge University Press, 2013), pp. 21–33.
Taylor, Jenny Bourne. *In the Secret Theatre of Home: Wilkie Collins, Sensation Narrative, and Nineteenth-Century Psychology* (London and New York: Routledge, 1988).
Wagner, Tamara. 'Clinical Gothic: Sensationalizing Substance Abuse in the Victorian Home', *Gothic Studies* 11.2 (2009), pp. 30–40.

Serialisation

Baker, William. 'The Manuscript of Wilkie Collins's *No Name*', *Studies in Bibliography* 43 (1990), pp. 197–208.

Delafield, Catherine. 'Novel/Magazine Interfaces: The "Long" Serialisation of Wilkie Collins's *Armadale*', *Australasian Journal of Victorian Studies* 23.1 (2019), pp. 1–13.

Hargreaves, Geoffrey. 'Wilkie Collins in Smith, Elder Boards 1865–66', *Studies in Bibliography* 59.1 (December 2015), pp. 269–80.

Law, Graham. 'The Professional Writer and the Literary Marketplace', in Jenny Bourne Taylor (ed.), *The Cambridge Companion to Wilkie Collins* (Cambridge University Press, 2006), pp. 97–111.

Sutherland, John. 'Two Emergencies in the Writing of *The Woman in White*', *Yearbook of English Studies* 7 (1977), pp. 148–56.

Index

Wilkie Collins is abbreviated to WC throughout the index. For the other abbreviations used, please see the List of Abbreviations at the front of the book. Unless otherwise stated, the literary works cited in the index were written by Wilkie Collins.

adoption laws, 217
affective transference (shared feelings), 41–2, 45–7, 112, 212, 221
After Dark and Other Stories
   critical reception, 90
   narrative framework, 61, 64
   'Nun's Story of Gabriel's Marriage, The', 64–6
   preface, 61
   publishers and editions, 22, 23, 24, 30
Ainsworth, William Harrison, 154
Alicia Warlock and Other Stories, 31
All the Year Round (periodical)
   Christmas numbers, 59–60, 164, 186
   Dickens's editorship, 161–2, 164, 184, 187–8, 189
   The Moonstone serialised in, 161, 162, 164, 187
   WC as temporary editor, 5, 162, 186
   WC's contributions generally, 59, 73, 162
   The Woman in White serialised in, 71–2, 161–3, 187, 201
Allan, Janice M., 81
Altick, Richard, 250
amateur theatricals. *See also* plays of WC
   Harriet Collins's interest in acting, 4, 84
   WC's first meeting with Dickens through, 5, 173–4, 184, 185
   WC's membership of Dickens's theatre company, xviii, 62, 79–80, 186
amnesia, 119, 222
Angel in the House stereotype, 190, 193, 216
Antiquary, The (Scott), 179–80
Antonina; or, The Fall of Rome
   anachronisms in, 36
   critical reception, 89, 170, 181
   dialogue v. descriptions in, 39
   English publishers and editions, 19, 21, 22–3, 26, 28
   overseas editions, 28, 29, 30
   religious conflict in, 36
   Roman setting, 35–6, 37, 271–2
Antrobus & Co. (tea merchant), 4, 33, 38, 69, 178
anxiety, 45, 48, 220, 299–300
Archer, Frank, 17
Armadale
   characters. *See* Gwilt, Lydia; Midwinter, Ozias
   critical reception, 92–3, 97, 98, 106, 160, 172–3
   dedicated to John Forster, 149
   as detective fiction, 109
   Lady Audley's Secret (Braddon) compared with, 190–2
   music in, 247
   politics in, 256
   publication success, 7, 141
   publishers and editions, 22, 23, 24, 27, 29, 30
   science in, 220–2
   serialised publication, 160–1, 162, 163–4, 165, 223
   settings, 275, 277–8, 285–6
   social identity destabilisation in, 303–4
   stage version (*Miss Gwilt*), 78, 80, 140
   WC's earnings from, 92, 202
Arrowsmith (publisher), 19
art in WC's works
   artistic v. commercial success theme, 35, 38, 73–4, 120, 171
   artists, depictions of, 35, 239–41, 242
   landscapes, 178–9, 283–6, 288–90
artists, WC's relationships with
   Henry Brandling. *See* Rambles Beyond Railways
   brother and father. *See* Collins, Charles Allston; Collins, William
   Augustus Egg, 5, 185, 242, 274

Index

Daniel Maclise, 239
Millais. *See* Millais, John Everett
other Pre-Raphaelite painters, xviii, 15, 17, 62, 81
Ashley, Robert P., 105, 309
Asylum, The (Harwood), 143
Awakening Conscience, The (Hunt), 241–2

Baccani, Egisto (character, HS), 256
Bachman, Maria, 44
Bain, Alexander, 222, 226
Baker, William, 11–12, 148, 163, 179
Bakhtin, Mikhail, 169
Balzac, Honoré de, 177, 273
Barickman, Richard, 110
Barnard, Fred, 63
Bartley, Henry, 9, 148–9
Basil
   critical reception, 89–90, 91, 170, 188
   English publishers and editions, 19, 21, 22–3, 26
   film adaptation, 135
   inspiration for, 241–2
   overseas editions, 30, 31
   preface, 35, 91–2, 231
   A Rogue's Life compared with, 306
   as sensation fiction, 140, 221
      realism blended with sensationalism, 37–8, 84–5, 181, 231, 272
   settings, 274, 286
   social identity destabilisation in, 301
Beacham, Rod, 136
Beard, Francis Carr (Frank), 12, 148–9, 205
Beecheno, Yaxley & Co. (wine merchant), 14
Beethoven, Ludwig van, 247
Belgravia (periodical), 24
Belinfante Brothers (publisher), 202–3
Beller, Anne-Marie, 171–2, 190, 195, 196
Bellini, Vincenzo, 247
Bells, The (Lewis), 81
Benjamin, Walter, 174
Benjulia, Dr Nathan (character, HS), 54
Bennett, M. L., 148, 150
Bentley, George, 17
Bentley, Richard. *See* Richard Bentley & Son
Bentley's Miscellany (periodical), 20, 62, 70, 202, 239
Ben-Yishai, Ayelet, 119
Besant, Walter, 9, 25
Betteredge, Gabriel (character, M), 45–6, 253, 259, 305
Bharadwaj, Radha, 135
Bigelow, Jane, 14–15
Billings, Jesse, 148
Bilston, Sarah, 286
biographies of WC, 105, 107–8
Bisla, Sundeep, 232

Black and White (with Fechter), 78, 297
Black Robe, The, 8, 24, 31, 152, 225, 246, 274
Blackwood, James, 20
Blake, Franklin (character, M), 43, 124, 223–4, 259
Bleak House (Dickens), 217
Bligh, William, 33
blind characters, 38, 224, 310–11
Blind Love
   English publishers and editions, 24, 25, 26, 27
   finished by Walter Besant, 9
   moral insanity in, 54–5
   overseas editions, 31
   politics in, 48, 258–9, 263
   preface, 56
   realism and sensationalism blended in, 48
   settings, 259, 280
Blyth, Madonna (character, H&S), 38–9, 180, 309
Blyth, Valentine (character, H&S), 35, 38, 217, 247–8, 253
Bodenheimer, Rosemarie, 3
'Bold Words by a Bachelor', 6
Bonaparte, Napoleon, 254–5
book collection of WC. *See* library of WC
Boucher, Abigail, 263–4, 269
Boucicault, Dion, 174
Bourne Taylor, Jenny, 43–4, 110–11, 190, 227, 318
Bowles, Thomas Gibson, 168–9
Braddon, Mary Elizabeth
   influence on WC's work, 190–3
   stage version of *Lady Audley's Secret*, 174
   WC's influence on, 41, 141, 190, 195
   WC's works compared with, xvii, 120, 195
Brandling, Henry, 4, 274, 288
Brantlinger, Patrick, 233
Bride of Lammermoor, The (Scott), 180
Brody, J. DeVere, 296
Bronkhurst, Judith, 241–2
Brontë, Charlotte, 196
Brontë, Emily, 217
Broughton, Rhoda, 195
Brown, Daniel, 182
Brown, John, 15
Browne, H. K., 21
Bulwer-Lytton, Edward
   detention of wife in lunatic asylum, 134
   influence on *Antonina*, 35, 62, 181
   Not so Bad as We Seem, 5, 79–80, 173–4, 185
   A Strange Story, 162
Bulwer-Lytton, Rosina, 134
Byatt, A. S., 196

Caine, Hall, 25, 180
Calovini, Susan, 190
Carlyle, Thomas, 297
Carpenter, William, 34, 220, 222, 223–4
Caspary, Vera, 130
Cassell's Magazine (periodical), 20, 94, 157, 160
Catherick, Anne (character, WW)
  association with Laura Fairlie, 43, 134, 212–13, 319, 322
  first meeting with Walter Hartright, 41–2, 299, 319–20
Cavendish, Ada, 77, 82
Cecioni, Adriano, 168
champagne, WC's love of, 13–15, 206–8
Chapman, Fredric, 187
Chapman & Hall (publisher), 34, 69
characters in WC's works. *See also* disabled characters; female characters; illegitimate characters; male characters; outcast characters; racialised characters
  generally, 7, 48–9, 83, 109
  identities destabilised. *See* identity destabilisation
  particular characters. *See* character names
Chartism, 36, 259–60
Chartres, H., 98, 100
Chatto, Andrew, 12, 17, 24
Chatto & Windus (publisher)
  cheap editions of WC's works, 24–5, 26, 27–8
  copyright purchases, 20, 22, 23, 25
  first editions of WC's works, 19, 20–1, 23–4
  superior editions of WC's works, 25–7
Chesterton, G. K., 101, 142
child custody law, 216–17, *See also* marriage law reforms
Chorley, Henry F., 170, 172, 246, 248
Christie, Agatha, 142
Christmas tales, 5, 59–60, *See also* shorter fiction of WC
cigars, WC's love of, 13–14, 179, 208
clairvoyance and mesmerism, 5, 34, 70–1, 117, 223–4
Clarke, William M., 11–12, 107–8, 148
class identity. *See* social identity destabilisation
Clique, The (art group), 81
Clow, Joseph, 6
Cobbett, William, 284
Cochrane, Alexander, 267–8
collaborations with Dickens. *See* Dickens and WC, collaborations
Collected Letters of Wilkie Collins (Intelex digital edition), 11
Collected Letters of Wilkie Collins: Addenda and Corrigenda 11

collective narratives. *See also* narrative forms
  generally, 43–4
  The Moonstone, 43, 112, 188
  reproduced texts, 236
  theoretical studies of, 44, 108, 111
  witness statements, 119, 132, 230–1, 262–3, 302
  The Woman in White, 43, 119, 230–1, 236, 262–3
  women's writing, 44, 165, 191, 196, 234–6
Collins, Charles Allston
  artistic career, xviii, 238, 284
  marriage to Katey Dickens, 185, 188–9
  physical appearance, 3
  religious beliefs, 5, 151
  WC's letters to, 13–14
Collins, Harriet
  acting, interest in, 4, 84
  dinner party for Millais hosted by, 242–3
  marriage to William Collins in Scotland, 178
  WC educated by, 177–8
  WC's inheritance from, 201–2, 209
  WC's letters to, 12, 151
  on his writing, 15–16, 162, 201, 202
  requests for money, 34, 208–9
  other mentions, 3, 6, 8, 164
Collins, Richard, 122
Collins, Wilkie
  amateur theatricals, involvement in. *See* amateur theatricals
  apprenticeship at Antrobus & Co. (tea merchant), 4, 33, 38, 69, 178
  artists, relationships with. *See* artists, WC's relationships with
  biographical sketch in *Vanity Fair*, 168–9
  biographies of, 105, 107–8
  book collection. *See* library of WC
  as character in neo-Victorian fiction, 144, 184–5
  Dickens, relationship with. *See* Dickens, Charles; Dickens and WC, collaborations
  fiction works. *See* titles of works
  health problems and laudanum addiction, 7–9, 13, 161, 164, 205, 309
  influences on. *See* influences on WC's work
  journalism. *See* journalism of WC
  late years and death, 8–9, 98
  legal studies, 4, 262
  letters. *See* letters of WC
  musical tastes. *See* music, WC's interest in
  personal finances. *See* personal finances of WC
  personality, 3–4, 13, 16
  philosophical and scientific interests, 5–6, 9, 15, 70, 117
  physical appearance, 3, 168

polyamorous relationships. *See* Graves, Caroline; Rudd, Martha
travels. *See* travels of WC
Collins, William (WC's father)
  artistic career, 3, 4, 178–9, 238, 271, 284
  investments, WC's dividend income from, 201–2, 203, 204
  marriage to Harriet Geddes in Scotland, 178
  religious beliefs, 5, 65–6, 151
  Scott, acquaintance with, 178
  WC's biography of. *See Memoirs of the Life of William Collins, Esq., R.A.*
Collins, William (WC's grandfather), 292
Compton-Rickett, Arthur, 101–2
Cook, James, 33
Cooper, James Fenimore, 177, 273
copyright
  Chatto & Windus purchases, 20, 22, 23, 25
  French law protecting playwrights, 79
  performance rights, 133
  Society of Authors foundation, 8
  US pirating of English works, 29, 31, 74, 77
  WC's strategies to protect, 7, 83, 140–1, 163, 202–3, 278
Corelli, Marie, 196
Cornhill Magazine (periodical), 157, 163–4, 202, 223
Cornwallis, Caroline Frances, 268
correspondence of WC. *See* letters of WC
Court Duel, A, 78
Crabbe, George, 151–2
Craik, Dinah, 217
criminality, Victorian theories of, 220–1
Crimson Petal and the White, The (Faber), 144
critical reception of WC's works, contemporary
  Dickens's works compared. *See* Dickens and WC, works compared
  early works, 89–91, 170, 188
  late works, 94
  mid-career works, 91–4, 100, 172–3
  play reviews, 77, 81–2
  puzzle plots critique, 90–1, 92, 93, 172–3, 230
  Quilter's review of WC's career, 97–8
  sensation fiction critique, xvii–xviii, 89, 91–2, 93, 139, 170–1
  serialisation, critics' views on, 160
  WC's view of critics, 15–16, 73–4, 91–2
critical reception of WC's works, posthumous 1889-1927, 97–102
  disability studies, 121–2, 311, 313, 314–15
  T.S. Eliot's essay (1927) and other reappraisals, 100, 102, 105–8, 173–4
  law and literature studies, 118–19, 148
  post-1990 studies generally, 115–17
  postcolonial criticism, 109, 122–4

poststructuralist criticism, 111–12, 116–17
psychoanalytical readings, 108–11, 112
queer studies, 122, 143–4, 217
reader-response criticism, 109
sensation fiction critique, 99–101
Victorian knowledge forms, studies on, 117–19
WC's professional identity, studies on, 119–20
WC's relationship with Dickens, studies on, 120–1, 184–5
Crowne, John, 154
'Cruise of the *Tomtit*, The', 275
Cuff, Sergeant (character, M), 9, 107, 111–12, 133, 305
Cvetkovich, Ann, 112, 116–17

Dallas, E. S., 165
Daly, Nicholas, 117–18, 169
Dames, Nicholas, 119
Dana, R. H., 33
Danes, Roger, 135
Daniel Deronda (Eliot), 196, 217
Dark Clue, The (Wilson), 130, 143, 144
Darwin, Charles, 16, 45, 283, 297
D'Avenant, Sir William, 154
David Copperfield (Dickens), 106, 216
Davis, Jim, 78
Davis, Lennard, 311
De la Mare, Walter, xviii, 106
Dead Alive, The, 31, 148, 280
Dead Secret, The
  English publishers and editions, 21, 22–3, 26, 28
  music in, 247, 248
  overseas editions, 28, 30, 31
  politics in, 254
  as sensation fiction, 4, 140, 225
  serialised publication, 157
  settings, 274, 286
  social identity destabilisation in, 302
  WC's *Household Words* byline as author of, 5, 187
  women's writing theme, 196
deaf characters, 38–9, 53–4, 180, 309
Delamayn, Geoffrey (character, M&W)
  aristocratic status, 260
  lack of feelings, 45, 266
  masculinity, 82, 213, 217–18, 226
  power over wife, 267
Detective and Mr Dickens, The (Palmer), 144
detective fiction. *See also* sensation fiction
  critics as 'detectives', 116
  detective characters in WC's works
    female detectives, 8, 51, 218, 314
    Walter Hartright (WW), 109, 256, 322–3

detective fiction. *See also* (cont.)
  influence of WC's work on, 105, 106–7, 132, 133–4, 142
  The Moonstone as, 7, 9, 105, 106–7, 108
  neo-Victorian. *See* neo-Victorian fiction
  The Woman in White, *No Name*, and *Armadale* as, 109
'Devil's Spectacles, The', 224
Dexter, Miserrimus (character, LL)
  disability and mental instability aligned, 225, 309–10, 313
  duality of appearance and personality, 218, 254, 312–14
  nervousness, 45, 313
  as outcast, 42–3, 213, 314–15
  suburban home, 287, 313–14
  as WC self-parody, 314
Dickens and WC, collaborations. *See also* All the Year Round; Household Words
  critical studies of, 120–1, 184–5
  The Frozen Deep. *See Frozen Deep, The*
  Lazy Tour of Two Idle Apprentices, 5, 72, 186, 187, 275
  A Message from the Sea, 78
  No Thoroughfare. *See No Thoroughfare*
  plays, 78, 188, 189
  WC's account of joint writing process, 187
  WC's work accredited to Dickens, 78, 187
Dickens and WC, works compared
  Dickens as sensation fiction writer, xvii, 171–2, 188, 189
  differences celebrated, 99, 102
  WC placed on lower literary rank, xvii, 90, 92, 99, 106, 171
    Dickens as 'genius', WC as 'ingenious', 106, 172–4
    'Wilkie Collins and Charles Dickens' (Eliot), 100, 102, 105–6, 108, 173–4
Dickens, Catherine (Katey), 185, 188–9
Dickens, Charles
  amateur theatre company of, 5, 79–80, 186
  artists, friendships with, xviii, 239, 242–3, 274
  as character in neo-Victorian fiction, 144, 184–5
  collaborations with WC. *See* Dickens and WC, collaborations
  commencement of friendship with WC, 5, 173–4, 184, 185
  correspondence with WC, 15, 16, 185, 189, 234
  as editor of *All the Year Round*, 161–2, 164, 184, 187–8, 189
  as editor of *Household Words*, 71–2, 74, 90, 184, 189
  Forster's biography of, 149–50, 185
  holidays with WC, 35–6, 79, 186–7, 188, 245, 273, 274–5
  library of, 154–5
  North American reading tour, 278–9
  relationship with Ellen Ternan, 5, 6, 188
  sensation fiction works, xvii, 171–2, 188, 189
  WC's works, views of, 38, 90, 188
  WC's works compared with. *See* Dickens and WC, works compared
  works held in WC's library, 154
Dickinson, Frances, 5
disabled characters
  blindness, 38, 224, 310–11
  deafness, 38–9, 53–4, 180, 309
  disability studies applied to WC's work, 121–2, 311, 313, 314–15
  elective mutism, 268
  generally, 38, 309, 311, 315
  Miserrimus Dexter. *See* Dexter, Miserrimus (character, LL)
  physical deformity, 122, 220–3, 312, 314
  in *Poor Miss Finch*, 124, 224, 297, 310–11
divorce law reform, 118–19, 254, *See also* marriage law reforms
Dolin, Tim, 81
domestic violence, 118–19, 123, 134, 144, 267–8
Donizetti, Gaetano, 247
Doyle, Arthur Conan, 136, 141
Drabble, Margaret, 196
Dracula (Stoker), 44
dramatic works. *See* plays of WC
dreams, WC's representation of, 37, 52, 108–9
Drood (Simmons), 144, 184–5
drugs
  dreams and trances induced by, 52, 223–4
  Lydia Gwilt's laudanum addiction, 191
  WC's laudanum addiction, 8
Duncan, Ian, 123
Duncombe, Thomas Slingsby, 255–6

Eagland, Jane, 143
East Lynne (Wood), 141, 174, 193–4
editions of WC's works. *See* publishers and editions of WC's works
effeminate male characters, 42–3, 112, 122, 212, 218, 305–6, 313
Egg, Augustus, 5, 185, 242, 274
electromagnetism, 220–3
Eliot, George
  realism of, 182, 284
  relationship with G. H. Lewes, 6, 154
  WC's influence on, 196
  WC's works compared with

by contemporary critics, 92, 99, 100, 139,
      172
  by later critics, 15, 250, 286
  other mentions, 154, 186, 217
Eliot, Sir John, 149
Eliot, T. S., 100, 102, 105–6, 108, 173–4
Elliotson, John, 34, 220, 223–4
Ellis, S. M., 107
Ellis, Sarah Stickney, 214
Ellis, William, 33–4
Ellis & Co. (publisher), 19, 23
Elton, Oliver, 102
Elyot, Kevin, 133–4
Emrys, A. B., 319
Engels, Friedrich, 284
Ernouf, Alfred-Auguste, 78–9
Esmail, Jennifer, 39
Esquirol, Jean-Etienne, 36
ethical chaos of *The Woman in White*, 318–23
Eustace Diamonds, The (Trollope), 106–7, 141
Evans, Mary Ann. *See* Eliot, George
Evil Genius, The
  divorce and child custody law in, 48, 216–17
  Herbert Linley's moral weakness, 55–6
  publication success, 94
  publishers and editions, 24, 30–1
  stage version, 78, 83
evolutionary theory, 45, 117, 224, 225, 283, 297
Eyre, Edward, 296

Faber, Michel, 144, 196
Fairlie, Laura (character, WW)
  ethical dilemma of, 320–1
  identity loss, 112, 212–13, 236, 264, 299, 319, 322–3
  relationships with other characters, 43, 112, 134, 212, 248
Fallen Leaves, The
  dedicated to Caroline Graves, 216
  music in, 246, 250
  publishers and editions, 21, 24, 31
  Scott's work referenced in, 147, 180
  sequel contemplated, 215
  settings, 276, 280
  social identity destabilisation in, 306–7
Faraday, Michael, 227
Farquhar, George, 154
Fechter, Charles, 77, 78, 279, 297
Felix Holt (Eliot), 196
female characters. *See also* gender identity destabilisation; male characters; women
  collectives formed by, 43
  detectives, 8, 51, 218, 314
  fallen women and prostitutes, 82, 215–16, 306–7

lonely women, 41–3
moral decline examined (late novels), 49–53, 218, 226–7
musical instruments played by, 248, 249–50
narratives of, 44, 165, 191, 196, 234–6
omitted from stage versions of novels, 82–3, 84
particular characters. *See* character names
revolutionaries, 256–8
roles and disguises adopted by, 42, 44–5, 83–4, 193, 299, 303, 304
scientists, 50–1, 226–7
Ferrier, David, 220, 227
film adaptations. *See* modern media adaptations of WC's works
finances. *See* personal finances of WC
Fingersmith (Waters), 130, 143–4
Finley, Matthew, 264
'First Officer's Confession, The', 60
first-person narratives, 37, 39, 42, 44, 74
Fitzball, Edward, 150–1, 153
Fitzgerald, Percy, 164
Flowerday, Rachel, 132–3
Fontaine, Madame (character, JD), 49–50, 218
Forbes, Sally Bonetta, 291
foreign editions of WC's works, 28–31
foreign travel of WC. *See* travels of WC
Forgues, E. D., 90, 91
Forster, John, 149–50, 185, 221
Fosco, Count (character, WW)
  effeminacy, 112
  physical descriptions of, 222, 255
  relationship with Sir Percival Glyde, 190, 321–2
  spying work and death, 255–6, 258–9, 272–3
  subversive attractiveness, 109, 110, 169, 323
Foucault, Michel, 111, 116
Frankenstein (Shelley), 37
Franklin, John, 224
Franklin Square Library, 31
French realist theatre and literature, 78–9, 80, 273
Freudian readings of WC's works, 108–9, 112
Frith, William Powell, xviii
Frozen Deep, The (with Dickens)
  inspiration for, 224
  music in, 249
  productions, 7, 78, 80–1, 188
  published editions, 20, 24, 28, 31
  radio adaptation, 135
  realism and sensationalism blended in, 81
  A Tale of Two Cities influenced by, 188
  WC's work often attributed to Dickens, 78
Fryer, Peter, 291

'Gabriel's Marriage', 186
Gallilee, Mrs (character, HS), 50–1, 217, 226–7, 287
Galpin, Thomas Dixon, 161
Garibaldi, Giuseppe and Anita, 256–7
Garland-Thomson, Rosemarie, 122
Gaskell, Elizabeth, 182, 186, 218, 284
Gasson, Andrew, 11
gender identity destabilisation
   affective transference across gender boundaries, 41–2, 45, 112, 212, 221
   disability depictions contributing to, 121–2
   effeminate men and masculine women, 42–3, 112, 122, 212, 218, 305–6, 313
   narrative forms contributing to, 111
   stereotypes, subversion and containment, 109–10, 112, 119–20, 215–16
      Angel in the House, 190, 193, 216
      muscular Christianity, 45, 82, 213, 217–18
   unconventional family structures, 43, 216–17
   Victorian gender ideology, 213–15
Genest, John, 153
geography in WC's works. *See* travels of WC; Victorian environments in WC's works
German music, WC's dislike of, 245–7
Gerzina, Gretchen Holbrook, 291
Ghost's Touch and Other Stories, The, 30
'Ghost's Touch, The' (alternatively 'Mrs Zant and the Ghost'), 66–7
Gibbon, Edward, 35, 181, 271
Gilbert, John, 21–2
Gilbert, Sandra M., 196
Glyde, Sir Percival (character, WW)
   illegitimacy, 135, 264, 302, 319
   political career aspirations, 253
   villainy, 134, 248, 277, 297, 320–2
Goldsmid, Lady Louisa, 14
Gordon, George William, 296
Gore, Clare Walker, 122, 312, 313
Gothic novels, 195–6, *See also* sensation fiction
Graphic, The (periodical), 63, 157, 160
Graves, Caroline
   European tour with WC (1863), 8, 203–5, 278
   holidays with WC, 275, 276–7, 278
   homes shared with WC, 205–6
   WC's first meeting with, 216
   WC's relationship with, 6, 8, 15, 107, 188, 206, 216
   WC's will provision to, 9, 209–10
Graves, Carrie, 6, 8, 9, 203
Graybrook, Natalie (character, MM), 296–7
Great Exhibition, 293–4, 300
Great Expectations (Dickens), 162, 171–2, 215, 217

Gubar, Susan, 196
Guilty River, The
   The Lodger (character), 53–4, 218, 274
   publication success, 94
   publishers and editions, 19, 30–1
   other mentions, 59, 61, 64, 178–80, 280
Gwilt, Lydia (character, A)
   Lady Audley compared with, 191–2
   Beethoven, love of, 247
   critical reception of, 93, 109, 110, 160
   diary of, 44, 165, 191, 234–6, 304
   first appearance, 277–8
   roles and disguises adopted by, 42, 83–4, 193, 304

Hack, Daniel, 120
Hails, Sasha, 132–3
Halcombe, Marian (character, WW)
   diary of, 165, 234, 274–5, 277
   masculine appearance and qualities, 112, 212, 216
   queer studies readings of, 122, 143–4
   relationships with other characters, 43, 110, 134
Hardy, Thomas, xvii, 284, 286
Harper's (publishers), 28–31
Harper's Weekly (periodical), 163
Harris, Joanne, 143
Hartright, Walter (character, WW)
   as detective, 109, 256, 322–3
   feminine nervousness transferred to, 41–2, 112, 212, 221, 319–20
   landscape painting, views on, 284–5, 288, 289
   social mobility of, 112, 302–3
   witness testimonies compiled by, 43, 230–1, 262–3
Harwood, John, 143
Haunted Hotel, The
   American temperament described in, 280
   English publishers and editions, 24, 26
   overseas editions, 28, 29, 31
   radio adaptation, 136
   serialised publication, 160
   unconscious mind, depictions of, 222, 224–5
   Venice setting, 275
Heart and Science
   English publishers and editions, 24, 28
   Mrs Gallilee's moral decline, 50–1, 226–7
   medical experimentations in, 54, 222, 224, 227
   music in, 246–7, 249
   politics in, 256
   preface, 180, 227
   other mentions, 94, 217, 256
Heller, Tamar, 42, 119–20, 121, 195, 196

Helmholtz, Herman von, 227
Henley, Iris (character, BL), 54–5
Hennelly, Mark M., 109
Herncastle, John, 46
Hewitt, Martin, 184
Hide and Seek
  Madonna Blyth (character), 38–9, 180, 309
  Valentine Blyth (character), 35, 38, 217, 247–8, 253
  critical reception, 90
  dedicated to Dickens, 38, 188, 189
  Dickens's praise for, 38, 90
  English publishers and editions, 19–20, 21, 22–3, 26, 33
  overseas editions, 30
  patriarchal authoritarianism in, 254
  as sensation fiction, 140
  settings, 286, 287
Hollingshead, John, 184
Holmes, Martha Stoddard, 121–2, 309
Holt, Victoria, 143
Hooks, Walter Farquar, 153
'House to Let, A' (with Dickens), 187
Household Words (periodical)
  Dickens's editorship, 71–2, 74, 90, 184, 189
  Lazy Tour of Two Idle Apprentices (with Dickens), 5, 72, 186, 187, 275
  'Sermon for Sepoys', 294–5
  'To Think or Be Thought For', 73–4
  'Unknown Public, The', 72–3, 90, 157, 180
  WC's contributions generally, 5, 59–60, 61, 185–6, 202
Huett, Lorna, 72–3
Hughes, Thomas, 217
Hughes, Winifred, 109, 195
Hunt, Thornton, 70
Hunt, William Holman, xviii, 15, 17, 241–2
Hurst & Blackett (publisher), 19
Hutchinson, Linda, 131
Hutter, Albert D., 108–9
Hyder, Clyde K., 107
'hysteria', 111, 313

identity destabilisation. *See also* insanity
  amnesia, 119, 222
  drug-induced, 52, 223–4
  gender identity. *See* gender identity destabilisation
  generally, 117, 299
  mistaken identities, 124, 212–13, 236, 319, 322
  racial identity, 124, 296–7, 305–6
  roles and disguises, adoption of, 42, 44–5, 83–4, 192–3, 299, 303, 304
  social identity. *See* social identity destabilisation

illegitimate characters
  Sir Percival Glyde (Sir Percival Glyde WW), 135, 264, 302, 319
  inheritance rights denied, 192, 264–5
  parental love for, 216
  Magdalen Vanstone ((character, NN), 84, 92, 192, 233–4, 264–5, 303
Illuminated Magazine, The (periodical), 69
Illustrated London News, The (periodical), 63, 69
Inchbald, Elizabeth, 153–4
India Fan, The (Holt), 143
Indian Rebellion, WC's response, 46, 294–5
industrialisation, 194, 283, 286
influence of WC's works
  on detective fiction, 105, 106–7, 132, 133–4, 142
  on early 20th-century authors, 142, 196
  generally, 9
  on neo-Victorian fiction. *See* neo-Victorian fiction
  on sensation fiction. *See* sensation fiction, WC's influence on
influences on WC's work
  artists. *See* artists, WC's relationships with
  Balzac, 273
  book collection. *See* library of WC
  Braddon, 190–3
  Bulwer-Lytton, 35, 62, 181
  Dickens, 189, *See also* Dickens and WC, collaborations
  female Gothic fiction authors, 195–6
  Méjan, 241, 273–4
  Scott. *See* Scott, Sir Walter
  Wood, 193–4
insanity. *See also* identity destabilisation
  criminality linked to, 220–1, 268
  of Miserrimus Dexter. *See* Dexter, Miserrimus (character, LL)
  incarceration of women for, 134, 221
  insurrections linked to, 36
  monomania, 66, 110, 221
  moral insanity, 49, 54–5, 56
  nature v. nurture debate, 52–4, 217, 225–6
  treatments for, 50–1, 110–11, 224–5
  WC's research on, 151
Ioláni; or, Tahíti as it was
  influences on, 33–4, 181
  memory and unconscious mind depictions, 34
  minimal dialogue in, 39
  racial stereotypes in, 271, 295
  rejected by publishers, 34, 181
Irvin, Darcy, 236
Isaacs, Jorge, 124
Iser, Wolfgang, 109

Italy
  Antonina's Roman setting, 35–6, 37, 271–2
  Italian opera, WC's taste for, 247
  Italian settings of WC's works, 274–5
  refugees and revolutionaries from, 255–8
  WC's residence in, 4, 35–6, 238, 271

James, Henry, 91, 216–17
James, Sir John Kingston, 150
Jane Eyre (Brontë), 195–6
Jauss, Hans Robert, 169–70
Jefferies, Richard, 284, 286
Jenkins, Ray, 135
Jennings, Ezra (character, M), 43, 133, 224, 225, 305–6
Jerrold, Blanchard, 184
Jewsbury, Geraldine, 90, 217
Jezebel's Daughter
  Madame Fontaine's moral decline, 49–50, 218
  medical experimentations in, 226
  origins as play *The Red Vial*, 79
  serialised publication, 157
  other mentions, 48, 215–16, 226, 227
'John Jago's Ghost; or, The Dead Alive, An American Story', 148
Jones, Anna Maria, 116
journalism of WC
  on art criticism, 73–4
  collection of. *See My Miscellanies*
  early career, 62, 69–71, 74
  genres blended in, 59, 69, 72, 73–4
  for *Household Words*. *See Household Words*
  on marriage laws, 6
  on sensation fiction, 72–3, 90, 157, 180
  on US copyright law, 74

Karim, Abdul, 291–2
Kean, Edmund, 80
Kelly, Fanny, 84
Kemble, John Philip, 80
Kendrick, Walter, 232, 234, 236
Kent, Charles, 17, 152
King, Andrew, 72
Kingsley, Charles, 218, 284
Kitto, John, 38
Knoepflmacher, U. C., 109–10
Knox, Robert, 297
Kucich, John, 117, 118

Lacan, Jacques, 108
Lady Audley's Secret (Braddon), 41, 141, 174, 190, 195
Laird, Karen, 130
Landor, Walter Savage, 149
landscapes in WC's work, 178–9, 283–6, 288–90

Lang, Andrew, 56, 98, 100
Langland, Elizabeth, 318
'Last Stage Coachman, The', 69, 179
laudanum, 8, 191
Law, Graham, 11, 72, 169, 179, 181
law and literature studies on, 118–19, 148
Law and the Lady, The
  anxiety in, 45
  critical reception, 160
  disability and insanity in. *See* Dexter, Miserrimus (character, LL)
  East Lynne (Wood) compared with, 193–4
  English publishers and editions, 20, 24, 25
  female characters in, 8, 42, 218, 225, 314
  law in, 265–6, 311–12
  music in, 247, 249
  overseas editions, 30, 31
  radio adaptation, 135
  Scott's work referenced in, 180
  serialised publication, 160
  settings, 179, 276, 287
law in WC's works. *See also* politics in WC's works
  collective narratives of witness statements, 119, 132, 230–1, 262–3, 302
  generally, 262–4, 269
  illegitimate children denied inheritance rights, 192, 264–5
  law books in WC's library, 148, 149, 262
  lawyers, depictions of, 263, 265, 266–7
  marriage law reforms. *See* marriage law reforms
  Méjan's account of French trials, influence of, 241, 273–4
  'not proven' verdict in Scotland, 311–12
  social identity destabilisation via law, 42, 264, 265–6, 268–9, 302, 303
  wrongful convictions, 148
Lawson, Lewis A., 108
Lazy Tour of Two Idle Apprentices (with Dickens), 5, 72, 186, 187, 275
Le Fanu, Sheridan, 175
Leader, The (periodical), 59, 62, 70–1, 151, 202
Legacy of Cain, The
  critical reception, 94
  English publishers and editions, 24–7, 28
  nature v. nurture debate in, 48, 51, 52–3, 217, 225–6
  settings, 280
legacy of WC's works. *See* influence of WC's works
Lehmann, Frederick, 5, 17, 272
Lehmann, Nina
  WC's friendship with, 5, 249, 272
  WC's letters to, 14, 17, 80–1, 247
Leitch, Thomas, 131
Leonard, Hugh, 133

letters of WC
  collections of, 11–12
  correspondents, 12, 16, 17
  Dickens, correspondence with, 15, 16, 185, 189, 234
  extent and composition data, 12, 16–17
  gaps and blind spots, 15–16
  'Magnetic Evenings at Home' letter series (with Lewes), 5, 70, 223
  topics and tone, xix, 12–15, 16, 147, 206–8
Letters of Wilkie Collins, The, 11–12
Lever, Charles, 154, 162
Lewes, George Henry, 5, 6, 70, 154
Lewis, Leopold, 81
Lewis, Paul, 11
Library Edition (Chatto & Windus), 26–7
library of WC
  catalogue records, 147–52, 153
  Eliot's and Dickens's libraries compared, 154–5
  Forster's works, 149–50, 185
  law books, 148, 149, 262
  medical books, 151, 220
  music books, 248–9
  novels and poetry, 147, 151–2, 154, 179
  theatre history and plays, 153–4
  theological books, 151, 152, 153
Life of Walter Scott, The (Lockhart), 180–1
Lighthouse, The, 7, 78, 81, 188
Linley, Herbert (character, EG), 55–6
Linsell, Annie, 12–13
Linton, W. J., 256
Little Novels, 24, 59, 61, 66–7
'Living Story-Teller, A' (Quilter), 97–8
Locker, Frederick, 160, 162
Lockhart, J. G., 180–1
Lodger, The (character, GR), 53–4, 218, 274
Longman (publisher), 15, 19, 34
Longmuir, Anne, 179, 265
Lonoff, Sue, 71
Losseff, Nicky, 249
Lucas, Audrey, 135
Lucie, Doug, 135–6

MacCarthy, Justin, 168
MacDonald, Susan, 110
MacDonald, Tara, 190
Maclise, Daniel, 239
'Mad Monkton', 135, 185–6, 221, 274
madness. *See* insanity
magazine publication. *See* serialised novels of WC
'Magnetic Evenings at Home' (letters series), 5, 70, 223

male characters. *See* female characters; gender identity destabilisation
  caring fathers, 217
  doctors, 222–5, 227, 305–6, 311
  effeminate men, 42–3, 112, 122, 212, 218, 305–6, 313
  masculine ideal satirised, 45, 82, 213, 217–18
  particular characters. *See* character names
  relationships between, 43, 190–1, 223
  scientists, 54, 118, 222–5
Man and Wife
  critical reception, 94, 98, 100, 267
  English publishers and editions, 19, 23, 24, 26, 27, 28
  marital violence in, 42, 43, 144, 267
  marriage law exploitation in, 82, 216, 254, 263, 265, 266–9
  masculinity ideal satirised in. *See* Delamayn, Geoffrey (character, M&W)
  music in, 249
  overseas editions, 28, 29, 31, 74, 202–3
  preface, 231, 266, 269
  serialised publication, 160, 164
  settings, 179, 286
  stage version, 7, 77, 78, 82–3, 140
Mansel, H. L., 92
María (Isaacs), 124
marital violence, 118–19, 123, 134, 144, 267–8
marriage law reforms
  child custody, 216–17
  divorce availability, 118–19, 254
  incarceration of wives for insanity, 134, 221
  married women's property rights and autonomy, 118, 123, 134, 216, 254, 263, 264, 266–9
  parental consent, 178
  prohibited degrees, 66
  WC's support generally, 6, 110, 269
Marryat, Frederick, 154
Martineau, Harriet, 33
Marxist reading of *The Woman in White*, 112
masculinity. *See* gender identity destabilisation; male characters
Maudsley, Henry, 54, 220–1, 313
Maunder, Andrew, 179, 181
Mazzini, Giuseppe, 255–6, 257
Meadows, Elizabeth, 195
media adaptations. *See* modern media adaptations of WC's works
medicine. *See* science and medicine
Mehta, Jaya, 123
Méjan, Maurice, 241, 273–4
melodrama. *See* plays of WC; sensation fiction
Melville, Herman, 33

Memoirs of the Life of William Collins, Esq. R. A.
  critical reception, xviii, 89
  depiction of WC's father in, xviii, 35, 178–9
  publication, 4, 15, 19, 33
memory loss, 119, 222
Mendelssohn, Felix, 247
mental illness. *See* insanity
Meredith, George, 168
Merrick, Mercy (character, NM), 82, 84, 225, 307
mesmerism and clairvoyance, 5, 34, 70, 117, 223–4
Message from the Sea, A (with Dickens), 78
Meyler, Bernadette A., 148
Micale, Mark S., 313
Midwinter, Ozias (character, A)
  performance skills, 83–4
  racial identity, 43, 45, 191, 295–6, 304
  relationships with other characters, 43, 190–1, 192, 223, 235
Mill, John Stuart, 297
Millais, John Everett
  illustrations for WC's works, 20, 21, 22, 62, 63, 239
  meeting with Dickens, 242–3
  WC's friendship with, xviii, 15, 241, 242
Miller, D. A., 42, 105, 111–12, 116
Milley, Henry J. W., 106–7
Milnes, Richard Monckton, 221
mind reading, 44–5, 220–3
Miss Gwilt (stage version of *Armadale*), 78, 80, 140
Miss or Mrs? and Other Stories in Outline
  German music derided in, 245–6
  preface, 61
  publishers and editions, 20, 24, 63, 203, 204
  racial identity destabilisation in, 296–7
  other mentions, 59, 160
Mitchell, David, 314–15
Mitford, Mary Russell, 33
modern media adaptations of WC's works
  generally, 130–2, 142
  The Moonstone, 130–6
  radio adaptations, 135–6
  videogame adaptations, 136
  WC's stage adaptations used for, 133
  The Woman in White, 130, 131–2, 134–5
Moonstone, The
  books consulted for, 147, 152–3, 220, 223–4
  characters. *See* Betteredge, Gabriel; Blake, Franklin; Cuff, Sergeant; Jennings, Ezra; Spearman, Rosanna
  collective narrative of, 43, 112, 188
  critical reception, 93–4, 98, 106–7, 108, 173
  as detective fiction, 7, 9, 105, 106–7, 108

  English publishers and editions, 19, 23, 24, 26, 28
  influence of, 106–7, 138, 141, 142, 143, 144
  modern media adaptations, 130, 131, 132–6
  overseas editions, 28, 29, 30
  politics in, 253, 259, 260
  postcolonial studies of, 109, 122–3, 124
  poststructuralist studies of, 111–12
  psychoanalytical studies of, 108–9
  publication success, 8
  racialised characters in, 45–6, 122–3, 124, 295, 297
  science in, 220–4
  serialised publication, 161, 162, 164, 165, 187
  settings, 276–7, 285–6
  social identity destabilisation in, 304–6
  stage version, 78, 82–3, 133, 140
  subtitle 'A Romance', 181–2
moral insanity, 49, 54–5, 56, *See also* insanity
Morland, George, 292
Morley, John, 102
Mossman, Mark, 122
Mozart, Wolfgang Amadeus, 247–9
Mr Wray's Cash-Box; or, The Mask and the Mystery
  frontispiece and title page, 61–2, 63, 239
  plot summary, 63
  publishers and editions, 19, 31, 62–3
  other mentions, 59, 61, 80
'Mrs Zant and the Ghost' (alternatively 'The Ghost's Touch'), 66–7
multiple narratives. *See* collective narratives
music, WC's interest in
  dislike of German music, 245–7
  favourite composers, 247–9
  gendered instruments, 249–50
  generally, 245, 250
  professional musicians, suspicion of, 249
My Lady's Money, 30–1, 59, 63–4
My Miscellanies
  genres blended in, 59, 61, 73–4
  preface, 70
  publishers and editions, 21, 23–4, 26, 30
  other mentions, 74, 274
Mystery of Edwin Drood, The (Dickens), 141, 188, 189
'Mystery of Marmaduke, The', 20–1

Nadel, Ira B., 34, 181
Napoleon I of France, 254–5
narrative forms
  collective narratives. *See* collective narratives
  comic monologues, 59, 62
  dialogue v. description, 39
  experiments with, 46–7, 48, 67
  first-person narratives, 37, 39, 42, 44, 74

fragmentary narratives, 225
omniscient narrators, fallibility exposed, 232–4
puzzle plots critique, 90–1, 92, 93, 172–3, 230
'National Wrong, A' (with Payn), 74
Nayder, Lillian, 118, 120–1, 123, 124, 184, 185, 187
Nelson, Claudia, 214
Nemesvari, Richard, 122, 231–2
neo-Victorian fiction
  'neo-Victorian' term, 138–40
  WC and Dickens as characters in, 144, 184–5
  WC's influence on, 130, 136, 142–4, 196
nervousness, 45, 48, 220, 299–300
'New Dragon of Wantley, The', 62
New Illustrated Library (Chatto & Windus), 24–5, 26
New Magdalen, The
  critical reception, 98
  English publishers and editions, 20, 24, 28
  Mercy Merrick (character), 82, 84, 225, 307
  overseas editions, 29–31
  serialised publication, 161
  social identity destabilisation in, 306–7
  stage versions, 77, 78, 80, 82
  other mentions, 215, 225
Newbery, Linda, 143, 144
Nie, Zhenzhao, 318, 323
Nikolopoulous, Anastasia, 174–5
Nine Tailors, The (Sayers), 142
No Name
  critical reception, 7, 92, 93, 97, 98, 172
  as detective fiction, 109
  English publishers and editions, 21, 22–3, 24, 27
  Lady Audley's Secret (Braddon) compared with, 192–3
  law in, 192, 263, 264–5
  music in, 247
  narrative style analysed, 232–4
  overseas editions, 29, 30
  politics in, 252, 259, 260
  preface, 46, 48, 231
  publication success, 7, 141
  radio adaptation, 135
  science in, 226–7
  serialised publication, 160, 162, 163
  settings, 151–2, 275, 276, 286
  social identity destabilisation in, 303
    Magdalen as disrupter. *See* Vanstone, Magdalen (character, NN)
  stage version, 78, 82, 84, 140
No Thoroughfare (with Dickens)
  De la Mare's assessment of, 106
  realism and sensationalism blended, 81, 215
  stage version, 78

WC's account of writing process, 187
WC's work accredited to Dickens, 78, 187
other mentions, 162, 164, 186
non-fiction of WC. *See* Collins's non-fiction works
Norland, Lord Harry (character, BL), 54–5, 258
nostalgia, 119
Not so Bad as We Seem (Bulwer-Lytton), 5, 79–80, 173–4, 185
Nottidge, Louisa, 134
novellas. *See* shorter fiction of WC
'Nun's Story of Gabriel's Marriage, The', 64–6

Oliphant, Margaret, 91, 160, 171–2, 195–6, 267
O'Neill, Philip, 263
Opium Wars, 293
Orsini, Felice, 255, 257
Orwell, George, 287–8
'Ostler, The', 186
Otway, Thomas, 154
Ouida (Marie Louise de la Ramée), 175, 195
outcast characters
  acting performances by, 42, 44–5, 83–4
  collectives formed by, 43
  disabled characters. *See* disabled characters
  fallen women and prostitutes, 82, 215–16, 306–7
  illegitimate characters. *See* illegitimate characters
  lonely women, 41–3
  racialised characters as outcasts, 42–3, 51–4
  WC's self-image as outcast, 117, 120, 314
overseas editions of WC's works, 28–31

Page, Norman, 90, 93–4, 269
painters. *See* artists, WC's relationships with
Palmer, Beth, 196
Palmer, William J., 144
Paris, WC's visits to
  with Dickens, 79, 187, 188, 273
  with Caroline Graves, 203–5
  'Passage in the Life of Perugino Potts, A', 35, 239–41
  as young man, 4, 208–9, 238–9, 272–3
Patmore, Coventry, 216
Payn, James, 25, 74, 161, 184
Pellico, Silvio, 255
'penny bloods'. *See* sensation fiction
Percy and the Prophet, 30
'Perils of Certain English Prisoners, The', 187–8, 295
periodical publication. *See* serialised novels of WC
personal finances of WC
  earnings and other income, 22, 24, 28, 201–4
  expenditure, 203–8

personal finances of WC (cont.)
  monetary value, 210
  money management, 9, 208–10
Pesca (character, WW), 253, 256, 258–9
Peters, Catherine, 262
Peveril of the Peak (Scott), 180
Phillips, Walter C., 102
Piccadilly Novels (Chatto & Windus), 25–6
Pictorial Boards (Yellowbacks) (Chatto & Windus), 27
Pigott, Edward
  as editor of *The Leader*, 62, 70–1, 151
  holidays with WC, 275
  WC's letters to, 13, 17, 71
Pinero, Arthur, 85
Pirate, The (Scott), 178–9
pirating of English copyright works, 29, 31, 74, 77
Pirie, David, 135
plays of WC. *See also* titles of plays
  amateur theatricals, WC's involvement in. *See* amateur theatricals
  British theatre, poor standards deplored, 78–80, 174
  collaborations with Dickens, 78, 188, 189
  list of, 77–8
  metadrama in novels, 42, 44–5, 83–4
  productions, 7, 77
  realist drama, WC's advocacy of, 77, 80–2, 84–5
  stage versions of novels. *See* stage versions of WC's novels
'Plea for Sunday Reform, A', 70
Plunkett, John, 72
'Poetry Did it: An Event in the Life of Major Evergreen, The' 180
politics in WC's works. *See also* law in WC's works
  Chartism and domestic radicalism, 36, 259–60
  continental spies, exiles and revolutionaries, 255–9
  generally, 252–3
  marriage law reforms. *See* marriage law reforms
  Napoleon, view of, 254–5
  parliamentary and constitutional reform, 253–4
  vivisection debates. *See* Heart and Science
Poor Miss Finch
  disabled and racialised characters in, 124, 224, 297, 310–11
  English publishers and editions, 20, 24, 28, 160
  music in, 247
  narrator (Madame Pratolungo, character, PMF), 46, 248, 253–4, 256–8, 286
  overseas editions, 29, 30
  politics in, 256–8
  preface, 49, 55
  serialised publication, 164
  settings, 276, 286
  WC's earnings from, 203, 204
Popular Edition (Chatto & Windus), 27
'Portrait of an Author, Painted by his Publisher', 273
postcolonial criticism, 109, 122–4
poststructuralist criticism, 111–12, 116–17
Pratolungo, Madame (character, PMF), 46, 248, 253–4, 256–8, 286
Prichard, James Cowles, 49, 55–6
Procter, Bryan, 221
prostitute characters, 82, 215–16, 306–7
psychoanalytical readings of WCs' works, 108–11, 112
Public Face of Wilkie Collins: The Collected Letters, 11
publishers and editions of WC's works
  Chatto & Windus superior editions, 25–7
  cheap editions, 20, 21–5, 27–8
  first editions, 19–20, 21, 22, 23–4
  overseas editions, 28–31
  of particular works. *See under* title of work
  particular publishers. *See* publisher names
Pullman, Philip, 143
Punch (periodical), 69
puzzle plots critique, 90–1, 92, 93, 172–3, 230
Pykett, Lyn
  on critical reception of WC's work, 89, 91, 97
  on sensation fiction, 170, 195–6
  on WC's childhood reading, 177–8

Queen of Hearts, The
  critical reception, 12, 90–1
  publishers and editions, 19, 21, 22–3, 30
  other mentions, 59, 61
queer studies, 122, 143–4, 217
Quilter, Harry, 97–8, 99, 101, 152
racialised characters
  destabilised racial identities, 124, 296–7, 305–6
  emotions of, 45–6, 190–1, 295–6
  Indian Rebellion, WC's response, 46, 294–5
  in *The Moonstone*, 45–6, 122–3, 124, 295, 297
  as outcasts, 42–3, 51–4
  postcolonial criticism on, 109, 122–4
  race and empire, Victorian discourse, 291–4, 296, 297

Radcliffe, Ann, 177, 195
radio adaptations, 135–6
'railway spine', 313
Rambles Beyond Railways
  Cornish settings of WC's works, 37, 274
  landscape descriptions, 288–90
  publishers and editions, 19, 70
  other mentions, 4, 282
Ramée, Marie Louise de (Ouida), 175, 195
Rank and Riches, 78, 83
Ranke, Leopold von, 152
Reade, Charles, xvii, 14, 25, 99, 102, 120, 175
reader-response criticism, 109
Readings in America, 31
  Balzac's realism admired by WC, 273
  politics. *See* politics in WC's works
  realism. *See also* sensationalism
  realist drama, WC's advocacy of, 77, 80–2, 84–5
  Victorian literature valorising, xvii–xviii, 182, 284
  WC's sensationalism blended with, 36–8, 41, 48, 81–2, 231–4, 273–4
Recueil des causes célèbres (Méjan), 241, 273–4
Red Vial, The, 7, 79, 81–2, 188
  novelistic adaptation. *See* Jezebel's Daughter
Reed, John R., 109
Reeve, Wybert, 273–4
Régnier, François-Joseph, 77, 78, 80
Reissiger, Karl Gottlieb, 247
Richard Bentley & Son (publisher), 19–21, 24, 35, 70
Ritson, Joseph, 150
Robertson, Tom, 85
Robinson, Kenneth, 107
Robson, Michael, 135
Rogue's Life, from his Birth to his Marriage, A, 20, 21, 23, 24, 26, 306
Rome
  Antonina's Roman setting, 35–6, 37, 271–2
  WC's residence in, 4, 35–6, 238, 271
Rossini, Gioachino, 247
Roy, Ashish, 122–3
Ruby in the Smoke, The (Pullman), 143
Rudd, Martha
  WC's first meeting with, 206, 277
  WC's relationship with, 6, 15, 107–8, 206, 216, 275
  WC's will provision to, 9, 209–10, 265
Ruskin, John, 214, 284

Said, Edward, 123
Sala, George Augustus, 71, 184
Sampson Low (publisher), 19, 21–2, 201

Saunders, J. Maynard, 208
Sayers, Dorothy L., 105, 108, 142
Schlesinger, Sebastian, 14, 17, 148–9
Schlicke, Paul, 72
Schubert, Franz, 247
Schumann, Clara, 245–6
Schumann, Robert, 245–6, 247
science and medicine
  amnesia, 119, 222
  electromagnetism, 220–3
  evolutionary theory, 45, 117, 224, 225, 283, 297
  insanity. *See* insanity
  mesmerism and clairvoyance, 5, 34, 70, 117, 223–4
  scientists, depictions of, 50–1, 54, 118, 226–7
  doctors, 222–5, 227, 305–6, 311
  in sensation fiction, 117–18, 227
Scott, Sir Walter
  acquaintance with WC's father and godfather, 178
  influence on WC's works, 179, 181–2
  Lockhart's biography of, 180–1
  referenced in WC's works, 180
  WC's childhood reading of, 177–8
  WC's praise for, 177, 179–80, 181, 185, 273
  WC's visit to Scotland inspired by, 178–9
  works held in WC's library, 147, 179
screenplay adaptations. *See* modern media adaptations of WC's works
Seacole, Mary, 296
sensation fiction
  Christmas ghost stories, 60
  class boundaries, perceived as threat to, 72–3, 174, 300
  Dickens's works as, xvii, 171–2, 188, 189
  Eliot's works as, 196
  influence of, 142, *See also* detective fiction; neo-Victorian fiction
  law, engagement with, 264
  marriage law reform, relationship with, 118–19
  poststructuralist reading of, 116–17
  readers, WC's essay on ('The Unknown Public'), 72–3, 90, 157, 180
  science and medicine in, 117–18, 227
  serialisation, suitability for, 164
  stage melodramas, 169, 171, 174
  WC and. *See* sensation fiction, WC's influence on; sensation fiction, WC's works as
sensation fiction, WC's influence on
  Braddon, 190, 195
  Dickens, 188, 189
  Eliot, 196
  generally, 119–20, 141–2, 195

sensation fiction, WC's influence on (cont.)
    neo-sensation fiction. *See* neo-Victorian fiction
sensation fiction, WC's works as
    Braddon's influence, 190–3
    female Gothic fiction authors' influence, 195–6
    'inventor' of genre appellation, 41, 168–71, 174–5
    law, engagement with. *See* law in WC's works
    posthumous reputation, 99–101
    puzzle plots critique, 90–1, 92, 93, 172–3, 230
    realism blended with sensationalism, 36–8, 41, 48, 81–2, 231–4, 273–4
    rebukes from contemporary critics, xvii–xviii, 89, 91–2, 93, 139, 170–1
    Scott's influence. *See also* Scott, Sir Walter
    subversion of tropes. *See* sensationalism
    The Woman in White reviewed as, 91, 98, 100, 139, 318
    Wood's influence, 193–4
sensationalism. *See also* realism
    anxiety, 45, 48, 220, 299–300
    dreams and buried memories, 34, 37, 52, 108–9, 222, 225–6
    identity destabilisation. *See* gender identity destabilisation; identity destabilisation
    insanity. *See* insanity
    mind reading, 44–5, 220–3
    realism blended with, 36–8, 41, 48, 81–2, 231–4, 273–4
    science and medicine. *See* science and medicine
    shared feelings (affective transference), 41–2, 45–7, 112, 212, 221
Seres, Fiona, 134–5
serialised novels of WC
    commodification of texts, 158–63
    composition and context, 161–3
    economics of serialisation, 160–1
    list and details, 158–9
    WC's adoption of serial format, 157–60
Seringapatam siege (1799), 46
'Sermon for Sepoys', 294–5
Set in Stone (Newbery), 143, 144
Setterfield, Diane, 143, 144
settings of WC's works. *See* travels of WC; Victorian environments in WC's works
shared feelings (affective transference), 41–2, 45–7, 112, 212, 221
Shaw, George Bernard, 82, 85
Shelley, Mary, 195
Shivering Sands, The (Holt), 143
shorter fiction of WC. *See also* titles of works
    Christmas tales, 5, 59–60
    exemplary longer tales, 62–4
    exemplary shorter tales, 64–7
    list of, challenges to compiling, 59–60
    publishing format and literary form, 60–2, 67
sign language debates, 39, 309
Sign of Four, The (Doyle), 141
Simmons, Dan, 144, 184–5
Simons, Eric M., 135
Sismondi, Jean Charles Léonard de, 35
'Sister Rose', 186
Sixpenny and Shilling Editions (Chatto & Windus), 27–8
Skilton, David, 313
slave trade, 292
Sleep, Pale Sister (Harris), 143
Small, William, 164
Smith, Alison, 241
Smith, George, 17, 162
Smith, W. H., 20
Smith, Elder & Co. (publisher), 19, 22–3, 24, 35, 202, 203, 204
Snyder, Sharon, 314–15
social commentary. *See* politics in WC's works
social identity destabilisation
    anxiety over, 299–300
    disguises facilitating, 193, 299, 303
    economic basis of class exposed, 306–7
    Walter Hartright's social mobility (WW), 112, 302–3
    law facilitating, 42, 264, 265–6, 268–9, 302, 303
    in *The Moonstone*, 304–6
    redundant hereditary status, 301–4
    A Rogue's Life satirising, 306
    sensation fiction, perceived threat of, 72–3, 174, 300
    social class turbulence of Victorian era, 300
Society of Authors, 8
Sor, Francine de (character, ISN), 51–2
Southerne, Thomas, 154
Southey, Robert, 152, 153, 178
Spearman, Rosanna (character, M)
    ambiguous social class, 42, 299, 305
    death, 106, 285
    omitted from stage version, 82
    physical deformity, 220–3, 309
St. Clair, William, 177
stage versions of WC's novels. *See also* plays of WC
    adaptation approach, 78–83, 140–1
    characters and scenes omitted, 82–3, 84, 133
    as copyright protection strategy, 7, 83, 140–1
    The Evil Genius, 78, 83
    list of, 78
    Man and Wife, 7, 77, 78, 82–3, 140
    The Moonstone, 78, 82–3, 133, 140

Miss Gwilt (stage version of *Armadale*), 78, 80, 140
modern media adaptations based on, 133
The New Magdalen, 77, 78, 80, 82
No Name, 78, 82, 84, 140
and WC's reputation for melodrama, 171, 174
The Woman in White, 7, 78, 80, 133, 140–1, 203, 204, 206
Stark, Myra, 110
Steere, Elizabeth, 193
Steinlight, Emily, 195, 196
Steinmetz, Andrew, 152
Steven, Alasdair, 134
Stewart, Mary, 143
Stoker, Bram, 44
Straley, Jessica, 118
Strovas, Karen Beth, 234
suburban settings of WC's works, 286–8
'Sunday Under Three Heads' (Dickens), 38
Surridge, Lisa, 118–19
Sutherland, John, 163, 223
Swinburne, A. C., 98, 100–1, 315

Tale of Two Cities, A (Dickens), 106, 161–2, 171, 186, 188, 189
Taylor, Jeremy, 151, 152
telepathy, 44–5, 220–3
television adaptations. *See* modern media adaptations of WC's works
Temple Bar (periodical), 20, 161
Ternan, Ellen, 5, 6, 188
Thackeray, William Makepeace
North American reading tour, 278–9
WC's acquaintance with, 186
WC's works compared with, 90, 99, 100, 172, 182
The Woman in White, praise for, 230
works held in WC's library, 154
Thérèse Raquin (Zola), 81
Thirteenth Tale, The (Setterfield), 143, 144
Thomas, Ronald, 118
Thompson, David M., 134
Thomson, Joseph John, 227
Tillotson, W. F., 66
Tindell, William, 12, 14, 206–8
Tinsley (publisher), 19, 23
'To Think or Be Thought For', 73–4
Tom Brown's School Days (Hughes), 217
translations of WC's works, 4, 31, 77
'Traveller's Story of a Terribly Strange Bed, The', 142, 185, 242
travels of WC
Cornwall trip with Brandling. *See* Rambles Beyond Railways
English seaside towns, 151–2, 275–8

European tour with Caroline Graves, 8, 203–5, 278
holidays with Dickens, 35–6, 79, 186–7, 188, 245, 273, 274–5
holidays with Pigott, 275
North American reading tour, 8, 15, 29–30, 278–80
Scotland trip with father, 178–9
youth in Italy and France, 4, 35–6, 208–9, 238, 271, 272–3
Trodd, Anthea, 71, 72, 121
Trollope, Anthony
The Eustace Diamonds, influence of *The Moonstone*, 106–7, 141
puzzle plots critique of WC, 161
WC's works compared with, 99, 102
works not in WC's library, 154
Tromp, Marlene, 118
Troost, Linda V., 132
True Detective (HBO television series, 2014), 132
Tucker, Irene, 123–4
Turow, Scott, 148
'Twin Sisters, The', 62
Two Destinies, The
English publishers and editions, 20–1, 24, 26
overseas editions, 29–31
other mentions, 225, 280

unconscious mind, representation of, 34, 37, 52, 108–9, 222, 223–6
United States
editions of WC's works, 28–31
pirating of English copyright works, 29, 31, 74, 77, 278
WC's North American reading tour, 8, 15, 29–30, 278–80
'Unknown Public, The', 72–3, 90, 157, 180
urbanisation, 194, 283, 286, 300

Vanity Fair biographical sketch of WC, 168–9
Vanstone, Magdalen (character, NN)
Lady Audley compared with, 192–3
contemplates suicide, 276
critical reception of, 92, 109
illegitimacy, 84, 92, 192, 233–4, 264–5, 303
moral strength, 52
omitted from stage version, 84
roles and disguises adopted by, 42, 192–3, 252, 299, 303
talent for mimicry, 44–5, 84
Victoria, Queen, 7, 291–2
Victorian environments in WC's works
English seaside towns, 151–2, 275–8
industrialisation and urbanisation impacts, 194, 283, 286, 300

Victorian environments in WC's works (cont.)
  introduction to study, 282–3
  landscapes, 178–9, 283–6, 288–90
  suburbia, 286–8
videogame adaptations, 136
Vining, George, 77
violence towards women, 118–19, 123, 134, 144, 267–8
vivisection
  Heart and Science addressing. See *Heart and Science*
  opposition to, 224, 227
  sensation fiction compared to, 118
'Volpurno; or, The Student', 4, 60

Wagner, Richard, 247
Ward, Charles
  WC's letters to, 13, 17, 209
  WC's trips to Paris with, 4, 272
Ward, Jane, 5, 14
Warden, Rob, 148
Ware, J. M., 133
Waters, Sarah, 130, 143–4, 196
Watt, A. P., 12
Welsh, Alexander, 119
Weston, Nancy, 239
Wheatley, Helen, 132
Wheeler, James Talboys, 152
White Mario, Jessie, 257
Wildthorn (Eagland), 143
Wilkie, David, 178, 238
'Wilkie Collins and Charles Dickens' (Eliot), 100, 102, 105–6, 108, 173–4
Wills, W. H., 5, 71, 164, 186
Wilson, James, 130, 143, 144
wine, WC's love of, 13–15, 206–8
Winslow, Forbes, 36, 151
Winter, William, 179
Wiseman, Cardinal, 152
Wollstonecraft, Mary, 195
Woman in White, The
  books consulted for, 151
  characters. See Catherick, Anne; Fairlie, Laura; Fosco, Count; Glyde, Sir Percival; Halcombe, Marian; Hartright, Walter; Pesca
  collective narrative of, 43, 119, 230–1, 236, 262–3
  critical reception, 91, 98, 100, 139, 230
  as detective fiction, 109
  English publishers and editions, 20, 21–3, 26, 27, 28
  ethical chaos of, 318–23
  influence of, 138, 140, 141, 143–4, 190
  insanity theme, 221–2
  inspiration for, 216, 241, 262, 273–4
  Lady Audley's Secret compared with, 195
  marriage law exploitation in, 134, 263, 264
  mistaken identities in, 124, 212–13, 236, 319, 322
  modern media adaptations, 130, 131–2, 134–5
  music in, 247
  opening line, 130, 161–2, 318
  overseas editions, 29, 30
  publication success, 6–7, 71–2, 91, 201
  referenced on WC's tombstone, 9
  serialised publication, 71–2, 161–3, 165, 187, 201
  settings, 221–2, 272, 275, 277, 285
  spying in, 255–6
  stage versions, 7, 78, 80, 133, 140–1, 203, 204, 206
women
  female characters. See female characters
  Gothic fiction authors, 195–6
  gynaecological surgery, 224
  'hysteria' of, 111
  incarceration of, 134, 221, 267–8
  marriage law reforms. See marriage law reforms
  musical instruments suitable for, 249–50
  sensation fiction authors. See Braddon, Mary Elizabeth; Wood, Ellen (Mrs Henry)
  Victorian gender ideology, 213–15
  violence towards, 118–19, 123, 134, 144, 267–8
Wood, Ellen (Mrs Henry), xvii, 120, 141, 174, 175, 193–4, 195
Wragge, Captain (character, NN), 120, 303
Wraxall, Sir Nathaniel William, 150
'Wreck of the Golden Mary, The' (with Dickens), 72
Wuthering Heights (Brontë), 217
Wynne, Anne (Nannie), 66

Yates, Edmund, 71, 90, 184
yellowbacks (pictorial boards) (Chatto & Windus), 27
Yonge, Charlotte, 218
Young Adult (YA) fiction, 143

Zieger, Susan, 116
Zola, Émile, 81

Milton Keynes UK
Ingram Content Group UK Ltd.
UKHW020951030823
426186UK00007B/14